APPLICATIONS OF RASCH MEASUREMENT IN EDUCATION

EDUCATION IN A COMPETITIVE
AND GLOBALIZING WORLD

Additional books in this series can be found on Nova's website under the Series tab.

Additional E-books in this series can be found on Nova's website under the E-books tab.

EDUCATION IN A COMPETITIVE AND GLOBALIZING WORLD

APPLICATIONS OF RASCH MEASUREMENT IN EDUCATION

RUSSELL WAUGH
EDITOR

Nova Science Publishers, Inc.
New York

LIBRARY OF CONGRESS CATALOGING-IN-PUBLICATION DATA
Applications of Rasch measurement in education / editor, Russell Waugh.
p. cm.
Includes index.
ISBN 978-1-61668-026-8 (hardcover)
1. Educational tests and measurements. 2. Education--Mathematical models.
3. Rasch models. I. Waugh, Russell.
LB3051. A738 2009
371.26--dc22
2009054146

Published by Nova Science Publishers, Inc. ✦ *New York*

CONTENTS

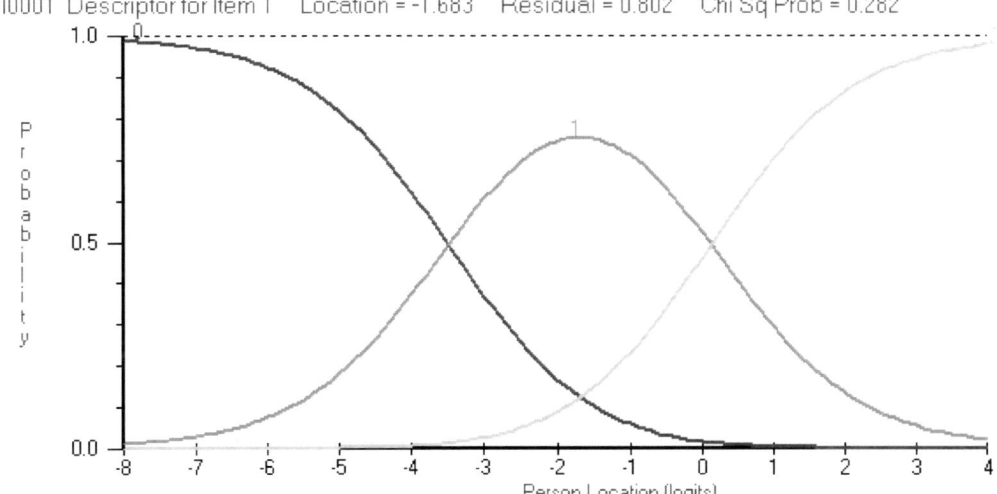

A 3-Category Response Curve for an Item in Rasch Measurement

PREFACE

This book contains Rasch measurement research papers that were based on part of some of my recent doctoral student theses that I supervised within the Faculty of Education and Arts at Edith Cowan University and the Graduate School of Education at the University of Western Australia (2007 to 2009). My doctoral students worked very hard on their theses investigating the relevant literature, mastering Rasch measurement and the Rasch Unidimensional Measurement Models (RUMM) computer program with its relevant statistics. Most of the doctoral students had families and jobs at the same time as they performed their research and, while all would say that it was a wonderful, rewarding experience during which time they learned a lot, they would also say that it was very hard work writing and re-writing their research output. In this book, they share some of their research output with you. To the best of our knowledge, all the Rasch measures reported here have not been performed by any other researcher in the world, up to the time of the thesis.

In making a Rasch measure of a variable, items are designed to be conceptually ordered by difficulty along an increasing continuum from easy to harder for that variable. For the purpose of explanation here, I shall use three items ordered from easy to medium to hard. In designing the items, one keeps in mind that the respondent measures of the variable are conceptualised as being ordered along the continuum from low to high according to certain conditions. The conditions in the three-item example are that respondents with low measures will have a high probability of answering the easy items positively, and a low probability of answering the medium and hard items positively. Respondents with medium measures will have a high probability of answering the easy and medium items positively, and a low probability of answering the hard items positively. Respondents with high measures will have a high probability of answering the easy, medium and hard items positively. These conditions are tested through a Rasch analysis. Data are collected from respondents on the items and scored dichotomously (0/1), as in, for example, but not limited to, wrong/right, no/yes, none/a lot, disagree/agree, some/often, bad/good, slow/fast, or the items can be scored with three or more responses as, for example, with none (0), some (1), most (2) and always (3). It is better to have an ordered response set and the RUMM computer program will test whether the response categories are being answered consistently and logically for each item.

I hope that the Rasch measurement papers in this book will help you in your desire to make some good, uni-dimensional and linear measures of variables that improve our knowledge in education for the benefit of young people.

Best wishes from sunny Perth, Western Australia
Russell Waugh
May 2010

AUTHOR BIOGRAPHIES

Chaowprapha Chuesathuchon is Assistant Professor at Rajabhat Ubon Ratchathani University in north-eastern Thailand. She holds the degrees of Grad. Dip. in Science, BEd, MEd, and PhD. Her PhD thesis (2008) was titled Computerized Adaptive Testing in Mathematics for Primary Schools in Thailand. She investigated item banking and computerized adaptive testing with primary mathematics in the north eastern section of Thailand (Ubon Ratchathnai Province) and the children represented in her thesis had their first ever experience with computerized adaptive testing. And there are no CAT/item banking programs commercially available with Thai output and so Chaowprapha designed the CAT and item bank in Thai from 'scratch'. Since her first language is Thai, it all had to be translated into English for me and the thesis!

Ahdielah Edries is Principal of one of three campuses of the Australian Islamic College in Perth, Western Australia and a current Fulbright Scholar. She holds the degrees of BSc, Grad. Dip. Ed., MEd, and EdD. Many of her students come from war torn countries like Somalia, Ethiopia and Lebanon, and some have not been to school before coming to Australia. Ahdielah works very hard to build up the Australian Islamic College so that its students have the same standard and the same opportunities as other Australian students. Her Doctor of Education thesis (2009) was titled Student and Teacher Identified Attitudes and Needs at the Australian Islamic College. Her research involved investigating the attitudes, interests and needs of the students (but not all of this is reported here). Only some Rasch measures about student self-views based on some Gardner Intelligences are reported in this book.

Natalie C. Leitao teaches at Edith Cowan University in the Faculty of Education and Arts and she has extensive experience in primary school education. She holds the degrees of Diploma of Teaching, BEd (Hons.) and PhD. Her PhD thesis (2008) was titled Teacher-Student Relationships in Primary Schools in Perth. Natalie Leitao taught at primary schools in Perth (she now teaches part-time at Edith Cowan University). While she completed her doctorate on student teacher relationships, Natalie raised her young family. In the paper reported here, Natalie designed a questionnaire to ascertain students' views about their relationships with teachers. The questionnaire is conceptually comprised of items in an ordered pattern from easy to hard, using both attitude and behavior perspectives together on the same items. The data were analyzed with the RUMM computer program to test this conceptualization which was, in the main, supported.

Leung Kin Man Thomas is the Head of Academic Affairs Committee of Ching Chung Hau Po Woon Secondary School in Hong Kong. He teaches biology and provides career counseling for students. Before taking his present position, he was a Teaching Consultant in Faculty of Education of the University of Hong Kong where he taught student guidance and science teaching methodology. He holds the degrees of B.Sc., PG.Dip.Ed., Cert. School Guidance, P.Dip.Psychology, M.Ed. (Counseling), M. Ed. (TESOL) and EdD. His Doctor of Education thesis (2007) was titled A Rasch Measurement of Career Maturity for Secondary School Students in Hong Kong. Thomas Kin Man Leung lives with his family and works in Hong Kong. He translated the Career Decision-Making Self-efficacy Scale (Rochleon, Mohr & Hargrove, 1999) and the Attitude towards Career Counseling Scale (Betz, Klein & Taylor, 1996) into Chinese to apply it to students in Hong Kong. Thomas applied the RUMM computer program to the data for the Career Decision-Making Self-Efficacy and the Attitude towards Career Counseling sections in this book to investigate its validity and reliability. He intends to improve the inventories for subsequent use in the Hong Kong context.

Ong Chun Ghee is the Academy Head of Bicultural Studies at Dunman High School in Singapore and he has wide experience in teaching talented and gifted secondary and pre-university students. He is currently running two national special programmes at Dunman High, namely the Bicultural Studies Programme and Chinese Language Elective Programme. He holds the degrees of BA (Hons.), MA (Distinction) and Postgraduate Dip. Ed. and EdD. His Doctor of Education thesis (2009) was titled Chinese Language Tests in Singapore: A Rasch Analysis of Mock 'A' Level and Equivalent Authentic Tests. Ong Chun Ghee lives with his family in Singapore where he specializes in teaching Chinese linguistics, literature and language to talented students. Ong Chun Ghee investigated both an 'ordinary' Mock Chinese Examination and an Authentic Chinese Examination at Cambridge "A" Level standard using Rasch measurement. While the 'Intermediate Mock A Level' examination was reliable and had a wider range of item difficulties, the 'Intermediate Authentic Test' was also reliable and was better supported by the students.

Tan Hock Chye is a teacher at one of the premier secondary schools in Singapore, the Hwa Chong Institution, Chinese High School. He holds the degrees of BSc (Hons.), MEd, EdD. His Doctor of Education thesis (2008) was titled: Science and Mathematics Research Programme (SMRP): Does it Motivate Students in Science and Mathematics? Tan Hock Chye lives and works in Singapore. The Singapore Government wanted schools there to improve student motivation in Science and Mathematics. Consequently, some Singapore schools implemented special programs to focus on improving student motivation. Tan Hock Chye teaches at one such premier school and he investigated motivation through a pretest/posttest, control experimental group approach, but only the motivation measure is reported here.

Russell F. Waugh works at two universities in Perth, Western Australia. He is a Professor at Edith Cowan University in the Faculty of Education and Arts and a Senior Research Fellow in the Graduate School of Education at the University of Western Australia, and he supervises doctoral students at both. He holds the degrees of BSc, MSc, BEd, MEd, and PhD (UWA). Russell is a former Fulbright scholar and now specializes in Rasch measurement using the Rasch Unidimensional Measurement Models (RUMM) computer program developed by Professors David Andrich, Barry Sheridan and Guanzhong Luo, mainly applied to psychological and educational variables in the human sciences. Russell has published widely through journals, conferences and books, mostly with Rasch measures. Russell can be contacted at r.waugh@ecu.edu.au

In: Applications of Rasch Measurement in Education
Editor: Russell Waugh

ISBN: 978-1-61668-026-8
© 2010 Nova Science Publishers, Inc.

Chapter 1

ITEM BANKING AND COMPUTERIZED ADAPTIVE TESTING WITH RASCH MEASUREMENT: AN EXAMPLE FOR PRIMARY MATHEMATICS IN THAILAND

Chaowprapha Chuesathuchon[1] and Russell Waugh[2]
1. Rajabhat Ubon Ratchathani University, Thailand
2. Faculty of Education and Arts, Edith Cowan University, Western Australia

ABSTRACT

This study was conducted in Thailand in three parts (creating an item bank, designing a Computerized Adaptive Test (CAT) and analysing an attitude to CAT questionnaire). In the first part, 290 multiple-choice test items on mathematical equations were created for an item bank for use in part two. They consisted of nine aspects: (1) identifying an equation; (2) identifying the true equation; (3) identifying equations with an unknown; (4) finding the value of an unknown that satisfies the equation; (5) identifying a method to solve an equation; (6) finding the solutions to equations; (7) finding a solution to an equation related the given condition; (8) selecting an equation converted from a verbal problem or a verbal problem related to an equation; and (9) solving an equation problem. Seven papers with 50 items each, containing 40 different items and 10 common items, were administered to 3,062 students of Year 6 (Prathom Suksa 6). There were 409, 413, 412, 400, 410, 408, and 610 students taking part in the 1st to the 7th tests respectively. The data were analysed with the Rasch Unidimensional Measurement Model (RUMM 2010) computer program. Ninety-eight test items fitted the measurement model and were installed in the item bank. In part two, a computer program for CAT was created, tested, and modified after trialling. A controlled experiment involving the use of CAT with 400 Prathom Suksa 6 students from two primary schools in Ubon Ratchathani province, Thailand, was implemented. In part three, the RUMM 2010 computer program was used to create a linear scale of Student Attitude towards Computerized Adaptive Testing. Attitude was conceptualised from five aspects: (1) Like and Interest in CAT; (2) Confidence with and Use of CAT; (3) CAT as Modern and Useful; (4) CAT is Reliable; and (5) CAT Recommendations. Data were collected from

400 Prathom Suksa 6 students and an interval scale was created with 30 items. Students were very supportive of the use of CAT with an item bank.

ITEM BANKING AND COMPUTERIZED ADAPTIVE TESTING: AN EXAMPLE FOR PRIMARY MATHEMATICS IN THAILAND

Item banks are potentially very helpful for teachers and test developers. The idea of item banking is associated with the need for making test construction easier, faster and more efficient. In the United States, for example, the concept of item banking has been associated with the movements to both individualized instruction and behavioural objectives in the 1960s (Hambleton, 1986; Umar, 1999). Van der Linden (1986, cited in Umar, 1999) viewed item banking as a new practice in test development, as a product of the introduction of Rasch measurement (Rasch, 1960/1980) and the extensive use of computers in modern society. It was suggested that, when a large collection of good items is available to either teachers or test developers, much of the burden of test construction can be removed. The quality of tests used in the schools, for example, could be expected to be better than it would be without an item bank. When a calibrated item bank is developed with Rasch measurement, testing programs can be made more flexible and appropriate, because different groups of students can take different tests which are suitable to each of them and the results can still be compared on the same scale.

Traditional assessment (as in True Score Theory) can cause many problems in education, such as, a circular dependency: (1) the person statistic (observed score) is item sample dependent; and (2) the item statistics (item difficulty and item discrimination) are examinee sample dependent (Fan, 1998, pp. 357-381); (3) the items are not conceptualised in order from easy to hard; (4) the theoretical ordering of item difficulties is not tested with the 'real' data to create a linear scale; and (5) the item difficulties (from easy to hard) and the person measures (from low to high) are not calibrated on the same interval-level scale.

Rasch measurement (Rasch, 1960/1980) coupled with item banking and CAT has the potential to overcome some of these problems. It is possible to produce high quality items that not only ensure more accuracy in evaluating learning achievement but also provide an alternative way to enhance the educational system as a whole. Item banking coupled with Rasch measurement could result in improvements in school learning and in school reporting of achievement (Umar, 1999).

A large collection of good items will help teachers to concentrate more on their teaching without having to spend much time on item construction. It could also ensure that only high quality items are used. When such a collection (popularly referred to as an "item bank") consists of items measuring the same thing and calibrated onto a common scale, it could help test developers in solving many of the practical testing problems. Use of a calibrated item bank could thus affect policies in educational testing and assessment (Umar, 1999, p.207).

What is an Item Bank?

Generally, the words item banks and item pools are used interchangeably in the research literature. Scholars generally identify the term, Item Bank, as a large collection of good test items for which their quality is analysed and known, and which are systematically stored in a computer and made accessible to students for measuring their achievement or ability (Choppin, 1981, 1985; Department of Academics, 1991; Millman and Arter, 1984, pp.315-316; Paeratkool, 1975; Rudner, 1998a,b; Wibroonsri, 2005). The items can be stored and retrieved by different aspects, such as subject area, instructional objective measurement, measurement traits, and significant item statistics such as item difficulty and discriminating power. The item bank is intended to ease the search and application of various testing procedures and to serve the users' needs (Department of Academics, 1991, p.4; Gronlund, 1998, p.130).

Some scholars state that item collection is not only a 'warehouse' or 'storage house' of items but, in a proper item bank, the items are systematically organized through the processes from the start. In a proper item bank, each of the items is codified and classified by subject matter assessed, objectives, and the psychometric traits of the items. The well-selected items are normally stored in the memory unit of the computer so that they can be later easily used when needed (Ebel and Frisbie, 1986, p.927). Ideally, the advancement of item banking could be achieved in that the statistical processes will be applied to differentiate and aggregate the items with the same difficulty level. This contributes to the possibility of the assessment comparison, although the results are gained from different test items (Shoemaker, 1976 cited in Lila, 1996, p.36; Wright and Bell, 1984, p.331).

The concept of item banking can be divided into two categories: conventional (with Classical test Theory) and 'temporary' (with Rasch measurement) (van der Linden,1994 cited in Srisamran, 1997, p.7). In a conventional item bank, there is standardization of the items, their construction and their storage. An emphasis is placed on experimental control consisting of four components. One, a test blueprint table of specifications (or a two dimensional table) is constructed to indicate the relationship between the subject matter being tested and the behavioural objectives needing to be measured. It indicates the test's content validity. Two, test items are created in accordance with the table of specifications. Three, then the following procedures are performed: (1) measurement of each item's quality in regard to accuracy, objectivity, index of item of content and objective congruence by experts; (2) The item and its overall test are then analysed based on Classical Test Theory (True Score Theory) in order to seek its item difficulty, its discriminating power, and the reliability of the test (Lord, 1980, p.8). Four, the investigation of norms are performed in order to compare and interpret the scores obtained with the common standardized scores. Two main problems here are that Classical Test Theory can only produce a non-linear scale and the item difficulties are sample dependent for each test (not directly comparable), thus limiting the usefulness of this type of item bank.

In a 'temporary' Rasch item bank, a new paradigm of test construction has been derived and test item banking has been developed with the application of Rasch measurement. Each test item is statistically calibrated to be linked on the same interval level scale. This can be easily processed with a specially developed computer program (such as RUMM, Andrich, Sheridan and Luo, 2005) which shows each item of the test that fits the measurement model. The test is flexible, and appropriate to Rasch measurement and its implementation, and it is applicable for school use. This has been explained by van der Linden (1986 cited in Umar, 1999, p.209) who viewed item banking as a new practice in test development, as a product of the introduction of Rasch measurement and the extensive use of computers in modern society. The items which cover every aspect of the domains are categorised and stored into the same domain of knowledge or ability. They are also located on a common, linear scale. In the selection of the items for testing, using Computerized Adaptive Testing, a certain statistical value namely difficulty is considered to be appropriate for the ability or competence level of the student. The result of the test even though different items are used can be compared since each of the test items is on a common, calculated linear scale. An item bank at this level could be considered as a model of a 'measurement system'. In this system, any new items intended for measuring the same attribute could be validated and calibrated onto the existing scale of the bank. Since the items are calibrated, it is possible to compare results from tests consisting of different subsets of items from the bank (Hambleton, Sawaminathan, and Rogers, 1991). As such, a calibrated item bank when developed with Rasch measurement makes the testing programs flexible and appropriate, because different groups of students can take different items which are suitable to each of them and the results can still be compared on the same scale. Together with sophisticated computer software, application of Computerized Adaptive Testing could be made possible at the school or district level (Hambleton et al., 1991).

Potential Benefits of Item Banking

It is believed that item banking can potentially bring several advantages to educational assessment. The students could directly benefit from such an evaluation tool since the well-developed test items can potentially accurately measure and compare their true competence or achievement level. There are ten potential benefits of item banking gleaned from the literature.

(1) Teachers can select good test items which meet the measurement objectives and the content from the item bank to suit their students' abilities in each of the area of testing.

(2) Item banking can reduce time spent on the construction of the test items by teachers. This could result in teachers having more time available for the students and their teaching tasks (Umar, 1990).

(3) The items analyzed using Rasch measurement will help create a test which contains items located on a common, linear scale and based on a variety of options or objectives (Rudner, 1998a) which in turn contribute to the comparison of the test results of the students who take the different test items, since the Rasch model used will assure items from multiple tests can be placed on a common scale and indicate the relative difficulty of the items (Rudner, 1998a).

(4) Item banking will enable teachers to build a test which contains items located on a common, linear scale and based on a variety of options or objectives by using a Rasch measurement model which is highly effective in item analysis and unidimensionality assessment (Njiru and Romanoski, 2007, pp.3-4; Rudner, 1998a,b).

(5) Item banking displays the advancement and standards in a school's measurement of student achievement; that is, valid longitudinal achievement inferences can be made from it.

(6) Teachers and measurement experts will be able to easily improve the item bank either by increasing or improving the test items to update them and make them relevant to the changing curriculum, as is required by State Systems, schools and the public at school and national levels (Njiru and Romanoski, 2007, pp.3-4).

(7) A well-developed item bank enhances effective measurements because the test items can be improved in both validity and reliability to meet educational higher standards (Umar, 1990). This consequently assures the accuracy and reliability of the measurement.

(8) Security is guaranteed because there are a lot of items in the bank. It is unlikely that the students who take the test can remember all of the items from one or several testings. Item banks can therefore protect item leakage, at least to a large extent (Choppin,1981 cited in Millman and Arter, 1984; Umar, 1999, p.210).

(9) Item banking is a product of a new innovation in measurement, namely Rasch measurement coupled with improvements in computing power (Computerized Adaptive Testing), and is easily applied to school state and national educational assessment; each student can complete different test items but the results from the testing can be compared (Umar, 1999).

(10) Item banking potentially allows for the creation of a test which is adaptive to any group of students who have different learning abilities and for students with disabilities (Umar, 1990).

Limitations of Item Banks

Although these two types of item banks are an improvement on existing individual assessment methods, they do have some limitations and restrictions. For example, the test constructed is fixed both in terms of content and items. Additionally, when the curriculum and the content are developed or changed, it consequently influences the validity of the test, if used again. The flexibility of the test is also problematic, since it cannot be again used with the same group of the test takers. Also, in the case where the competence of the students varies greatly, the measures gained from the test can vary greatly from the likely true scores (Lord, 1980, p.8; Lord and Novick, 1968).

Item banking involves equating various tests and items. It is entirely possible, mathematically, to equate tests which cover entirely different subject matter. At the practical level, this means that it is also possible to equate items which assess subtly, but significantly different skills. In order to avoid this undesirable situation, the item review process must also include a careful evaluation of the skills assessed by each item and tests must be carefully formulated (Lawrence, 1998; Njiru and Romanoski, 2007a,b).

While it is possible for a school or state to implement very successful item banks and Rasch calibrated testing programs without knowing much about Rasch measurement, good practice calls for a staff that is comfortable with, and a knowledgeable of, what they are doing. A school or state that decides to undertake an item banking project should have full understanding of the practical as well as the mathematical and theoretical aspects of item banking (Lawrence, 1998; Njiru and Romanoski, 2007a,b).

An item bank really consists of multiple collections of items with a reasonable unidimensional content area, such as mathematic computations or vocabulary. In order to develop the bank, many tests must be calibrated, linked (or equated), and organized. This requires a great deal of work in terms of preparation and planning and in terms of computer time and expertise. Once the item bank is established, however, test development time, effort, and costs are reduced (Lawrence, 1998; Njiru and Romanoski, 2007a,b).

Most of the problems on Item Banking are technical or practical (Njiru and Romanoski, 2007a,b). Hiscox (1983) pointed out that it is not all that easy to implement several aspects of a successful item bank, such as securing or developing a sound and useful collection of items, having knowledgeable people to maintain the item bank, publicizing the item bank, and using the items appropriately and effectively. Some of these concerns, however, apply to tests constructed by traditional means as well.

Item Banking in Thailand

In the case of Thailand, the concept of item banking apparently emerged in 1957 and was widely known in 1982-1984 when Thailand was assigned by her neighbouring Asean countries to initiate a testing program for the entire ASEAN education region, but its use in any Asian country is still very limited, probably because of the large cost involved in development (Boonprasert, 1988). Throughout the 1982-1984 project, there were several training seminars and further educational seminars, including the proceedings for the meetings. Since then the Thai Ministry of Education has been very slowly developing item banking with a view to eventually expanding it to the regional and local levels (Department of Academics, 1991, p.5). At the Provincial level, for example, the Item Banking and Examination Online System Chiang Mai Examination Center was established in Chiang Mai Province in 2007 (Sangphueng and Chooprateep, 2007), and the Project of Item Banking Development of Nong Khai Superintendents was established in 1997 (Srisamran, 1997), but these have not been developed to the stage where they can be used by teachers and students in schools on a continual basis. They are still in the developing and trialling stage.

On Thai university campuses, there has been some limited research of item banking such as the Online Test Bank at Sura Nari University of Technology (Chansilp, 2006). The test items in this university were standardized on the basis of Traditional Measurement Theory which can only produce non-linear scores and so it is difficult to see how this item bank project can be useful and it would have been better if the researchers had used Rasch measurement to create linear measures. Other item bank projects in Thai universities have used Rasch measurement, but they have used the now discredited and so-called 2-parameter Rasch model (involving item difficulty, item discrimination and one parameter of person ability) or the so-called 3-parameter Rasch model (involving item difficulty, item discrimination, a guessing parameter and one parameter of person ability) (see Wright, 1999a for a discussion and discrediting of these models). The best Rasch model to use is the so-called 1-parameter Rasch model (actually one parameter of item difficulty and one parameter of person ability) (see Andrich, 1988a, 1988b; Wright, 1999a,b). In Thailand, the 2-parameter and 3-parameter Rasch models were used by research students to develop trials of item banks for Mathematics (Maneelek, 1997; Songsang, 2004; Supeesut, 1998, 1999; Tuntavanitch, 2006), English (Phungkham, 1988), and Chemistry (Suwannoi, 1989).

COMPUTERIZED ADAPTIVE TESTING (CAT)

CAT consists of a computer program that allows a student to 'interrogate' an item bank (Embreston and Reise, 2000; Weiss, 2004, 2003,1982). The test items are constructed and adapted to the ability level of the individual test-taker and administered using a computer (Beevers, McGuire, Stirling, and Wild, 1995; Lord, 1971, 1980; Nering, 1996; Shermis et al., 1996; Stocking and Swanson, 1998, p.271; Wainer, 1990, 1993; Weiss and Kingsbury, 1984). Examinees do not have to answer exactly the same test items as any other examinees and the number of test items to be answered by different examinees are not equal, they depend on the result of the test items that an examinee chooses to answer (Karnjanawasri, 2002; Lord, 1980; Weiss, 1983; Weiss and Kingsbury, 1984).

Advantages of Computerized Adaptive Testing (CAT)

There has been some research in the area of Computerized Adaptive Testing conducted over the last several years. Some suggest that using CAT with an item bank is more efficient than conventional paper-and-pencil tests, because the itemsare tailored to an individual examinee's ability level. CAT also offers advantages to test developers in regards to improved test reliability, improved test security and data collection, better opportunity to control cheating, and cost saving with regard to printing and shipping. Convenience and flexibility of scheduling an appointment to test, anytime testing, immediacy in test scoring and reporting, faster score reporting service, potentially shorter tests, reduced scheduling and supervision, fewer test items to arrive at a more accurate estimate of test taker proficiency, and reduction of teacher time on marking are also the advantages offered by CAT (Green, 1984; Karnjanawasri, 2002; Leung, 2001; Meijer and Nering, 1999; Owen, 1975; Patsula and Steffen, 1997; Wainer, 1990; Weiss, 1982).

Some scholars such as Meijer and Nering (1999), credit CAT with various benefits which it has over traditional testing or paper-and-pencil tests. Enhanced measurement precision, and testing on demand also make CAT an attractive proposition. In terms of reduction of test length, Shermis, Stemmer, and Webb (1996) conducted a pilot study of CAT in the Michigan Educational Assessment Program (MEAP). Over 500 volunteer students in grade 9-12 answered 97 items by using five paper-and pencil forms of mathematical content. Each form consisted of 23-25 items. All forms consisted of six similar items. A computerized adaptive version (HYPERCAT) was used by 122 volunteers in a different group. The data from paper and pencil forms were calibrated and vertically equated by using RASCAL. They found that CAT could reduce test length by 25%. They also found that the CAT version assessed student achievement better than the paper and pencil form. Moreover, exams based on CAT can achieve at least as good precision as a paper-and-pencil test, using only half of the number of items (Embreston and Reise, 2000; Weiss, 2004). However, the initial costs of implementing and launching CAT can be high. Considerable financial and human resources are needed to staff and organized a CAT program. In many cases, complicated technical, economic, and political changes are also needed (Sands, Waters, and McBride, 1997). For example, although test security initially seemed to be one of the greatest advantages of CAT, it became one of its major problems. Item banks needed to be continually updated to ensure item and test security. This greatly increased the cost of implementing an operational CAT. Although CAT applications do have certain problems, their advantages outweigh their disadvantages according to Meijer and Nering (1999).

In addition, CAT offers a mathematical programming approach that creates a model to take care of many questions concerning the test, such as feasibility, accuracy and time of testing, as well as item pool security (Cordova, 1998). CAT could be used to obtain the most information about a single test taker compared to paper and pencil tests including methods for estimating an examinee's ability, based on the dichotomous responses to the items in the test.

In an unpublished by the Center for Advanced Research On Language Acquisition, Office of International Programs, the University of Minnesota (1999), CAT is claimed to have better scoring measures than conventional tests. It takes not only the number of items answered correctly into account, but also the difficulties of the items which are correctly answered. A test-taker who correctly answers a harder set of questions will score higher than a test-taker who correctly answers an easier set of questions. Student data and feedback over time can be stored for easy access using a computer. Moreover, CAT has been found to improve test-taking motivation, to increase average test score differences across ethnic groups (Pine, Church, Gialluca, and Weiss, 1979; Pine and Weiss, 1978, cited in the University of Minnesota, 1999, unpublished paper). Psychologically, CAT helps lessen the stress of the test-taker since those with lower ability do not have to answer the items that are too difficult for their level of ability. This makes CAT go hand-in-hand with the view that each student is challenged at his or her own level because items that are too difficult or too easy for a given student don't have to be administered (Eggen and Verschoor, 2006; Karnjanawasri, 2002; van der Linden and Pashley, 2000).

In terms of the reliability, validity, fairness and feasibility, CAT takes advantage of technology and modern measurement theory to deliver tests that are more reliable. Since only items of appropriate difficulty are administered to test takers, lower measurement error and higher reliability can be achieved using fewer items. When items are targeted to the ability level of the examinee, the standard error of measure (SEM) is minimized and test length can be minimized without loss of precision. Thus CAT can substantially reduce test length compared to paper and pencil tests (Gershon, 2005, p.112; Olsen, Maynes, Slawson, and Ho, 1986; Weiss, 1983; Weiss and Kingsbury, 1984).

Test validity includes (1) the test measures what it purports to measure; (2) the inferences made from the test scores are meaningful and useful, and; (3) the content of the test reflects critical aspects of the crucial skills or knowledge. Shorter tests with acceptable precision, possible with CAT, can enhance validity when examinee fatigue or test anxiety may introduce construct irrelevant variance (Gershon, 2005, p.112; Gershon and Bergstrom, 1995; Huff and Sireci, 2001).

Computer adaptive tests also have characteristics that enhance fairness. Since tests are administered via the computer from a large bank of items, there is no human intervention on the selection of test forms. Given the existence of a well constructed item bank, each test taker has the same opportunity to demonstrate ability or achievement as any other test taker. Recent improvements in electronic test publishing ensure that banks can be changed easily (in and out) allowing compromised items to be removed from circulation in real time (Gershon, 2005, p.113).

From a cost perspective, adaptive tests are feasible for many organizations. The cost for administering adaptive tests is spread out over several areas that roughly conform to the test development and administration cost structure of any exam at a comparable level of security: test content development, test administration, scoring and reporting. Test content development for CAT differs in terms of the number of items required to create an item bank large enough to cover the range of abilities, and also large enough to insure overall bank security. For criterion referenced mastery tests, the test may only need to have a large number of items near a pass point, but for a norm referenced test, a large number of items may be required across the ability or trait continuum. For high stakes tests, administered to thousands of examinees, it may be necessary to have thousands of items to merely insure test security. At the other extreme are low stakes and/or self-assessment tests where a very small bank of less than 100 items may be sufficient (Gershon, 2005).

The cost consideration for item development is primarily of concern for high stakes norm referenced testing programs. Once items have been written, the next cost relates to calibrating the item response theory parameters for every item. In the case of an established testing program using previously administered items, the calculation of bank parameters may simply require re-analysing old datasets. At the other extreme, all newly written items may have to be piloted on hundreds of examinees. While it is clear that many organizations will experience increased up front costs to create their CAT program, they may similarly encounter decreased costs in the future, as the necessity to write completely new tests each year is replaced by lesser bank maintenance tasks such as insuring the currency of existing items (getting rid of items that are now outdated), and writing a greatly reduced number of new items each year to insure content coverage and to further increase security by keeping the bank fresh.

The cost of test administration is also related to the security level of the test. High stakes tests must be administered in highly arranged settings. Third-party test delivery vendors, with test administration centers located in thousands of cities throughout the United States and around the world, act as sub-contractors to provide a secure high stakes test environment. Alternatively, a test administration organization can set up its own private center on a full-time or part time basis. Lower stakes CAT exams can now be administered over the internet. While the testing time for a CAT is typically shorter than its fixed length test equivalent, test administration time at a testing vendor is often paid for based upon the maximum time allotted for testing. The cost of scoring a CAT is basically nonexistent, since the scoring burden is born in the test administration process itself. There are no answer sheets to collect and scan, and indeed, for many organizations, the final score report is produced on screen or on paper at the time of testing; removing the cost of generating reports altogether (Gershon, 2005, p.113).

History of CAT with Item Banking

The history of item banking and CAT can be traced back to the 1960s, following the development of the Rasch measurement model (Rasch, 1960; Wright and Stone, 1979; Choppin, 1985). The two notions have provided a theoretical structure for building large scale calibrated item banks (Choppin, 1985). One of the first adaptive tests to be discussed was the ASVAB (Armed Services Vocational Aptitude Battery, 1975, see Gershon, 2005). The stimulus for producing a CAT test for personal selection and classification in the Armed Services was to increase the accuracy of test scores, reduce test compromise and reduce testing time. The first conference of CAT researchers for the ASVAB, held in 1975, was followed by several years of research. In addition to designing the test, the Navy Personnel Research and Development Center (NPRDC) researchers designed a complete delivery system (Gershon, 2005).

In 1979, computer technology was simply not ready to address CAT- ASVAB requirements. Much of the early effort by NPRDC and Service researchers served as a learning experience, while they waited for computer hardware to catch up with the functional requirements of the CAT-ASVAB. (Gershon, 2005, p.27).

From 1979 to 1992, the NPRDC researched, developed, tested and implemented several generations of the CAT-AS VAB. By the mid-1980's experimental CAT-ASVAB data from over 7,500 military recruits from all Services had been collected and analyzed. The CAT-ASVAB system remained in operational use until 1996 when it was replaced by the 'next generation' system (Gershon, 2005, p.112). This included several other works of scholars in the late 70s to the early 90s. A meta- analysis of 20 studies published from 1977 to 1992 compared results from paper and pencil administrations to CAT administrations, and consistently found that both modes of test administration yielded similar results (Bergstrom and Lunz, 1992 cited in Gershon, 2005, p.112). For example, English, Reckase, and Patience (1977) published a study of undergraduate students enrolled in a course entitled "Introduction to Educational Measurement and Evaluation" at the University of Missouri. Bejar and Weiss (1978) reported on achievement test results for students enrolled in a large introductory biology class at the University of Minnesota. The Californian Assessment Program used mathematics application items to create tests in a pencil and paper administered format, a computer administered format, and a computer adaptive format (Olsen, Maynes, Slawson, and Ho, 1986). Comparability of CAT and pencil and paper versions of the math computation section of the College Level Academic Skills Test (CLAST) at the University of Florida were reported by Legg and Buhr (1987). The results of computer administered and pencil and paper versions of the Differential Aptitude Test, a battery of eight ability tests, were reported by Henly, Klebe, McBride and Cudeck (1989). Baghi, Gabrys and Ferrara (1992) conducted research done with the Maryland Functional Testing Program, a statewide competency testing program used as a high school graduation requirement. The study compared pencil and paper versions and computer adaptive versions of math and reading tests and illustrated the previously mentioned issues with long text reading passages. Both the American Society of Clinical Pathologists (Lunz and Bergstrom, 1991) and the National Council State Boards of Nursing (National Council of State Boards of Nursing, 1991; Zara, 1994) reported on studies that supported the validity of CAT programs with item banking.

When looking closer, we can see that each of these studies (despite differences in test content, age of test-takers, and study design) demonstrated comparability of measures obtained using both CAT and pencil and paper test versions. Indeed, what is most remarkable in reviewing the literature comparing these two test modalities is the marked absence of any significant studies demonstrating the inability of CATs to show different achievement levels from assessed using paper-and-pencil tests. Even performance realized with long reading passages in CAT supports the view that the CAT format better captures reading comprehension. The paper format may benefit the test taker who is quick to re-scan the material, and the CAT version may benefit the examinee who is better able to commit the material to memory (Gershon, 2005, p.112).

RASCH ANALYSIS FOR THE ITEM BANK (PRESENT STUDY)

The present study involved an initial analysis with 250 mathematics items involving six tests with 50 items each. For linking the scales, each test contained 10 common items first, and then the six data sets were combined. Responses for the mathematics tests came from 2,452 Prathom Suksa 6 (Grade 6) students in Thailand which were entered into an Excel file, as per the response category codes (zero for wrong and one for right) and then converted to a text file. The data pattern had 254 columns: columns 1-4 were for the ID; columns 5-14 were for 10 answers of common test items; columns 15-54 were for 40 answers of test 1; columns 55-94 were for 40 answers of test 2; columns 95-130 were for 40 answers of test 3; columns 135-174 were for 40 answers of test 4; columns 175-214 were for 40 answers of test 5; and columns 215-254 were for 40 answers of test 6. The data were analysed using the Rasch Unidimensional Measurement Model (RUMM2010, Andrich, Sheridan and Luo, 2003) computer program. The non-performing items of the mathematics test (172 items out of 250) were deleted from the scale, leaving 78 items that fitted the measurement model.

Because 172 items (out of 250) were deleted, as not fitting a Rasch measurement model, only 78 items were stored in the item bank. To improve the bank, a further 50 items were created and analysed. For linking the scales, 10 common items from the 78 set were added to the 50 set for calibration together. Data from 610 students were analysed using the RUMM computer program. Of these 50 items, 30 were deleted as not fitting a Rasch measurement model, leaving 20 good fitting items to be add to the set of 78 items.

The presentation begins with two descriptions of the analysis for the mathematics achievements that are reported for 78 items in the first and 20 items in the second. The Rasch analysis provides data on global item and person fit to the measurement model, individual item fit, dimensionality, reliability, Student Separation Index and targeting.

In Rasch analysis, the items are designed in a conceptual order by difficulty and this order is tested. The data for the items have to also fit the measurement model in order to create a linear scale and this is tested. The person measures and item difficulties were calibrated on the same scale by the RUMM 2010 program, thus providing the creation of a linear measure of achievement for primary school equations.

The results of the analysis are set out in Tables 1 and 2, and Figures 1 to 4. Table 1 presents a summary of the global fit statistics of the measure of mathematics achievement in the first and second testings, including the item-trait test of fit to the measurement model. The item difficulties in order of the 78 items are shown in Table 2. Figure 1 shows person measures of ability and item difficulty map for the mathematics test (78 items, 2,452 students), with the mathematics measures on the LHS and the difficulties on the RHS. Figures 2 and 3 show response category curves for item 76 (good-fitting item) and item 180 (not-so-good fitting item). Figure 4 shows item locations on the lower side (LS) and mathematics measures on the upper side (US) on the same scale in logits for the test.

RASCH ANALYSIS: 78 ITEMS SCALE

The final analysis with the RUMM program tested the 78 items (N=2,452) in order to create a linear scale of mathematics achievement from an initial bank of 250 items. The residuals were examined; the residuals being the difference between the expected item score calculated according to the Rasch measurement model and the actual item score of the students. This is converted to a standardized residual score in the computer program. The global item fit residuals and global student fit residuals have a mean near zero and a standard deviation near one, when the data fit the measurement model. In this case, the global item and person fit residuals indicate a satisfactory, but not excellent, fit to the measurement model (see Table 1). The individual probability of fit of items to the measurement model was then checked. Of the 78 items, 71 fitted the measurement model with probability p>0.04.

Item Trait Test-of-Fit

The item-trait test of fit examines the consistency of the item difficulties across the student mathematics measures along the scale. This determines whether there was agreement amongst the students as to the difficulties of all items along the scale. The item-trait interaction was not statistically significant at 0.01 level [Chi-square (df =690) =760.34, p =0.03]. This means that a dominant trait was measured and that overall fit to the measurement is acceptable, but not excellent.

Table 1. Summary of fit statistics for mathematics achievement scale (78 items)

	Items	students
Number	78	2,452
Location mean	0.00	0.58
Standard deviation	0.62	1.64
Fit statistic mean	0.63	0.08
Fit statistic standard deviation	1.23	0.73

Item-trait interaction chi square = 760.34, df=690, p=0.03
Person Separation Index =0.83
Power of test-of fit: Good (based on the Separation Index)

1. The item means are constrained to zero by the measurement model.
2. When the data fit the model, the fit statistics approximate a distribution with a mean near zero and a standard deviation near one. The item fit and student fit are satisfactory, but neither is an excellent fit.
3. The item-trait interaction indicates the agreement displayed with all the items across all students from different locations on the scale (acceptable for these data). This means that a dominant trait has been measured.
4. The Student Separation Index is the proportion of observed student mathematics variance considered true (in this scale, 83% and is acceptable). It tells us that the measures are well separated compared to the errors.
5. Numbers are given to two decimal places because the errors are between 0.11 and 0.14.

```
--------------------------------------------------------------------------
LOCATION          PERSONS                  ITEM DIFFICULTIES
--------------------------------------------------------------------------
5.0      High Achievement      |              Hard items



                        XX  |
4.0                      X  |
                      XXXX  |
                      XXXXX  |
               XXXXXXXXXXXX  |

3.0                     XX  |
                        XX  |
                       XXX  |
                      XXXX  |
                    XXXXXX  |
2.0               XXXXXXXX  |
                     XXXXX  |
                     XXXXX  |
                      XXXX  |  34
                XXXXXXXXXXX  |  233 97
1.0                 XXXXXX  |  164 112
               XXXXXXXXXXX  |  134 73 60
                        XX  |  75 121 156 71 182 83
   XXXXXXXXXXXXXXXXXXXXXXX  |  140 236 183
                     XXXXX  |  76 74 48 106 104 117 185 212 81 223 142 172
0.0       XXXXXXXXXXXXXXXX  |  115 129 171 170  47 29 90 224
               XXXXXXXXXXX  |  109 141 103 132 249 127 126 197 130 13 68 248 100 180
             XXXXXXXXXXXX  |  92 85 150 125
      XXXXXXXXXXXXXXXXXXX  |  241 220 218 45 202 157
                XXXXXXXX  |  116 135 200 14 87 122 53 91
-1.0      XXXXXXXXXXXXXXX  |  16 139 88 51 174 119
               XXXXXXXX  |  138 214
               XXXXXXX  |  59
               XXXXXXX  |
                      XX  |
-2.0                   XX  |
                      XXX  |
                       XX  |
                        X  |

-3.0                       |

                         X  |


-4.0                       |



-5.0     Low Achievement      |              Easy items
--------------------------------------------------------------------------
```

1. The scale is in logits, the log odds of answering positively.
2. Measures are ordered from low to high on the LHS and item difficulties are ordered from easy to hard on the RHS.
3. Each x represents 11 students.

Figure 1. Person measures of achievement and item difficulty map for mathematics test (N=2,452, I=78).

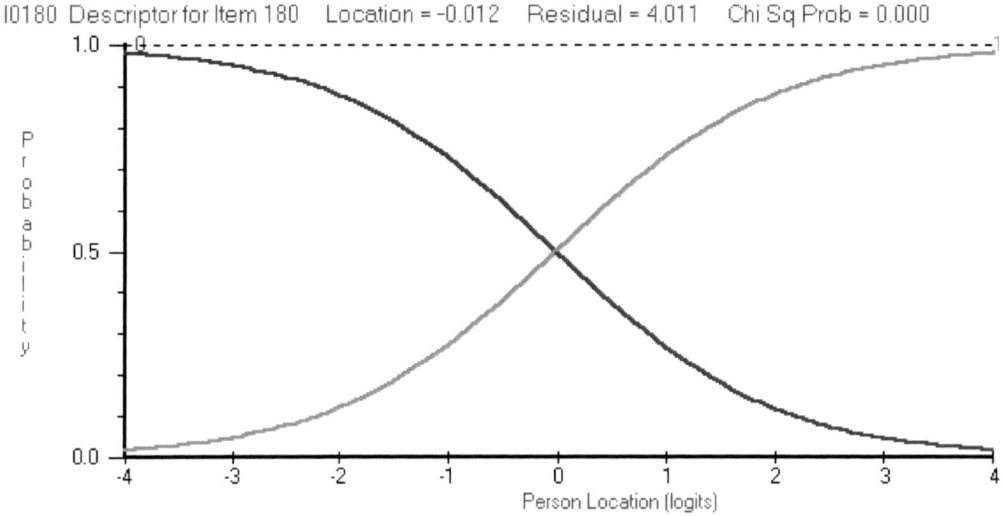

Figure 2. Response category curve for item 180 (not-so-good fitting item).

Targeting

The item difficulties range from −1.3 logits (SE=0.12) to + 1.6 logits (SE=0.14) and the student measures range from −3.4 logits to +4.2 logits. There are some students (34%) whose mathematics abilities are more than +1.6 logits and less than −1.3 logits and hence not 'matched' against an item location on the scale. In Figure 1, there are no items matching persons at either the lowest end (-1.5 to −3.5 logits) or the highest end (+1.5 to +4.4 logits) of the scale, indicating the improvements that are needed for the test. That is, both easy items and hard items need to be added to improve the targeting of the items for these Prathom Suksa 6 students. There are approximately 600 students who found these test items easy and approximately 180 who found who found them hard. The item difficulties were appropriate for the rest of the students, approximately 1,770 students.

Category Response Curves

The RUMM program provides a category response curve for each item, which makes it possible to view the ordering of the thresholds, and to check whether the category responses are being answered consistently and logically. A perusal of the category response curves for the 78 items indicates that the students answered the response categories consistently and logically. The items contained two response categories, 0 for wrong and 1 for correct. Figure 2 shows the category response curve for the item 180, a moderately difficulty item (difficulty = -0.01 logits) that doesn't fit the measurement model as well as one would like. Nevertheless, the Response Category Curve is good showing that the marking for this item is consistent and logical.

Item Characteristic Curves

The item characteristic curve for Item 76 (good-fitting item) of the mathematics scale is shown on Figure 3. The line indicates the *expected* score of mathematics ability groups, ranging from the lowest to highest ability groups, for each *observed* measure of a student ability group. When the observed scores closely follow the curve of expected values, the group is performing as expected on the item. Item 76 shows a good-fitting item to the model with all groups of mathematics ability close to the expected scores.

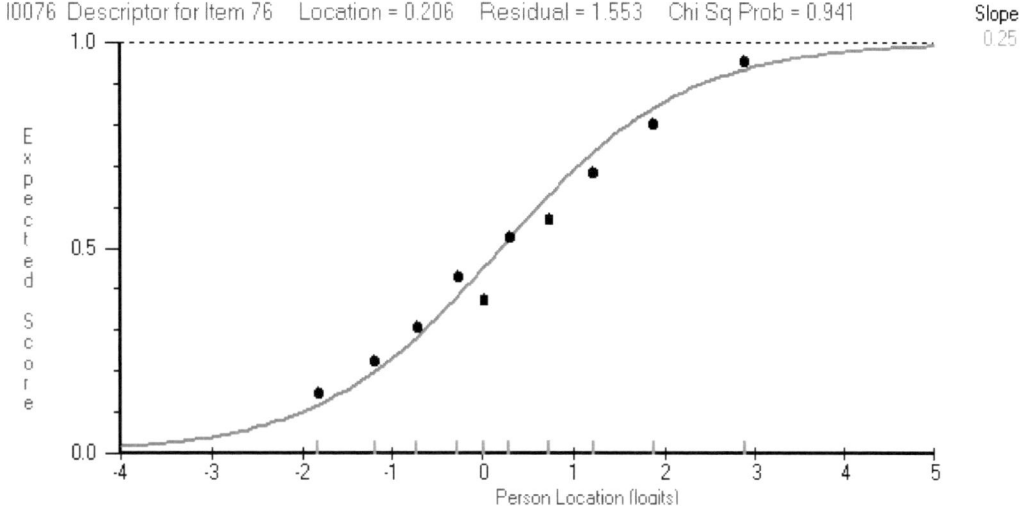

Figure 3. Characteristic curve for item 76 (a Good-Fitting Item).

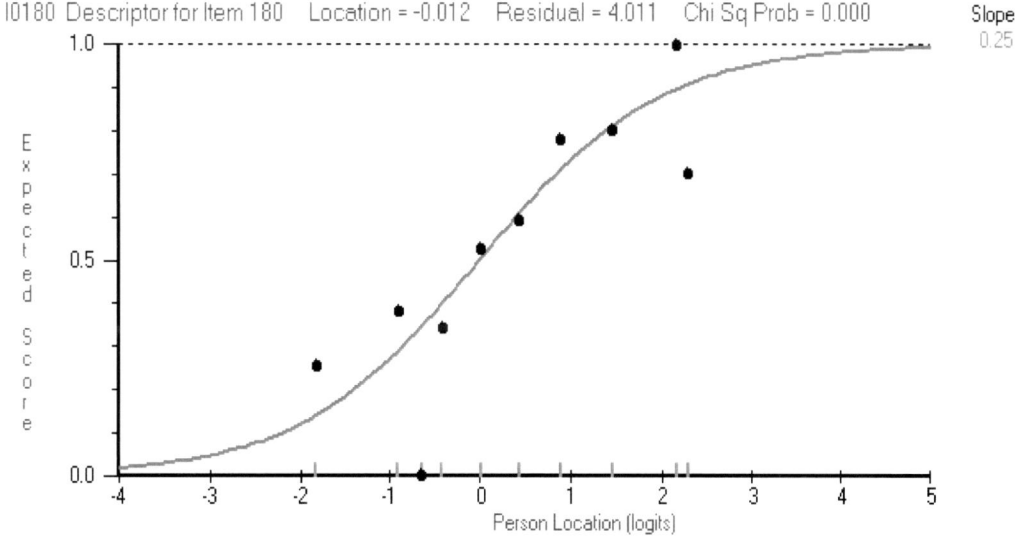

Figure 4. Characteristic curve for item 180 (a Poor-Fitting Item).

Item 180 is a not-so-good-fitting item of the mathematics scale. The item characteristic curve is shown on Figure 4. Four groups had higher expected scores and two groups had lower than expected scores. This explains the poor fit of this item to the measurement model since many students did not perform as expected on this item.

Item Difficulties

After the Rasch analysis, the items were ordered in terms of their calibrated item difficulties (see Tables 2 – 10) by sub-groups.

The items relating to the identification of the equation were found to be ordered from very easy (item 51) to moderately hard (item 172) (see Table 2). For example, the students found it very easy to identify the equations, item 51, item 91, and item 92. They found it easy (but harder) to identify the equations, item 132. For items 171, 212, and 172, they found it moderately hard to identify the equations, as would be expected.

Table 2. Item difficulties for identifying an equation from given choices (I=7, N=2,452)

Item Number	Item content	Difficulty
1(51)	Identification of an equation from given choices	-0.85
2(91)	Identification of an equation from given choices	-0.61
3(92)	Identification of both equations from given choices	-0.33
4(132)	Identification of both equations from given choices	-0.10
5(171)	Identification of an equation from given choices	+0.12
6(212)	Identification of both equations from given choices	+0.27
7(172)	Identification of both equations from given choices	+0.39

Table 3. Item difficulties for identifying the true equation (I=11, N=2,452)

Item Number	Item content	Difficulty
1(214)	Identification of the true equation from given choices	-1.07
2(174)	Identification of the true equation from given choices	-0.83
3(53)	Identification of the true equation from given choices	-0.62
4(13)	Identification of the true equation from given choices	-0.05
5(74)	Selecting the true equation from given equations	+0.22
6(71)	Selecting the true equation from given equations	+0.68
7(134)	Identification of the true equation from given choices	+0.85
8(73)	Selecting the true equation from given equations	+0.85
9(112)	Selecting the true equation from given equations	+1.08
10(233)	Selecting the true equation from given equations	+1.37
11(34)	Selecting the true equation from given equations	+1.57

Table 4. Item Difficulties for identifying an equation with an unknown (I=3, N=2,452)

Item Number	Item content	Difficulty
1(16)	Identification of two equations with unknowns	-0.96
2(135)	Identification of an equation with an unknown	-0.71
3(14)	Identification of an equation with an unknown	-0.66

**Table 5. Item Difficulties for finding the true equation in different circumstances
(I=8, N=2,452)**

Item Number	Item content	Difficulty
1(59)	Finding the true equation when an unknown is replaced by 5	-1.27
2(138)	Finding the value of X which satisfies the equation $X \times 6 = 6$	-1.12
3(139)	Finding the true equation when an unknown is replaced by 100	-0.93
4(220)	Finding the true equation when an unknown is replaced by 79	-0.50
5(218)	Finding the value of an unknown which satisfies the equation $121 \div Y = 11$	-0.48
6(180)	Finding the true equation when an unknown is replaced by 12	-0.01
7(83)	Finding the value of an unknown which satisfies the equation $Z \div 6 = 42$,	+0.74
8(97)	Finding the value of an unknown which satisfies the equation $\frac{Y}{5} = 60$	+1.37

The items relating to the identification of the true equation were found to be ordered from very easy (item 214) to very hard (item 34) (see Table 3). For example, the students found that it very easy to identify the true equation from the given choices of item 214. They found it very easy (but harder) to identify the true equation of items 174 and 53, moderately easy for item 13, hard for item 74, and very hard for items 71, 134, 73, 112, 233 and 34, as would be expected.

The items on identifying equations with an unknown were found to be all very easy (items 16, 135 and 14) (see Table 4). The students found it very easy to identify the two equations with unknowns (item 16) and harder (but still very easy) to identify the equations with unknowns from items 135 and 14.

The items on finding the value of an unknown that satisfies an equation were found to be ordered from very easy (item 59) to very hard (item 97) (see Table 5). For example, the students found it very easy to find the true equation when an unknown is replaced by the number 5 (item 59). They found it harder (but still very easy) to find the value of X which satisfies the equation $X \times 6 = 6$ (item 138), the true equation when an unknown is replaced by the number 100 (item 139), the true equation when an unknown is replaced by the number 79 (item 220) and the value of Y which satisfies the equation $121 \div Y = 11$ (item 218). They found it moderately easy (but harder) to find the true equation when an unknown is replace by the number 12 (item 180). They found that it very hard to find the value of Z which satisfies the equation $Z \div 6 = 42$ (item 83) and the value of Y which satisfies the equation $\frac{y}{5} = 60$ (item 97).

The items relating to the identification of the method to solve the equations were found to be ordered from easy (item 150) to very hard (item 60) (see Table 6). Some examples are given now. Item 109 (Find the method to solve the equation $X \div 29 = 174$) and item 103 (Find the method to solve the equation $96 + L = 386$) were found to be easy. Item 224 (Find the method to solve the equation $56 + B = 168$) and item 104 (Find the method to solve the equation $J - 35 = 105$) was found to be of moderate difficulty. Item 183 (Find the method to solve the equation $125 + E = 250$) and item 182 (Find the method to solve the equation $X + 61 = 122$) were found to be very difficult.

The items relating to finding the solutions to equations are ordered in difficulty from very easy (item 119) to moderately hard (item 117) (see Table 7). For example, the students found it very easy to find the solutions to the equations $Q \times 24 = 168$ (item 119), $Y + 14 = 140$ (item 116), and $21 + Z = 63$ (item 200), $25 \times F = 25$ (item 122), $7 + R = 84$ (item 241), $11 \times D = 88$ (item 202), and $A - 10 = 100$ (item 157). They found it moderately easy to find the solution to the equation $M - 38 = 152$ (item 197) and they found it moderately hard to find the solution to the equation $175 = E - 5$ (item 117).

Table 6. Item difficulties for finding a method to solve the equations (I= 17, N=2,452)

Item Number	Item Content	Difficulty
1(150)	Finding the method to solve the equation $J \div 65 = 130$	-0.28
2(109)	Finding the method to solve the equation $X \div 29 = 174$	-0.15
3(141)	Finding the method to solve the equation $P + 100 = 200$	-0.13
4(103)	Finding the method to solve the equation $96 + L = 386$	-0.12
5(68)	Finding the method to solve the equation $16 \times Q = 64$	-0.04
6(100)	Finding the method to solve the equation $X + 45 = 90$	-0.02
7(29)	Finding the method to solve the equation $Z \div 73 = 365$	+0.14
8(224)	Finding the method to solve the equation $56 + B = 168$	+0.19
9(106)	Finding the method to solve the equation $Z \times 35 = 140$	+0.24
10(104)	Finding the method to solve the equation $J - 35 = 105$	+0.24
11(185)	Finding the method to solve the equation $L - 47 = 188$	+0.27
12(223)	Finding the method to solve the equation $80 + F = 240$	+0.29
13(142)	Finding the method to solve the equation $75 + D = 375$	+0.37
14(140)	Finding the method to solve the equation $Y + 40 = 80$	+0.47
15(183)	Finding the method to solve the equation $125 + E = 250$	+0.54
16(182)	Finding the method to solve the equation $X + 61 = 122$	+0.73
17(60)	Finding the method to solve the equation $X + 100 = 100$	+0.95

Table 7. Item difficulties for finding a solution to an equation (I=9, N=2,452)

Item Number	Item content	Difficulty
1(119)	Find the solution of $Q \times 24 = 168$	-0.82
2(116)	Find the solution of $Y + 14 = 140$	-0.77
3(200)	Find the solution of $21 + Z = 63$	-0.70
4(122)	Find the solution of $25 \times F = 25$	-0.62
5(241)	Find the solution of $7 + R = 84$	-0.54
6(202)	Find the solution of $11 \times D = 88$	-0.45
7(157)	Find the solution of $A - 10 = 100$	-0.41
8(197)	Find the solution of $M - 38 = 152$	-0.06
9(117)	Find the solution of $175 = E - 5$	+0.25

The items relating to finding a solution to an equation involving a given condition (see Table 8) were found to be ordered from moderately hard (item 115) to very hard (item 164). For example, the students found it moderately hard to find the equation in which E has the highest value (item 115). They found it hard to find the value of $X + 10$, given $X + 69 = 138$ (item 76) , $Y - 5$, given $Y \times 7 = 49$ (item 81), and to find the equation in which F is less than 90 by 6 (item 236). They found it very hard to find an equation which has the same solution as the equation C − 11= 22 (item 75), the value of E+10, given E × 12 = 60 (item 121), the value of X + 10, given X + 21 = 105 (item 156), and the value of B − 5, given B ÷ 5 = 60 (item 164).

Table 8. Item difficulties for finding the solution or equation which relates to the given conditions (I=8, N=2,452)

Item Number	Item content	Difficulty
1(115)	Find the equation where E has the highest value	+0.08
2(76)	Find the value of X + 10, given X + 69 = 138	+0.21
3(81)	Find the value of Y − 5, given Y × 7 = 49	+0.28
4(236)	Find the equation which F is less than 90 by 6	+0.51
5(75)	Find the equation which is the same solution as the equation C − 11= 22	+0.63
6(121)	Find the value of E+10, Given E × 12 = 60	+0.65
7(156)	Find the value of X + 10, Given X + 21 = 105	+0.67
8(164)	Find the value of B − 5, Given B ÷ 5 = 60	+1.01

Table 9. Item difficulties for selecting an equation which is converted from a verbal problem or a problem which is converted from an equation (I=8, N=2,452)

Item Number	Item content	Difficulty
1(88)	Select an equation of the statement " Y students in a classroom were divided into 8 equal groups with 5 students each.	-0.86
2(45)	Select an equation in finding out the value of X from a problem "Dang had X Baht and had 10 Baht more from selling eggs. The total sum of his money was 30 Baht."	-0.45
3(85)	Select an equation which shows how many items did Peter had solve more from a problem "Peter solved 5 items and solved Y more. In total, he solved 12 items".	-0.32
4(125)	Select an equation which shows how many pieces of paper did Pooh collect from a problem "Pooh had 3 pieces of paper. She collected Z pieces more. The total pieces were 20".	-0.21
5(126)	Select an equation which shows the temperature of yesterday from a problem "Today's temperature is 19c. Yesterday was Xc. The total temperatures were 41c".	-0.07
6(129)	Select an equation which shows the total sum of John from a problem "John had the sum Y Baht. He bought a flashlight for 120 Baht and two bags for 70 Baht. 55 Baht remains."	+0.10
7(170)	Select an equation which shows how many pieces did Adam buy from a problem "Adam bought Z pieces of pork, costing 3 Baht per each. The sum used was 54 Baht."	+0.14
8(48)	Select a verbal problem which is related the equation X ÷ 5 = 7	+0.22

The items on selecting an equation converted from a verbal problem, or a problem converted from an equation, were found to be ordered from very easy (item 88) to hard (item 48) (see Table 9). Some examples are now given. The students found it very easy to select an equation which is converted from a verbal problem "Y students in a classroom were divided into 8 equal groups with 5 students each" (item 88). They found it easy to select an equation in finding out the value of X from a problem "Dang had X Baht and had 10 Baht more from selling eggs. The total sum of his money was 30 Baht." (item 45) and found it easy (but harder) to choose an equations which shows how many pieces of paper did Pooh collect from a problem "Pooh had 3 pieces of paper. She collected Z pieces more. The total pieces were 20" (item 125). They found it moderately hard to select an equation which shows the total sum of John from a problem "John had the sum Y Baht. He bought a flashlight for 120 Baht and two bags for 70 Baht. 55 Baht remains." (item 129) and an equation which shows how many pieces did Adam buy from a problem "Adam bought Z pieces of pork, costing 3 Baht per each. The sum used was 54 Baht." (item 170). They found it hard to select a verbal problem which is related the equation $X \div 5 = 7$ (item 48).

The items on problem solving were found to be ordered from very easy (item 87) to moderately hard (item 90) (see Table 10). For example, the students found it very easy to find the original amount from the problem "Dang had X Baht in his account and deposited 115 Baht more. The total was 321 Baht"(item 87). They found it moderately easy (but harder) to solve the problem "A man has cash of 4,650 Baht. After having it deposited in a bank, he has 3,500 Baht remaining. How much money did he deposit in a bank?" (item 249), and the problem "A teacher wants to divide 100 boy scouts into equal groups with 9 members a group, which keeps one scout from a group. How many groups will she have?' (item 248).

Table 10. Item difficulties for problem solving (I=7, N=2,452)

Item Number	Item content	Difficulty
1(87)	Dang had X Baht in his account and deposited 115 Baht more. The total was 321 Baht. What is the original amount?	-0.66
2(249)	A man has cash of 4,650 Baht. After depositing some of it in a bank, he has 3,500 Baht remaining. How much money did he deposit in the bank?	-0.09
3(127)	One fence post is 180 cm. long. 40 cm. of the post is buried in the soil and Y cm. is above the soil. How many centimetres are above the soil?	-0.07
4(130)	Sopon wants to buy a 360 Baht slack. But he had only 180 Baht. How many flowers garlands does he have to sell to earn enough money if each garland costs 10 Baht?	-0.05
5(248)	A teacher wants to divide 100 boy scouts in to equal groups with 9 members a group. Which keep one scout from group. How many groups will he divide?	-0.03
6(47)	"A" had X Baht, "B" had 5 Baht more than "A". The total sum of the two was 65 Baht. How much money did "A" have?	+0.14
7(90)	A rope is M metres long. It is cut into 18 ropes with the length of 2 metres each. What is the length of the rope?	+0.16

They found it moderately hard to solve the problems "A" had X Baht, "B" had 5 Baht more than "A". The total sum of the two was 65 Baht. How much money did "A" have? (item 47) and the problem "A rope is M metres long. It is cut into 18 pieces with a length of 2 metres each. What is the length of the rope M?" (item 90).

RASCH ANALYSIS FOR THE 20 EXTRA ITEMS
(LINKED TO THE 78 ITEM SCALE)

Further analysis with the RUMM program tested the extra 50 items (N=610) in order to create a linear scale of mathematics achievement with the 20 items that fitted the measurement model. Ten common items from the set of 78 items were included as part of the 50 items. The residuals were examined. The global item fit residuals and global student standardised fit residuals have a mean near zero and a standard deviation near one indicating a reasonable fit to the measurement model. The probability of fit of items to the measurement model was then checked to identify items that fitted the model. Of the 20 items, 19 fitted the measurement model with probability p>0.04. The item-trait test of fit examines the consistency of the item difficulties across the student mathematics measures along the scale. This determines whether there was agreement among student as to the difficulties of all items along the scale. The item-trait interaction was not statistically significant [Chi-square (df =160) =178.34, p =0.15]. This means that a unidimensional trait was measured with good linkage to the 78 item scale.

Table 11. Item difficulties for finding a solution to an equation (I=3, N=6 10)

Item Number	Item content	Difficulty
1(18)	Find the solution of $\dfrac{2X}{8} + \dfrac{5X}{20} = 6$	-0.53
2(17)	Find the solution of $Y - 9 = \dfrac{1}{4}$	-0.46
3(20)	Find the solution of $\dfrac{X+2}{6} = \dfrac{2X-1}{6}$	-0.11

The items on finding the solution to an equation were found to be all easy (items 18, 17 and 20) (see Table 11). The students found it easy to find the solutions to the equations $\dfrac{2X}{8} + \dfrac{5X}{20} = 6$ (item 18) and the equation $Y - 9 = \dfrac{1}{4}$ (item 17). They found it easy (but harder) to find the solution to the equation $\dfrac{X+2}{6} = \dfrac{2X-1}{6}$ (item 20).

The items relating to finding a solution to an equation which relating to a given condition (see Table 12) were found to be ordered from moderately easy (item 47) to moderately hard (item 22). For examples, the students found it moderately easy to find the equation which has the same solution as the equation $5X + 10 = 40$ (item 47) and the equation which Y equal to 10 (item 42). They found it moderately hard to find the different solution between the equations $3Y - 6 = Y + 4$ and $2Y - 5 = 35$ (item 37), the value of the equation 2X – 14, Given X – 7 = 3 (item 24), the equation which X equal to 18 (item 45), the value of X which makes $\dfrac{X}{6} + \dfrac{5X}{6} = 3$ less than $2X - 5 = 43$ (item 41), the value of X which makes $5X = 4X + 9$ more than $5X + 3 = 3X + 9$ (item 36), and the value of X which makes $5X - 5 = 30$ more than $5X = 3X + 6$ (item 40). They found it hard to find the value of x, Given $6X - 24 = 6 - 4X$ (item 32) and the two equations in the choice have the same solutions (item 50). They also found it hard to find the equation which has different solution from the others equations (item 43), and the equation which has the least solution (item 23). They found it moderately hard to find the equation which has the solution more than 40 (item 46), the value of $3A + 3B$, Given $A = 4 - B$ (item31), and the equation which has the least value of X (item22).

Table 12. Item difficulties for finding the solution or equation which related to the given condition (N=610)

Item Number	Item content	Difficulty
1(47)	Find the equation which has the same solution as the equation $5X + 10 = 40$	-0.23
2(42)	Find the equation where Y is equal to 10	-0.15
3(37)	Find the different solution between the equations $3Y - 6 = Y + 4$ and $2Y - 5 = 35$	+0.09
4(24)	Find the value of 2X – 14, Given X – 7 = 3	+0.11
5(45)	Find the equation which X equal to 18	+0.12
6(41)	Find the value of X which makes $\dfrac{X}{6} + \dfrac{5X}{6} = 3$ less than $2X - 5 = 43$	+0.12
7(36)	Find the value of X which makes $5X = 4X + 9$ more than $5X + 3 = 3X + 9$	+0.15
8(40)	Find the value of X which makes $5X - 5 = 30$ more than $5X = 3X + 6$?	+0.18
9(32)	Find the value of $4X - 2$ Given $6X - 24 = 6 - 4X$	+0.28
10(50)	Find the choice which has two equations in which choice have the same solutions	+0.31
11(43)	Find the equation which has different solution from others	+0.31
12(23)	Find the equation which has the least solution	+0.39
13(46)	Find the equation which has the solution more than 40	+0.42
14(31)	Find the value of $3A + 3B$, Given $A = 4 - B$	+0.43
15(22)	Find the equation which has the least value of X	+0.51

The students found it extremely easy to select an equation which is converted from a verbal problem "John had the sum Y Baht. He bought a flashlight for 120 Baht and two bags for 70 Baht. 55 Baht remains. What is the total sum that John had?" (item 7). They found it moderately easy to select an equation which is converted from a verbal problem "A had X Baht. B had 50 Baht more two times of A. The sum of the two equals to four times of A's"(item 45).

Table 13. Item difficulties for selection an equation which is converted from a verbal problem (I=2, N=610)

Item Number	Item content	Difficulty
1(7)	Select the equation which shows the total sum of John from a problem "John had the sum Y baht. He bought a flashlight for 120 baht and two bags for 70 baht. 55 baht remains."	-1.65
2(12)	Find the equation of the statement " A had X baht. B had 50 baht more two times of A. The sum of the two equals to four times of A's"	-0.29

ITEM BANK CONTENT

The item bank for mathematics on equations for the year 6 (Prathom Suksa 6) students contained 98 items which fitted the measurement model and consisted of:

1. Seven items relating to the identification of an equation, ordered from very easy (difficulty = -0.85) to moderately hard (difficulty = +0.39);
2. Eleven items relating to the identification of the true equation, ordered from very easy (difficulty = -1.07) to very hard (difficulty = +1.57) ;
3. Three items on identifying equations with an unknown were all very easy (difficulties from
4. -0.96 to -0.66);
5. Eight items on finding the value of an unknown that satisfies the equation, ordered from very easy (difficulty = -1.27) to very hard (difficulty = +1.37);
6. Seventeen items relating to Identify the Method to solve the Equation, ordered from very easy (difficulty = -0.28) to extremely hard (difficulty = +0.95);
7. Twelve items relating to finding the solutions to equations, ordered from very easy (difficulty = -0.82) to moderately hard (difficulty = +0.25);
8. Twenty-three items relating to finding a solution of an equation which related the given condition, ordered from moderately easy (difficulty = -0.23) to very hard (difficulty = +1.01);
9. Ten items on selecting an equation converted from a verbal problem or a verbal problem related to an equation, ordered from very easy (difficulty = -0.86) to hard (difficulty = +0.22);
10. Seven items on problem solving, ordered from very easy (difficulty = -0.66) to moderately hard (difficulty = +0.16).

DATA ANALYSIS (PART II)
THE COMPUTERIZED ADAPTIVE TESTING RESULTS

The SPSS computer program (Pallant, 2001) was used to analyse data from 400 Prathom Suksa 6 students. The frequencies and percentages of mathematics ability were used as the indicators to examine mathematics competencies of the students. A one-way ANOVA was used to examine differences in test length and testing times among the different groups relating to stopping criteria and mathematics competencies, and also to examine in differences mathematics competencies among the different groups of stopping criteria. ANOVA is the appropriate statistic to use because there are more than two groups of the students and test length, testing times and because mathematics competencies were measured on ratio or interval scales (Cavana et al., 2001). Because the F statistics were significantly different, the Sheffe Multiple Range test was used to determine between which groups the true differences lie (Cavana et al., 2001). The frequency of Mathematics competencies of the students, one-way ANOVA, and Sheffe Multiple Range test results are shown through tables and descriptive text. The presentation begins with a description of the analysis for the mathematics achievement that is reported for 400 Prathom Suksa 6 students. The ANOVA and the Sheffe Multiple Range are used to show the mean differences in test length and testing times, among stopping criteria and mathematics competencies, and the mean difference of mathematics competencies for different groups of stopping criteria.

Table 14. Frequency Table for Mathematics Competencies

Achievement	Frequency	Percent	Cumulative Percent
Low	67	16.75	16.75
Moderately high	301	75.25	92.00
High	32	8.00	100.00
Total	400	100.00	

Table 15. Test length for the different groups by stopping criteria

Source of Variation	Sum of Squares	df	Mean Square	F	p
Between Groups	1560.31	3.00	520.10	191.30	.00*
Within Groups	1076.63	396.00	2.72		
Total	2636.94	399.00			

Note: p means significance based on the F value. * p < 0.05.

MATHEMATICS COMPETENCY

The result of the analysis of mathematics competencies of Prathom Suksa 6 students is set out in Table 14. It presents frequencies and percentages of mathematics competencies of the students in the three groups (low, moderately high, and high).

The results showed that there are 67 (16.75%) students who can be regarded as having a low mathematics achievement (mathematics measures were from -1.02 to 0.00 logits). From 0.00 to +1.00 logits, there are 301 (75.25%) students and they can be regarded as having a moderately high mathematics achievement. From +1.00 to +3.00 logits, there are 32 (8.00%) students and they can be regarded as having a high mathematics achievement.

DIFFERENCES IN TEST LENGTH AND TESTING TIMES AMONG DIFFERENT GROUPS BY STOPPING CRITERIA AND MATHEMATICS COMPETENCIES

The results of the analysis of the test relating to different test lengths and testing times among four groups for stopping criteria and three groups of mathematics competencies of the students with the Mathematics Computerized Adaptive Testing are set out in Tables 15 to 22. Tables 15, 17, 19, and 21 show the F values to examine the difference in test length and testing times among the different groups for stopping criteria and mathematics competencies, while the Sheffe Multiple Range test results for the differences are set out in Tables 16, 18, 20, and 22.

Table 16. Differences in test length by stopping criteria

Stopping criteria		(2)	(1)	(4)	(3)
	Mean	3.14	4.34	6.83	8.14
$SEE \leq 0.30$ (2)	3.14		1.20*	3.69*	5.00*
$SEE \leq 0.20$ (1)	4.34			2.49*	3.80*
$SEE_m - SEE_{m-1} \leq 0.005$ (4)	6.83				1.31*
$SEE \leq 0.40$ (3)	8.14				

Note * The mean difference was significant at the 0.05 level.

As can be seen from Table 16, the F test shows that the difference in the means of the students for the four groups by stopping criteria, $SEE \leq 0.20$ (1), $SEE \leq 0.30$ (2), $SEE \leq 0.40$ (3), and $SEE_m - SEE_{m-1} \leq 0.005$ (4), were significantly different at the 5 per cent significance level in regards to test length (F = 191.30, df = 3, 396, p = 0.00). That is, there were significant differences in the mean test length levels of students in the four groups by stopping criteria. To determine between which groups test lengths are significantly different, the Sheffe Multiple Range test was performed.

As can be seen from Table 16, the results showed that mean test length (number of items) for the four groups by stopping criteria was 4.34 for the first criteria, 3.14 for the second, 8.14 for the third, and **7.83** for the fourth. There were six main points of difference in test length by stopping criteria. The third group was significantly different from groups 2, 1, and 4 at p=0.05; the fourth group was significantly different from groups 2 and 1 at p=0.05; and the first group was significantly different from group 2 at p=0.05.

Table 17. Testing times for the different groups by stopping criteria

Source of Variation	Sum of Squares	df	Mean Square	F	p
Between Groups	755.89	3.00	251.96	53.85	.00*
Within Groups	1,852.78	396.00	4.68		
Total	2,608.67	399.00			

Note p means significance based on the F value. * p < 0.05.

Table 18. Differences in testing time by stopping criteria

Stopping criteria		(2)	(1)	(4)	(3)
	Mean	2.38	3.33	5.26	5.74
$SEE \leq 0.30$ (2)	2.38		0.95*	2.88*	3.36*
$SEE \leq 0.20$ (1)	3.33			1.93*	2.41*
$SEE_m - SEE_{m-1} \leq 0.005$ (4)	5.26				0.48
$SEE \leq 0.40$ (3)	5.74				

Note * The mean difference was significant at the 0.05 level.

Table 19. Test length for the different groups of mathematics competency

Source of Variation	Sum of Squares	df	Mean Square	F	p
Between Groups	207.04	2	103.52	16.91	.00*
Within Groups	2429.89	397	6.12		
Total	2636.94	399			

Note p means significance based on the F value. * p < 0.05.

Table 20. Differences in test length by mathematics competencies

Mathematics competencies		2	3	1
	Mean	5.21	6.31	7.07
Moderately high (2)	5.21		1.10	1.86*
High (3)	6.31			0.76
Low (1)	7.07			

Note * The mean difference was significant at the 0.05 level.

Table 21. Testing times for the different groups by mathematics competency

Source of Variation	Sum of Squares	df	Mean Square	F	p
Between Groups	52.40	2	26.20	4.07	0.02*
Within Groups	2556.27	397	6.44		
Total	2608.67	399			

Note p means significance based on the F value. * p < 0.05.

As can be seen from Table 18, the F test shows that the difference in the means of the students for the four groups by stopping criteria, $SEE \leq 0.20$ (1), $SEE \leq 0.30$ (2), $SEE \leq 0.40$ (3), and $SEE_m - SEE_{m-1} \leq 0.005$ (4), were significantly different at the 5 per cent significance level, in regards to testing time (F = 53.85, df = 3, 396, p = 0.00). That is, there were significant differences in the mean testing time levels of students in the four groups by stopping criteria. To determine between which groups, testing times are significantly different, the Sheffe Multiple Range test was performed.

As can be seen from Table 20, the results showed that mean testing times for the four groups by stopping criteria was 3.33 minutes for the first criteria, 2.38 minutes for the second, 5.74 minutes for the third, and 5.26 minutes for the fourth. There were five main points of difference in testing times by stopping criteria. The third group and the fourth group were significantly different from groups 2 and 1 at p=0.05; and the first group was significantly different from group 2 at p=0.05. The third group with the stopping criteria of $SEE \leq 0.40$ was not significantly different from group 4.

As can be seen from Table 20, the F test shows that the difference in the means of the students in the different groups of mathematics competency, high, moderately high, and low, were significantly different at p=0.05 (at the 5 per cent significance level) in regards to test length (number of items)(F = 16.91, df = 2, 397, p = 0.00). That is, there were significant differences in the mean test length levels of students in the three groups of the mathematics competency.To determine between which groups, test lengths are significantly different, the Sheffe Multiple Range test was performed. The results are shown in Table 19.

Table 22. Differences in testing time by mathematics competencies

Mathematics competencies		2	3	1
	Mean	3.97	4.50	4.92
Moderately high (2)	3.97		0.53	0.94*
High (3)	4.50			0.41
Low (1)	4.92			

Note * The mean difference was significant at 0.05 level.

Table 23. Mathematics competencies for the different groups by stopping criteria

Source of Variation	Sum of Squares	df	Mean Square	F	p
Between Groups	3.41	3.00	1.14	5.09	.00*
Within Groups	88.46	396.00	.22		
Total	91.87	399.00			

Note p means significance based on the F value. * p < 0.05.

As can be seen from Table 22, the results showed that mean test length (number of items) for the three groups of mathematics competency was 7.07 for the first (low), 5.21 for the second (moderately high), and 6.31 for the third (high). The test length of the students in the first group with the low mathematics competency was significantly different from that in group2 (moderately high) at the 5 per cent significance level.

As can be seen from Table 22, the F test shows that the difference in the means of the students in the different groups of, high, moderately high, and low mathematics competency, were significantly different. at the 5 per cent significance level, in regards to testing times (F = 4.07, df = 2, 397, p = 0.02). That is, there were significant differences in the mean testing time levels of students in the three groups of the mathematics competency. To determine between which groups, testing times are significantly different, the Sheffe Multiple Range test was performed.

As can be seen from Table 22, the results showed that mean testing time for the three groups of mathematics competency was 4.92 minutes for the first (low), 3.97 minutes for the second (moderately high), and 4.50 minutes for the third (high). There was one main point of difference in testing time by mathematics competencies. The first group with the low mathematics competency was significantly different from group 2 (moderately high) at the 5 per cent significance level.

DIFFERENCES IN MATHEMATICS COMPETENCIES AMONG DIFFERENT GROUPS BY STOPPING CRITERIA

The results of the analysis of the test of different mathematics competencies among four groups for stopping criteria of Mathematics Computerized Adaptive Testing are set out in Tables 23 and 24. Table 23 shows the F values to examine the difference in mathematics competencies among the different groups for stopping criteria, while the Sheffe Multiple Range test results for the differences are set out in Table 24.

Table 24. Differences in mathematics competency by stopping criteria

Stopping criteria	Mean	(2) 0.38	(3) 0.54	(1) 0.57	(4) 0.63
$SEE \leq 0.30$ (2)	0.38		0.16	0.19*	0.25*
$SEE \leq 0.40$ (3)	0.54			0.03	0.09
$SEE \leq 0.20$ (1)	0.57				0.06
$SEE_m - SEE_{m-1} \leq 0.005$ (4)	0.63				

Note * The mean difference was significant at the 0.05 level.

As can be seen from Table 24, the F test shows that the difference in the means of the students for the four groups by stopping criteria, $SEE \leq 0.20$ (1), $SEE \leq 0.30$ (2), $SEE \leq 0.40$ (3), and $SEE_m - SEE_{m-1} \leq 0.005$ (4), were significantly different at the 5 per cent significance level in regards to mathematics competency (F = 5.09, df = 3, 396, p = 0.00). That is, there were significant differences in the mean mathematics competency levels of students in the four groups by stopping criteria. To determine between which groups mathematics competencies are significantly different, the Sheffe Multiple Range test was performed.

The results showed that mean mathematics competency for the four groups by stopping criteria was 0.57 logits for the first criteria, 0.38 logits for the second, 0.54 logits for the third, and 0.63 logits for the fourth. There were two main points of difference in mathematics competency by stopping criteria. The second group was significantly different from group 1 and group 4 at p=0.05.

SUMMARY OF RESULTS

Mathematics Competencies

There were 72.25 %, 16.75%, and 8% of the Prathom Suksa 6 students having a moderately high, low, and high mathematics achievement respectively.

Test Length, Testing Times and Mathematics Competencies in Different Groups by Stopping Criteria

The four groups of stopping criteria were $SEE \leq 0.20$ (group 1), $SEE \leq 0.30$ (group 2) $SEE \leq 0.40$ (group 3) and $SEE_m - SEE_{m-1} \leq 0.005$ (group 4).

1. Test lengths were significantly different at p=0.05 among four groups of stopping criteria (F = 191.30, df = 3, 396, p = 0.00).
2. The mean highest test length (8.14 items) and the mean lowest test length (3.14 items) were in group 3 (stopping criteria is $SEE \leq 0.40$) and group 2 (stopping criteria is $SEE \leq 0.30$). Each group was significantly different at p=0.05 from the others.
3. Testing times were significantly different at p=0.05 among the four groups of stopping criteria (F = 53.85, df = 3, 396, p = 0.00).
4. The mean highest testing time (5.74 minutes) and the mean lowest testing time (2.38 minute) were in group 3 (stopping criteria is $SEE \leq 0.40$) and group 2 (stopping criteria is $SEE \leq 0.30$). Each group was also significantly different at p=0.05 from the others.
5. Mathematics competencies were significantly different at p=0.05 among the four groups of stopping criteria (F = 5.09, df = 3, 396, p = 0.00).
6. The mean highest mathematics competency (0.63 logits) and the mean lowest mathematics competency (0.38 logits) were in group 4 (stopping criteria is $SEE_m - SEE_{m-1} \leq 0.005$) and group 2 (stopping criteria is $SEE \leq 0.30$). Students mathematics competency in group 2 (stopping criteria is $SEE \leq 0.30$) was significantly different from group 1(stopping criteria is $SEE \leq 0.20$) and group 4 (stopping criteria is $SEE_m - SEE_{m-1} \leq 0.005$) at p=0.05.

Test Length and Testing Times in Different Groups by Mathematics Competencies

The three groups of mathematics competencies were low (group1), moderately high (group 2), and high (group 3).

1. Test lengths were significantly different at p=0.05 among three groups of mathematics competencies (F = 16.91, df = 2, 397, p = 0.00).
2. The mean highest test length (7.07 items) and the mean lowest test length (5.21 items) were in group 1 (low mathematics competency) and group 2 (moderately high mathematics competency). There was an only one significantly different test length at p=0.05 between students in group 1 (low mathematics competency) and group 2 (moderately high mathematics competency).
3. Testing times were significantly different at p=0.05 among the three groups of mathematics competencies (F = 4.07, df = 2, 397, p = 0.02).
4. The mean highest testing time (4.92 minutes) and the mean lowest testing time (3.97 minutes) were in group 1 (low mathematics competency) and group 2 (moderately high mathematics competency). There was an only one significantly different testing

times at p=0.05 between students in group 1 (low mathematics competency) and group 2 (moderately high mathematics competency).

ATTITUDE TO COMPUTERIZED ADAPTIVE TESTING

At the end of the Computerized adaptive testing, an attitude questionnaire was given to 400 students and the results were Rasch analysed. There was a good fit to the measurement model (item-trait interaction chi-square =165.4, df=150, p=0.18) showing that there reasonably good agreement with the item difficulties all along the scale. The Person Separation Index was 0.92 and the Cronbach Alpha was 0.92 showing that the scale data were reliable. The thresholds between the response categories were ordered in line with the ordering of the response categories showing that the response categories were used logically and consistently by the student respondents.

The items are well targeted against the attitude measures (that is, the range of item thresholds match the range of attitude measures of the students on the same scale). The item threshold values range from -2.04 logits (SE=0.07) to + 2.18 logits (SE=0.07) and the student measures range from -1.96 logits to +5.82 logits. There are only 38 students whose attitude measures are more than +2.18 logits and hence not 'matched' against an item threshold on the scale. These results indicate that a good measurement scale of attitude has been created, that the data are reliable and consistent, that the errors are small relation to the measures, and so valid inferences can be made from the scale data.

Item Difficulties

After the Rasch analysis, the items were ordered in terms of their calibrated item difficulties by sub-groups so that a reader can see which items are easy and which are hard.

The students found it very easy to say that Computerized Adaptive Testing is very interesting (item 3) and they are happy with it (item 14). They found it easy (but harder) to say that they like it because of its immediate feedback (item 8). They found it moderately easy (but harder) to say that they enjoyed doing the Computerized Adaptive Test (item 2) and moderately hard to say that they are lucky to have the chance to take a Computerized Adaptive Test (item 12). They found it harder to say that they were enthusiastic about taking part in a Computerized Adaptive Test (item 1) and this was expected because the attitude is linked to a behaviour which is theoretically harder than a similar attitude (compare item 3 and item 8). They found it very hard to say that they liked the Computerized Adaptive Test because it was not too difficult (item 6) because this again is linked to a behaviour (compare item 3 and item 8).

The students found it very easy to say that they want Computerized Adaptive Testing for all other subjects (item 13) and much harder (but still moderately easy) to say that they feel it is worth taking a Computerized Adaptive Test (item 9). They found it moderately easy to say that they feel like using their full ability with the Computerized Adaptive Test (item 10) and much harder to say that Computerized Adaptive Testing makes them want to study Mathematics (item 11). They found it hard to say that after finishing the Computerized

Adaptive Testing, they want to do another (item 7), in line with their answer to item 11. They found it extremely hard to say that they believe they can do the Computerized Adaptive Test well (item 5) and that they took the Computerized Adaptive Test with confidence (item 4), as would be expected.

Table 25. Item difficulties in order for Like and Interest in CAT (N=400)

Item No.	Item wording	Difficulty
	Like and Interest in CAT	
1. (3)	The Computerized Adaptive Testing is very interesting.	-0.53
2. (14)	I am happy doing the Computerized Adaptive Test without limited time.	-0.29
3. (8)	I like the Computerized Adaptive Test because of its immediate feedback.	-0.11
4. (2)	I am happy and enjoyed doing a Computerized Adaptive Test.	+0.03
5. (12)	I feel lucky to have the chance to take a Computerized Adaptive Test.	+0.14
6. (1)	I am enthusiastic about taking part in a Computerized Adaptive Test.	+0.23
7. (6)	I liked the Computerized Adaptive Test because it was not too difficult for me.	+0.48

The students found it very easy to say that Computerized Adaptive Testing is modern (item 17) and a little easier to say that it is appropriate for these days (item 20), and useful (item 15). They found it moderately easy to say that Computerized Adaptive Testing allows students to spend less time on testing (item 23) (with the implication that they can then spend more time on learning) and that it provides students with appropriate items (item 24). Students found very hard to say that Computerized Adaptive Testing saves money (item 18).

Table 26. Item difficulties in order for Confidence with and Use of CAT (N=400)

Item No.	Item wording	Difficulty
	Confidence with and Use of CAT	
1. (13)	I want Computerized Adaptive Testing to be used for my other subjects.	-0.41
2. (9)	It is worth taking a Computerized Adaptive Test.	-0.06
3. (10)	I feel like using my full ability with the Computerized Adaptive Test.	+0.01
4. (11)	The Computerized Adaptive Testing makes me want to study Mathematics.	+0.28
5. (7)	After finishing the Computerized Adaptive Testing, I feel like wanting to do another.	+0.37
6. (5)	I believe that I can do the Computerized Adaptive Test well.	+0.72
7. (4)	I took the Computerized Adaptive Test with confidence.	+0.75

Table 27. Item difficulties in order for CAT as Modern and Useful (N=400)

Item No.	Item wording	Difficulty
	CAT as Modern and Useful	
1. (17)	Computerized Adaptive Testing is modern.	-0.73
2. (20)	The Computerized Adaptive Testing is currently appropriate for these days.	-0.56
3. (15)	Computerized Adaptive Testing is very useful.	-0.53
4. (23)	Computerized Adaptive Testing allows students to spend less time on testing.	+0.07
5. (24)	Computerized Adaptive Testing provides examinees with appropriate items.	+0.08
6. (18)	Computerized Adaptive Testing saves money.	+0.61

Table 28. Item difficulties in order for CAT as Reliable, Fair and Good (N=400)

Item No.	Item wording	Difficulty
	CAT as Reliable, Fair and Good	
1. (21)	Computerized Adaptive Testing is fair for all students.	-0.36
2. (19)	Computerized Adaptive Testing gives reliable results.	-0.32
3. (25)	Computerized Adaptive Testing makes examinees careful when doing the test.	-0.01
4. (16)	Computerized Adaptive Testing is challenging.	+0.05
5. (22)	Computerized Adaptive Testing inspires the students to do the test.	+0.08

Students found it very easy to say that Computerized Adaptive Testing is fair for all students (item 21) and that it gives reliable results (item 19). They found it moderately easy to say that Computerized Adaptive Testing makes student take care in testing (item 25), provides a challenge (item 16), and inspires the students to do the test (item 22).

Table 29. Item difficulties in order for CAT Recommendations (N=400)

Item No.	Item wording	Difficulty
	CAT Recommendations	
1. (30)	I am ready to apply the knowledge from Computerized Adaptive Testing.	-0.43
2. (28)	If possible, I 'd rather take a Computerized Adaptive Test.	-0.13
3. (29)	If I have a chance, I will introduce my younger friends to Computerized Adaptive Testing.	-0.11
4. (26)	I wish I could take a Computerized Adaptive Test in a Mathematics test competition.	+0.33
5. (27)	I will tell my friends about Computerized Adaptive Testing.	+0.36

Students found it very easy to say that they were ready to apply their knowledge of Computerized Adaptive Testing (item 30). They found it moderately easy to say that they would rather take a Computerized Adaptive Test (item 28) (than an ordinary test) and that they would introduce their younger friends to Computerized Adaptive Testing (item 29). Students found it very hard to say that they could take a Computerized Adaptive Test in a mathematics competition (item 26) and that they would tell their friends about Computerized Adaptive Testing (item 27).

REFERENCES

Andrich, D., Sheridan, B., and Luo, G. (2003). *RUMM2010: A windows-based item analysis program employing Rasch unidimensional measurement models.* Perth, Western Australia: RUMM Laboratory.

Andrich, D., Sheridan, B., and Luo, G. (2005). *RUMM2020: A windows-based item analysis program employing Rasch unidimensional measurement models.* Perth, Western Australia: RUMM Laboratory.

Beevers, C. E., McGuire, G. R., Stirling, G., and Wild, D. G. (1995). Mathematical ability assessed by computer. *Computers and Education, 25*(3), 123-132.

Bergstrom, B. A., and Lunz, M. E. (1999). CAT for certification and licensure. In F. Drasgow and J. B. Olson-Buchanan (Eds.), *Innovations in computerized assessment* (pp. 67-91). Mahwah, New Jersey: Lawrence Erlbaum Associates.

Boonprasert, U. (1988). *The construction of item banking*. Bangkok: Chulalongkorn University.

Cavana, R.Y., Delahaye, B.L, and Sekaran, U. (2001). Applied business research: qualitative and quantitative methods. Singapore: Markono Print media Pty Ltd

Chansilp, S. (2006). *Online Test Bank SUT*. Retrieved 20/5/2007, from http://library.sut.ac.th/central/HeaderFrame.html

Choppin, B. (1981). Educational measurement and the item bank model. In C. Lacey and D. Lawton (Eds.), *Issues in evaluation and accoutability*. Methuen, London.

Choppin, B. (1985). Principles of item banking. *Evaluation in Education, 9*, 87-90.

Cordova C. M. J. (1998). *Applications of network flows to computerized adaptive testing (Item Response, test assembly)*. Unpublished PhD, Rutgers The State University of New Jersey, NJ.

Department of Academics. (1991). *Local item bank for schools*. Bangkok: Khurusapha press.

Ebel, R. L., and Frisbie, D. A. (1986). *Essentials of educational measurement* (4th ed.). Englewood Cliffs, New Jersey: Prentice-Hall.

Eggen, T. J. H. M., and Verschoor, A. J. (2006). Optimal testing with easy or difficult items in computerized adaptive testing. *Applied Psychological Measurement, 30*(5), 379-393.

Embreston, S. E., and Reise, S. P. (2000). *Item response theory for phychologists*. Mahwah, NJ: Erlbaum.

Fan, X. (1998). Item Response Theory and Classical Test Theory: An empirical comparison of their item/person statistics. *Educational and Psychological Measurement, 58*(3), 357-381.

Gershon, R. C. (2005). Computer adaptive testing. *Journal of Applied Measurement, 6*(1), 109-127.

Gershon, R. C., and Bergstrom, B. A. (Artist). (1995). *Does cheating on CAT pay: Not!* [ERIC Document Reproductions No. TM024692].

Green, B. F. (1984). Technical guidlines for assessing computerized adaptive test. *Journal of Educational Measurement, 21*, 72, 97, 347,352.

Gronlund, N. E. (1998). *Assessment of student achievement* (6 ed.). Boston: Allynand Bacon.

Hambleton, R. K. (1986). The changing conception of measurement : A commentary. *Applied Psychological Measurement, 10*, 415-421.

Hambleton, R. K., Sawaminathan, H., and Rogers, J. H. (1991). *Fundamental of item response theory*. Newbury Park, CA: Sage Publications.

Hambleton, R. K., and Swaminathan, H. (1985). *Item response theory : Principles and application*. Boston: Kluwer-Nijhoff Publishing.

Hiscox, M. D. (1983). *A balance sheet for educational item banking*. Paper presented at the annual meeting of National Council for Measurement in Education, Montreal.

Huff, K. L., and Sireci, S. G. (2001). Validity issues in computer-based testing. *Educational Measurement: Issues and Practice, 20*, 16-25.

Karnjanawasri, S. (2002). *Modern test theories* (2 ed.). Bangkok, Thailand: Chulalongkorn University Press.

Kyungsu, W. (1996). *Computerized adaptive testing : A comparison of item response theoretic approach and expert systems approach in polytomous grading.* Unpublished PHD, Indiana University.

Lawrence, R. (1998). *Item Banking. Practical Assessment, Researchand Evaluation, 6(4).* Retrieved February, 14, 2007, from *http://PAREonline.net/getvn.asp?v=6andn=4.*

Leung Chi Keung, E. (2001). *Computerized adaptive testing as a means for mathematics assessment.* Retrieved 11 May, 2001, from *http://www.fed.cuhk.edu.hk/~flle e/mathfor/edumath/9812/05leungck.html*

Lila, S. (1996). *The developement of computerized item banking system.* Unpublished Doctor of Education, Srinakarinwirote University.

Lord, F. M. (1971). Robins-monro procedures for tailored testing. *Journal of Educational and Psychological Measurement, 31,* 80-120.

Lord, F. M. (1980). *Applications of item response theory to practical testing problems.* Hillsale New Jersey: Erlbaum.

Lord, F. M., and Novick, M. R. (1968). *Statistical theories of mental test score.* Massachusetts: Addison-Wesley Publishing Company.

Maneelek, R. (1997). *The effect of some variables on concurrent validity and item number of computerized adaptive testing.* Unpublished Ed.D, Srinakharinwirot, Thailand.

Master, G., and Evans, J. (1986). Banking non-dichotomously scored items. *Applied Psychological Measurement, 10,* 355-367.

Meijer, R. R., and Nering, M. L. (1999). Computerized adaptive testing : overview and introduction. *Applied Psychological Measurement, 23,* 187-194.

Mertens, D. M. (1998). *Research methods in education and psychology.* California: SAGE Publications, Inc.

Millman, J., and Arter, J. A. (1984). Issues in item banking. *Journal of educational measurement, 21*(4), 315-330.

Nering, M. L. (1996). *The effect of person misfit in computerized adaptive testing.* Unpublished PhD, University of Minnesota.

Njiru, J., and Romanoski, J. (2007a). *Development and calibration of Physics items to create an item bank, using a Rasch measurement model.* Paper presented at the The International Conference on Learning, Johannesburg, South Africa, June 26-29, 2007.

Njiru, J., and Romanoski, J. (2007b). *Development and calibration of Physics items to create an item bank, using a Rasch measurement model.* The International Journal of Learning, 14 (2), 19-29.

Olsen, J. B., Maynes, D., Slawson, D., and Ho, K. (1986, April). *Comparison of paper-administered, computer-administered and computerized adaptive tests of achievement.* Paper presented at the the annual meeting of the American Educational Research Association, San francisco, CA.

Owen, R. J. (1969). *A Baysian approach to tailored testing (Research Bulletin No. 69-92).* Princeton, NJ: Educational Testing Service.

Paeratkool, C. (1975). *Measurement techniques* (6 ed.). Bangkok: Wattanapanich.

Pallant, J. (2001). *SPSS survival manual: a step by step guide to data analysis using SPSS.* Crows Nest, NSW: Allen and Unwin.

Patsula, L. N., and Steffen, M. (1997). *Maintaining item and test security in a cAT environment: A simulation study* (report No. 309). Chicago, IL: National Council on Measurement in Education.

Phungkham, N. (1988). *A comparison of the quality of CAT and Classicat Testing in English vocabulary ability of Mathayom Suksa 3 students.* Unpublished Master in Education, Chulalongkorn University, Thailand.

Rasch, G. (1960). *Probabilistic models for some intelligence and attainment tests.* Copenhagen: Denish Institute for Educational Research.

Rasch, G. (1980/1960). *Probabilistic model for some intelligence and attainment tests.* Chicago: The University of Chicago.

Richichi, R. V. (1996). *An analysis of test bank multiple-choice items using Item Response Theory* (Research /Technical No. ED 405367). USA.

Rudner, L. (1998a). *Item Banking* (No. EDO-TM-98-04). USA: Eric Clearinghouse on Assessment and Evaluation, Washington ,DC.

Rudner, L. (1998b). *Item banking. Practical Assessment, Researhand Evaluation, 6(4).* Retrieved June 9, 2007, from *http://PAREonline.net/getvn.asp?v=6andn=4* .

Sands, W. A., Waters, B. K., and McBride, J. R. (1997). *Computerized adaptive testing: From inquiry to operation.* Washington DC: American Psychological Association.

Sangphueng, S., and Chooprateep, J. (2007). *Item bank in examination online system Chiangmai examination center.* Retrieved 20/05/2007, from http;//www.chiangmaiexam. com

Shermis, D., Stemmer, M., and Webb, M. (1996). Computerized adaptive skill assessment in a statewide testing program. *Journal of Research on Computing in Education, 29,* 49-67.

Songsang, K. (2004). *The Information Fuction of Computerized Adaptive Testing.* Unpublished Doctor of Education, Srinakharinwirot University.

Srisamran, P. (1997). *The evaluation of the project of item banking developement of the year1995-1997.* Sakonnakorn, Thailand

Stocking, M. L., and Swanson, L. (1998). Optimal design of item banks for computerized adaptive tests. *Applied Psychological Measurement, 22,* 271-279.

Supeesut, N. (1998). *Construction of tailored test package and test administering through microcomputer in Mathematics for Mathayom Suksa 1 Level.* Unpublished Master Degree, ChiangMai University.

Supeesut, N. (1999). *Construction of tailored test package and test administering through microcomputer in Mathematics for Mathayom Suksa 1 Level.* Unpublished Master Degree, ChiengMai University.

Suwannoi, P. (1989). *A computerized peramidal testing in Chemistry for Mattayom Suksa 5 students.* Unpublished Master Degree, Khon Kaen University.

Tuntavanitch, P. (2006). *A Estimation of Elementary Students Efficacy in Division Skill using Computer Programing Method and Usual Testing Method.* Surin: Faculty of Education, Surin Rajabhat University, Thailand.

Umar, J. (1990). *Development of an examination system based on calibrated item bank networks* (Unpublished Project report): SIDEC, Standford University.

Umar, J. (1999). Item banking. In G. N. Masters and J. P. Keeves (Eds.), *Advances in measurement in educational research and assessment.* New York: Pergamon Press.

van der Linden, W. J. (1999). Computerized educational testing. In G. N. Masters and J. P. Keeves (Eds.), *Advances in Measurement in Educational Research and Assessment* (pp. 138-150). New York: PERGAMON.

van der Linden, W. J., and Pashley, P. J. (2000). Item selection and ability estimation in adaptive testing. In W. J. van der Linden and C. A. W. Glas (Eds.), *Computerized adaptive testing: Theory and practice* (pp. 1-25). Dordrecht, the Netherlands: Kluwer Academic.

Wainer, H. (1990). Introduction and History. In H. Wainer, N. J. Dorans, R. Flaugher, B. F. Green, R. J. Mislevy, L. Steinberg and D. Thissen (Eds.), *Computerized Adaptive Testing: A Primer* (pp. 1-22). Hillsdale, NJ: Lawrence Erlbaum Associates.

Wainer, H. (1993). Some practical considerations when covering a linearly administered test to an adaptive format. *Journal of Educational Measurement, 12*, 15-20.

Wainer, H., and Wright, B. D. (1980). Robust estimation of ability in the Rasch model. *Psychometrika, 45*, 373-391.

Waugh, R. F. (2006). Rasch measurement. In N. J. Salkind (Ed.), *The Encyclopedia of Measurement and Statistics*. Thousand Oaks, CA: Sage Publications.

Waugh, R. F. (Ed.). (2003). *On the forefront of educational psychology*. New York: Nova Science Publishers.

Waugh, R. F. (Ed.). (2005). *Frontiers in educational psychology*. New York: Nova Science Publishers.

Waugh, R. F., and Chapman, E. S. (2005). An analysis of dimensionality using factor analysis (True Score Theory) and Rasch measurement: What is the difference? Which method is better? *Journal of Applied Measurement, 6*(1), 80-99.

Weiss, D. J. (1982). Improving measurement quality and efficiency with adaptive testing. *Applied Psychological Measurement, 4*, 273-285.

Weiss, D. J. (2004). Computerized adaptive testing for effective and efficient measurement in counseling and education. *Measurement and Evaluation in Counseling and Development, 37*, 70-84.

Weiss, D. J. (Ed.). (1983). *New horizons in testing: Latent trait test theory and computerized adaptive testing*. New York: Acadamic Press.

Wiboonsri, Y. (2005). *Measurement and achievement test construction* (4th ed.). Bangkok, Thailand: Chlalongkorn University Press.

Wise, S. L. (1997, March, 25-27). *Overview of practical issues in CAT program.* Paper presented at the The Annual Meeting of the National Council on Measurement in Education, Chicago.

Wright, B. D. (1999a). Fundamental measurement of psychology. In S. E. Embretson and S. L. Hershberger (Eds.), *The new rules of measurement*. Mahwah, NJ: Lawrence Erlbaum Associates.

Wright, B. D. (1999b). Rasch measurement models. In G. N. Masters and J. P. Keeves (Eds.), *Advance in measurement in educational research and assessment* (pp. 85-97). Oxford, UK: Elsevier Science.

Wright, B. D., and Bell, S. R. (1984). Item banks: what, why, how. *Journal of Educational Measurement, 21*, 331-345.

Wright, B. D., and Stone, M. H. (1979). *Best test design: Rasch measurement*. Chicago, Illinois: Mesa Press.

In: Applications of Rasch Measurement in Education   ISBN: 978-1-61668-026-8
Editor: Russell Waugh   © 2010 Nova Science Publishers, Inc.

Chapter 2

RASCH MEASURES FOR INTER-PERSONAL AND INTRA-PERSONAL STUDENT SELF-VIEWS BASED ON GARDNER INTELLIGENCES

Ahdielah Edries[1] and Russell F. Waugh[2]
1. Australian Islamic College
2. Faculty of Education and Arts, Edith Cowan University,
Mount Lawley, Western Australia

ABSTRACT

The Australian Islamic College is a co-educational Islamic Independent school with three campuses which cater for migrant students from war-torn countries and others with culturally and linguistically, diverse backgrounds. This paper is part of a larger study to identify the strengths and interests of Islamic students, across eight of Gardner's intelligence domains, as perceived by the students, so that the College could better meet the needs of these students. This study is important for the Islamic College because it is hoped that the study will lead to the provision of opportunities for students to increase their confidence, self-esteem and motivation, and to achieve better in academic and non-academic areas. Student self-views were based on three aspects: (1) Things I really like; (2) Things I enjoy; and (3) Things I prefer, with items answered in two perspectives What I would like to do and What I actually do. This paper reports a Rasch analysis of student self-views based on two Gardner Intelligences: inter-personal and intra-personal (N=321). Only 8 out 12 items fitted the measurement model for inter-personal self-views and 10 out of 12 items for intra-personal self-views. For all items, students found it easier to say what they would like to do than to actually do it. The item-trait interaction chi-squares are respectively: $x^2 = 38.77$, df=32, p=0.19; and $x^2 = 57.65$, df = 40, p= 0.03 showing no significant interaction between student measures and item difficulties along the scale, thus supporting uni-dimensional scales. The Person Separation Indices are respectively 0.78, and 0.85 with standard errors of about 0.09 logits showing acceptable separation of measures compared to errors, and improvements could be made by adding more items to all measures.

BACKGROUND FOR CHAPTERS TWO AND THREE

The Australian Islamic College has three campuses which operate and work together by following the same policies to provide a holistic education for all the students by integrating Islamic values and information technology in all the subject matter. The first campus opened its doors in February, 1986. This campus was established with two teachers and 50 students and it delivered an academic education based on a framework of Islamic ethos and values. Its students have now been incorporated into three main campuses. An addition was constructed in 1990 with its Technological Centre being developed in 1994. Its total enrolment in 2009 is 550 students.

The second campus was established in 1996 and a new double-storey building on the school ground was opened in March 2003 to accommodate the increasing number of enrolments. This college caters for students between Kindergarten and Year 10 (5 to 15 years old), total enrolment in 2009 is 708 students. The third campus is the most recent addition and this was purchased in 2000 to cater for the increasing number of Islamic high school students. This College offers Kindergarten through to Year 12 and has been successful in producing graduates who have entered tertiary education in recent years (N=120). This year (2009), the three campuses of the Australian Islamic College have approximately 2300 students, over 200 teachers and supporting staff (Magar, 2008 p. 13). Small class sizes in the Colleges enable students and teachers to interact more efficiently and productively then they could with larger classes. Class sizes range from around 25-30 students in Lower Primary with a Teacher and Teacher Aide per class (Kindy – Year 1) to 20-25 students in Middle Primary and in High School (Edries, 2008).

The philosophy, *Islamic Values and Academic Excellence for Your Children's Success in this Life and the Hereafter*, sums up how the Islamic Colleges govern themselves and educate their students. All classroom curricula are based on the Western Australian Curriculum Framework (Curriculum Framework, 2008), outcome-based teaching and learning where teachers plan, conduct lessons and assess their students through outcomes. Portfolios, fortnightly assessments, formal testing (English literacy and numeracy), National English Testing (National Assessment Program Literacy and Numeracy), Interschool Competitions (University of New South Wales) and progress maps are used to record students' academic performance throughout their education at the Colleges.

Islamic values are integrated in all the different subject areas, thus allowing students to learn classroom concepts and relate them to life and their faith. The students are encouraged to excel in secular and non-secular subjects, integrate with other communities and strive towards a goal in life. The Islamic Colleges encourage academic excellence in all areas, as well as good behaviour and conduct through a reward system amongst the students where positive points may be accumulated to be exchanged for a prize at the end of a week (Edries, 2008). On the other hand, a negative-point system also exists to discourage anti-social behaviour and to monitor the students' conduct through parent-teacher conferences and shared concerns. The school conducts several inter-school visits with neighbouring government and private schools, where students meet to exchange ideas about religion and form friendships outside their Islamic communities. Other types of visits include celebratory occasions such as Harmony Day, and Inter-Faith Sports for Peace Carnival (Edries, 2008). In the primary Islamic colleges, students attend English, Mathematics, Science, Society and

Environment lessons. In addition to these core subjects, the students have to attend the LOTE (Arabic), Islamic Studies, Sports, Health, Art and Computing classes (Deria, 2006a). Each college day includes six, 45-50 minute periods, a recess and lunch break, prayers after lunch and morning and afternoon assemblies. Most of the teachers are trained in Australia and they are encouraged to utilise the best and latest pedagogy in their classrooms, share resources and promote the best teaching methods at the weekly meetings after school (Deria, 2006a).

In the secondary Islamic colleges, qualified teachers are employed to give the students the best education possible, especially in Senior School (Deria, 2006b). The boys and girls are separated into single-sex classes and are taught by male and females teachers respectively. The aim is to discourage any distraction in class and allow more comfortable interactions between staff and students than might be possible with mixed boys and girls classes. Secondary college subjects taught at Middle school level are English, Mathematics, Science, Society and Social Environment, Computing, Art, Health, Sports and Islamic Studies (Deria, 2006b). In the senior years (Years 11 and 12), the subjects vary a little depending on student choices and numbers; examples of Tertiary Entrance Ranked subjects include LOTE-Arabic, English, Senior English, English as a Second Language (ESL), English Literature, Geography, History, Political and Legal Studies, Calculus, Geometry and Trigonometry, Physics, Chemistry, Biology, and Human Biology (Deria, 2006c).

Each College runs its own education support system where the educational and emotional needs of the students are catered for by a school psychologist through consultations and testing. Education support classes are provided for the weaker students from each year group and, while gifted and talented classes are offered for the advance students of each year group, resources are limited and the Colleges would like to do more in this regard (Edries, 2008). Behaviour management consultations (such as the National Safe School's Friendly Policy, 2008) are provided where needed.

Although all the students share the same faith of Islam, they originate from various cultural groups. A small percentage (20%) of students' are Australian-born (first generation Australians) and the next largest group (30%) of students was born in Iraq and Somalia. The remaining students (50%) come from all the continents of the world such as Africa, America, Asia, Europe and the Pacific Islands. Due to this diversity of cultures, the students speak a variety of languages and dialects, as well as conforming to different customs in areas of community life.

The wide variety of cultural groups in the Australian Islamic College has positive aspects and limitations. Such a diverse group of students in one College makes the teaching of diversity, multiculturalism and tolerance easier because the students can learn from each other and they bring their own 'voice' to the classroom. Celebrations of multiculturalism brings a deeper meaning when the students come dressed in their cultural clothing, bring home-cooked food of their nations and share experiences from their country of origin. However, such a diverse cultural mix also has its problems because of difficulties in communication, low English literacy acquisition and cultural conflicts. College Parent-Teacher conferences require translators and newsletters sent home have to be translated in other languages such as Bosnian, Somali, Arabic and Afghan (Edries, 2009). The Islamic Colleges also spend a lot of funds purchasing and maintaining literacy and numeracy programs that are IT-based for every classroom, such as the *Accelerated Reader* and *Accelerated Mathematics Programs* (Edries, 2008). These programs encourage users to take some charge of their learning and become independent learners to a greater extent. The *Accelerated Reader Program* is linked to the

Colleges' library catalogues and students borrow a book every week to read and then sit for a computer quiz that assesses their reading level and directs them to another reading level book. The *Accelerated Mathematics Program* is a collection of Mathematics topics (categorized by year groups) that the computer produces, such as exercises, tests and revision questions for students to complete and that are later marked through the computer program (Edries, 2008). Every student has a different Mathematics level and can progress at his or her own pace, thus making their learning less stressful and more positive. These programs are conducted as extension exercises to the students' usual study load.

The Australian Islamic Colleges' have New Arrivals classes that are an essential starting point for many of its migrant students. In these classes, specialist teachers help to integrate the students into the formal education system and provide the basic English literacy skills to cope with their age-level classes in six months to a year's time. However, this time duration isn't sufficient for most of these students to achieve at the mainstream standard. They often find it very difficult to cope at the standard of the mainstream, not because they are academically incapable, but because they simply haven't mastered the English language yet (Edries, 2009; personal observation as Principal). Many of the classroom teachers have to adapt their pedagogy to suit the multiple student needs in their classrooms.

In the Islamic Colleges' mainstream classrooms, the assumption that all the students who have come from overseas, or government schools in Perth, have basic English literacy and numeracy skills is challenged when these students still fall into the lower percentile of academic performance compared with their same year level peers across Western Australia. In addition to the usual pressure to produce excellent results nationally (Tertiary Entrance Ranking table), the College also has to contend with national testing such as the *National Assessment Program in Literacy and Numeracy* (previously known as *Western Australian Literacy and Numeracy Assessment*) each year (Edries, 2008). The Islamic Colleges have taken this challenge to improve English Literacy and Numeracy standards by adapting their hiring policy to encourage very motivated teachers, and by retaining excellent staff through meritocracy-based salary reviews (Magar, 2008a).

Handling such a dependent and disadvantaged group of students (and their families) is also draining on the resources of the Australian Islamic College as there are insufficient funds and staffing to implement all that is considered necessary. Computers are essential tools for the IT-based programs and the growing number of students will require more access to up-to-date computers and computer programs. The computer programs are expensive and have to be maintained by support staff, thus adding further staffing costs. To prepare the students for national testing and general school work, the Islamic Colleges also run after-school, weekend and holiday classes that see committed teachers volunteer their time and effort to help the students achieve a better understanding of their school work. All these mean that the Colleges run almost all day, every day, and this accrues high energy costs (Edries, 2009; personal observation as Principal).

Cultural conflicts and misunderstandings are unavoidable in the Islamic Colleges, especially when new students and families arrive in Australia for the first time. These people bring their own conceptions about education and social interactions, and handling confrontations is an acquired skill at the Colleges. The administration, Heads of schools and teachers have to deal with these interactions sensitively to avoid escalation in conflict (Edries, 2009; personal observation as Principal). Education Support services are essential in this area but often there is a lack or unavailability of resources, including interpreters and mediators.

The Islamic Colleges often have to rely on external services offered by independent organizations, or small government funded associations, to assist with helping these new families adapt to new life in Australia and therefore ease their children into the Australian school system. Families who come from war-torn countries, or who have lived in refugee camps for several years, tend to arrive with children who have emotional and social difficulties at school thus affecting their already limited schooling and literacy acquisition (Edries, 2009; Haig and Oliver, 2007).

Generally, the Intensive English classes are small in number (N=15) and the students are given quality time, thus affording them the opportunity to make some progress. However, some students still experience great difficulty in their learning, and continue to struggle throughout the mainstream classes (Edries, 2009). This is why interventions involving programs based on multiple intelligence theory could be important to the Islamic College students. If student abilities across Gardner's intelligences can be ascertained, then programs can be tailored to give each student some success in at least one subject, involving at least one of the intelligences.

RATIONALE FOR THE STUDY

There are few significant studies (Haig & Oliver, 2007) which have dealt with the attitudes and needs of students from cultural and linguistically diverse (CALD) backgrounds in Australia (especially migrants and refugees from war-torn countries); and no recent studies in Australia could be found that have investigated how Australian schools could effectively improve and enhance the learning of these migrant students. Since the majority of the students within the Islamic Colleges are born overseas (particularly from war-torn countries), or live in families with parents born overseas, the students' English literacy and numeracy limitations have to be addressed by the Islamic College, as little help comes from the homes. In particular, research has never been undertaken in the Western Australian Islamic Colleges to investigate the intelligences, strengths and interests of the students, and the teacher perceived needs of their students. Cook-Sather (2002, p.3) stated that there are certain pedagogical merits in understanding and utilising student perspectives in schools. Choe (2006) in his recent study in Singapore asserts that hearing and listening to student voices is important in education because of the various ways it can improve educational practices, re-inform existing conversations about educational reform, and point to the discussions and reform efforts yet to be undertaken. Students' who feel engaged with what they are learning, feel empowered because their views are valued, or teachers who, in seeing the world from the students' point of view, adopt more effective instructional approaches to teach their students, but these statements arose from research with advantaged students, not migrant students with poor English and numeracy skills.

Secondly, there is a need to address the issues that students from Culturally and Linguistically Diverse Backgrounds have to contend with in a traditional classroom. On a daily basis, the administration and staff at the Islamic Colleges grapple with issues such as helping students deal with their past traumatic experiences and their new way of life in Australia; the consequences of severely disrupted prior schooling; a lack of social understanding and learning strategies to process content; and poor literacy in their first language (which is needed to support the acquisition of a second language); meeting classroom demands for literacy and communication; obtaining appropriate learning resources; and a lack of parental support due to lack of education. According to Haig and Oliver (2007) these deficiencies are compounded by the complexity and specificity of cognitive academic knowledge used in schools. Cognitive development which has taken place over many years in the classroom is clearly one of the key elements which students from Non-English speaking backgrounds are missing when they have had interrupted (or no prior) schooling (Miller, Mitchell, and Brown, 2005). This makes it difficult for staff at the Australian Islamic College to target learning at the right level, as students in their classes have variable skills and gaps in their learning.

It is hoped that the current study will provide some information to develop and implement effective school and educational practices to cater for its students at the Islamic colleges in Perth. Student learning, motivation and engagement in a variety of academic and non-academic areas are important for success at school (Bragg, 2005). Whilst there are numerous factors that impact on the wellbeing, learning and teaching of students, it is not in the scope of the present study to investigate all of these. The present study will only focus on the need to determine student interests in relation to some Gardner intelligence areas and their perceived interests and strengths. Gardner views "intelligence" as a biological and psychological potential that is capable of being realized to a greater or lesser extent in everyone, depending on one's experience, education, social environment, and other factors (Gardner, 1993a).

The majority of students attending the Islamic Colleges in Perth overcome obstacles such as adjusting to their host country, facing confronting rules and issues in school (something to which a large proportion of these students have not been exposed to in their own countries); and, coupled with compliance to learning from a traditional curriculum (which often does not take into account their prior background and past experiences) makes school difficult for them. When students' views, strengths and interests are known, action can be taken to address difficulties that students might be facing and further develop their strengths. Consequently, this study attempts to use students' and teachers' perspectives on what can be done to enhance student learning, and how their needs can be effectively met within the school environment.

Unidimensional, linear scales for self concepts relating to Interpersonal, Intrapersonal, English, Mathematics, Art, Sport, Music, and Drama domains were created using a Rasch Measurement Model computer program, RUMM 2020 (Andrich, Sheridan and Luo, 2005). This paper reports on the RUMM 2020 output, that is, the statistics showing a good fit to the measurement model for the data relating to the Interpersonal and Intrapersonal domains. These domains were chosen to present first because they are important to students who come from war-torn countries like Lebanon, Somalia, Iraq and Ethiopia. While the academic subject self concepts and sports self-concepts are important too, it was considered, more important to be able to make valid inferences about student Interpersonal and Intrapersonal self-concepts first. Rasch measures for student self-views based on other Gardner Intelligences were made as part of a larger study, but not reported here.

GARDNER INTELLIGENCES

Definitions of Gardner's Intelligence Domains

The Intelligence Domains are based on Gardner's Multiple Intelligence Theory (1993, 1999, 2004) and the definitions below are taken from his work.

Linguistic Intelligence refers to the capacity to use words effectively, whether orally or in writing. This includes the ability to manipulate the structure and syntax of language, the sounds of language, the meanings of language, and the practical uses of language, such as for explaining, remembering, and persuading. This intelligence is evident in children who demonstrate strength in the language arts: speaking, writing, reading, listening. They learn best by saying, hearing and seeing words and they are good at memorizing names, places, dates and trivia. These students have always been successful in traditional classrooms because their intelligence lends itself to traditional teaching.

Logical/Mathematical Intelligence refers to the capacity to use numbers effectively and to reason well. This includes awareness of logical patterns and relationships, functions, and cause and effect. This intelligence is evident in children who display an aptitude for numbers, reasoning and problem solving. They like to participate in experiments, figure things out, ask questions, explore and discover patterns and relationships. They learn best by categorizing, classifying, and working with abstract patterns. These children typically do well in traditional classrooms where teaching is logically sequenced and students are asked to conform.

Visual/spatial Intelligence refers to the ability to perceive the visual and spatial world accurately, including sensitivity to colour, line, shape, form, space, and the relationships between them. Includes the capacity to visualize, make graphic representations, and orient oneself in spatial surroundings. This intelligence is evident in children who learn best visually and organise things spatially. They like to see what you are talking about in order to understand. They enjoy charts, graphs, maps, tables, illustrations, art, imagining things, puzzles, costumes (basically anything that is eye catching). Students learn best by visualizing, dreaming, working with colours and pictures.

Bodily/Kinesthetic Intelligence refers to the ability to use one's whole body to express ideas and feelings, and the ability to fashion or transform with one's hands. This includes skills such as coordination, balance, dexterity, strength, flexibility, speed, and other physical skills. This intelligence is evident in children who experience learning best through activity: games, movement, hands-on tasks, building. They learn best by touching, moving, interacting with space and processing knowledge through bodily sensations. These children are often labelled 'overly active' in traditional classrooms where they are told to sit and be still.

Musical Intelligence refers to the ability to perceive, distinguish between, and express oneself in musical forms. It includes sensitivities to rhythm, pitch or melody, timbre, and tone colour. It can apply to either an intuitive grasp of music, or an analytic or technical understanding of it, or both. This intelligence is evident in children who learn well through songs. They like to sing, hum tunes, listen to music, patterns, rhythm, play an instrument and respond to musical expression. These children are good at picking up sounds, remembering melodies, noticing pitches and rhythms and keeping time. It is easy to overlook children with this intelligence in traditional education.

Interpersonal Intelligence refers to the capacity to perceive and distinguish differences in the moods, intentions, motivations, and feelings of others. It includes sensitivity to facial expressions, gestures, and body language. This intelligence also includes the ability to respond to these cues effectively, to work well with others, and to lead. This intelligence is evident in children who are noticeably people orientated and outgoing, and do their learning cooperatively. They are good at understanding people, leading others, organizing, communicating, manipulating and mediating conflicts. They learn best sharing, helping others and asking for help. These children may have typically been identified as 'talkative' or 'too concerned about being social' in a traditional setting.

Intrapersonal Intelligence refers to the capacity for self-knowledge and understanding, and the ability to act on the basis of that knowledge. It includes having an accurate picture of one's own strengths and limitations, inner moods, intentions, feelings, motivations, needs, and desires, and a capacity for self-discipline and self-esteem. This intelligence is evident in children who are especially in touch with their own feelings, values, and ideas. They may tend to be more reserved, like to work alone and reflect on problems, but they are actually quite intuitive about what they learn and how it relates to themselves. They are good at being independent, and learn best by being given time to think.

Naturalist Intelligence refers to the capacity of children to love the outdoors, to be with animals, and to go on field trips. They are good at categorizing, organizing a living area, planning a trip, preservation and conservation. Learns best by studying natural phenomenon in a natural setting learning about how things work. These children love to pick up on subtle differences in meanings. The traditional classroom has not been accommodating these children.

Existentialist Intelligence refers to the capacity of children to learn in the context of where humankind stands in the 'big picture' of existence. They ask, "Why are we here?" and "What is our role in the world?" This intelligence is seen in the discipline of philosophy.

Gardner (1999) suggested that the nine intelligences very rarely operate independently. Rather, the intelligences are used concurrently and typically complement each other as individuals develop skills or solve problems. Viewed in this way human intelligence is not restricted to only the more narrow linguistic and mathematical abilities measured by the common standardized tests in which high scores traditionally described students in school as being 'smart'. There are research studies that confirm that by addressing students' culture, language, and social status with appreciation, inclusion, and sensitivity increases students' academic successes (Grant and Tate, 1995; Jimenez, 1997).

Rasch Measurement Fit Statistics

For student self-views in the Interpersonal domain, only 8 out of 12 items fitted the measurement model and items 3, 6, 7 and 12 were deleted. For self-views in the Intrapersonal domain, 10 out of 12 items fitted the measurement model and items 2 and 6 were deleted. For both self-concepts, linear uni-dimensional scales were created with 10 items.

Dimensionality

The RUMM 2020 program calculates an item-trait interaction chi-square to determine whether a uni-dimensional trait has been measured. This examines the consistency with which students with measures all along the scale agree with the calculated difficulties of the items along the scale. That is, it provides a check that all the students agree that particular items are easy, of medium difficulty or hard. For the item-trait interaction for the Interpersonal domain the ($x^2 = 38.77$, df $= 32$, p $= 0.19$), and the item-trait interaction for the Intrapersonal domain the ($x^2 = 57.65$, df $= 40$, p $= 0.03$) respectively. This means that a good scale has been constructed with good agreement about the alignment of items from easy to medium to hard along the scale. Each item is given a difficulty parameter and each student a self-view parameter that together give a good prediction of student answers for each item along the scale for all students. This is what it means to have a unidimensional scale and this scale is calibrated in standard units (logits) that are linear. That is, equal differences between numbers on the scale represent equal amounts of self-views in logits.

Person Separation Index

In a good measure, the measures of self-concept are well separated in comparison to the errors. That is, the errors are small in comparison to separation of measures. The standard errors of measurement are about 0.10 logits for Interpersonal self-concept and about 0.09 for Intrapersonal self-concept. The Person Separation Indices are respectively 0.78 and 0.85, indicating good separation of measures in comparison to the errors.

Item Fit to the Measurement Model

The RUMM 2020 program calculates individual item fits to the measurement model and these are given in Table 1 and 2 respectively for the Interpersonal and Intrapersonal self-concepts. For Interpersonal Self-Views, the eight items fitted the measurement model with probabilities greater than, or equal to, p=0.04. For the Intrapersonal Self-Views, the ten items fitted the measurement model with probabilities greater than, or equal to, p=0.03. These item fits support the other fits to the measurement indicating that reasonably consistent scales have been created.

Table 1. Fit of items to Rasch Measurement Model (Interpersonal Self-Views)

Item	Location	SE	Residual	df	Chi-Square	Probability
1	-0.74	0.12	-0.69	226.42	6.81	0.15
2	-1.12	0.14	-1.34	226.42	10.01	0.04
3	No Fit					
4	0.03	0.10	0.55	226.42	5.38	0.25
5	No Fit					
6	No Fit					
7	0.77	0.09	1.67	226.42	2.79	0.59
8	-0.07	0.10	-0.87	226.42	2.35	0.67
9	0.60	0.11	0.05	225.55	4.30	0.37
10	0.19	0.10	-0.03	222.95	2.56	0.63
11	0.35	0.10	0.87	226.42	4.59	0.33
12	No Fit					

Table 2. Fit of items to Rasch Measurement Model (Intrapersonal Self-Views)

Item	Location	SE	Residual	df	Chi-Square	Probability
1	-0.05	0.09	1.68	267.20	3.61	0.46
2	No Fit					
3	0.02	0.10	-0.46	267.20	4.26	0.37
4	-0.11	0.09	0.67	267.20	4.48	0.34
5	-0.18	0.09	1.32	267.20	6.06	0.19
6	No Fit					
7	0.34	0.09	0.79	267.20	1.65	0.80
8	-0.06	0.08	-0.04	267.20	10.58	0.30
9	0.12	0.09	0.92	267.20	3.07	0.55
10	-0.08	0.09	-0.80	267.20	11.15	0.03
11	0.13	0.09	-0.05	267.20	9.17	0.06
12	-0.13	0.09	-0.53	267.20	3.63	0.46

Explanatory Notes for Tables 1 and 2.
1. Location refers to the difficulty of the item on the linear scale.
2. SE refers to standard error, that is, the degree of the uncertainty in a value: in this case, the standard error for each of the items is reasonable, ranging from 0.09 to 0.14 logits (for table 6.1) and 0.08 to 0.1 logits (for table 6.2) respectively.
3. Residual represents the difference between the expected value on an item, calculated according to the Rasch measurement model, and its actual value.
4. df (degrees of freedom) refers to the number of scores in a distribution that are free to change without changing the mean of the distribution.
5. Chi-Square is the probability statistic of fit to the model.
6. Probability refers to the levels of certainty to which an item fits the measurement model, based on its chi-square.
7. For no fit, the item was deleted
8. All values are given to two decimal places because the errors are to two decimal places.

Item-Person fit Interactions

The item-student interaction tests-of-fit provided by the RUMM 2020 program shows the response patterns for items across students, and the student-item test-of-fit examines the response patterns for students across items. The standardized fit residuals for both the item difficulties and the person measures have a mean near zero and a standard deviation near one, supporting the good fit to the measurement model (see Tables 3 and 4). The residuals are the differences between the actual values and the expected values, calculated according to the measurement model and, when they are standardized, they have an approximately normal distribution (mean = 0, SD =1), if the data fit the measurement model. The standardized fit residual data for Interpersonal Self-Views has a mean of 0.03 and a standard deviation of 0.99, and the data for Intrapersonal Self-Views has a mean of -0.22 and a standard deviation of 0.91 respectively. This means that there is a good consistency of student responses to the items.

Table 3. Global Item and Person Fit to the Measurement Model Interpersonal Item-Person Interaction

	Item locations	Item residuals	Student locations residuals	Student
Mean	0.00	0.03	1.38	-0.22
SD	0.64	0.10	1.21	0.91

Table 4. Intrapersonal Item-Person Interaction

	Item locations	Item residuals	Student	locationsStudent
Mean	0.00	0.35	-0.05	-0.40
SD	0.16	0.84	1.28	2.33

Explanatory Notes on Tables 3 and 4.
1. Item location is item difficulty in logits
2. Student location is the measure in logits
3. SD is standard deviation
4. The mean item difficulty is constrained to zero by the RUMM 2020 program
5. Fit residuals are the difference between the actual values and the expected values calculated according to the measurement model (standardised the data fit the measurement model (a good fit for these data). They have a mean near zero and an SD near 1.
6. All values are given to two decimal places because the errors are to two decimal places.

Consistency of Use of Response Categories

Thresholds (see Tables 5 and 6) are points between adjacent response categories where the odds are 1:1 of answering the adjacent categories. The thresholds should be ordered in line with the conceptual ordering (from low to high) of the response categories, if the students answer the response categories consistently and logically. Tables 5 and 6 show that the thresholds are ordered in line with the response categories and so students used the response categories consistently and logically.

Table 5. Item Thresholds for Interpersonal Self-View

Item	Mean	Threshold 1	Threshold 2
1	0.74	-1.14	-0.34
2	0.12	-1.30	-0.93
3	No Fit		
4	0.03	-0.28	0.33
5	No Fit		
6	No Fit		
7	0.77	0.58	0.95
8	-0.07	-0.35	0.21
9	0.60	-0.64	1.83
10	0.19	-0.37	0.76
11	0.35	-0.38	1.09
12	No Fit		

Table 6. Item Thresholds (Intrapersonal Self-Views)

Item	Mean	Threshold 1	Threshold 2
1	-0.05	-0.75	0.65
2	N/F	N/F	N/F
3	0.02	-0.99	1.04
4	-0.11	-0.47	0.24
5	-0.18	-0.75	0.39
6	N/F	N/F	N/F
7	0.34	-0.16	0.83
8	-0.06	-0.25	0.13
9	0.12	-0.70	0.93
10	-0.08	-0.51	0.36
11	0.13	-0.43	0.70
12	-0.13	-0.42	0.16

Explanatory Notes on Table 5 and 6.

1. Thresholds are points between adjacent response categories where the odds are 1:1 of answering the adjacent categories.
2. Mean thresholds are the item difficulties in logits
3. The thresholds for each item are ordered in line with the ordering of the response categories.
4. For no fit, the item was deleted
5. All values are given to two decimal places because the errors are to two decimal places.

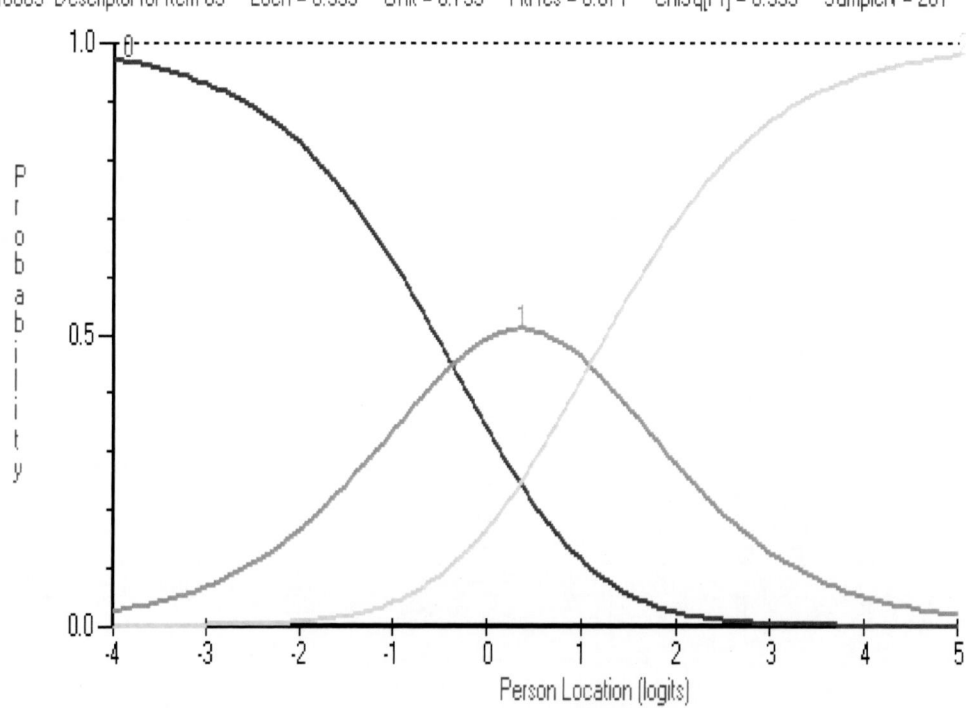

I0083 Descriptor for Item 83   Locn = 0.353   Unit = 0.733   FitRes = 0.871   ChiSq[Pr] = 0.333   SampleN = 261

Figure 1. Response Category Curve for Item 11 for Interpersonal Self-Views.

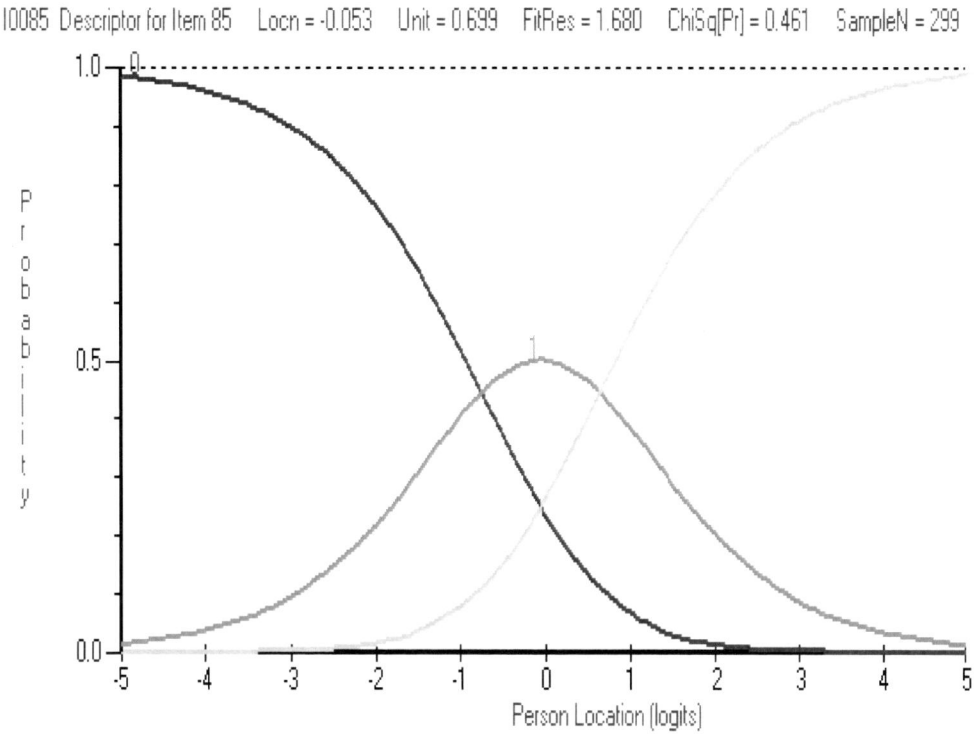

Figure 2. Response Category Curve for Item 1 for Intrapersonal Self-Views.

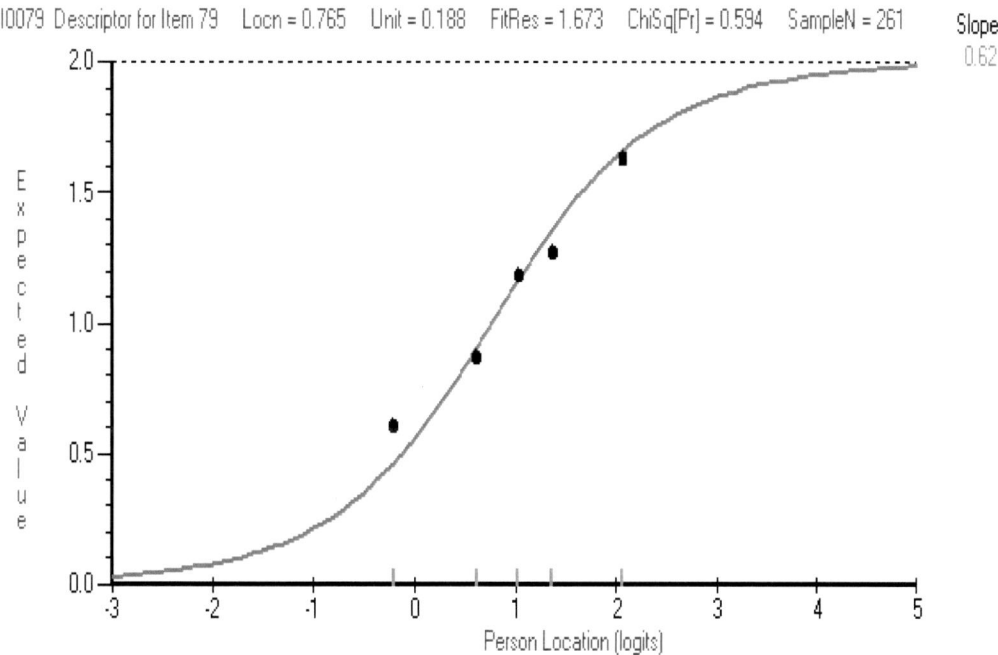

Figure 3. Item Characteristic Curve for Item 11 Interpersonal Self-Views.

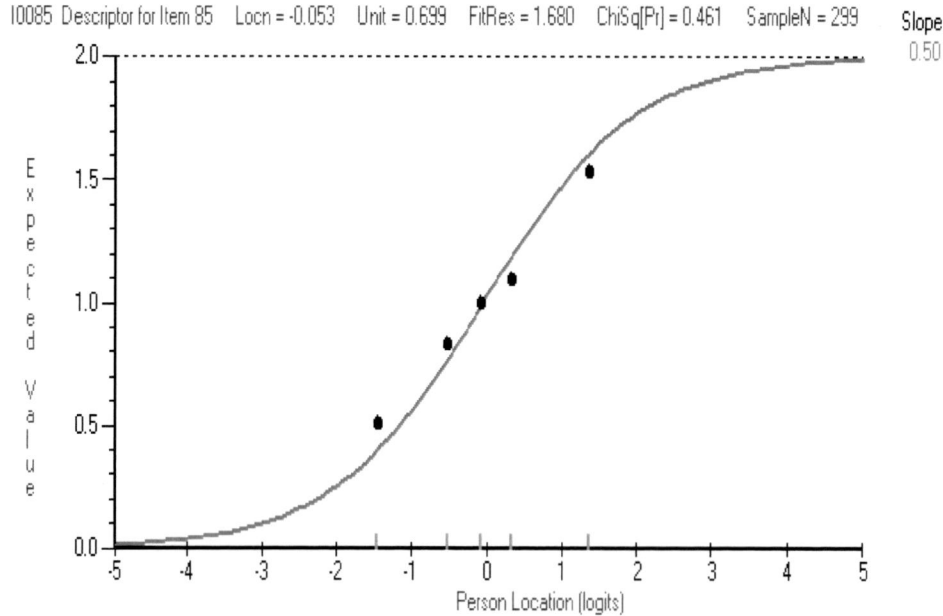

Figure 4. Item Characteristic Curve for Item 1 Intrapersonal Self-Views.

The RUMM 2020 program also produces category response curves for each item showing the relationship between the probability of answering each category in relation to the measure for Interpersonal and Intrapersonal Self-Views respectively. The response category curves for one item only for each of the Interpersonal and Intrapersonal self-views are shown below in Figures 1 and 2 respectively, supporting the view that the response categories were used consistently and logically. The other response category curves were checked for consistency but they are not shown here to avoid repetition.

Discrimination

The RUMM 2020 program produces an item characteristic curve for each item showing the relationship between the expected response score and the Student Self-View measure. Examples are given for the Interpersonal and Intrapersonal Self-Views in Figures 3 and 4 for item 79 and item 85 respectively. These curves show how the item discriminates for groups of persons near the item difficulty. In both cases, the items are functioning as intended (that is, the items discriminated well for students with different measures).

Targeting
The RUMM 2020 program produces a Person Measure/Item Threshold graph which shows the item thresholds instead of item difficulties. This graph (see Figure 5) shows the item thresholds for the Interpersonal Self-Concept range from easy (about -1.5 logits) to reasonably hard (about +2 logits); and the student measures calibrated on the same scale from low (about -3.2 logits) to high (about + 3.4 logits). These measures indicate that some harder items need to be added to better target the attitudes and behaviours of students with high measures.

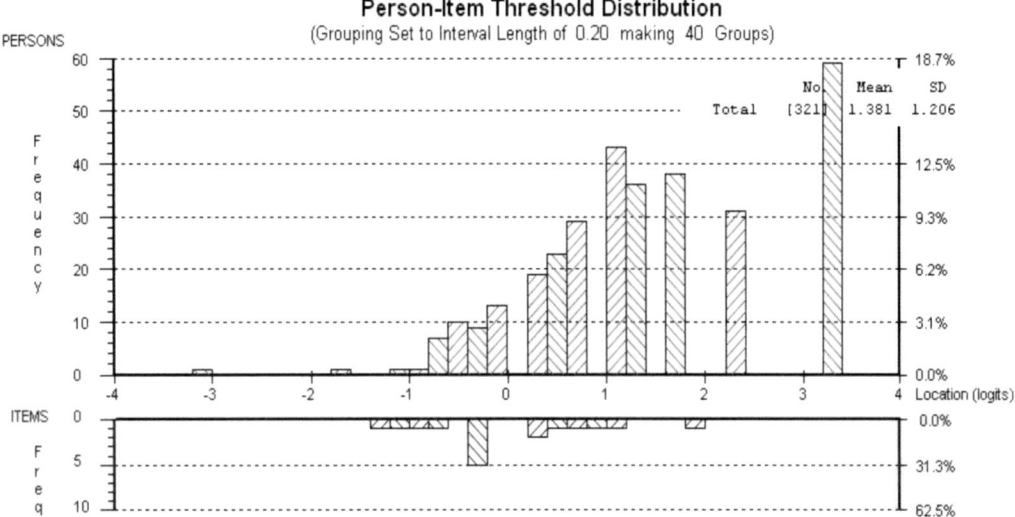

Figure 5. Person measure / Item Threshold Graph for Interpersonal Self-Views.

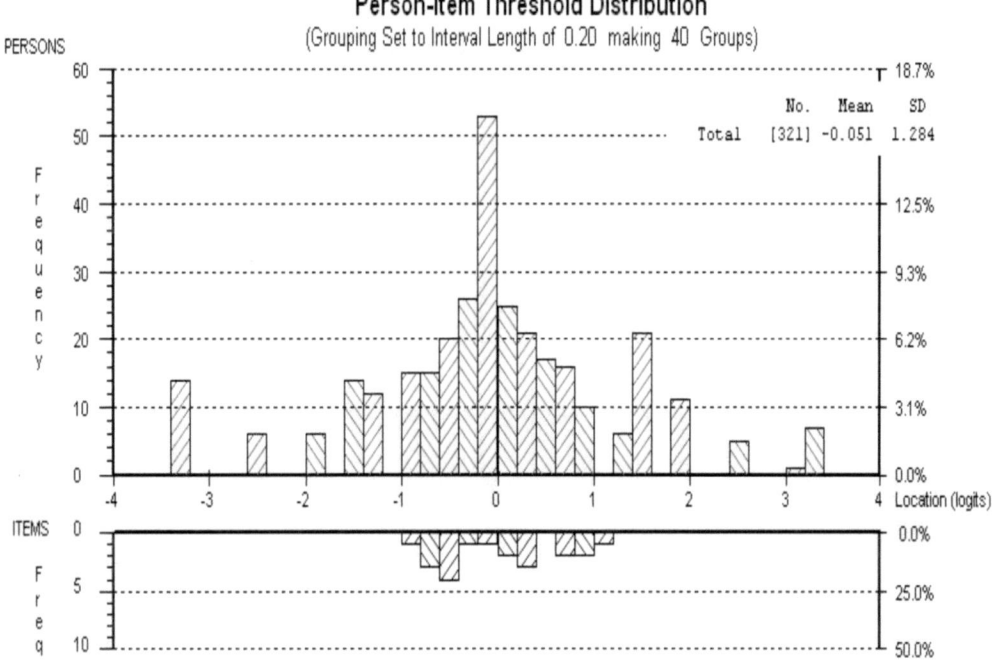

Notes on Figures 5 and 6.
1. The scale is in standard Rasch units of logits.
2. Person measures (low to high) are given on the upper side in logits.
3. Item thresholds (easy to hard) are given on the lower side in logits.

Figure 6. Person measure / Item Threshold Graph for Intrapersonal Self-Views.

It can be seen from the distribution of items in Figure 6 that the item difficulties mostly cover the middle range (-1 to +1.2 logits) of Intrapersonal Self-View measures. Therefore, some easier and harder items need to be added in any revision of the scale to cover the students with the lowest and the highest measures (+1.2 to +3.4 logits). That is, targeting could be improved by adding some easy and hard items appropriate for students with the lowest and the highest measures and this would improve the measure.

Construct Validity

The construct validity of the Interpersonal Self-View measure can be tested by comparing the order of the item difficulties with those used in the design of the questionnaire because the item difficulties are measured on the same scale. For Interpersonal Self-Views, there is partial agreement (see Table 7). First, only eight items out of 12 fitted the measurement model and so there is some disagreement there. There is a prediction that the attitude items should be easier than the behaviour items and, where both fit the model, there is strong agreement. Attitudes are easier than corresponding behaviours and the measurement shows that attitudes influence corresponding behaviour.

Table 7. Item Difficulties for Student Interpersonal Self-Views

Item	INTERPERSONAL SELF-VIEWS	What I actually do	What I'd like to do
	Things that I really like		
1	Being with my friends	-0.74	-1.12
2	Joining in with groups of people	N/F	+0.03
	Things I enjoy		
3	Watching TV shows like *Friend, Home and Away and Neighbours*	N/F	N/F
4	Watching TV shows with my friends	+0.77	-0.07
	Things I prefer		
5	Working with others in groups to make or prepare things.	+0.60	+0.19
6	Working with, playing with, and joining with others in groups	+0.35	N/F

Table 8. Item Difficulties for Student Intrapersonal Self-Views

Item	INTRAPERSONAL SELF-VIEWS	What I actually do	What I'd like to do
	Things that I really like		
1	Working on my own	-0.05	N/F
2	Just doing my own thing by myself	+0.02	-0.11
	Things I enjoy		
3	Choosing and working my own individual work	-0.18	N/F
4	Walking and exploring on my own	+0.33	-0.06
	Things I prefer		
5	Preparing things on my own, without help from others	+0.12	-0.07
6	Being by myself and thinking by myself about the world	+0.13	-0.13

Notes for Tables 7 and 8.

1. N/F means no fit (hence, the item was deleted).

2. All values are given to two decimal places because the errors are to two decimal places.

For Intrapersonal Self-Views, there is partial agreement between the predicted and actual item difficulty order (see Table 8). First, only ten items out of 12 fitted the measurement model and so there is some disagreement there. There is a prediction that the attitude items should be easier than the behaviour items and, where both fit the model, there is strong agreement. Attitudes are easier than corresponding behaviours and the measurement shows that attitudes influence corresponding behaviour.

Inferences from the Linear Rasch Measures

Good linear scales were created for Interpersonal and Intrapersonal Self-Views that showed a good fit to the measurement model. Valid inferences can now be made about item difficulties and student measures of self-views (see Tables 7 and 8).

Item Difficulties

For the Interpersonal Self-View attitudes (What they would like to do), students found it very easy to say that they liked to be with their friends, moderately easy to say that they liked to watch TV shows with their friends and moderately hard to say that they liked to work with others in groups to make or prepare things. In contrast, for actual behaviour (What they actually do), they found it easy to be with their friends, moderately hard to work play or join with others in groups, and very hard to watch TV shows with their friends and work with others in groups to make or prepare things.

For the Intrapersonal Self-View attitudes (What they would like to do), students found it moderately easy to say that they liked to be by themselves and think by themselves about the world, moderately easy to just do their own thing by themselves, moderately easy to walk and explore on their own, and moderately easy to prepare things on their own, without help from others. In contrast, for actual behaviour (What they actually do), they found it easy to work on their own individual work, moderately easy to work on their own and to just do things by themselves. They found it moderately hard to prepare things on their own without help from others, moderately hard to be by themselves and think about the world by themselves, and very hard to actually walk and explore on their own.

Student Measures of Self-Views

Each student's raw score, based on the items that fit the measurement model, has been converted to a linear measure, expressed in logits. Table 9 shows the lowest 25 student measures for Interpersonal Self-Concept and Table 10 shows the 25 highest student measures. Students with the lowest measures have a low Interpersonal Self-Views and these students can be identified (but only by numbers here for ethical reasons). These are the students who may need extra help to improve their Interpersonal Self-Views.

Table 11 shows the lowest 25 student measures for Intrapersonal Self-Views and Table 12 shows the 25 highest student measures. Students with the lowest measures have a low Intrapersonal Self-Views and these students can be identified (but only by numbers here for ethical reasons). These are the students who may need extra help to improve their Intrapersonal Self-Views. For the purposes of this analysis the 25 number cut-off is somewhat arbitrary, but the highest measure of these (7) represents answers of 'some of the time' to only 7 of the 16 items which represents a low self-concept.

Table 9. Students with Lowest 25 Measures for Interpersonal Self-Views

ID	Raw Score	Student Measure	SE	Residual
230	0	-3.07	1.20	-
232	2	-1.78	0.69	+0.13
262	4	-1.06	0.56	+0.31
214	4	-0.93	0.58	+2.00
142	5	-0.78	0.54	+0.73
260	5	-0.78	0.54	+0.68
250	5	-0.78	0.54	-1.20
228	5	-0.78	0.54	+0.17
248	5	-0.78	0.54	-1.20
179	5	-0.78	0.54	-0.20
251	5	-0.62	0.57	+0.52
172	6	-0.52	0.52	-1.25
14	6	-0.52	0.52	-2.11
102	6	-0.52	0.52	-0.35
175	6	-0.52	0.52	+0.12
124	6	-0.52	0.52	+0.76
163	6	-0.52	0.52	+0.23
242	6	-0.52	0.52	+0.46
268	6	-0.52	0.52	-2.00
46	6	-0.52	0.52	-1.00
180	6	-0.52	0.52	-0.30
213	7	-0.27	0.51	-1.91
255	7	-0.27	0.51	+0.25
259	7	-0.27	0.51	+1.60
51	7	-0.27	0.51	+1.77

Table 10. Students with 25 Highest Measures for Interpersonal Self-Views

ID	Raw Score	Student Measure	SE	Residual
104	16	3.25	1.29	-
123	16	3.25	1.29	-
117	16	3.25	1.29	-
115	16	3.25	1.29	-
96	16	3.25	1.29	-
194	16	3.25	1.29	-
257	16	3.25	1.29	-
256	16	3.25	1.29	-
237	16	3.25	1.29	-
219	16	3.25	1.29	-
ID	Raw Score	Student Measure	SE	Residual
161	16	3.25	1.29	-
202	16	3.25	1.29	-
114	16	3.25	1.29	-
170	16	3.25	1.29	-
195	16	3.25	1.29	-
173	16	3.25	1.29	-
192	16	3.25	1.29	-
190	16	3.25	1.29	-
69	16	3.25	1.29	-
189	16	3.25	1.29	-
74	16	3.25	1.29	-
75	16	3.25	1.29	-
77	16	3.25	1.29	-
39	16	3.25	1.29	-
198	16	3.25	1.29	-

Table 11. Students with Lowest 25 Measures for Intrapersonal Self-Views

ID	Raw Score	Student Measure	SE	Residual
184	0	-3.25	1.19	-
257	0	-3.25	1.19	-
299	0	-3.25	1.19	-
235	0	-3.25	1.19	-
234	0	-3.25	1.19	-
216	0	-3.25	1.19	-
188	0	-3.25	1.19	-
186	0	-3.25	1.19	-
308	0	-3.25	1.19	-
182	0	-3.25	1.19	-
148	0	-3.25	1.19	-
117	0	-3.25	1.19	-
318	0	-3.25	1.19	-
185	0	-3.25	1.19	-
316	1	-2.45	0.86	-0.35
267	1	-2.45	0.86	-0.35
199	1	-2.45	0.86	-0.35
66	1	-2.45	0.86	-0.35
43	1	-2.45	0.86	-0.35
31	1	-2.45	0.86	-0.35
133	2	-1.90	0.68	+0.84
198	2	-1.90	0.68	+0.84
141	2	-1.90	0.68	+0.84
280	2	-1.90	0.68	+0.84
169	2	-1.90	0.68	-0.26

Table 12. Students with 25 Highest Measures for Intrapersonal Self-Views

ID	Raw Score	Student Measure	SE	Residual
269	17	1.52	0.59	+0.06
15	18	1.90	0.68	-0.28
113	18	1.90	0.68	-0.27
24	18	1.90	0.68	-0.53
178	18	1.90	0.68	-0.19
155	18	1.90	0.68	-0.27
88	18	1.90	0.68	-0.13
41	18	1.90	0.68	+0.05
145	18	1.90	0.68	+0.05
64	18	1.90	0.68	-0.34
215	18	1.90	0.68	-0.12
95	18	1.90	0.68	-0.65
320	19	2.47	0.86	-0.55
81	19	2.47	0.86	+0.06
129	19	2.47	0.86	-0.31
149	19	2.47	0.86	-0.55
159	19	2.47	0.86	-0.61
138	19	3.08	1.25	-
153	20	3.28	1.2	-
110	20	3.28	1.2	-
96	20	3.28	1.2	-
312	20	3.28	1.2	-
71	20	3.28	1.2	-
241	20	3.28	1.2	-
12	20	3.28	1.2	-

Gender Differences

The RUMM program provides graphical data where the measures are placed on the upper-side and the item thresholds are placed on the lower-side on the same scale. The measures are separated by gender so that inferences can be made in regard to gender. Figure 7 shows this graphical approach for Interpersonal Self-Views and Figure 8 for Intrapersonal Self-Views.

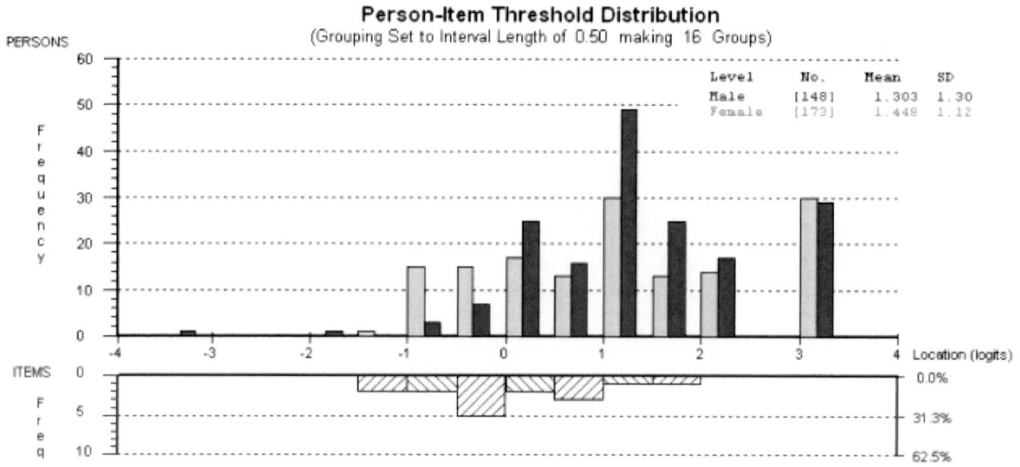

Figure 7. Target Graph by Gender for Interpersonal Self-Views.

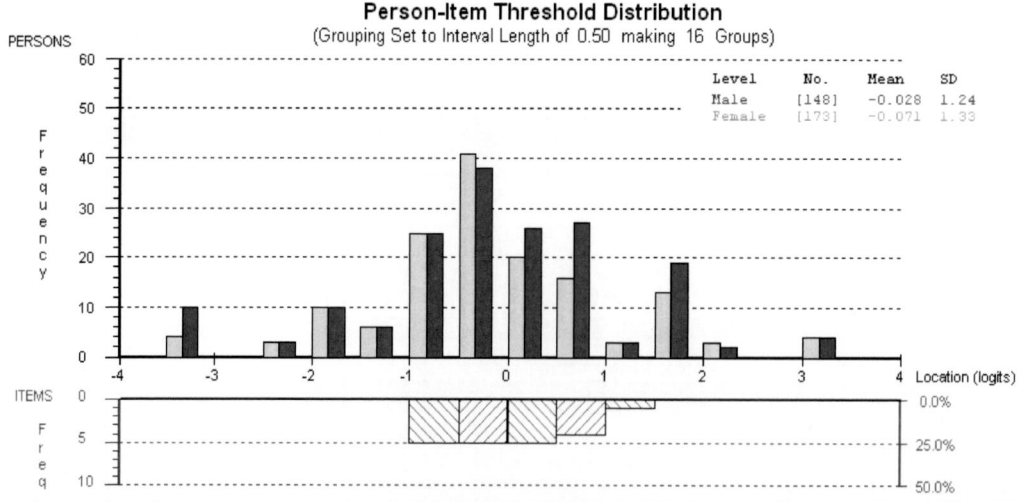

Note: There is a colour error in the RUMM program. Purple corresponds to red (female) and green corresponds to blue (male).

Figure 8. Target Graph by Gender for Intrapersonal Self-Views.

Taking the data from figure 7 for Interpersonal Self-Views, female students do not have statistically significantly higher mean measures than the male students (t=1.07, df=319, p=0.15). From the graph, further conclusions can be made. From about -1.00 to -3.07 logits, there are 12% of students (1 male and 2 females), who have extremely low levels of Interpersonal Self-Views. From -1 to 0 logits, 44% of students (32 males and 9 females) have low levels of Interpersonal Self-Views. From 0 to +1.0 logits, there are 30.5 % of students (29 males and 41 females) who have a fairly high level of Interpersonal Self-Views. From+1.0 to +2.0 logits, there are 13% of students (57 males and 91 females) who have high levels of Interpersonal Self-Views. From +3.0 to +4.0 logits, there are 30 males and 29 females who have very high levels of Interpersonal Self-Views.

Taking the data from Figure 8 for Intrapersonal Self-Views, female students do not have statistically significantly higher mean measures than the male students (t=0.30, df=319, p=0.38). From the graph, further conclusions can be made. There were 89 students (44 males and 45 females) who were able to answer the hard items easily in the +3.0 to + 4.0 logits range. In the 0.0 to 2.0 logits range, more females (133) than males (86) were able to answer the medium questions. There were 33 boys who were only able to answer the easy items, compared to their female counterparts (11). The majority of students (56%) were able to only answer the easy items.

SUMMARY OF FINDINGS

The RUMM 2020 computer program (Andrich, Sheridan, and Luo, 2005) was particularly helpful in conducting the analysis to create separate linear, uni-dimensional scales for Interpersonal Self-Views (8 items) and Intrapersonal Self-Views (10 items). The reliability of the scale data was shown by:

1. Good global and person item fit to the measurement model;
2. Good individual fit to the measurement model;
3. The three category responses being answered consistently and logically;
4. Good Person Separation Indices indicating that the person measures were well separated in comparison to the errors;
5. Good item-trait interaction chi-squares indicating the measurement of a uni-dimensional trait.
6. Reasonable targeting of the items against the person measures, although some easier and harder items need to be added for any future use of the two scales.

Since the scale data were shown to be reliable, the following valid inferences were drawn from the scales:

1. All attitude relationships (What I would like to do) were easier than their corresponding actual behaviours (What I actually do).
2. The easiest attitude item (What I would like to do) for Interpersonal Self-Views was being with their friends (and very easy).
3. The hardest attitude item (What I would like to do) for Interpersonal Self-Views was working with others in groups to make or prepare things (and moderately hard).

4. The easiest behaviour item (What I actually do) for Interpersonal Self-Views was being with their friends (and very easy).

5. The hardest behaviour item (What I actually do) for Interpersonal Self-Views was watching TV shows with their friends (and very hard).

6. The easiest attitude item (What I would like to do) for Intrapersonal Self-Views was being by themselves and thinking by themselves about the world (and moderately easy).

7. The hardest attitude item (What I would like to do) for Intrapersonal Self-Views was walking and exploring on their own (and moderately easy).

8. The easiest behaviour item (What I actually do) for Intrapersonal Self-Views was choosing and working on their own individual work (and moderately easy).

9. The hardest behaviour item (What I actually do) for Intrapersonal Self-Views was walking and exploring on their own (and hard).

Girls did not have statistically significantly higher mean Interpersonal and Intrapersonal Self-Views than boys.

REFERENCES

Allerup, P. (1997). Rasch meassurement theory. In J. P. Keeves (Ed.), *Educational Research, Methodology, and Measurement: An International Handbook* (2nd ed., pp. 863-874). Cambridge University Press, UK: Elsevier Science Ltd Publishers.

Andrich. (1988a). *Rasch models for measurement.* Paper presented at the Sage university on quantitative applications in the social sciences, series number 07/068, Newbury Park, CA: Sage Publications

Andrich, D. (1988b). A general form of Rasch's Extended Logistic Model for partial credit scoring. *Applied Measurement in Education, 1*(4), 363-378.

Andrich, Sheridan, B., and Luo, G. (2005). *RUMM: A windows-based item analysis program employing Rasch unidimensional measurement models.* Perth:WA: RUMM Laboratory.

Armstrong, T. (1994). *Multiple Intelligences in the classroom.* Alexandria, VA: Association for Supervision and Curriculum Development.

Armstrong, T. (2000). *Multiple intelligences in the classroom.* (2nd ed.). Alexandria, VA: Association for Supervision and Curriculum Development.

Bragg, J. (2005). The Effects of Problem-Based Learning on Student Engagement and Motivation. In L. P. McCoy (Ed.), *Studies in Teaching 2005 Research Digest.* Winston-Salem, NC: Wake Forrest University.

Campbell, B., Campbell, L., and Dickinson, D. (1992). *Teaching and Learning Through Multiple Intelligences.* Australia: Hawker Brownlow Education.

Choe, K. C. (2006). *Student Engagement with Project Work in a Junior College in Singapore.* Unpublished Doctor of Education thesis, Graduate School of Education, University of Western Australia.

Christodoulou, J. A. (2009). Applying multiple intelligence: how it matters for schools today, 25 years after its introduction by Howard Gardner. *School Administrator, 66*(2), 22-25.

Cook-Sather, A. (2002). Authorising Students' Perspectives: Toward trust, dialogue, and change in education. *Educational Researcher, 31*(4), 3-14.

Curriculum Framework. (2008). Retrieved 25 March, 2008, from http://www.curriculum. wa.edu.au/pages/framework00.htm

Deria, A. (2006a). *Australian Islamic College Primary Student Handbook*. Perth, WA: Australian Islamic College

Deria, A. (2006b). *Australian Islamic College Middle School Student Handbook*. Perth, WA: Australian Islamic College

Deria, A. (2006c). *Australian Islamic College Senior School Student Handbook*. Perth, WA: Australian Islamic College

Edries, A. (2008). *Australian Islamic College (Dianella) Annual Report*. Perth, WA: The Australian Islamic College.

Edries, A. (2009). *Personal observation as Principal*. Unpublished memo, Australian Islamic College, Perth, WA

Furnham, A., Clark, K., and Bailey, K. (1999). Sex differences in estimates of multiple intelligences. *European Journal of Personality, 13*, 247-259.

Furnham, A., and Ward, C. (2001). Sex differences, test experience and self-estimation of multiple intelligence. *New Zealand Journal of Psychology, 30*, 52-60.

Furnham, A., Wytykowska, A., and Petrides, K. V. (2005). Estimates of multiple intelligences: A study of Poland. *European Pyschologist, 10*, 51-59.

Gardner, H. (1983). *Frames of Mind: The Theory of Multiple Intelligences* (Second ed.). London: Fontana Press.

Gardner, H. (1993a). *Frames of Mind: The Theory of Multiple Intelligences* (2 ed.). London: Fontana Press.

Gardner, H. (1999). Multiple Intelligence Theory. *Australian Journal Of Education, 43*(1), 289.

Gardner, H. (2004). Audiences for the Theory of Multiple Intelligences. *Teachers College Record, 106*(1), 212-220.

Gardner, H., Goleman, D., and Csikszentmihalyi, M. (1998). Optimising Intelligences: Thinking, Emotion and Creativity. On *Video* [Video]: National Professional Resources, Inc.

Goodnough, K. (2001). Multiple intelligence theory: a framework for personalising science curricula. *School Science and Mathematics, 101*(4), 180-193.

Grant, C. A., and Tate, W. E. (1995). Multicultural education through the lens of the multicultural education research literature. In J. A. Banks and C. A. M. Banks (Eds.), *Handbook of Research on Multicultural Education*. New York: MacMillan, Harvard University Library.

Haig, Y., and Oliver, R. (2007). *Waiting in Line: African Refugee Students in Western Australian Schools*. Bunbury: WA.

Hickey, M. G. (2004). "Can I pick more than one Project?" Case Studies of Five Teachers Who Used Multiple Intelligence-Based Instructional Planning. *Teachers College Record, 106*(1), 77-86.

Jimenez, R. T. (1997). The strategic reading abilities and potential of five low-literacy Latino readers in middle school. *Reading Research Quarterly, 32*(3), 363-383.

Johnson, M. (2007). *An Extended Lietarure Review: The Effect of Multiple Intelligences on Elementary Student Performance.* Unpublished Master of Science in Education, Dominican University of California, San Rafael, CA.

Kornhaber, M. L., Fierros, E., and Veenema, S. (2004a). *Multiple Inteligences: Best ideas from theory and practice.* Needham Heights: MA: Allyn and Bacon.

Leitao, N. C. (2008). *Teacher-Student Relationships in Primary Schools in Perth.* Unpublished Doctor of Education thesis, Edith Cowan University, Perth.

Loori, A. A. (2005). Multiple intelligences: A comparison study between the preferences of males and females. *Social Behaviour and Personality, 33*(1), 77-88.

Luo, G. (2007). The relationship between the Rating Scale and the Partial Credit Models, and the implication for disordered thresholds of Rasch models for polytomous items. In E. V. Smith and R. M. Smith (Eds.), *Rasch measurement: Advanced and specialized applications* (pp. 181-201). Maple Grove, MN: JAM Press.

Magar, A. (2008a). *Australian Islamic College Annual School Report.* Perth, WA: Australian Islamic College

Magar, A. (2008b). *Teacher Induction Booklet.* Perth, WA: Australian Islamic College

Masters, G. N. (1982). A Rasch model for partial credit scoring. *Psychometrica, 47*, 149-174.

Masters, G. N. (1988). The analysis of partial credit scoring. *Applied Measurement in Education, 1*(4), 279-297.

Masters, G. N. (1997). Partial Credit Model. In J. P. Keeves (Ed.), *Educational Research, Methodology and Measurement: An International handbook* (2nd ed., pp. 857-863). Cambridge, UK: Cambridge University Press.

Michell, J. (1990). *An introduction to the logic of psychological measurement.* Hillsdale, NJ: Lawrence Erlbaum Associates.

Michell, J. (1997). Quantitative science and the definition of psychology. *British Journal of Psychology, 88*, 355-383.

Michell, J. (1999). *Measurement in psychology: A critical history of a methodoological concept.* Cambridge, UK: Cambrige University Press.

Miller, J., Mitchell, J., and Brown, J. (2005). African Refugees with interrupted schooling in the highschool mainstream:Dilemmas for teachers. *Prospect, 20*(2), 19-33.

Moran, S., Kornhaber, M., and Gardner, H. (2007). Multiple Intelligences: building active learners. *Teacher, 177*, 26-30.

Nolen, J. L. (2003). Multiple Intelligences in the Classroom. *Education (Chula Vista, Calif.), 124*(1), 115-119.

Park, J., and Niyozor, S. (2008). Madrasa education in South Asia and Southeast Asia: Current issues and debates. *Asia Pacific Journal of Education, 28*(4), 323-351.

Rasch, G. (1960/1980). *Probabilistic Models for Intelligence and Attainment Tests.* Chicago: IL: MESA Press.

Shah, S. (2008). Leading multi-ethnic schools: Adjustments in concepts and practices for engaging with diversity. *British Journal of Sociology of Education, 29*(5), 523-536.

Waterhouse, L. (2006). Multiple Intelligences, the Mozart Effect, and Emotional Intelligence: A critical review. *Educational Psychologist, 41*(4), 207-225.

Waugh, R. F. (2003a). Measuring Attitudes and Behaviours to Studying and Learning for University Students: A Rasch Measurement Model Analysis. *Journal of Applied Measurement, 4*(2), 164-180.

Waugh, R. F. (2003b). *On the Forefront of Educational Psychology.* New York: Nova Science Publishers.

Waugh, R. F. (2005b). *Frontiers in Educational Psychology.* New York: Nova Science Publishers.

Waugh, R. F. (2006). Rasch Measurement. In N. J. Salkind (Ed.), *Encyclopedia of Measurement and Statistics* (Vol. 3, pp. 820-825). Thousand Oaks, CA: Sage Publications.

Whitaker, D. (2002). *Multiple intelligences and after-school environments.* Nashville: TN: School-Age NOTES.

White, J. (1998). *Do Howard Gardner's multiple intelligences add up?* London: Institute of Education, University of London.

Wikipedia. (2009). *Theory of multiple intelligences.* Retrieved 23 April, 2009, from *http://www.en.wikipedia.org/wiki/Theory_of_multiple_intelligences*

Wright, B. D. (1999). Fundamental Measurement for Psychology. In S. E. Embretson and S. L. Hershberger (Eds.), *The New Rules of Measurement: What every psychologist and educator should know* (pp. 65-104). Mahwah, NJ: Lawrence Erlbaum Associates.

In: Applications of Rasch Measurement in Education   ISBN: 978-1-61668-026-8
Editor: Russell Waugh   © 2010 Nova Science Publishers, Inc.

Chapter 3

RASCH MEASURES FOR STUDENT SELF-VIEWS IN MATHEMATICS, ENGLISH AND ARTS BASED ON GARDNER INTELLIGENCES

Ahdielah Edries[1] and Russell F. Waugh[2]
1. Australian Islamic College
2. Faculty of Education and Arts, Edith Cowan University,
Mount Lawley, Western Australia

ABSTRACT

The Australian Islamic College is a co-educational Islamic Independent school with three campuses which cater for migrant students from war-torn countries and others with culturally and linguistically, diverse backgrounds. This paper is part of a larger study to identify the strengths and interests of Islamic students, across eight of Gardner's intelligence domains, as perceived by the students, so that the College could better meet the needs of these students. This study is important for the Islamic Colleges because it is hoped that the study will lead to the provision of opportunities for students to increase their confidence, self-esteem and motivation, and to achieve better in academic and non-academic areas. Student self-views were based on three aspects: (1) Things I really like; (2) Things I enjoy; and (3) Things I prefer, with items answered in two perspectives What I would like to do and What I actually do. This paper reports a Rasch analysis of student self-views based on three Gardner Intelligences: Mathematics, English and Arts (N=321). 12 out of 12 items fitted the measurement model for Mathematics Self-Views, 9 out of 12 for English Self-Views and 10 out of 12 items for Arts Self-Views. For all items, students found it easier to say what they would like to do than to actually do it. The item-trait interaction chi-squares are respectively: $x^2 =39.02$, df=48, p=0.82; $x^2 =33.27$, df=36, p=0.60; and $x^2 = 56.36$, df = 40, p= 0.05 showing no significant interaction between student measures and item difficulties along the scale, thus supporting uni-dimensional scales. The Person Separation Indices are respectively 0.78, 0.57 and 0.83 with standard errors of about 0.09 logits showing acceptable separation of measures compared to errors, except for Arts Self-Views, and improvements could be made by adding more items to all measures.

THE BACKGROUND TO THIS CHAPTER IS GIVEN AT THE BEGINNING OF CHAPTER TWO

Chapter Three reports on the RUMM 2020 output for the data relating to Student Self-Views for Mathematics, English and Arts, based on Gardner Intelligences. The same analysis and outputs was used here as for the Interpersonal and Intrapersonal Self-Views as reported in Chapter Two, but are not reported here in the same detail to lessen repetition of similar output presentations. This Chapter will present a summary and some interesting data for the Mathematics, English and Art Self-Views. Essential measurement data are presented through a series of tables and figures accompanied by some explanatory notes. Important inferences that can validly be made from the reliable Rasch measures are outlined in Part A. Part B reports on The RUMM 2020 output for item difficulties (easiest and hardest), the (worst 25 and best 25) student measures, and the targeting graphs by gender from which valid inferences was made by identifying the easy and hard items, the weak students who need help, and the weaker gender measures.

RASCH MEASURES

Linear Scales

Linear scales relating to Mathematics, English and Art Self-Views were created using a Rasch Measurement Model computer program, RUMM 2020 (Andrich, Sheridan and Luo, 2005). This section reports on the statistics showing a good fit to the measurement model for the data relating to the Mathematics, English and Art, Self-Views.

Dimensionality

The item-trait interactions for Mathematics, English and Art Self-Views are presented below in Tables 1, 2, and 3 respectively.

Table 1. Summary Test-of-fit Statistics for Mathematics Self-Views

Number of Items	12
Item-trait interaction chi- square (x2)	39.02
Probability of item-trait chi-square (p)	0.82
Degrees of freedom (df)	48.00

Table 2. Summary Test-of-fit Statistics for English Self-Views

Number of Items	9
Item-trait interaction chi- square (x2)	33.27
Probability of item-trait chi-square (p)	0.60
Degrees of freedom (df)	36.00

Table 3. Summary Test-of-fit Statistics for Art Self-Views

Number of Items	10
Item-trait interaction chi- square (x2)	56.36
Probability of item-trait chi-square (p)	0.05
Degrees of freedom (df)	40.00

Explanatory Notes for Tables 1, 2, and 3.

1. The item-trait interaction indicates the agreement displayed with all items across all students from different locations on the scales (acceptable for this scale).
2. df (degrees of freedom) refers to the number of scores in a distribution that are free to change without changing the mean of the distribution.
3. Chi-Square determines the probability of significant interaction.
4. Probability refers to the levels of certainty to which an item fits the measurement model, based on its chi-square.
5. All values are given to two decimal places because the errors are to two decimal places.

Table 4. Reliability Indices for Mathematics, English and Arts

Self-Concept	Standard Error of Measurement	Person Separation Index	Power of test-of-fit
Maths	0.09	0.78	Good
English	0.09	0.57	Reasonable
Art	0.09	0.83	Good

The tables above indicate that there is a consensus amongst students with regard to the difficulty of items (that is, items are easy, of medium difficulty or hard) and that the items for each of the Academic Self-Views (Mathematics, English and Art) have a level of certainty with which it fits the measurement model, based on the chi-square values ($x^2 = 39.02$, $x^2 = 33.27$, $x^2 = 56.36$) for Mathematics, English and Art respectively. The fit of items for the 12 items of Mathematics and the 10 items of Art Self-Views are good, and the fit of items for the 9 items of English Self-View is reasonable, but acceptable.

Reliability

Table 4 reports on the reliability of each of the self-view measures in Mathematics, English and Art. The standard errors of measurement are about 0.09 logits for Mathematics, English and Art Self-Views. The Person Separation Indices are respectively 0.78 and 0.57, and 0.83, indicating good (or acceptable) separation of measures in comparison to the errors.

Targeting

The Person Measure/Item Threshold graphs (see Figures 1, 2, and 3 respectively) for Mathematics, English and Art, were significant in showing the range of item thresholds and student measures. The graphs were also helpful in showing which students had a negative self-concept towards their academic subjects; and which students excelled in the areas of Mathematics, English and Art. These results are now explained.

It can be seen from the distribution of items in Figure 1 that the item difficulties mostly cover the middle range (-1.2 to +1.8 logits) of Mathematical Self-View measures. Therefore, some easier and harder items need to be added in any revision of the scale to cover students with the lowest measures (-3.36 logits) and students with the highest (+3.44 logits) measures.

For example, there were 13 students who were not able to identify with the items asked, their raw scores ranged from 0 (extremely low) to a score of 4 for the lower end of the scale. Similarly, 5 students obtained an extremely high score of 24. Hence, targeting could be improved by adding some easy and hard items appropriate for students with the lowest and the highest measures and this would improve the measure.

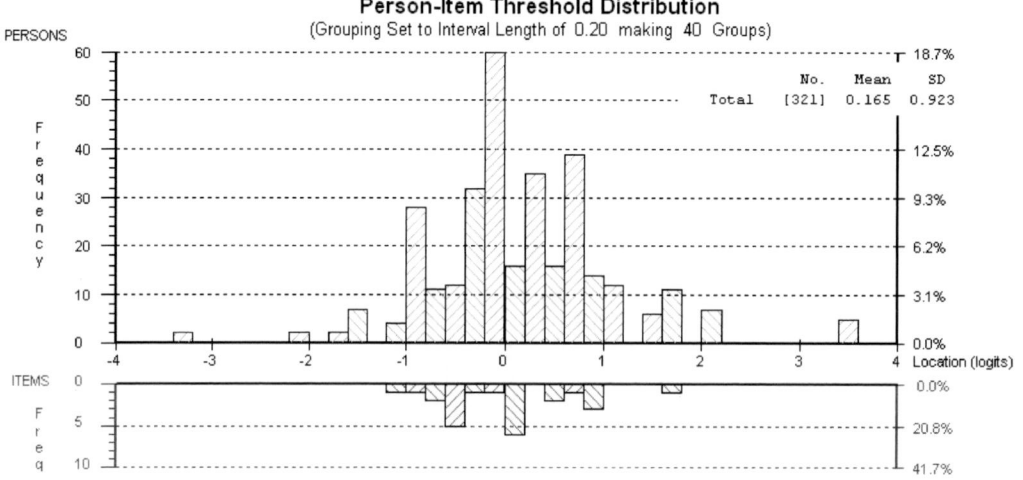

Figure 1. Person measure / Item Threshold Graph for Mathematics Self-View.

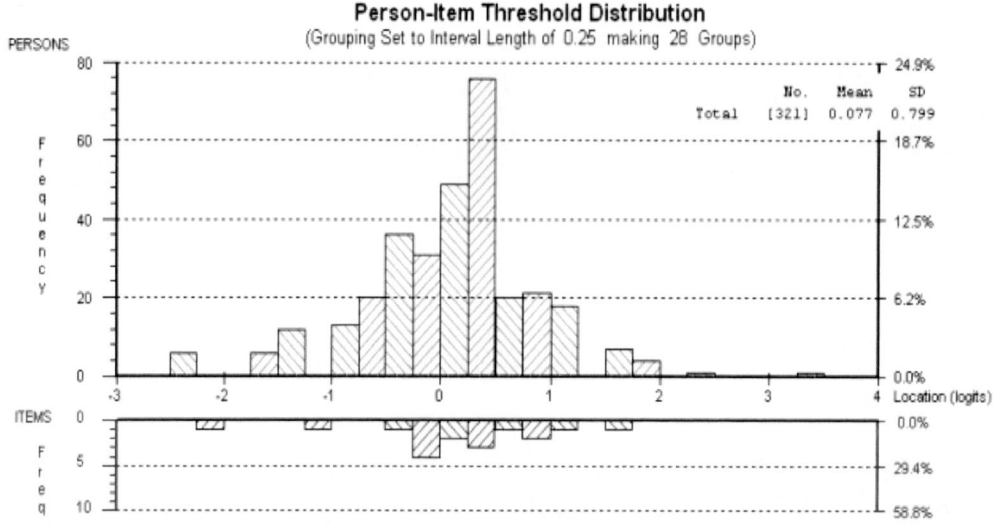

Figure 2. Person measure / Item Threshold Graph for English Self-View.

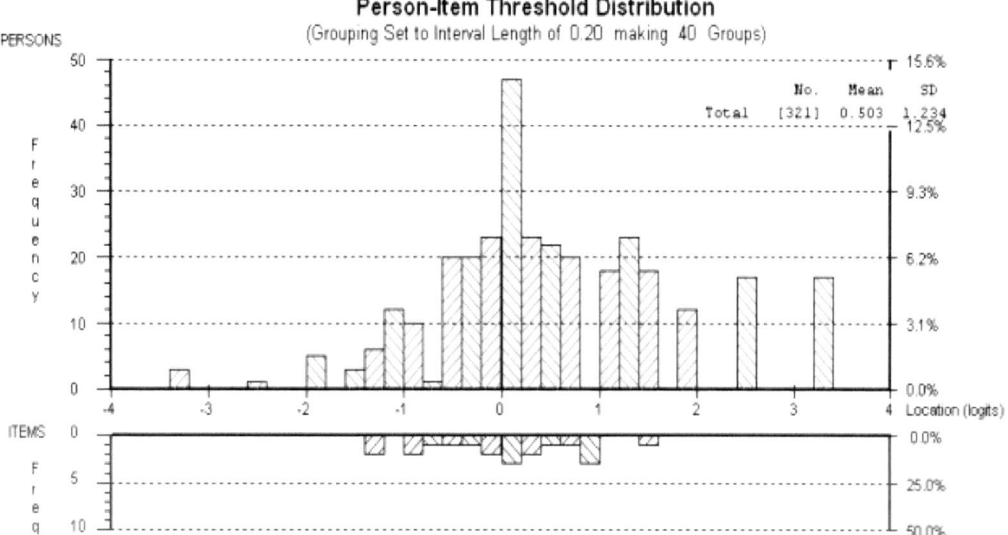

Person-Item Threshold Distribution
(Grouping Set to Interval Length of 0.20 making 40 Groups)

Notes on Figures 1, 2, and 3.
1. The scale is in logits, that is, the log odds of answering the response categories.
2. Person measures (low to high) are given on the upper side in logits.
3. Item thresholds (easy to hard) are given on the lower side in logits.

Figure 3. Person measure / Item Threshold Graph for Art Self-View.

Figure 2 shows that the item thresholds for English Self-View range from easy (about -2.2 logits) to reasonably hard (about +1.8 logits); and the student measures calibrated on the same scale from low (about -2.35 logits) to high (about + 3.26 logits). These measures indicate that some harder items need to be added to better target the attitudes and behaviours of students with high measures (that is, students who obtained scores from 15 to 17).

Two-hundred and sixty-three students out of a total of three-hundred and twenty-one students (see Figure 3) were able to easily answer the items relating to the Art Self-View (that is, the item difficulties mostly covered the middle range (-1.4 to +1.6 logits) of Art Self-View measures. Twelve students fell in the lower range (-1.4 logits to -3.27 logits) of the scale, and forty six students fell in the higher range of the scale (+1.6 logits to 3.30 logits) indicating that some easier and harder items need to be added in any revision of the scale to cover the students with the these measures.

Inferences from the Linear Scales

Valid inferences can be made about item difficulties and student measures of Mathematics, English and Art Self-View that showed a good fit to the measurement model (see Tables 5, 6 and 7 respectively). There is a prediction that the attitude items should be easier than the behaviour items and, where both fit the model, attitudes are easier than their corresponding behaviours showing that attitudes influence corresponding behaviour.

Table 5. Item Difficulties for Student Mathematics Self-View

Item	MATHEMATICS SELF-CONCEPT	What I actually do	What I'd like to do
	Things that I really like		
1	Doing computer games and Maths games	-0.48	-0.79
2	Working out maths problems by logic	+0.21	-0.28
	Things I enjoy		
3	Watching TV programs like Documentaries and Quiz Shows like *Who wants to be a Millionaire*	+0.04	-0.32
4	Solving maths problems that are hard	+0.20	-0.11
	Things I prefer		
5	Creating charts and graphs for group presentations	+0.53	-0.11
6	Communicating through charts and graphs	+1.01	+0.10

Table 6. Item Difficulties for Student English Self-View

Item	ENGLISH SELF-CONCEPT	What I actually do	What I'd like to do
	Things that I really like		
1	Telling stories and jokes	+0.27	-0.37
2	Writing stories or poems for others to read	+1.03	+0.30
	Things I enjoy		
3	Watching TV programs with witty scripts: sitcoms like *The Simpsons and Raven*	N/F	-2.06
4	Reading books like Harry Potter	+0.44	-0.00
	Things I prefer		
5	Writing and library research for group presentations	+0.33	+0.06
6	Reading a variety of books and good stories	N/F	N/F

Table 7. Item Difficulties for Student Art Self-Views

Item	ART SELF-CONCEPT	What I actually do	What I'd like to do
	Things that I really like		
1	Drawing and creating	-0.65	-1.12
2	Making models, murals and collages	+0.46	-0.42
	Things I enjoy		
3	Watching TV programs involving art and craft demonstrations	+0.63	+0.09
4	Creating my own art works	-0.40	N/F
	Things I prefer		
5	Drawing pictures and art for group presentations	+0.44	N/F
6	Communicating by using drawings, diagrams and pictures	+0.83	+0.14

Notes for Tables 5, 6 and 7.
1. N/F means no fit (hence, the item was deleted).
2. All values are given to two decimal places because the errors are to two decimal places.

Item Difficulties

For the Mathematics Self-View attitudes (What they would like to do), students found it very easy (-0.79 logits) to say that they really liked to do Maths and Computer games, moderately easy (-0.32 logits) to say that they enjoy watching TV programs like documentaries and Quiz shows such as "Who wants to be a Millionaire'. They found it moderately easy (-0.11 logits) to say that they liked to create charts and graphs for group presentations, and to solve Maths problems (-0.11 logits). Students found it hard to say that they would like to be able to communicate through charts and graphs (+0.11 logits). In contrast, for actual behaviour (What they actually do), students found it very easy (-0.48 logits) to like Maths and Computer games, moderately easy (+0.04 logits) to enjoy watching TV programs like documentaries and Quiz shows such as "Who wants to be a **Millionaire**". They found it moderately hard (+0.53 logits) to actually create charts and graphs for group presentations, and very hard (+1.01 logits) to actually communicate through charts and graphs.

For the English Self-View attitudes (What they would like to do), students found it very easy to say that they liked to watch television programs with witty scripts, such as, 'The Simpsons' and 'Raven' (-2.06 logits). They found it easy to say that they really like to tell stories and jokes (-0.37 logits), moderately hard to say that they prefer to write and do library research for group presentations (+0.06 logits), and hard to write stories and poems for others to read (+0.30 logits). In contrast, for actual behaviour (What they actually do), they found it hard to actually tell stories and jokes (+0.27 logits), hard to actually write and do library research for group presentations (+0.33 logits), hard to read books like Harry Potter (+0.44 logits), and very hard to write stories and poems for others to read (+1.03 logits).

For Art Self-View attitudes (What they would like to do), students found it very easy to say that they really liked to draw and create things (-1.12 logits), moderately easy to say that they like making models, murals and collages (-0.42 logits). They found it moderately hard to say that they enjoy watching TV programs that involve art and craft demonstrations (+0.09 logits), and that they prefer to communicate by using drawings, diagrams and pictures (+0.14 logits). In contrast, for actual behaviour (What they actually do), they found it easy to actually enjoy drawing and creating things (-0.65 logits), and easy to create their own art works (-0.40 logits). Students found it hard to say that they do actually enjoy watching TV programs that involve art and craft demonstrations (+0.63 logits), and very hard to actually communicate by using drawings, diagrams and pictures (+0.83 logits).

Student Measures of Self-Views

The lowest 25 and the highest 25 student measures have been identified by converting each student's raw score, based on the items that fit the measurement model, to a linear measure, expressed in logits. These students are identified here only by number for ethical reasons. Tables 8, 9, and 10 are presented below for Mathematics, English and Art Self-Views respectively. To complement the tables a descriptive analysis is provided for the lowest twenty-five students who require extra support to improve their academic self-views, and the twenty-five highest achieving students in Mathematics, English and Art.

Table 8. Students with Lowest 25 Measures for Mathematics Self-View

ID	Raw Score	Student Measure	SE	Residual
299	0	-3.358	1.18	-
250	0	-3.358	1.18	-
308	2	-2.057	0.66	-1.064
90	2	-2.057	0.66	-0.362
103	3	-1.699	0.57	-0.541
187	3	-1.699	0.57	-0.363
300	4	-1.420	0.51	-0.969
145	4	-1.420	0.51	0.591
294	4	-1.420	0.51	-0.960
133	4	-1.420	0.51	-0.407
39	4	-1.420	0.51	0.270
267	4	-1.420	0.51	-1.203
230	4	-1.420	0.51	1.203
55	5	-1.188	0.48	-0.570
202	5	-1.188	0.48	-0.175
9	5	-1.188	0.48	0.199
301	5	-1.188	0.48	0.925
272	6	-0.985	0.45	0.483
40	6	-0.985	0.45	0.023
69	6	-0.985	0.45	0.252
174	6	-0.985	0.45	1.309
207	6	-0.985	0.45	-0.543
33	6	-0.985	0.45	-0.044
56	6	-0.985	0.45	-0.935
17	6	-0.985	0.45	-0.022

Table 9. Students with Lowest 25 Measures for English Self-View

ID	Raw Score	Student Measure	SE	Residual
250	1	-2.355	0.93	-1.064
260	1	-2.355	0.93	-1.064
181	1	-2.355	0.93	-1.064
179	1	-2.355	0.93	0.046
230	1	-2.355	0.93	-0.531
226	1	-2.355	0.93	-0.531
158	2	-1.701	0.73	-0.579
130	2	-1.701	0.73	-0.531
267	2	-1.701	0.73	-1.096
9	2	-1.701	0.73	0.286
35	2	-1.701	0.73	-0.579
3	2	-1.701	0.73	-0.123
115	3	-1.259	0.63	1.103
247	3	-1.259	0.63	-1.008
ID	Raw Score	Student Measure	SE	Residual
294	3	-1.259	0.63	-0.267
103	3	-1.259	0.63	-0.438
33	3	-1.259	0.63	0.215
299	3	-1.259	0.63	-1.008
178	3	-1.259	0.63	-0.438
87	3	-1.259	0.63	-1.017
303	3	-1.259	0.63	-0.243
117	3	-1.259	0.63	-1.008
319	3	-1.259	0.63	-0.139
175	3	-1.259	0.63	-1.017
116	4	-0.919	0.57	-1.043

Table 10. Students with Lowest 25 Measures for Art Self-View

ID	Raw Score	Student Measure	SE	Residual
118	0	- 3.265	1.19	-
187	0	-3.265	1.19	-
260	0	-3.265	1.19	-
35	1	-2.498	0.85	-0.840
120	2	-1.962	0.68	0.534
299	2	-1.962	0.68	0.116
132	2	-1.962	0.68	0.116
228	2	-1.962	0.68	-0.188
56	2	-1.962	0.68	-0.964
250	3	-1.588	0.59	-1.350
294	3	-1.588	0.59	-0.249
175	3	-1.588	0.59	-1.097
125	4	-1.289	0.54	0.415
116	4	-1.289	0.54	-1.283
308	4	-1.289	0.54	0.356
226	4	-1.289	0.54	0.215
41	4	-1.289	0.54	-0.457
151	4	-1.289	0.54	-0.514
158	5	-1.032	0.50	-1.989
168	5	-1.032	0.50	-0.963
262	5	-1.032	0.50	-0.110
58	5	-1.032	0.50	-1.188
17	5	-1.032	0.5	0.163
181	5	-1.032	0.5	-1.069
221	5	-1.032	0.5	-0.464

Comments on the 25 students who have been identified as having a low Mathematics Self-View are now given. Two students (one male and one female) had an extreme low raw score of 0 (-3.36 logits), and will require urgent extra help such as remediation classes to improve in this Self-View. Eleven students (five males and six females) had scores ranging from 2 to 4, and will also require extra support. Of the 12 students (raw scores of 5 and 6) who answered, 'some of the time' to the items, five were males and seven were females. These students will also benefit from extra support and attention in the strands of Mathematics. In contrast, the top 25 students (14 males and 11 females) who had a high Mathematics Self-View did remarkably well, with scores ranging from 20 to 24 (+1.48 logits to an extreme +3.44 logits). These results indicate that these students would require specialised extension classes.

There were more males than females who had a very low English Self-View (that is, 18 males compared with seven females), indicating that urgent intervention may be required as well as extra support with English for these males (and females). Raw scores for these students were quite low ranging from 1 to 4 (-2.36 logits to -0.92 logits). Twelve males and thirteen males attained high scores ranging from 13 to 17 (with one male having an extreme high score of 17 at +3.26 logits).

For the Art Self-View, three males had an extreme low score of 0, thus having a very low Art Self-View and would require urgent intervention. One female had a low score of 1 and would also require help in Art. Out of the 14 students who had a raw score ranging from 2 to 4, ten were males and four were females. The above results are indicative that males have different perceptions towards Art than females, and this needs to be reviewed. Seven students (five males and two females) have the highest measure of 5, which represents answers of 'some of the time' to only 5 of the 20 items, representing a low self-concept in Art. In contrast, females had a significantly high Art Self-View. That is, eight females had a score of 19 (+2.51 logits), and of the remaining 17 students who had an extreme high score of 20 (+3.29 logits), 10 were female. This means that these 17 students answered 'often, a lot of the time' to all 20 items, representing a very high concept in Art.

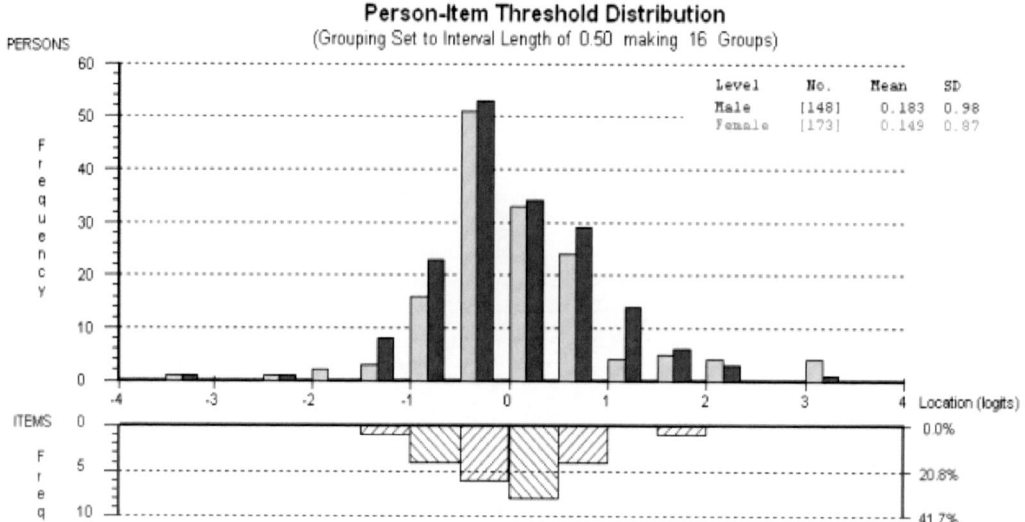

Note: There is a colour error in the RUMM program. Purple corresponds to red (female) and green corresponds to blue (male).

Figure 4. Target Graph by Gender for Mathematical Self-View.

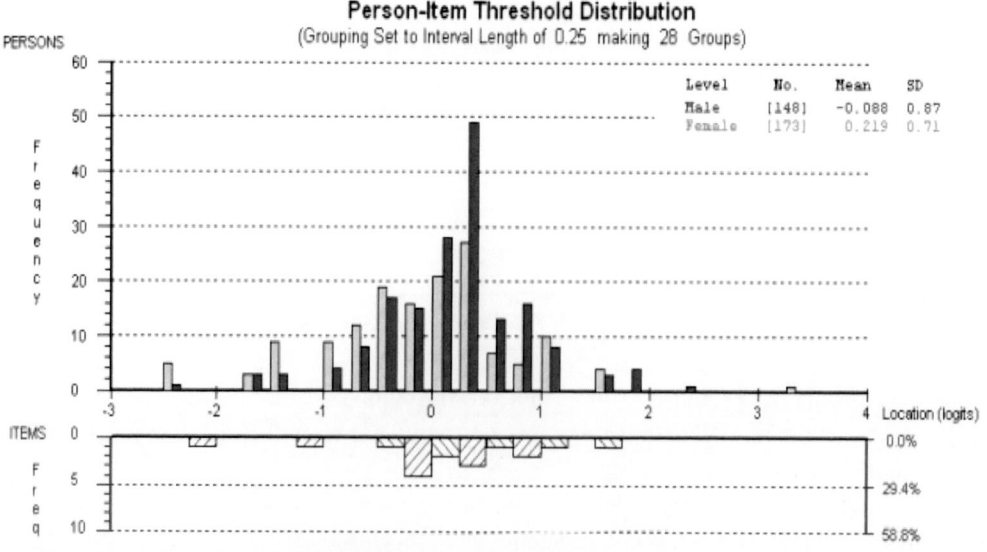

Note: There is a colour error in the RUMM program. Purple corresponds to red (female) and green corresponds to blue (male).

Figure 5. Target Graph by Gender for English Self-View.

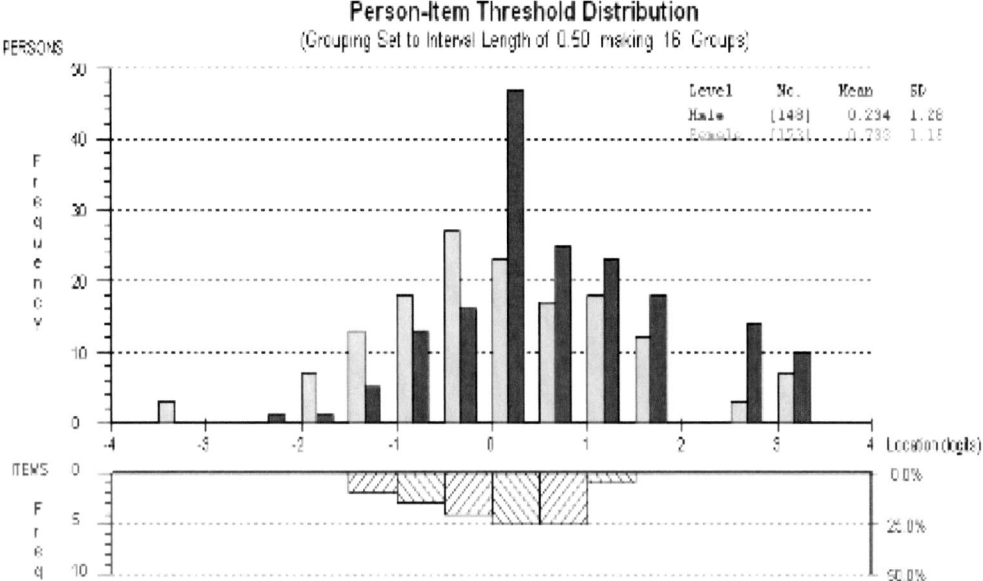

Person-Item Threshold Distribution
(Grouping Set to Interval Length of 0.50 making 16 Groups)

Level	No.	Mean	SD
Male	[148]	0.234	1.26
Female	[173]	-0.733	1.15

Note: There is a colour error in the RUMM program. Purple corresponds to red (female) and green corresponds to blue (male).

Figure 6. Target Graph by Gender for Art Self-Concept.

Gender Differences

The measures were separated by gender so that inferences can be made in regard to gender.

Data from the graph in Figure 4 for Mathematical Self-View shows that there were 148 males and 173 females who participated in this survey. Male students have statistically significantly higher mean Mathematical Self-Concept measures than their male counterparts ($t=3.28$, $df=319$, $p=0.00$). Further conclusions can be made from the graph. From about -1.00 to -3.36 logits, there are 4.1% of students (8 males and 10 females), who have extremely low levels of Mathematics Self-Concept. From -1 to 0 logits, 41.4% of students (66 males and 78 females) have low levels of Mathematics Self-Concept. From 0 to +1.0 logits, there are 49.5 % of students (55 males and 63 females) who have a medium level of Mathematics Self-Concept. From+1.0 to +2.0 logits, there are 4.1% of students (9 males and 20 females) who have moderately high levels of Mathematics Self-Concept. From +2.0 to +3.44 logits, there are 8 males and 4 females who have very high levels of Mathematics Self-Concept.

Taking the data from Figure 5 for English Self-Views, female students have statistically significantly higher mean measures than the male students ($t=12.4$, $df=319$, $p=0.000$). From the graph, further conclusions can be made. There were 12 % of students (17 males compared with 7 females) who were only able to answer the easy items (-1.00 to -2.35 logits). The majority of students (76%), comprising of 118 males and 148 females, were able to only answer the medium items in the -1.00 to $+1.00$ logits range. The remaining 12 % (15 males and 16 females) were able to answer the hard items easily in the $+1.0$ to $+3.26$ logits range, with only one male having an extreme score of 17.

Figure 6 for Art Self-Views shows that, female students have statistically significantly higher mean measures than the male students (t=4.03, df=319, p= 0.000). Valid conclusions were made from the graph in determining the best and the worst student measures for Art Self-Concept. There were 34 students (10 males compared to their (24) female counterparts) who were able to answer the hard items easily in the +2.0 to + 4.0 logits range. Seventeen students (7 males and 10 females) had an extreme high score of 17, in contrast to the 3 males who had an extreme low score of 0. In the 0.0 to -2.0 logits range, 45% of students (35 males compared to their female counterparts (64) were only able to answer the easy items. The medium questions were answered by 55 % of students in the 0.0 to 2.0 logits range, with more females (113) than males (70) responding to these medium questions.

SUMMARY OF FINDINGS

Linear scales, relating to Mathematics Self-View (12 items), English Self-View (9 items), and Art Self-View (10 items), were created using the Rasch Measurement Model computer program, RUMM 2020 (Andrich, Sheridan and Luo, 2005). The reliability of the scale data was shown by:

1. Good global and person item fit to the measurement model, and good individual fit to the measurement model. That is, the standardized fit residual data for Mathematics Self-View has a mean of 0.33 and a standard deviation of 0.72, the English Self-View has a mean of 0.26 and a standard deviation of 0.80, and the data for Art Self-View has a mean of 0.01 and a standard deviation of 0.92 respectively. This means that there is a good consistency of student responses to the items, and that the three category responses were being answered consistently and logically.
2. The standard errors of measurement were approximately 0.09 logits for Mathematics, English and Art Self-Views. The Person Separation Indices were 0.78 and 0.57, and 0.83 respectively, indicating good (or reasonable) separation of measures in comparison to the errors.
3. The items for each of the Academic Self-Views have good item-trait interaction chi-square values ($x2 = 39.02$, $x2 = 33.27$, $x2 = 56.36$) respectively for Mathematics, English and Art, indicating the measurement of a uni-dimensional trait on a linear scale.
4. Reasonable targeting of the items against the person measures, although some easier and harder items need to be added for any future use of the three scales.

Since the scale data were shown to be reliable, the following valid inferences were drawn.

1. All attitude relationships (What I would like to do) were easier than their corresponding actual behaviours (What I actually do), in line with the theoretical concept of the variables.
2. Males have statistically significantly higher Mathematical Self-Views than females.

3.   For the Mathematics Self-View attitudes (What I would like to do), students found it very easy to say that they really liked to do Maths and Computer games, they found it moderately hard to say that they prefer to communicate through charts and graphs. In contrast, for actual behaviour (What I actually do), students found it easy to say that they actually liked to do Maths and Computer games, and very hard to actually communicate through charts and graphs.

4.   Girls have significantly higher English Self-Views than boys.

5.   For the English Self-View attitudes (What I would like to do), students found it very easy to say that they liked to watch Television programs with witty scripts, such as, 'The Simpsons' and 'Raven', and they found it moderately hard to say that they would like to write stories and poems for others to read. In contrast, for actual behaviour (What I actually do), they found it hard to actually tell stories and jokes, moderately hard to enjoy reading books like Harry Potter, and very hard to actually write stories and poems for others to read.

6.   Females have significantly higher Art Self-Views than males.

7.   For the Art Self-View attitudes (What I would like to do), students found it very easy to say that they really liked to draw and create things. They found it moderately hard to say that they enjoy watching Television programs that involve art and craft demonstrations, and that they prefer to communicate by using drawings, diagrams and pictures. In contrast, for actual behaviour (What I actually do), they found it easy to actually enjoy drawing and creating things, and hard to say that they actually communicated by using drawings, diagrams and pictures.

In: Applications of Rasch Measurement in Education
Editor: Russell Waugh

ISBN: 978-1-61668-026-8
© 2010 Nova Science Publishers, Inc.

Chapter 4

A UNIDIMENSIONAL RASCH MEASURE OF MOTIVATION IN SCIENCE AND MATHEMATICS

Tan Hock[1] Chye and Russell F.Waugh[2]

1. Hwa Chong Institution, Singapore
2. Graduate School of Education,
University of Western Australia, Perth, Western Australia

ABSTRACT

Using a Rasch computer program, a linear, uni-dimensional scale of Motivation in Science and Mathematics was created with data from a self-report questionnaire modified for Secondary-Three (aged 15 years) students in a premier Singapore Junior High, based on *Striving for Excellence* (Standards, Goals, Tasks, Effort, Ability and Values), *Desire to Learn* (Interest, Learning from Others, and Responsibility for Learning) and Personal Incentives (Extrinsic Rewards, Intrinsic Rewards and Social Rewards). Thirty-four items out of 50, in a mixture of the ideal and actual perspectives, fitted the measurement model. The proportion of observed variance considered true was 0.92 and the item-trait chi-square was 192 (df=204) with p=0.71 showing a highly reliable and unidimensional scale. It was found that attitude items need to be designed as a prime influence on behaviour items in an easy/harder pattern to form a good model of Motivation suggesting a method of item design for measuring educational variables.

A UNI-DIMENSIONAL RASCH MEASURE OF MOTIVATION IN SCIENCE AND MATHEMATICS

The paper reports the creation of a linear, unidimensional scale to measure Motivation to Achieve Academically in Science and Mathematics at a premier high school in Singapore, using the Rasch Unidimensional Measurement Model (RUMM 2020) computer program (Andrich, Sheridan, and Luo, 2005). Rasch measures (Andrich, 1982, 1985, 1988a, 1988b; Rasch, 1960/1980) are currently the only known way to create a linear, unidimensional measure in the human sciences (and human psychology variables) (see Waugh, 2006; Wright, 1999).

Theoretical Framework of Motivation

The framework for the model of motivation was adopted and modified from Waugh's (2002) model for this study. The model had three main aspects: Motivation Aspect 1: *Striving for Excellence* (defined by the sub-aspects, Standards, Goals, Tasks, Effort, Ability and Values), Motivation Aspect 2: *Desire to Learn* (defined by the sub-aspects, Interest, Learning from Others, and Responsibility for Learning), and Motivation Aspect 3: *Personal Incentives* (defined by Extrinsic Rewards, Intrinsic Rewards and Social Rewards). The sub-aspects were conceptually ordered by difficulty in Guttman-like patterns, with direct links between attitude and behaviour. This was done through two perspectives, 'What I aim for' (expected to be 'easy' on average), which measures attitude, and 'What I actually do' (expected to be 'harder' on average), which measures behaviour, which together measure motivation.

'What I aim for' was expected to be stated by the students in terms of the number of Science and Mathematics subjects to which it applies. It was expected that this would reflect the students' needs, expectations, cognitions and desires, all internally and covertly contained within the students' minds, but now generally expressed in terms of what they aim for in their subjects. 'What I actually do' was expected to be stated by the students in terms of the number of Science and Mathematics subjects to which it applies too. It was expected that this would be decided by the students' personal beliefs, needs and cognitions, all now expressed as to what they actually do in their subjects. Thus the two response sets were in turn linked to an ordered set of subject response categories (in none, or only one of my science or mathematics subjects, in two, or three of my science and mathematics subjects and in four, or all of my science and mathematics subjects). The reasons for the design of the subject response categories in this study are explained below.

All secondary-three students in the premier high school where this study was based studied four Science and Mathematics subjects. They were Chemistry, Physics, Mathematics and Additional Mathematics. The fifth science subject, Biology was optional. Students opted to do Biology, an additional science subject, at the end of secondary two based on interest as well as the science grade obtained in the secondary two final examinations. So students doing Biology in secondary three would have five Science and Mathematics subjects to study in total, and students not doing Biology in secondary three would have four Science and Mathematics subjects to study in total. The response set was ordered from easy (in none, or only one of my science or mathematics subjects), indicated by the number '1', to hard (in four, or all of my science and mathematics subjects), indicated by the number '3'.

Expected Outcomes for Model of Motivation

The items under the sub-aspects were created and ordered from easy to hard, conceptually. For example under the sub-aspect, Standards, of Striving for Excellence, were three items: (1) I aim to do my best in science and mathematics; (2) I set, for myself, good grades in Science and Mathematics which I believe I can achieve; and (3) I evaluate my performance in Science and Mathematics against the grade that I set for myself. It was expected that most students would find it easy to say they aim to do their best in all their Science and Mathematics subjects, with some expected variation in student response around this. It was expected that most student would find it harder to say that they aim to achieve good grades for all their Science and Mathematics subjects, with some variation around this. This was because item (2) is more difficult than item (1). That is, to set the goal of achieving good grades involves a little more effort than just aiming to do one's best. It was expected that most students would find it harder still to say that they aim to evaluate their performance in Science and Mathematics against the good grade they have set for themselves in all their Science and Mathematics subjects, with some variation around this. The reason is that item (3) is more difficult than item (2). That is, to aim to evaluate my performance involves more than just aiming for good grades – it involves evaluating with an implication for improvement. Thus it was expected that these three items would form an ordered pattern of response by difficulty, on average, from easy to hard, when the student reported that this is 'What I aim for'.

Similarly, it was expected that this vertically ordered pattern in terms of difficulty for the students' self-views of 'What I aim for' in relation to the three items under the sub-aspect Standards (as explained above), would be repeated for their self-view of their behaviour when they responded to 'What I actually do' for the same three items (items 1, 2, and 3).

Rationale for Adopting the Scale of Motivation

Motivation has been measured both qualitatively and quantitatively in many studies. Ray (1986) reported over 70 scales; see also Blankenship, 1987; Clarke, 1973; Conoley and Impara, 1995; Fineman, 1977; Harper, 1975; Lian-Hwang Chiu, 1997; Piedmont, 1989, test numbers 226,244,245; Thibert and Karsenti, 1996. However, many of these scales do not give a comprehensive view of motivation and most of them involve only a relative simple range of aspects and items (Waugh, 2002). Also, the large majority of these scales are measured using True Score Theory which cannot produce a linear scale (Waugh and Njiru, 2005; Wright, 1996). Most scales measured using True Score Theory have poor reliability and validity (see Ray, 1986). Even though modern measurement programmes are available to create interval level measures in which item difficulties and student Motivation measures are calibrated on the same scale, all the above scales have been analyzed according to traditional measurement and not with modern Rasch computer programs. Lian-Hwang Chiu (1997) reported that reviews of literature showed that the score reliability and validity of many of the scales measured using True Score Theory varied from satisfactory to poor. Furthermore, many of these scales are not based on a sufficiently detailed model of motivation, and are not linked to behaviour which is almost always part of the definition of motivation (Waugh and Njiru, 2005).

The structure was designed to measure the motivation of a student who is highly motivated in one subject only and, at the same time, measure the motivation of other students who are motivated in some or many Science and Mathematics subjects. The subject response categories ('in none, or only one of my science or mathematics subjects', 'in two, or three of my science and mathematics subjects' and 'in four, or all of my science and mathematics subjects') cater for students motivated in one subject as well as many.

Likert (1932) response categories were not used because they contain a discontinuity between disagree and agree and are not ordered from low to high. That is, 'neutral' (between disagree and agree) does not necessarily represent more motivation than disagree, or less than agree. When a 'neutral' category is provided those who are undecided, unclear, don't want to answer or just neutral, will answer the middle (neutral) category, which will result in a measurement and interpretation problem.

The structure tests the linkage between attitude and behavior. Item difficulties relating to both 'What I aim for' (attitude of Motivation) and 'What I actually do' (behavior of motivation), are measured at the same time and calibrated on the same scale in Rasch measurement so they can be directly compared. This allows a direct test of the conceptually ordered item difficulties, much like is done in Science experiment.

In traditional questionnaires, positively and negatively worded items are mixed to avoid the fixed response syndrome. There is some evidence that this causes an interaction effect between items as shown in modern measurement models (Andrich and Van Schoubroeck, 1989). The reason for this is that negatively worded items evoke a stronger attitude than positively worded items. The items in the present study are all worded positively.

The analysis of most motivation data uses only traditional statistical programs and ordinal level scales (True Score Theory). Modern Rasch measurement programs (such as RUMM 2020, Andrich, Sheridan and Luo, 2005) are now available to create interval level measures in which item difficulties and student motivation measures can be calibrated on the same scale (Andrich, 1988a; Wright, 1996, 1999). They also test the conceptual structure of motivation, including its dimensional nature (see Andrich, 1988a, 1988b; Rasch, 1960/1980; Waugh, 1998a, 1998b, 2002). Rasch measurement model analysis has been shown as appropriate to use in measuring variables like motivation (see; Andrich, 1982, 1985; Waugh, 1998a, 1998b, 1999, 2001, 2002; Wright, 1999; Wright and Masters, 1981, 1982).

Rationale for Modifying the Scale of Motivation

There are three reasons for modifying the Waugh (2002) scale of motivation. One, the aim of this research is to measure the motivation of students in Science and Mathematics and not motivation in general. This study is more subject-specific than the Waugh (2002) model. Two, the questionnaire is mainly targeted at 15 year old students and not 18 year old students so the items have to be reworded and simplified so as not to be conceptually too difficult for them to understand. Three, this questionnaire has 25 items instead of the original 45 Motivation items in Waugh's (2002) questionnaire and, as the sample age is younger, the students need more time to think through the items before responding. Also, in Waugh's (2002), study the students took 15 minutes to complete the questionnaire. The target population in this study might tooka little longer time to complete the questionnaire as they were younger.

METHOD

A formal pilot test of the self-reported questionnaire was carried out in October 2006 with twenty students. Each student was asked to complete the 25 items in the questionnaire and provide verbal and written feedback on several aspects. The aspects were adapted from Bell (1987, p. 65) involving, for example, did each question make sense, were the response categories ordered satisfactorily, are there any main items omitted and does this set of items seem to measure your motivation.

Ethical approval was obtained for this study involving human participants from the Ethics Committee of the University of Western Australia through the submission of the online ethics form. This was submitted and approved in August 2006 together with the proposal for this study. As required, a letter was attached to the consent form outlining the purpose for the research and the rights of the participants. Consent was obtained from the principal of the premier high school, the parents of the participants, and the participants prior to the collection of data. The contact address of the researcher was included in the letter for further queries by the participants and parents involved in the research.

The participants in this study were Secondary-Three boys between the age of 14 and 15 years old. There were 478 students in secondary three in the year 2007. The questionnaires were administered in March 2007 with the help of the Physics teachers, taking about twenty minutes of their lesson time. The venues were the individual classrooms and the data collection lasted for about a week, depending on the schedule of the individual Physics teachers. Twenty-four students did not participate because they were either on sick leave or they were out representing the school in sports competition on the days the survey was carried out. Of the 454 participants, 41 submitted incomplete questionnaires. Thus subsequently only 413 responses to the questionnaire were entered into an Excel (Microsoft, 2004) file. Science and Mathematics Research Programme participants were assigned the code '1' and the non-Science and Mathematics Research Programme participants were assigned the code '2'. For each participant, the responses to the questionnaire were entered in terms of response categories, '1', '2' and '3'. '1' was for 'in none, or only one of my science or mathematics subjects', '2' was for 'in two, or three of my science and mathematics subjects', and '3' was for 'in four, or all of my science and mathematics subjects'.

Rasch Analysis

Summary of Fit Statistics
Of the 50 items, 34 items consisting of a mixture of the ideal and actual perspectives fitted the Rasch measurement model. Table 1 is a summary of the global standardized fit residuals.

When the data fit the measurement model, the standardized item and student fit residuals have a mean near zero and a SD near 1, as is the case in these data. This means that there is a very good consistency of item parameters across student motivation measures for this scale.

Table 1 also shows the Cronbach Alpha (0.92) and the Separation Index (0.92) for the 34 items. These are constructed essentially in the same way as for True Score Theory (Crobach, 1951; Andrich and van Schoubroeck, 1989). However Cronbach's Alpha can only be calculated on complete raw score data, whereas, the Separation Index is calculated using Rasch parameter estimates and this does not require every person to complete every item in the survey. The maximum value for both the Cronbach Alpha and the Separation Index is 1 and the values of 0.92 and 0.92 are high, showing that the student measures are well separated in comparison to the errors (about 0.1 logits).

Table 1. Summary of Fit Statistics for Motivation to Achieve in Science and Mathematics from the Rasch Analysis (N = 408, I = 34)

Item-Student Interaction				
Items			*Students*	
	Location	*Fit Residual*	*Location*	*Fit Residual*
Mean	*0.00*	*0.15*	*1.07*	*-0.24*
SD	*0.90*	*1.01*	*1.13*	*1.40*
Item-Trait Interaction			*Reliability Indices*	
Total Item Chi-Square		*192.18*	*Separation Index*	*0.92*
Total Degree of Freedom		*204.00*	*Cronbach Alpha*	*0.92*
Total Chi-Square Probability		*0.71*		
			Reliability Indices	
			Power is EXCELLENT	
			[Based on Separation Index of 0.92]	

1. The Separation Index is the proportion of observed variance that is considered true and is high (92%).
2. The item and student fit statistics have an expected mean of near zero and a standard deviation of near one, when the data fit the model. The fit statistics in this case are good.
3. The item-trait interaction test indicates that students of differing motivation level responded to the item difficulties accordingly to what is expected of them by the model and that a unidimensional trait has been measured.
4. All numbers are given to two decimal places because the errors are two decimal places (see Table 2).

Dimensionality

The item-trait interaction given by the total chi-square probability of 192 (df=204, p=0.71) (see Table 1) shows that there is no significant interaction between the student responses to the items in the questionnaire and the location values of the students calculated along the scale, called Motivation to Achieve in Science and Mathematics. This means that there was very good agreement about the difficulties of the items among the students for different measures along the scale. This, in turn, means that the difficulty of each item can be represented by a single parameter and the Motivation of each student can be represented by a single parameter that can be used to predict the students' responses to the items reasonably accurately. This is what it means to have a unidimensional scale.

Individual Item-Fit

In Table 2, the locations are the item difficulties in logits, the standard units in Rasch measurement. Of the 34 items, the easiest is item number 1 (difficulty -2.32 logits) and the most difficult is item number 34 (difficulty +1.48 logits). The table also shows the Standard Errors in conjunction with the estimates of the Locations (Difficulties) of the items. The Standard Errors are smaller in the region where there are more students.

Table 2 has a column that shows the Residuals. These are the differences between the actual response and the response estimated from the Rasch measurement parameters. Standardized Residuals are generally expected to be within the range of -2 and +2. The table shows that except for one item, item number 31, the rest of the items have acceptable residuals.

Table 2. Item Difficulties (Locations), Standard Errors (SE), Residuals and Fit to the Measurement Model

Item	Difficulty	SE	Residual	DegFree	DataPts	ChiSquare	Prob
1	-2.32	0.15	1.31	394.03	408	7.02	0.32
3	-0.31	0.09	0.51	394.03	408	3.74	0.71
4	1.11	0.08	1.45	394.03	408	4.24	0.64
5	-0.39	0.09	-0.60	394.03	408	5.94	0.43
7	-1.02	0.11	0.43	394.03	408	4.68	0.59
8	0.17	0.08	0.27	394.03	408	6.80	0.34
10	1.17	0.08	1.85	394.03	408	7.21	0.30
11	-0.92	0.11	0.59	394.03	408	7.77	0.26
14	0.48	0.08	0.42	394.03	408	7.80	0.25
15	-0.65	0.10	0.62	394.03	408	1.98	0.92
17	-0.98	0.10	-0.77	394.03	408	8.71	0.19
20	-0.00	0.08	-0.63	394.03	408	1.61	0.95
21	-0.46	0.09	-2.09	394.03	408	10.12	0.12
22	0.58	0.08	-1.21	394.03	408	3.60	0.73
23	0.09	0.08	0.55	394.03	408	4.33	0.63
24	1.48	0.08	0.56	394.03	408	4.63	0.59
25	-0.60	0.09	-0.92	394.03	408	6.05	0.42
27	0.33	0.08	1.37	394.03	408	8.39	0.21
30	1.16	0.08	-0.37	394.03	408	0.80	0.99
31	-0.26	0.09	1.45	394.03	408	7.59	0.27
33	0.07	0.08	1.43	394.03	408	2.61	0.86
35	-1.42	0.17	-1.23	394.03	408	10.27	0.11
36	-0.10	0.09	-0.31	394.03	408	6.14	0.41
37	-1.34	0.12	-0.90	394.03	408	5.42	0.49
38	-0.21	0.09	0.64	394.03	408	4.05	0.67
39	-0.69	0.10	-0.56	394.03	408	7.43	0.28
40	0.56	0.08	-0.79	394.03	408	9.93	0.13
42	1.09	0.08	-0.90	394.03	408	4.85	0.56
44	1.33	0.08	0.94	394.03	408	2.34	0.89
45	0.49	0.07	1.91	394.03	408	4.75	0.58
46	1.29	0.08	1.20	394.03	408	5.77	0.45
47	-0.69	0.10	-0.11	394.03	408	6.95	0.33
48	0.30	0.08	-0.78	394.03	408	5.76	0.45
50	0.66	0.08	-0.16	394.03	408	2.92	0.82

1. The Difficulty of each item is in logits (the log odds of giving a positive response to an item).
2. SE is standard error in logits. They are smaller in the region where there are more students.
3. Residual is the difference between the observed and expected response.
4. Probability is based on the chi-square fit to the measurement model and is dependent on sample size.

The individual item chi-squares and their associated probabilities are calculated from the discrepancies between the observed mean in the class intervals and the expected values according to the measurement model. If the probability has a value of less than 0.01, then it implies that the discrepancy between the observed mean and the expected value is large relative to chance and that item should be examined. However, for a large sample (N=408), this probability is often low, thus it is important to consider the graphical display before discarding the item (see Figures 1 and 2).

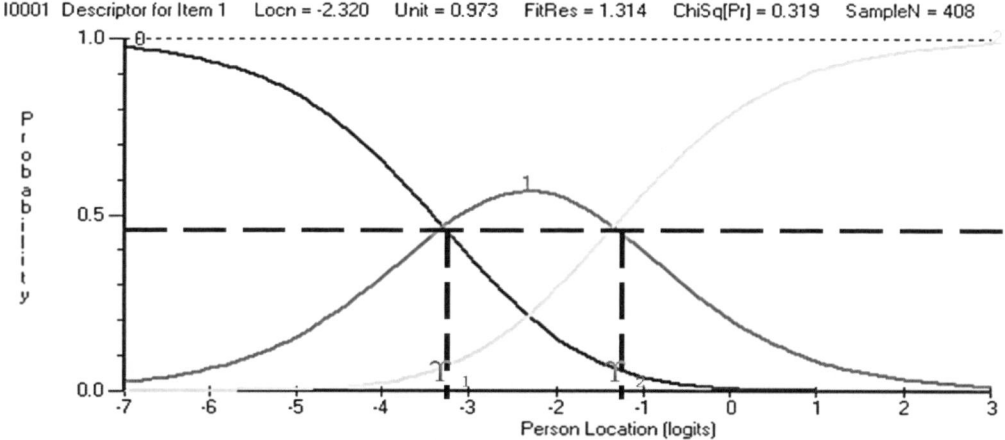

The category responses have been used logically and consistently.

Figure 1. Response Category Curves for Item 1.

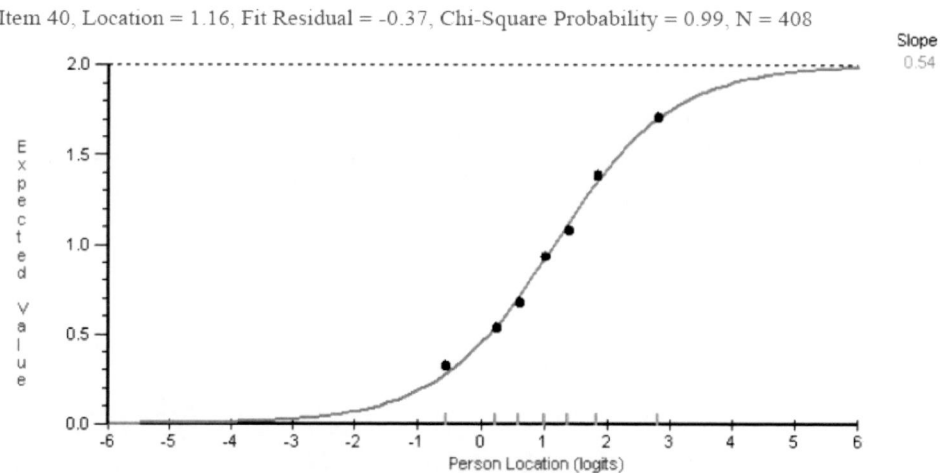

This item discriminates well, as specified by the Rasch measurement model.

Figure 2. Item Characteristic Curve for Item number 40.

Answering Response Categories Logically

Thresholds are points between adjacent response categories where the odds for answering in each response category are equal. Thresholds should be ordered in line with the conceptual ordering of the response categories indicating that the response categories are answered consistently and logically. Table 3 shows the thresholds for the 34 items that fit the measurement model. The first threshold shows the point between response categories '0' and '1', numbered according to the Rasch program, where there is equal probability of responding either a '0' or '1'. The second threshold shows the point between categories '1' and '2', numbered according to the Rasch program, where there is equal probability of responding either a '1' or '2'. The thresholds for each item are ordered in line with the conceptual order of the response categories (see table 3).

Table 3. Uncentralised Item Thresholds

Item Statement	Difficulty	Mean	Thresholds 1	2
Item 1	-2.32	-2.32	-3.29	-1.35
Item 3	-0.31	-0.31	-0.74	+0.11
Item 4	+1.11	+1.11	+0.30	+1.91
Item 5	-0.39	-0.39	-1.13	+0.34
Item 7	-1.02	-1.02	-1.65	-0.40
Item 8	+0.17	+0.17	-0.74	+1.08
Item 10	+1.17	+1.17	+0.63	+1.71
Item 11	-0.92	-0.92	-0.98	-0.85
Item 14	+0.48	+0.48	-0.62	+1.58
Item 15	-0.65	-0.65	-1.20	-0.10
Item 17	-0.98	-0.98	-1.56	-0.40
Item 20	-0.00	-0.00	-0.63	+0.62
Item 21	-0.46	-0.46	-1.02	+0.10
Item 22	+0.58	+0.58	-0.31	+1.48
Item 23	+0.09	+0.09	-0.44	+0.61
Item 24	+1.48	+1.48	+0.66	+2.29
Item 25	-0.60	-0.60	-1.29	+0.09
Item 27	+0.33	+0.33	-0.30	+0.96
Item 30	+1.16	+1.16	+0.61	+1.70
Item 31	-0.26	-0.26	-0.53	-0.01
Item 33	+0.07	+0.07	-0.48	+0.62
Item 35	-1.42	-1.42	-2.33	-0.51
Item 36	-0.10	-0.10	-1.24	+1.05
Item 37	-1.34	-1.34	-1.84	-0.85
Item 38	-0.21	-0.21	-0.86	+0.45
Item 39	-0.69	-0.69	-1.19	+0.19
Item 40	+0.56	+0.56	-0.30	+1.42
Item 42	+1.09	+1.09	+0.32	+1.86
Item 44	+1.33	+1.33	+0.87	+1.80
Item 45	+0.49	+0.49	+0.30	+0.68
Item 46	+1.29	+1.29	+0.61	+1.98
Item 47	-0.69	-0.69	-1.07	-0.31
Item 48	+0.30	+0.30	-0.39	+0.99
Item 50	+0.66	+0.66	-0.05	+1.36

There are two thresholds since each item has three response categories. The thresholds are ordered in line with the ordering of the response categories meaning that the students have answered the response categories consistently and logically.

A further test that the response categories are answered consistently and logically is given through Response Category Curves (see Figure 1 for item number 1, '*I aim to do my best in science and mathematics*'). The vertical axis represents the probability of responding in a particular response category and the horizontal axis represents the students' person location in logits. The Rasch program converts the response categories 1, 2, and 3 to 0, 1, and 2 respectively.

In Figure 1, the category 0 response curve indicates that a student with a Motivation in Science and Mathematics measure of -7.0 logits (Person Location) has about a 0.97 probability of responding in this category ('*In none, or only one of my science or mathematics subjects*'), whereas a student with a Motivation in Science and Mathematics measure of 0.0 logits has a near zero probability of responding in the same category for item 1. Category 1 curve of Figure 1 shows that a student with a Motivation in Science and Mathematics measure of about -2.4 logits has a probability of about 0.60 of responding in the category ('*In two or three of my science and mathematics subjects*') for item 1, whereas a student with a Motivation measure of -7.0 logits has a probability of about 0.04 of responding in the same category. Looking at category curve 2, a student with a Motivation measure of about -4.5 logits has a probability near zero of responding in the category ('*In four or all of my science and mathematics subjects*') for item 1, whereas a student with a Motivation measure of 3.0 logits has a probability of about 0.99 of responding in the same category. This shows that the students discriminated logically and consistently using the three response categories for item 1.

The Category Response Curves for all 34 items were checked and they were found to be satisfactory, and operating as they should (similar to Figure 1 for item 1).

Item Characteristic Curves

Figure 2 shows the item characteristic curve for item number 40. This is a difficult item (the location is +1.16 logits). The observed means, shown as dots, in the seven class intervals are close to the curve. This shows that the item fits very well to the theoretical curve of the Rasch model according to this criterion (the chi-square probability is 0.99). It means that the item discriminates between the students as well as specified by the model as measures increase; (item 40 wording is '*I like solving challenging science and mathematics problems which others have difficulties solving*'). The Characteristic Curves for all the 34 items were satisfactory.

As part of the study of the fit of the data to the Rasch measurement model, it was also necessary to check whether the items work in the same way for students in the Science and Mathematics Research Programme and as they do for students in the non-Science and Mathematics Research Programme. This can also be done graphically, in which the basic principle of the item characteristic curves is considered. The requirement is that, as best as can be estimated from the data, for the same location of a person, the expected value on an item should be the same, irrespective of what group the person belongs. The test is that there is no differential item functioning (DIF) relative to whether students are in the Science and Mathematics Research Programme group or not.

Figure 3 shows the same item number 40 where the two groups (students in the Science and Mathematics Research Programme and students in the non-Science and Mathematics Research Programme) effectively have the same functioning, except for the students in Science and Mathematics Research Programme in the lower class intervals. The item does not significantly discriminate between these students in the Science and Mathematics Programme and those not in the Programme (F=3.9, df=6,1, p=0.67).

There was no significant overall discrimination between the two groups on each of the 34 good-fitting items, as displayed by their Item Characteristic Curves.

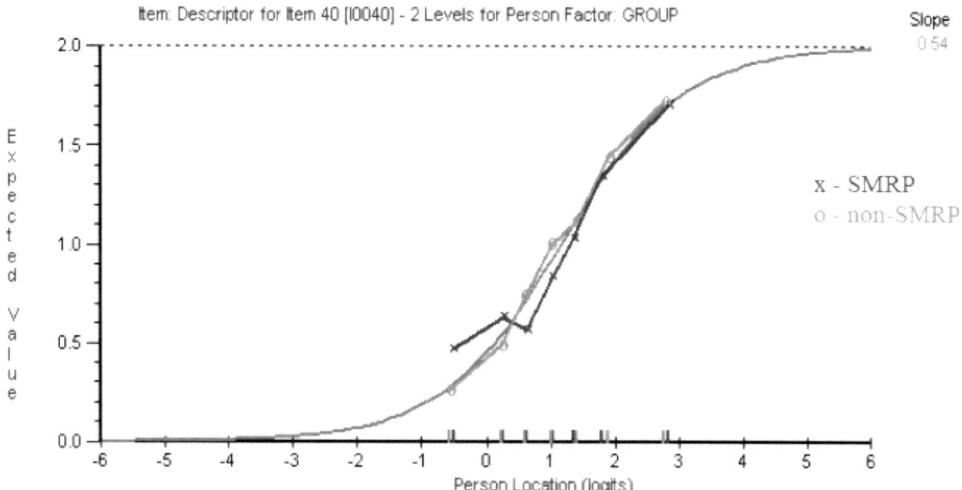

The same item does not significantly discriminate between the students in the Science and Mathematics Research Programme (SMRP) of the lower class intervals and those not in the Programme (F=3.9, df=6,1, p=0.67).

Figure 3. Characteristic Curve for Item 40 by Group.

Person-Item Threshold Distribution (Targeting)

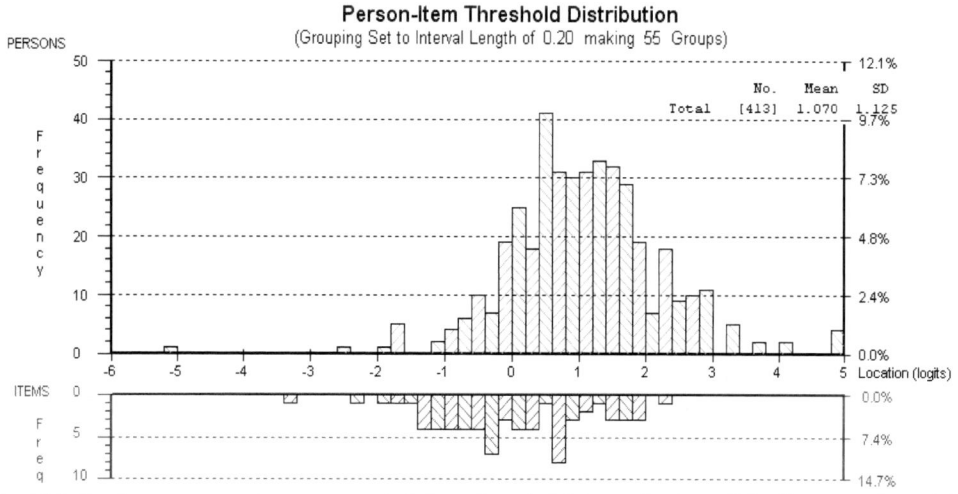

Student Motivation measures are represented from low to high on the top of the linear scale and item thresholds are represented from easy to hard on the bottom of the scale.

Figure 4. Person-Item Threshold Graph showing the distribution of 413 student measures and the 68 item thresholds.

Figures 4 and 5 show the distribution of student measures and item thresholds for the 413 secondary three students on the same linear scale. Student measures of motivation range from low to high on the top the scale and item thresholds range from easy to hard on the bottom of the scale. The distribution graphs show that there are insufficient hard items to cater for those students who have very high measures of Motivation in Science and Mathematics. There are enough easy items. This may be understandable as the students come from one of the top schools in Singapore.

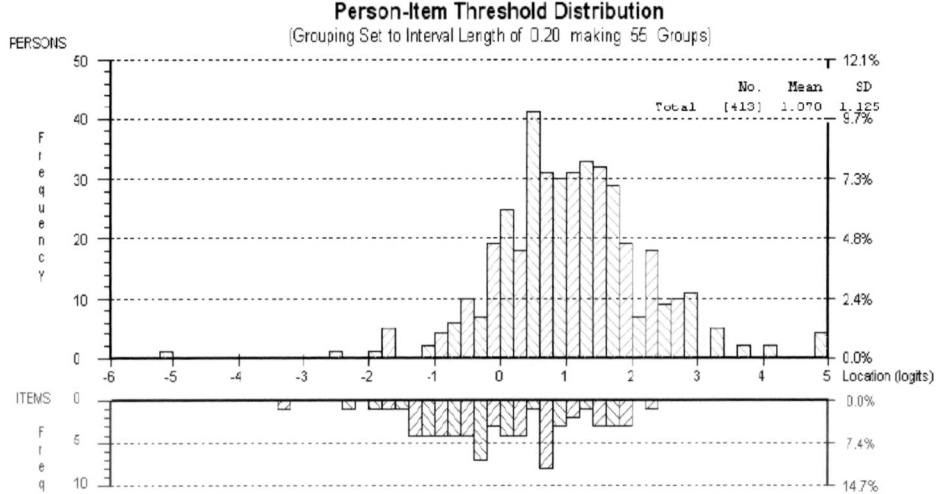

There is an error in the colouring of Figure 5 due to an error in the computer program. Green represents the SMRP students and black represents the non-SMRP students.

Figure 5. Person-Item Threshold Graph showing the distribution of student measures and item thresholds by groups (Science and Mathematics Research Programme and non-Science and Mathematics Research Programme).

Mean Rash Measures by Group

The mean Motivation measure for students in the Science and Mathematics Research Programme group is 1.27 logits (SD=1.06, N=179) and the mean Motivation measure for students in the non-Science and Mathematics Research Programme group is 0.92 logits (SD=1.15, N=234) (see Figure 5). In terms of groups, the Science and Mathematics Research Programme students have a significantly higher mean Motivation measure as compared to the mean Motivation measure of the non-Science and Mathematics Research Programme students (t=3.24, df=411, p=0.000). This is as expected since those students initially having a higher motivation for Science and Mathematics are more likely than the others to choose the Science and Mathematics Research Programme than the Humanities Programme.

Item Difficulties by Aspect

The item difficulties for Striving for Excellence and Desire to Learn are calculated on a linear scale (see Tables 4 and 5 respectively) and there is partial agreement between the conceptual item difficulty order and the actual measured order. In some items, only one perspective fits the measurement model, but where both perspectives fit the measurement model, then attitudes are easier than behaviour, as conceptualised.

Table 4. The Items on Motivational Aspect 1: Striving for Excellence, of the Motivation to Achieve in Science and Mathematics Scale and their Difficulties (Locations)

Motivation Aspect 1 : Striving for Excellence

Standards

Item No.	Item	What I aim for	What I actually do
1/2	I aim to do my best in science and mathematics.	-2.32	Did not fit
3/4	I evaluate my performance in science and mathematics test against the good grades I set for myself.	-0.31	+1.11

Goals

5/6	I set, for myself, realistic but challenging goals in science and mathematics.	-0.39	Did not fit
7/18	When I do not get what I expected in science and mathematics grades I work harder to achieve it.	-1.02	+0.17
9/10	When I do not get what I expected in science and mathematics grades I try different ways to achieve it	Did not fit	+1.17

Task

Item No.	Item wording	What I aim for	What I actually do
11/12	I try to complete all my science and mathematics homework all the time.	-0.92	Did not fit

Effort

13/14	I make strong demand on myself to do well in science and mathematics.	Did not fit	+0.48
15/16	I make an effort to get correct answers for all my science and mathematics homework.	-0.65	Did not fit
17/18	I make strong effort to achieve high grades in all science and mathematics tests.	-0.98	Did not fit

Values

Item No.	Item wording	What I aim for	What I actually do
19/20	I value doing well in my science and mathematics subjects.	Did not fit	-0.00

Ability

21/22	I have confidence in achieving the best possible grades in science and mathematics with my ability.	-0.46	+0.58
23/24	I receive positive feedback from my friends or teachers on my ability in science and mathematics.	+0.09	+1.48

1. Item difficulties are in logits.
2. Attitudes are easier than their corresponding behaviours, when both fit the model.

Table 5. The Items on Motivational Aspect 2: Desire to Learn, of the Motivation to Achieve in Science and Mathematics Scale and their Difficulties (Locations)

Motivation Aspect 2 (M2): Desire to Learn

Interest

Item No.	Item	What I aim for	What I actually do
25/26	I am interested in one or more of the science and mathematics topics	-0.60	Did not fit
27/28	I read widely on one or more of the science and mathematics topics.	+0.33	Did not fit
29/30	I show interest in the science and mathematics topics being taught.	Did not fit	+1.16

Learning from others

31/32	I learn from friends with more knowledge in science and mathematics.	-0.26	Did not fit
33/34	I seek help from my teachers whenever I have difficulties in science and mathematics.	+0.07	Did not fit
35/36	I pay attention in science and mathematics class so that I can understand what is being taught.	-1.42	-0.10

Responsibility for learning

37/38	I am responsible for my own learning in science and mathematics.	-1.34	-0.21
39/40	I seek out information on my own when necessary and take steps to master science and mathematics	-0.69	+0.56

1. Item difficulties are in logits.
2. Attitudes are easier than their corresponding behaviours, when both fit the model.

Table 6. The Items on Motivational Aspect 3: Personal Incentives, of the Motivation to Achieve in Science and Mathematics Scale and their Difficulties (Locations)

Item No.	Item	What I aim for	What I actually do
Motivation Aspect 3 (M3): Personal Incentives			
Extrinsic Rewards			
41/42	I try to do well in science and mathematics because I like the respect I get from others in doing these subjects well.	Did not fit	+1.09
43/44	I try to do well in science and mathematics because I like to compete with others.	Did not fit	+1.33
Intrinsic Rewards			
45/46	I try to solve problems in science and mathematics with friends because of the interaction I get out of it.	+0.49	+1.29
47/48	I try to do well in science and mathematics because I feel good knowing that I have done well.	-0.69	+0.30
Social Rewards			
49/50	I have fun as I study science and mathematic with my friends.	Did not fit	+0.66

1. Item difficulties are in logits.
2. Attitudes are easier than their corresponding behaviours, when both fit the model.

Motivational Aspect 3: Personal Incentives

Table 6 shows items representing the sub-aspects of Motivational Aspect 3 (M3): Personal Incentives that fit the Rasch model again in a mixture of both the ideal and actual perspectives. In this Motivational Aspect, the students found item 61 (*I try to do well in science and mathematics because I feel good knowing that I have done well*), in the ideal perspective, the easiest (-0.69 logits), and items 58 (*I try to do well in science and mathematics because I like to compete with others*) (+1.33 logits) and 60 (*I try to solve problems in science and mathematics with friends because of the interaction I get out of it*) (+1.29), the most difficult in the actual perspective for Motivation Aspect 3.

DISCUSSION

Scale Meaning

Good-fitting items were found in all three motivational aspects, namely: Striving for Excellence; Desire to Learn; and Personal Incentives. The 34 good fitting items, aligned along the scale from easy to hard, define Motivation in Science and Mathematics, in this measurement. Data from those 34 items were used to create a unidimensional, linear scale of Motivation in Science and Mathematics and there is a good fit to the measurement model. Equal numerical distances along the scale represent equal amounts of Motivation and this is a consequence of the mathematics behind the scale. Generally speaking, students who have the lowest measures can only answer the easy items positively (but not the medium and hard items). Students who have medium measures of Motivation can answer the easy and medium items positively (but not the hard items), and students who have the highest measures can answer all the items positively.

Item-Pair Interpretation where Both Fit

It was noted that some items fit the measurement in only one perspective (either the attitude of what I aim for or the behaviour of what I actually do) and some items fit the model in both perspectives. How are we to interpret this? Where an item fits the model, as conceptualized, in both perspectives such as an attitude (what I aim for) and a behaviour (what I actually do), then it can be inferred that this part of the conceptualized model is consistent with the scale data and that this attitude is an important influence on (and maybe the prime influence on) that behaviour. For example, items 37/38, I am responsible for my own learning in Science and Mathematics, fit the model in both perspectives and it seems reasonable to infer that students who aim to be responsible for their own learning should actually behave that way, and that the attitude is an important influence on that corresponding behaviour. Both the attitude and behaviour items fit the measurement model for item pairs 3/4, 7/8, 21/22, 23/24, 35/36, 37/38, 39/40, 45/46 and 47/48. Thus we infer that, for these item pairs, the attitude of Motivation is an important and, maybe the prime influence on, its corresponding behaviour of Motivation.

Item-Pair Interpretation where Only One Fits

It does seem unsatisfactory that, in what is expected to be a reasonable model of Motivation, one item of the attitude/behaviour pair doesn't fit the measurement model. How are we to interpret the cases where the behaviour of Motivation does not fit the measurement model but its corresponding attitude does, as occurs for item pairs 1/2, 5/6, 11/12, 15/16, 17/18, 27/28, 31/32, and 33/34? A reasonable way to interpret this is to say that the conceptual model is partly wrong because the data does not fit the Motivation model (even if it fits the measurement model). While it was conceptualized, for example, that I aim to do my best in Science and Mathematics (item 1) should be the prime part of the attitude of Motivation that influences this item in the behaviour perspective (item 2), it is probable that the behaviour perspective of this item is significantly more influenced by other attitude motivations than by this particular, corresponding attitude. Another example lies in item pairs 11/12, I try to complete all my Science and Mathematics homework all the time. The attitude of this Motivation probably is not the main or prime influence of its corresponding behaviour for many students. It is probable that other things like parental and teacher sanctions have more influence on this behaviour. This means that the wording of these items need to be changed (or modified) so that the attitude captures the main influence on the corresponding behaviour.

Similarly, in the cases where only the behaviour perspective fits the measurement model, it is probable that its corresponding attitude is not the prime influence on it. This occurs for item pairs 9/10, 13/14, 19/20, 29/30, 41/42, 43/44, and 49/50. For example, when students do not achieve what they expect in Science and Mathematics, then they try different ways to achieve (item pair 9/10), it is probable that many students do not start out with an attitude of

Motivation that they will try a different method that influences their behaviour if 'things do not work out'. It seems that that some other item of attitude Motivation is the prime influence on this behaviour of Motivation. Other motivation researchers should take note, modify these attitude items to comply with the influence requirement and re-test the questionnaire.

A New Model of Item Design

This now provides researchers with a model about how to design items in questionnaires to gather data for measurement, not only for Motivation, but also for other variables. Researchers should design items in pairs where the attitude is conceptualized as the prime influence on the corresponding behaviour, and where the attitude is conceptualized as easier than the corresponding behaviour. We then want the data to fit both the variable model (in this case of Motivation) and the Rasch measurement model to construct a linear, unidimensional scale. Only then will we have a good conceptual model of Motivation (or any other variable).

Item pairs can be created through the researcher' experience and thinking, or through interviewing students, and trying to discover what students think are the most likely prime behaviours from their corresponding attitudes. This would then give researchers ideas as to how to modify the items in the attitude perspective so that both the attitude and its corresponding behaviour provide a good model of Motivation (or some other variable). An example can be taken from item pair 7/8 (when I do not get what I expected in Science and Mathematics grades, I work harder to achieve it), which fit both the measurement model and the Motivation model. Here, the attitude of aiming to work harder to improve one's achievement is generally seen by the students as a prime influence on their actually doing this, when achievement falls below expectations and the attitude is easier than its corresponding behaviour. We can understand that there may be a number of other influences on students to improve their school work (such as parental pressure, sibling pressure, and upward social pressure), but here students are saying that the prime attitudinal influence to improve their school achievement, when it falls below expectations, is their own motivational aim. This doesn't mean to say that students' own motivational aims are not, further in turn, influenced by other things such as parental pressure, but only that, from the students' view, the prime influence is their own motivation. In the measurement model aspect, there has to be good agreement between students as to the difficulty of each item along the scale and so it's the prime influence that becomes important in the measurement, as well as in the conceptual model. If there is not enough agreement among the students, then the data from the item will not fit the measurement model.

Another example can be taken from item pair 21/22 (I have confidence in achieving the best possible grades in Science and Mathematics, with my ability), which fit both the Motivation and Measurement models. We can understand that achieving grades commensurate with ability might be influenced by a number of factors (namely parental comments, teacher comments and peer comments), but here students are generally saying that they aim to have confidence in receiving the best possible grades related to their ability and this is a prime influence on their actually receiving the best grades for their ability. There may be other aspects that influence this confidence but these other aspects vary too much between students on their influence on confidence for there to be strong enough agreement that they are the prime influence on the corresponding behaviour. So the measurement part of Motivation is telling us that there has to be some good agreement about the prime influence of the attitude on the corresponding behaviour in order for there to be good agreement about the difficulty of the items on the scale, and then the measurement model and the Motivation model can work together in helping us to understand student Motivation.

REFERENCES

Andrich, D. (1982). Using latent trait measurement to analyse attitudinal data: a synthesis of viewpoints. In Spearitt, D. (Ed.), *The improvement of measurement in education and psychology,* (pp. 89-126). Melbourne: ACER.

Andrich, D. (1985). A latent trait model for items with response dependencies: Implications for test construction and analysis. In S. E. Embretson (Ed.), *Test design: developments in psychology and psychometrics* (pp. 245-275). Orlando; Academic Press.

Andrich, D. (1988a). A General Form of Rasch's Extended Logistic Model for Partial Credit Scoring. *Applied Measurement in Education, 1*(4), 363-378.

Andrich, D. (1988b). Rasch models for measurement. Sage university paper on quantitative applications in the social sciences, series number 07/068. Newbury Park, California: Sage Publications.

Andrich, D., and Van Schoubroeck, L. (1989). The General Health Questionnaire: a psychometric analysis using latent trait theory. *Psychological Medicine*, *19*, 469-485.

Andrich, D., Sheridan, B., and Luo, G. (2005). *RUMM: A windows-based item analysis program employing Rasch unidimensional measurement models.* Perth: RUMM Laboratory.

Bell. J. (1987). *Doing your research project*. Philadelphia: Open University Press.

Blankenship, V. (1987). A computer-based measure of resultant achievement Motivation. *Journal of Personality and Social Psychology*, *53*, 361-372.

Clarke, D. E. (1973). Measures of achievement and affiliation Motivation. *Review of Educational Research*, *43*, 41-51.

Conoley, J. C. and Impara, J. C. (1995) (Eds.). *The twelfth mental measurements yearbook.* Lincoln, NE: Buros Institute of Mental Measurements.

Cronbach, L. J. (1951). Coefficient alpha and the internal structure of tests. *Psychometrika*, 16, 297-333.

Fineman, S. (1977). The achievement motive construct and its measurement: where are we now? *British Journal of Psychology*, *68*, 1-22.

Harper, E. B. W. (1975). The validity of some alternative measures of achievement Motivation. *Educational and Psychological Measurement*, *40*, 531-536.

Lian-Hwang Chiu (1997). Development and validation of the school achievement motivation rating sale. *Educational and Psychological Measurement*, *57*, 292-305.

Microsoft Office 2004 version 11.4.1 for Mac. (2004). [Computer software]. Redmond, WA: Microsoft Corporation.

Likert, R. (1932). A technique for the measurement of attitudes. *Archives of Psychology*, *140*, 1-55.

Piedmont, R. L. (1989). The Life Activities Achievement Scale: An act-frequency approach to the measurement of Motivation. *Educational and Psychology Measurement*, *49*, 863-874.

Rasch, G. (1960/1980). *Probabilistic models for intelligence and attainment tests (expanded edition)*. Chicago: The University of Chicago Press (original work published in 1960).

Ray, J. J. (1986). Measuring achievement motivation by self-reports. *Psychological Reports*, *58*, 525-526.

Thibert, G. and Karsenti, T. P. (1996). Motivation profile of adolescent boys and girls: gender differences throughout schooling. Paper presented at the Annual Conference of the American Educational Research Association in San Francisco, CA, April 8-12, 1996.

Waugh, R. F. (1998a). The Course Experience Questionnaire: A Rasch measurement model analysis. *Higher Education Research and Development,* 17 (1), 45-64.

Waugh, R. F. (1998b). A Rasch measurement model analysis of an Approaches to Studying Inventory for students in higher education. Paper presented at the Latent Trait Theory Conference: Rasch measurement, held at the University of Western Australia from January 22-24.

Waugh, R. F. (1999). Approaches to studying for students in higher education: A Rasch measurement model analysis. *British Journal of Education Psychology*, *69*(1), 63-80.

Waugh, R. F. (2001). Measuring ideal and real self-concept on the same scale, based on a multi-faceted, hierarchical model of self-concept. *Educational and Psychological Measurement*, *61*(1), 85-101.

Waugh, R. F. (2002). Creating a scale to measure motivation to achieve academically: Linking attitude to behaviour using Rasch measurement. *British Journal of Educational Psychology*, *72*, 65-86.

Waugh, R. F. (2006). Rasch Measurement. In Salkind N. J. (Ed.), *The Encyclopedia of Measurement and Statistics* (Vol. 3, pp. 820-825), Thousand Oaks, CA: Sage Publications, Inc.

Waugh, R. F., and Njiru, J. N. (2005). Measuring academic motivation to achieve for Malaysian high school students using a Rasch measurement model. In R. F. Waugh (Ed.), *Frontiers in Education* (pp. 3-35). New York: Nova Science Publishers.

Wright, B. D. (1996). Comparing Rasch measurement and factor analysis. *Structural Equation Modeling*, *3* (1), 3-24.

Wright, B. D. (1999). Fundamental measurement for psychology. In S. E. Embretson, and S. C. Hershberger (Eds.), *The new rules of measurement: What every psychologist and educator should know*, pp. 65-104. Mahwah, NJ: Lawrence Erlbaum Associates.

Wright, B. and Masters, G. (1981). *The measurement of knowledge and attitude (Research memorandum no. 30)*. Chicago: Statistical Laboratory, Department of Education, University of Chicago.

Wright, B., and Masters, G. (1982). *Rating scale analysis: Rasch measurement.* Chicago: MESA Press.

In: Applications of Rasch Measurement in Education   ISBN: 978-1-61668-026-8
Editor: Russell Waugh   © 2010 Nova Science Publishers, Inc.

Chapter 5

A RASCH MEASURE OF STUDENT VIEWS OF TEACHER-STUDENT RELATIONSHIPS IN THE PRIMARY SCHOOL

Natalie Leitão and Russell F. Waugh
Faculty of Education and Arts, Edith Cowan University,
Mount Lawley, Western Australia

ABSTRACT

This study investigated teacher-student relationships from the students' point of view at Perth metropolitan schools in Western Australia. The study identified three key social and emotional aspects that affect teacher-student relationships, namely, Connectedness, Availability and Communication Skills. Data were collected by questionnaire (N=139) with stem-items answered in two perspectives: (1) Actual: This is what does happen and (2) Idealistic: this is what I wish would happen, using four ordered response categories: not at all (score 1), some of the time (score 2), most of the time (score 3), and almost always (score 4). Data were analysed with a Rasch measurement model and a uni-dimensional, linear scale with 20 items (2 times 10 stem items), ordered from easy to hard, was created. The data were shown to be highly reliable, so that valid inferences could be made from the scale. The Person Separation Index (akin to a reliability index) was 0.90; there was good global student and item fit to the measurement model; there was good item fit; the targeting of the item difficulties against the student measures was good, and the response categories were answered consistently and logically. The difficulties of the items strongly supported the conceptualised structure of the variable. This study shows that research into teacher-student relationships is made possible using modern methods of measurement, and by considering primary students' points of view.

BACKGROUND

Teaching is a people profession that demands a large proportion of time being devoted to personal interaction. Positive teacher-student relationships are believed to be necessary for effective teaching and learning to take place (Arthur, Gordon, and Butterfield, 2003; McInerney and McInerney, 2006; Sztejnberg, den Brok, and Hurek, 2004). Effective teachers are those who, in addition to being skilled at teaching, are attuned to the human dimension of classroom life and can foster positive relationships with their students (Good and Brophy, 2000; Larrivee, 2005). But what is meant by positive teacher-student relationships? Why are teacher-student relationships important and how are they to be measured? This paper begins with some discussion to these questions as a background to the present study.

Teacher-Student Relationships

Positive teacher-student relationships are characterised by mutual acceptance, understanding, warmth, closeness, trust, respect, care and cooperation (Good and Brophy, 2000; Krause, Bochner, and Duchesne, 2006; Larrivee, 2005; Noddings, 2005; Smeyers, 1999). The success of any interpersonal relationship is dependent to a large extent upon input from both parties (Pianta, 1999). In the classroom setting, it is the teacher who has the opportunity, and indeed, the responsibility, to initiate positive interpersonal relationships (Barry and King, 1993; Krause et al., 2006; McInerney and McInerney, 2006; Smeyers, 1999). The teacher who is pro-active in demonstrating acceptance, understanding, warmth, closeness, trust, respect, care and cooperation towards his or her students not only works at initiating positive teacher-student relationships, but also increases the likelihood of building strong relationships that will endure over time (Barry and King, 1993).

Teacher-student relationships are important for many reasons. Teacher-student relationships greatly influence a student's ability to adjust to school, to do well at school, and to relate to peers (Entwisle and Hayduk, 1988; Howes, Hamilton, and Matheson, 1994; Pianta, 1999; Sztejnberg et al., 2004). Teacher-students relationships have an impact on classroom management and affect learning progress (Klem and Connell, 2004; Sztejnberg et al., 2004). From a developmental perspective, the establishment of a positive teacher-student relationship aids a student's cognitive, social and emotional growth and enhances their mental well-being (Brazelton and Greenspan, 2000; Lynch and Cicchetti, 1992; Pianta, 1999; Weare, 2000). Stable teacher-student relationships impact positively on a student's developing sense of self and promote resiliency in them (Pianta and Walsh, 1996; Rutter, 1979). Furthermore, the benefits of positive teacher-student relationships extend to teachers, contributing to an improved sense of job satisfaction (L. Goldstein and Lake, 2000).

Past research on teacher-student relationships has focused heavily on instructional aspects of the relationship, and largely ignored the social and emotional aspects of teacher-student relationships (Baker, 1999; Birch and Ladd, 1996; Pianta, 1999). As such, research into social and emotional aspects of teacher-student relationships is relatively new. This study, which takes place across Perth metropolitan schools in Western Australia, helps to address this gap in the research by identifying key social and emotional aspects of the teacher-student relationship from the literature and exploring these in more detail with data collected in Perth,

Western Australia. The three key social and emotional aspects of the teacher-student relationship that have been identified for inclusion in the present study are connectedness, availability and communication. These are explained in more detail in the following section.

A Theoretical Model of Teachers' Relationships with Students

There are many aspects that influence the quality and nature of personal relationships and, specifically in this study, relationships between teachers and students in the primary school. A complete understanding of how these aspects influence teachers' relationships with students is likely to be very complex. To fully understand the interconnections between all possible aspects would be very involved, and is beyond the scope of this study. However, it is possible to simplify these connections by creating a theoretical model and building into it a selected number of aspects that are considered most important. This simplified model provides an understanding of the interconnections between the selected aspects, gives direction to the research in the collection of data, and provides guidelines for the analysis and interpretation of the data. A simplified model was created using three aspects that were found to be necessary for the development of strong, healthy relationships between teachers and students. The three aspects are Connectedness, Availability and Communication. Each of these three areas is seen to be a key aspect likely to impact on a teacher's ability to develop relationships with the students in their classroom. The model showing the three key aspects have is depicted pictorially in Figure 1. An explanation of the model and an explanation of the inclusion of the three key aspects follows.

The Theoretical Model is a multi-levelled model. Incorporated in the first level are the three key aspects most expected to impact on teachers' relationships with students: Connectedness, Availability and Communication. The second level of the model features the expected mechanisms by which the key aspects were expected to be demonstrated by teachers as they relate with the students in their classes. Teachers who demonstrated the expected mechanisms were seen to be working towards achieving the key aspects in their relationships with students.

Connectedness refers to the connection that exists between a teacher and a student and, as indicated in the literature, is an important aspect in the development of teachers' relationships with students in the classroom (Fox, 1993; Howes, 2000). Connectedness encompasses how 'in-tune' a teacher may be with a student, and concerns the emotional tone of the relationship (Lynch and Cicchetti, 1992). A secure connection between a teacher and student contributes to an individual student's academic success, a student's ability to regulate his or her own behaviour, and a student's ongoing ability to develop social relationships with others (Entwisle and Hayduk, 1988; Shields et al., 2001; Thompson and Lamb, 1984; Valeski and Stipek, 2001). How well teachers connect with their students is considered to be a significant aspect to investigate when considering teachers' relationships with students in the primary school because positive connections enhance a student's sense of belonging and self value (Slater, 2004).

Availability is an important aspect influencing teachers' relationships with students as indicated in the literature (Good and Brophy, 2000; Pianta, 1999). In this study, availability means how available teachers are to their students. Put another way, it means how easily students are able to access their teacher. Availability includes a teacher being available to fulfil a need for a student, be it an academic need (for example, to help with school work), or a social or emotional need (for example, to talk about being rejected by a friend). By being available and spending time with students, teachers and students are able to get to know each other better (Good and Brophy, 2000; Pianta, 1999). In addition, ongoing contact with a caring adult, such as the classroom teacher, helps develop in children a protective mechanism thereby reducing psychosocial risk factors (Weissberg, Caplan, and Harwood, 1991).

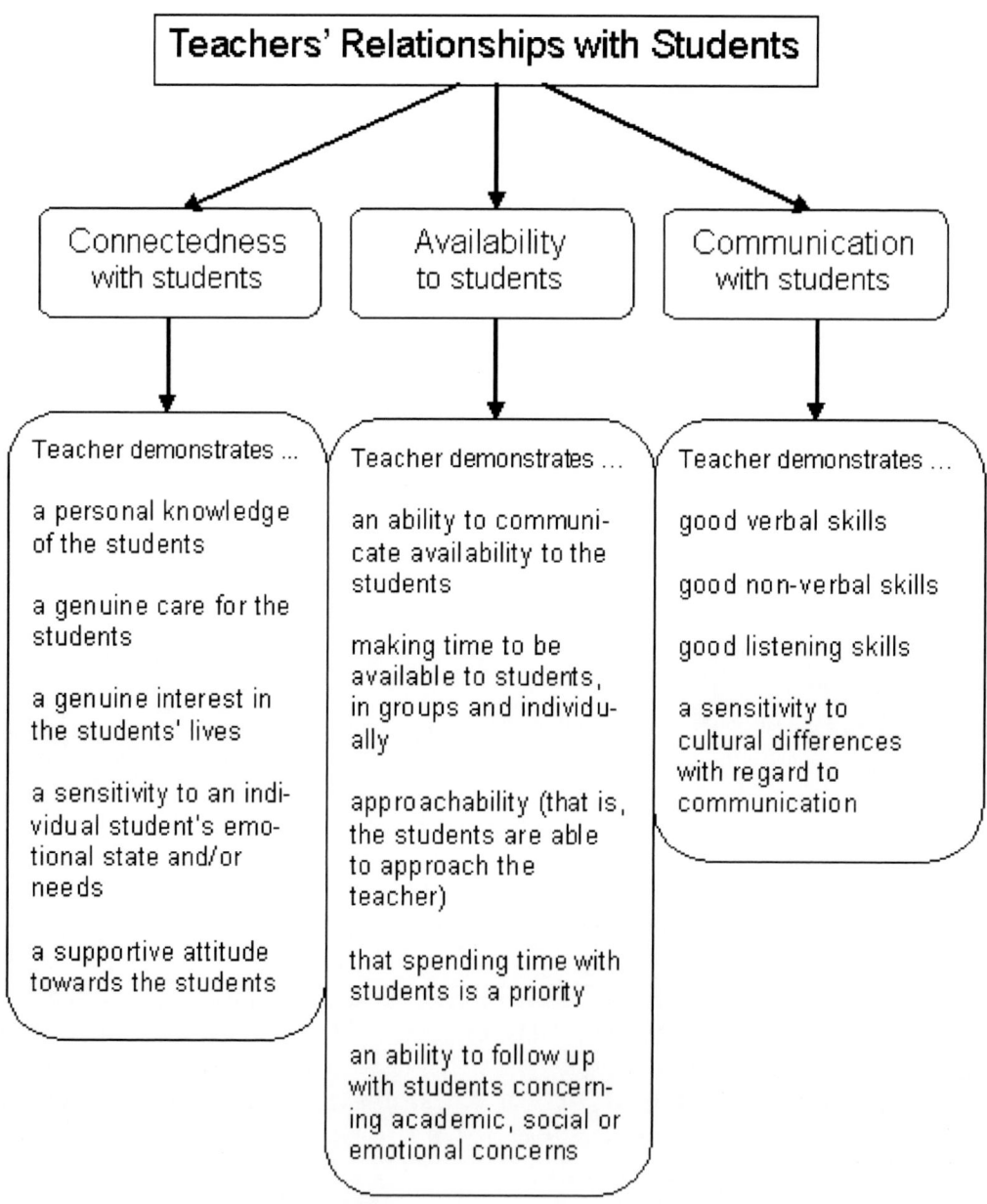

Source: Created by Natalie Leitão (2006).

Figure 1. Theoretical Model: Teachers' Relationships with Students.

Good communication is important to the ongoing development of relationships between teachers and students. Adler (1985) emphasises this point by stating "without communication, there can be no community. Human beings cannot form a community or share in a common life without communicating with one another" (p. 15). When done effectively, communication allows for the meeting of 'hearts and minds' (Adler, 1985). In the context of the classroom, ongoing communication is noted by Wynne (cited in Sroufe, 1989) as being a major process in the development of relationships.

Effective communication is based on a shared focus of attention that leads to shared meanings. By communicating effectively, people are able to relate to each other in meaningful ways. Communication that takes on "a quality of caring, openness, and authenticity … naturally engenders respect and love" (Campbell, 2005, p. xxix). Goldstein (1995) describes an effective teacher as being one who is able to communicate with their students "in positive, sensitive, and assertive ways" (p. 16). In the context of the classroom, communication of this kind is expected to strengthen a relationship of trust and respect between teacher and student (Good and Brophy, 2000).

A Structural Model of Teachers' Relationships with Students

In addition to the theoretical model, a structural model for the questionnaires has been constructed for use in the study. The structural model presents the theoretical basis for the construction of the questionnaires developed for this study. It is based on an expectation that attitudes influence behaviour (Ajzen, 1989; Clark and Peterson, 1986). More specifically, the theory of reasoned action purports that beliefs influence attitudes, attitudes influence intentions, and intentions influence behaviour (Ajzen, 1989). The structural model demonstrates the degrees of difficulty associated with each of these steps. For example, in this study, it was expected that attitudes would influence intentions and be easier than intentions, and that intentions would influence behaviour and be easier than behaviour. In this way, a pattern of difficulty emerges in the structural model from left to right. In addition, a pattern of difficulty emerges in the structural model from top to bottom, because the items within each key aspect are presented in order of difficulty. Within each key aspect, the initial item was expected to be the easiest to answer, the following items were expected to be harder to answer and the final item was expected to be the hardest of all to answer. Thus, what results is a structural model that maps out multi-directional expected levels of difficulty as shown in Table 1. Varying intensities of the colour blue have been used to represent the varying degrees of difficulty. The lightest shade of blue represents the easy to answer attitudes and the easy first items. The middle shade of blue represents the harder to answer intentions and the harder middle items. The darkest shade of blue represents the hardest to answer behaviour and the hardest to answer final items.

Although the structural model comprises three levels of difficulty from left to right, that is, attitudes, intentions and behaviour, a simplified form of this model has been used for the present study. In consideration of students' ongoing conceptual development, responses expected from them were limited to the two perspectives of attitudes and behaviour. Specifically, students were asked their views on easy to answer attitude items (What I wish would happen) and harder to answer behaviour items (This is what does happen).

In this way the questionnaire developed for students has been constructed to mirror the pattern of difficulty present in the structural model of teachers' relationships with students.

Table 1. Structural Model of Teachers' Relationships With Students

		Easy Attitudes	Harder Intentions	Hardest Behaviour
Easy	First item			
Harder	Middle item/s			
Hardest	Final item			

Source: Created by Natalie Leitão (2008).

The structural model interconnects closely with the Rasch measurement used in this study. Rasch measurement calculates item difficulties on the same scale as the measures and has been used to enable a true linear scale to be created with standard units. In this way, Rasch measurement provides a means for testing the structure of the questionnaire and, in turn, testing the structure of the teachers' relationships with students model, relating to the stated key aspects that were expected to influence teachers' relationships with students.

AIM

This paper reports on just one part of a larger study that investigated teachers' views and students' views of teacher-student relationships using linear scales and discussion data. The part of the study documented in this paper focuses on the students' views using a linear scale. As such, this part of the study had two main aims. The first aim was to create a theoretical model involving three aspects (connectedness, availability and communication skills) to determine student self-reported self-views in two perspectives (ideal and actual) with regard to the teacher-student relationship. The second aim was to create a linear scale of self-reported teacher-student relationships from the student's point of view in which the item difficulties are ordered from easy to hard and calibrated on the same scale as the measures from low to high.

SIGNIFICANCE

Given that research into the social and emotional aspects of teacher-student relationships is a relatively new area of study, it is understandable that there are few well-validated tools available. Calls have been made for the development of valid and reliable tools that can be used to better understand teacher-student relationships (Ang, 2005; Pianta, 1999). This study responds to those calls by employing world's best practice in measurement in the human sciences (Rasch measurement), to develop a linear scale from the point of view of the student. This is a significant aspect to the study as linear measures of teacher-student relationships using a Rasch measurement model have not been created before. In addition, a theoretical model of teachers' relationships with students and a structural model have been created for this study. In so doing this study offers a completely new approach to better understand relationships between teachers and students and the role these relationships play in the primary school classroom.

This study is important because it contributes new knowledge to the body of information about teachers' relationships with students in primary school classrooms in Perth, Western Australia. Of the research published on teacher-student relationships most of the studies have been conducted in the United States of America. My research provides information based on Western Australian teachers and students, resulting in greater local applicability than that of research conducted overseas.

METHOD

Prior to the commencement of the study, approval was sought at the university level and at the school level. Initial approval to conduct the study was given by the Edith Cowan University Ethics Committee. Subsequent approval was given by school principals, staff, students and the students' parents.

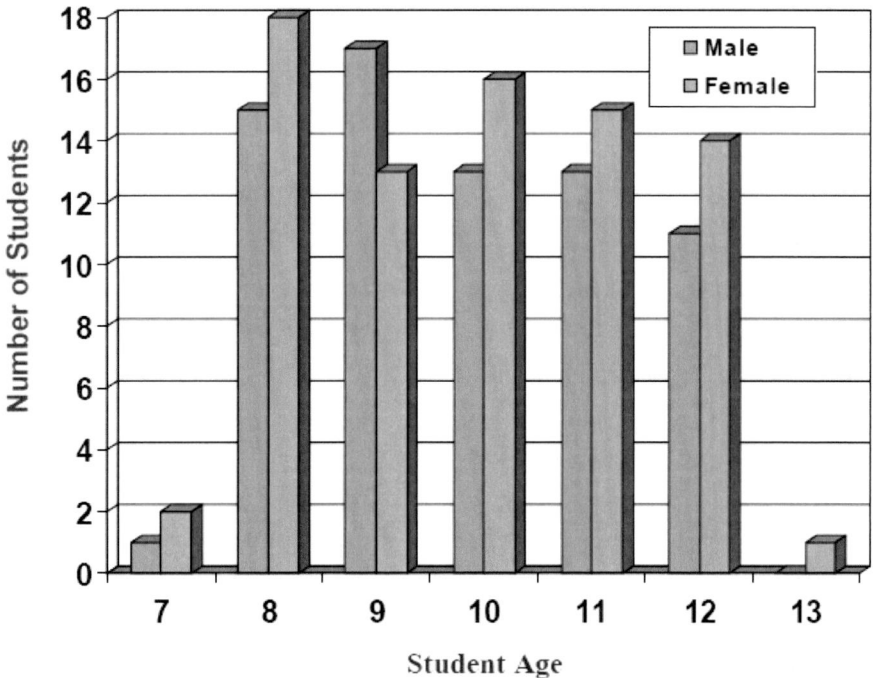

Figure 2. Age and Gender of Student Participants.

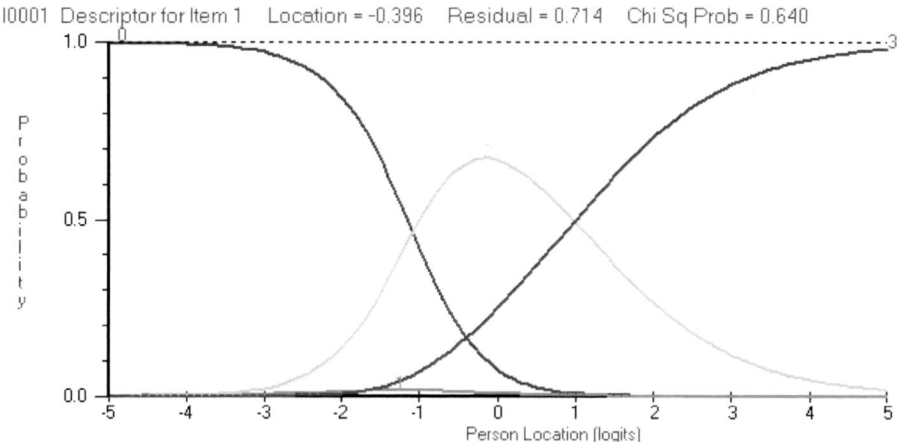

I0001 Descriptor for Item 1   Location = -0.396   Residual = 0.714   Chi Sq Prob = 0.640

Note: Students have not discriminated between response categories 0 (not at all) and 1 (some of the time). Consequently, those two response categories were combined for the final analysis.

Figure 3. Response Category Curve for Item 1 Showing Poor Discrimination.

Convenience sampling was used to find the 139 participants who were all from schools in the Perth Metropolitan area. A sub-sample of the 15 students tested the questionnaire. Of the total 139 students, 70 were male and 69 were female. The students ranged in age from 7 to 13 and came from a total of 26 schools, 13 of which were government schools, and 13 of which were independent schools. Figure 2 shows the break down of students by age and gender.

Students completed the Teachers' Relationships with Students Questionnaire: Student's View (see Appendix A). Each student completed a single questionnaire to report on how they perceived their relationship with their teacher to be. In this way a total of 139 questionnaires were completed.

The Rasch Unidimensional Measurement Models computer program (RUMM) (Andrich, Sheridan, and Luo, 2005) was used to analyse the data and create a scale of Teacher-Student Relationships from the students' view. Wright (1999) recommends the use of such computer programs, particularly as they may be a way of helping social scientists "to take the decisive step from unavoidably ambiguous, concrete raw observations to well-defined, abstract linear measures with realistic estimates of precision and explicit quality control" (p. 101).

RESULTS

Initial Rasch Analysis

The analysis started with ten items, each answered in two perspectives ('this is what does happen' and 'what I wish would happen'), giving 10 x 2 (20) items. Data were analysed with the RUMM 2020 computer program (Andrich et al., 2005). It was first checked to see whether the response categories were answered consistently and logically. The RUMM 2020 program assesses this with two outputs, namely, response category curves and thresholds. Response category curves show the probability of answering each response category by the Teacher-Student Relationship measure. These curves showed that students could not discriminate consistently between the two lowest categories ("never" and "some of the time"). An example of this is given in Figure 3. Thresholds are points between adjacent response categories where the odds are 1:1 of answering in either category. For good measurement, thresholds should be ordered in line with the ordering of the response categories. The thresholds, in this case, were not ordered in line with the ordering of the response categories, and this supported the evidence from the response category curves. Therefore, the two lowest response categories were combined giving score 1 for 'never or some of the time', score 2 for 'most of the time', and score 3 for 'always. Using these three response categories, the data were re-analysed with the RUMM 2020 program (note: the RUMM 2020 program converts the scores to 0, 1, 2). This re-analysis is now reported.

Final Analysis

The final analysis of the data for the model of Teachers' Relationships with Students: Students' View used 20 items (10 x 2 perspectives), three response categories and 139 students. The RUMM 2020 program produces outputs to assess fit to the measurement model, reliability and dimensionality. These are now explained.

Global Item and Person Fit

Table 2 shows the global item and person fit. The fit residuals for both the item difficulties and the person measures have a mean near zero and a standard deviation near one. The residuals are the differences between the actual values and the expected values, calculated according to the measurement model and, when they are standardised, they have an approximately normal distribution (mean = 0, SD =1), if the data fit the measurement model. These fit residual data for the measure of Teacher-Student Relationships have a good fit to the measurement model (see Table 2).

Individual Item Fit

The RUMM 2020 program calculates individual item fits to the measurement model and these are given in Appendix B. Nineteen items out of 20 fit the measurement model with a probability greater than 0.05, indicating that there is an excellent fit to the measurement model.

Table 2. Global Item and Person Fit to the Measurement Model

Item-Person Interaction			
Items Persons			
Location Fit Residual Location Fit Residual			
Mean	0.00	-0.16	1.54	-0.13
SD	1.78	0.95	1.53	0.93

1. Item location is item difficulty in logits.
2. Person location is person measure in logits.
3. SD is standard deviation.
4. The mean item difficulty is constrained to zero by the RUMM 2020 program.
5. Fit residuals are the difference between the actual values and the expected values calculated according to the measurement model (standardised). They have a mean near zero and an SD near 1 when the data fit the measurement model. (A good fit for these data).
6. All values are given to two decimal places because the errors are to two decimal places.

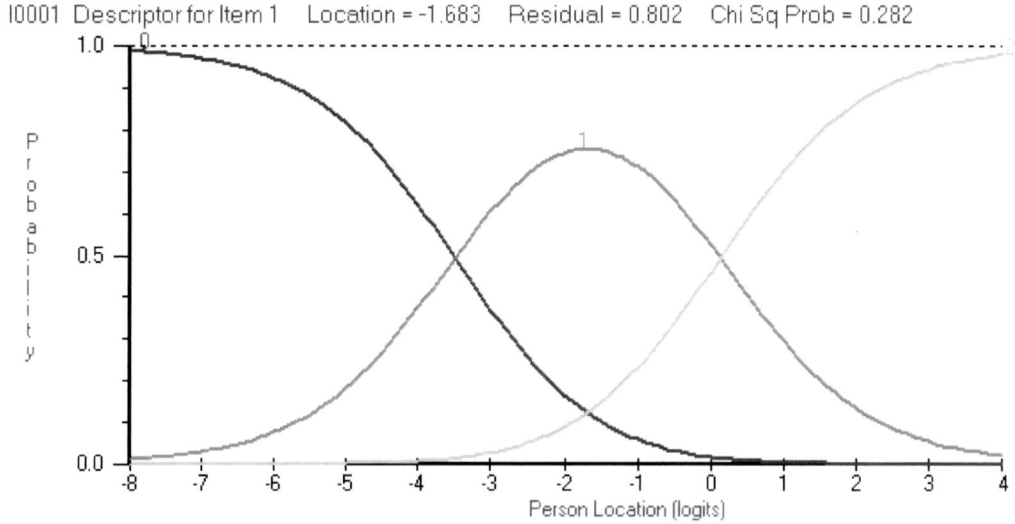

Figure 4. Response Category Curve for Item 1.

Consistency of Category Responses

The thresholds between category responses are given in Appendix C. The thresholds are ordered in line with the conceptual ordering from low to high (never/some of the time, most of the time and all the time). This indicates that the students answered the three response categories consistently and logically.

The RUMM 2020 program produces category response curves for each item showing the relationship between the probability of answering each category in relation to the Teacher-Student measure. An example is given in Figure 4.

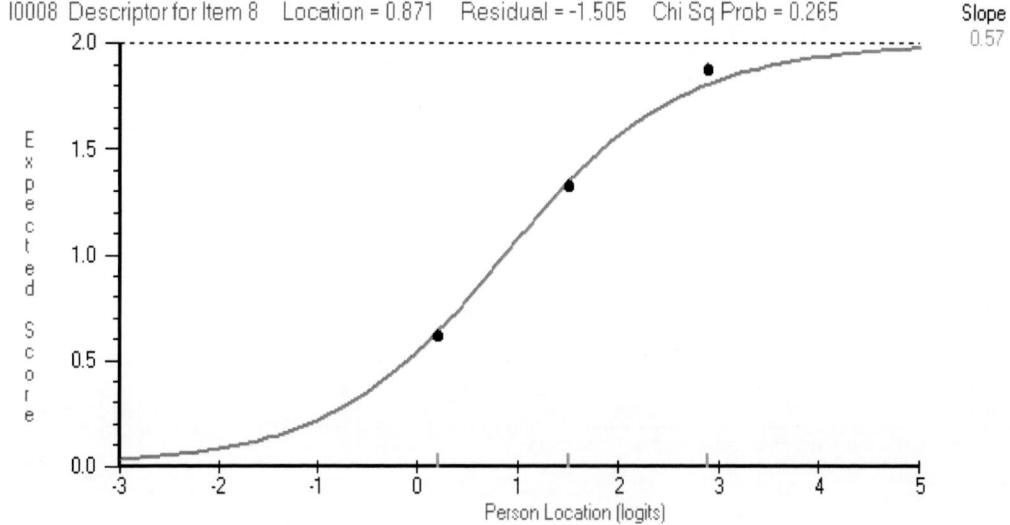

Figure 5. Characteristic Curve for Item 8.

Figure 4 shows that when the measure is low, then the probability is high that the student response is low (never/some of the time), that as the measure increases, the probability of answering in the lowest category decreases and the probability of answering in the next category increases, and that as the measure increases further still, the probability of answering category two (most of the time) decreases and the probability of answering category three (all the time) increases. This means that the students have answered the three response categories logically and consistently. The response category curves for all 20 items were good.

Item Characteristic Curves

The RUMM 2020 program produces an item characteristic curve for each item showing the relationship between the expected response score and the Teacher-Student measure. An example is given in Figure 5 for item 8. It shows how the item discriminates for groups of persons near the item difficulty. In this case, the item is functioning as intended. The item characteristic curves for all 20 items showed that the items were functioning as intended.

Dimensionality

The RUMM 2020 program calculates an item-trait interaction effect to determine whether a unidimensional trait has been measured. This examines the consistency with which students with measures all along the scale agree with the calculated difficulties of the items along the scale. That is, it provides a check that all the students agree that particular items are easy, of medium difficulty or hard. For the item-trait interaction, the total item chi-square was 45.00, and the probability was 0.27 (chi-square = 45, df = 40, p = 0.27). This indicates that there was no significant interaction of person measures with item difficulties along the scale and that, therefore, it can be concluded that a unidimensional trait was measured.

Person Separation Index

The Person Separation Index is 0.90 indicating that the measures are well separated along the scale in comparison to their errors of measurement. This also implies that the power of the tests-of-fit are strong and the RUMM 2020 program says that the power for these data are excellent.

Targeting

The RUMM 2020 program produces a Person Measure/Item Difficulty graph. This graph (see Figure 6) shows the scale of item difficulties from easy (about -1.8 logits) to hard (about +2.6 logits) and the student measures calibrated on the same scale from low (about -6.2 logits) to high (about + 5.6 logits). This shows that some hard items need to be added to the scale to better target those students with high measures.

The RUMM 2020 program also produces a Person Measure/Item Threshold graph (see Figure 7) which shows the item thresholds instead of item difficulties. The thresholds range from easy (about -3.6 logits) to hard (about +3.1 logits) and thus better cover the range of student measures. Nevertheless, in any future use of the scale, some harder items need to be added to better measure those students with high teacher-student relationships.

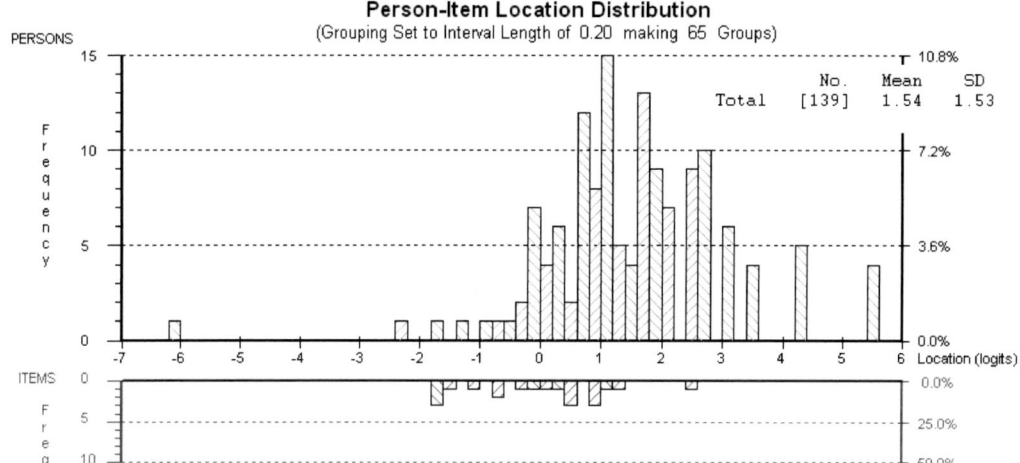

1. Person measures are given on the upper side in logits.
2. Item difficulties are given on the lower side in logits.
3. The mean ideal item difficulty for Connectedness is -1.10, for Availability is -0.43 and for Communication is -1.18.
4. The mean real item difficulty for Connectedness is 0.96, for Availability is 1.59 and for Communication is 0.44.
5. Refer to Table 3 for the full list of item difficulties.
6. Some harder items need to be added to the scale in future use to cover the higher measures.

Figure 6. Person Measure/ Item Difficulty Graph.

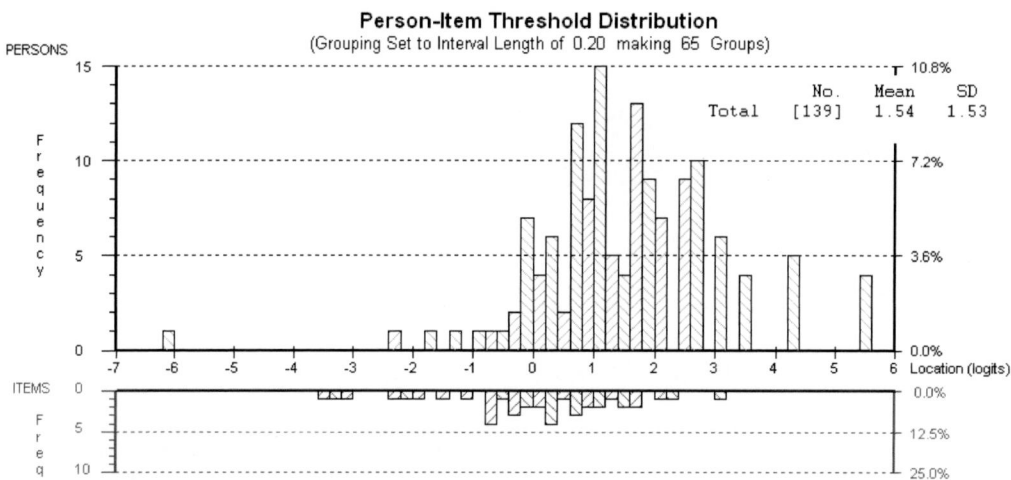

1. Person measures are given on the upper side in logits.
2. Item threshold are given on the lower side in logits.
3. The mean ideal item threshold for Connectedness is -1.10, for Availability is -0.43 and for Communication is -1.18.
4. The mean real item threshold for Connectedness is 0.96, for Availability is 1.35 and for Communication is 0.44.
5. Refer to Appendix C for the full list of item thresholds.

Figure 7. Person Measure/Item Threshold Graph.

The Teacher-Student Relationship Scale: Student's View

The Rasch analysis has calibrated the student measures on the same scale as the item difficulties and produced a linear, unidimensional scale (see Table 3), for which the data have a good fit to the measurement model. Since it has now been shown that the scale data are reliable (there is good individual and global fit to the measurement model, the separation of measures is good in comparison to the errors and the students have answered the response categories consistently and logically), valid inferences can be made from the scale.

Items

For each item, the ideal perspective ('what I wish would happen') was easier than the actual behaviour ('what does happen'), as conceptualised at the beginning of the study.

The four easiest attitude items (what students wish to happen) are, and these are very easy:

1. My teacher and I get along well together (item 2, difficulty -1.79 logits);
2. My teacher listens to me and helps me to feel better (item 10, difficulty -1.71 logits);
3. My teacher likes me (item 1, difficulty -1.68 logits);
4. My teacher listens to me (item 8, difficulty -1.47 logits).

Table 3. Item Wording and their Difficulties in Logits (Final Data Analysis)

Item no. Item Wording	Response	
	What I "wish" would happen	This is what does happen
Connectedness		
1 My teacher likes me.	-1.68	+0.83
2 My teacher and I get along well together.	-1.79	+0.99
3 My teacher is interested in what I think and feel, and in what I do.	-0.74	+1.15
4 My teacher and I care about each other.	-0.19	+0.87
Availability		
5 I can go up to my teacher any time.	-0.60	+1.30
6 I can ask my teacher for help.	-1.12	+0.92
7 If my teacher is busy, I can still go and get help.	+0.42	+2.57
Communication Skills		
8 My teacher listens to me.	-1.47	+0.37
9 My teacher listens when I talk about personal/private things.	-0.36	+0.55
10 My teacher listens to me and helps me to feel better.	-1.71	+0.41

The four hardest attitude items (what students wish to happen) are, although these are still moderately easy, except for item 7 which is hard:

1. If my teacher is busy, I can still go and get help (item 7, difficulty +0.42 logits);
2. My teacher and I care about each other (item 4, difficulty -0.19 logits);

3. My teacher listens when I talk about personal/private things (item 9, difficulty -0.36 logits);
4. I can go up to my teacher any time (item 5, difficulty -0.60 logits).

The four easiest behaviour items (what actually does happen) are, although still hard:

1. My teacher listens to me (item 8, difficulty +0.37 logits);
2. My teacher listens to me and helps me to feel better (item 10, difficulty +0.41 logits);
3. My teacher listens when I talk about personal/private things (item 9, difficulty +0.55 logits);
4. My teacher likes me (item 1, difficulty +0.83 logits).

The four hardest behaviour items (what actually does happen) are, still very hard:

1. If my teacher is busy, I can still go and get help (item 7, difficulty +2.57 logits);
2. I can go up to my teacher any time (item 5, difficulty +1.30 logits);
3. My teacher is interested in what I think and feel, and in what I do (item 3, difficulty +1.15 logits);
4. My teacher and I get along well together (item 2, difficulty +0.99 logits).

Persons

Each person's raw score has been converted to a student measure, expressed in logits. The student measures range from a lowest possible -6.01 logits to a maximum possible +5.49 logits. The lowest measures indicate a perception of a distant relationship while, conversely, the highest measures indicate a perception of a close relationship. The data on person measures is presented in Appendices D and E. Of the total 139 students who participated in the study, 20 students were measured at the lower end of the scale, indicating they perceived themselves to have a not-so-good relationship with their teacher. Twenty-nine students were measured at the higher end of the scale which indicates they perceived themselves to have a highly satisfactory relationship with their teacher.

SUMMARY

A Rasch measurement analysis was conducted with ten items, conceptually ordered from easy to hard, and answered in two perspectives ('what I wish would happen' and 'what actually happens') giving an effective scale of 20 items. The RUMM 2020 computer program (Andrich et al., 2005) was particularly helpful in conducting this analysis. It was concluded that a reliable linear, unidimensional scale of Teacher-Student Relationships was created using student views in which the measures were calibrated on the same scale as the item difficulties. The reliability of the scale data was shown by:

1. Good global and person item fit to the measurement model;
2. Good individual fit to the measurement model;
3. The three category responses being answered in a consistent and logical way;

4. A good Person Separation Index indicating that the person measures were well separated in comparison to the errors.
5. A good item-trait interaction indicating the measurement of a unidimensional trait;
6. Reasonable targeting of the items against the person measures, although some harder items need to be added for any future use of the scale.

Since the scale data were shown to be reliable, the following valid inferences were drawn from the scale.

1. All attitude relationships ('what I wish would happen') were easier than the actual behaviour relationship.
2. Students found it very easy to wish that they could get along well with their teacher.
3. Students found it moderately easy to wish that they and their teacher care about each other.
4. Students found it moderately hard to say that their teacher actually listens to them.
5. Students found it very hard to say that their teacher could be approached for help when the teacher was busy.

The distribution of Teacher-Student Relationship Measures makes it possible to describe a relationship as perceived by the student. Students with low measures perceive that they have a not-so-good relationship with their teacher. Students with a high measure perceive that they have a highly satisfactory relationship with their teacher. A closer look at the responses given by the students within the three aspects of Connectedness, Availability and Communication Skills may indicate which aspects specifically are sound and which may need attention in order for the relationship to be further enhanced.

CONCLUSION AND IMPLICATIONS

This study demonstrates that it is possible to create a linear measure of teacher-student relationships, based on a model involving three aspects, in order to better understand student's views of their relationships with teachers. A student's relationship with a teacher was defined in terms of 20 items forming a linear scale, created using a Rasch measurement model with data from 139 students who reported on their relationships with their teachers. Teacher-student relationship measures were calibrated from low to high on the same scale as the item difficulties that were calibrated from easy to hard. The linear measure supported the theoretical model of teachers' relationships with students as involving the three aspects of Connectedness, Availability and Communication to determine student self-reported self-views in two perspectives (ideal and actual). In addition the linear measure supported the structural model of teachers' relationships with students whereby attitudes influence behaviour, and whereby attitudes are easier than behaviour.

Implications from this research may be drawn for teachers and educational administrators, for policy makers and for those involved in future research.

Implications for Teachers and Educational Administrators

For teachers to effectively monitor the development of their relationships with students, they need information about their relationships. Teachers are typically not encouraged or supported in this kind of self-reflection (Pianta, 1999). This study provides a tool that is easy to use, is not time consuming, and may be used to pinpoint areas of strength and need within individual relationships. This study demonstrates that students are able to provide teachers with valuable insight into what students expect from the relationship, and how students might perceive things to be. Given that such insight can guide teachers in improving the way they relate to their students, an implication from this study is that teachers and educational administrators should engage students in the assessment process by giving them the opportunity and the means to provide information about their relationships with teachers.

Implications for Policy Makers

Recent school reform in the United States has added pressure to school stakeholders and policy makers by legislating detailed expectations for student performance and consequences for students, teachers, and schools who fail to meet those expectations (Klem and Connell, 2004). Similar legislative changes have been mooted here in Australia. Recent debate has covered such topics as the development of a National Curriculum to specifically raise literacy and numeracy standards across the country, and the introduction of merit pay or performance based salary for teachers (Department for Education Science and Training, 2007a, 2007b). Any changes that our policy makers make must guard against student achievement becoming the sole focus of attention. An educational system that determines its success by demonstrable evidence may direct the spotlight onto standards of academic achievement and direct attention away from social and emotional areas of development. As Hargreaves (2000) pointedly states:

> If we are serious about standards, we must become serious about emotions too and look again at the organizational conditions and professional expectations that can increase emotional understanding between teachers and their students as a basis for learning. By focussing only on cognitive standards themselves, and the rational processes to achieve them, we may, ironically, be reinforcing structures and professional expectations that undermine the very emotional understanding that is foundational to achieving and sustaining those standards. (p. 825)

In the push to raise teaching standards and levels of literacy and numeracy here in Australia, policy makers must not overlook the importance of the social and emotional involvement of teachers and students in the teaching and learning process. As Pianta (1999) suggests "No amount of focus on academics, no matter how strong or exclusive, will substantially change the fact that the substrate of classroom life is social and emotional" (p. 170). Goleman (1995) challenges schools to educate the whole child, "bringing together mind and heart in the classroom" (p. xiv). In helping to maintain a balanced approach to determining the success of our education system here in Australia it is vital that when policy makers debate National Curriculum, they must focus on strengthening academic learning alongside social and emotional development. The teacher-student relationship must be recognised as relevant to the success of instruction and seen as a powerful resource in the classroom. Not only must our policy makers be aware of the importance of teacher-student relationships with regard to student achievement and development, but they must also be committed to supporting teachers in harnessing this resource.

Implications for Future Research

Whilst this study has shown it is possible to create a linear measure of teacher-student relationships to better understand students' views of their relationships with teachers, more needs to be done in this area. Future studies could expand on the Teachers' Relationships with Students Questionnaire: Student's View and build in additional stem items. Furthermore, future studies could incorporate additional aspects that impact on the shared relationship between teachers and students. Examples include class size, length of contact between class teacher and the class, the timetabling of specialised staff, and the use of humour in the classroom. Given that a limitation to the present study concerns the small sample size, future studies would do well to draw on a larger number of participants from a broader range of schools.

To conclude, this study contributes new knowledge to the body of information about teachers' relationships with students in primary school classrooms in Perth, Western Australia. Further research in this area is needed to expand our understanding of how good teacher-student relationships can be recognised and promoted. To use the words of Pianta (1999), "Relationships with teachers are an essential part of the classroom experience for all children and a potential resource for improving developmental outcomes" (p. 21). The more that is known about how to identify and build positive teacher-student relationships, the better use can be made of this resource in our schools and in our communities.

REFERENCES

Adler, M. (1985). *How to Speak, How to Listen.* New York: Macmillan Publishing Company.

Ajzen, I. (1989). Attitude Structure and Behaviour. In A. Pratkanis, S. Breckler and A. Greenwald (Eds.), *Attitude Structure and Function* (pp. 241-274). Hillsdale, NJ: Lawrence Erlbaum Associates, Inc.

Andrich, D., Sheridan, B., and Luo, G. (2005). *Rasch Unidimensional Measurement Models: A windows-based item analysis program employing Rasch models (RUMM2020).* Perth, Western Australia: RUMM Laboratory.

Ang, R. (2005). Development and Validation of the Teacher-Student Relationship Inventory Using Exploratory and Confirmatory Factor Analysis. *Journal of Experimental Education, 74*(1), 55-73.

Arthur, M., Gordon, C., and Butterfield, N. (2003). *Classroom Management: Creating positive learning environments.* Southbank, Victoria: Thomson.

Baker, J. (1999). Teacher-student interaction in urban at-risk classrooms: Differential behavior, relationship quality, and student satisfaction with school. *The Elementary School Journal, 100*(1), 57-70.

Barry, K., and King, L. (1993). *Beginning Teaching* (2nd ed.). Wentworth Falls: Social Science Press.

Birch, S., and Ladd, G. (1996). Interpersonal Relationships in the School Environment and Children's Early School Adjustment: The role of teachers and peers. In J. Juvonen and K. Wentzel (Eds.), *Social Motivation: Understanding children's school adjustment* (pp. 199-225). NY: Cambridge University Press.

Brazelton, T., and Greenspan, S. (2000). *The Irreducible Needs of Children: What Every Child Must Have to Grow, Learn, and Flourish* (1st ed.). Cambridge, Massachusetts: Perseus Publishing.

Campbell, S. (2005). *Saying What's Real: 7 Keys to authentic communication and relationship success*. Novato, CA: New World Library.

Clark, C., and Peterson, P. (1986). Teachers' Thought Processes. In M. Wittrock (Ed.), *Handbook of Research on Teaching* (pp. 255-296). New York, NY: Macmillan Publishing Company.

Department for Education Science and Training. (2007a). Expert to Develop Performance-Based pay. Retrieved August 18, 2007, from http://www.dest.gov.au/Ministers/Media/Bishop/2007/06/B001120607.asp#

Department for Education Science and Training. (2007b). Performance-based rewards for teachers.

Retrieved August 18, 2007, from http://www.dest.gov.au/NR/rdonlyres/DE79EE9A-6D71-4BAC-8026-599FD4D4A366/16286/DESTPerformancebasedrewardsforteachers APRIL1.rtf#_Toc162950211

Entwisle, D., and Hayduk, L. (1988). Lasting Effects of Elementary School. *Sociology of Education, 61*, 147-159.

Fox, M. (1993). *Psychological Perspectives in Education*. London: Cassell Educational Ltd.

Goldstein, L., and Lake, V. (2000). "Love, love, and more love for children": exploring preservice teachers' understandings of caring. *Teaching and Teacher Education, 16*(8), 861-872.

Goldstein, S. (1995). *Understanding and Managing Children's Classroom Behaviour*. New York: John Wiley and Sons, Inc.

Goleman, D. (1995). *Emotional Intelligence: Why it can matter more than IQ*. New York: Bantam Books.

Good, T., and Brophy, J. (2000). *Looking In Classrooms* (8th ed.). New York: Longman.

Hargreaves, A. (2000). Mixed Emotions: teachers' perceptions of their interactions with students. *Teaching and Teacher Education, 16*, 811-826.

Howes, C. (2000). Social-emotional Classroom Climate in Child Care, Child-Teacher Relationships and Children's Second Grade Peer Relations. *Social Development, 9*(2), 191-204.

Howes, C., Hamilton, C., and Matheson, C. (1994). Children's Relationships With Peers: Differential Associations with Aspects of the Teacher-Child Relationship. *Child Development, 65*, 253-263.

Klem, A., and Connell, J. (2004). Relationships Matter: Linking Teacher Support to Student Engagement and Achievement. *The Journal of School Health, 74*(7), 262-273.

Krause, K., Bochner, S., and Duchesne, S. (2006). *Educational Psychology for Learning and Teaching* (2nd ed.). Southbank, Victoria: Nelson Australia Pty Ltd.

Larrivee, B. (2005). *Authentic Classroom Management: Creating a learning community and building reflective practice* (2nd ed.). Boston, USA: Pearson Education, Inc.

Lynch, M., and Cicchetti, D. (1992). Maltreated Children's Reports of Relatedness to Their Teachers. In R. Pianta (Ed.), *Relationships Between Children and Non-parental Adults: New Directions in Child Development* (pp. 81-107). San Francisco: Jossey-Bass.

McInerney, D., and McInerney, V. (2006). *Educational Psychology: Constructing Learning* (4th ed.). Frenchs Forest, NSW: Pearson Education Australia.

Noddings, N. (2005). *The Challenge to Care in Schools* (2nd ed.). New York, NY: Teachers College Press.

Pianta, R. (1999). *Enhancing Relationships Between Children and Teachers* (1st ed.). Washington, DC: American Psychological Association.

Pianta, R., and Walsh, D. (1996). *High-risk Children in Schools: Constructing and Sustaining Relationships*. New York: Routledge.

Rutter, M. (1979). Invulnerability, Or Why Some Children Are Not Damaged by Stress. In S. Shamsie (Ed.), *New Directions in Children's Mental Health* (pp. 55-75). New York: Spectrum Publications Inc.

Shields, A., Dickstein, S., Seifer, R., Giusti, L., Magee, K., and Spritz, B. (2001). Emotional Competence and Early School Adjustment: A Study of Preschoolers at Risk. *Early Education and Development, 12*(1), 73-96.

Slater, L. (2004). Relationship-Driven Teaching Cultivates Collaboration and Inclusion. *Kappa Delta Pi Record, 40*(2), 58-59.

Smeyers, P. (1999). 'Care' and Wider Ethical Issues. *Journal of Philosophy of Education, 33*(2), 233-251.

Sroufe, L. A. (1989). Relationships and Relationship Disturbances. In S. A.J and E. R.N (Eds.), *Relationship Disturbances in Early Childhood: A Developmental Approach* (pp. 97-124). New York: Basic Books.

Sztejnberg, A., den Brok, P., and Hurek, J. (2004). Preferred Teacher-Student Interpersonal Behaviour: Differences Between Polish Primary and Higher Education Students' Perceptions. *Journal of Classroom Interaction, 39*(2), 32-40.

Thompson, R., and Lamb, M. (1984). Infants, Mothers, Families and Strangers. In M. Lewis (Ed.), *Beyond The Dyad* (pp. 195-221). New Brunswick, NJ: Plenum Press.

Valeski, T. N., and Stipek, D. J. (2001). Young Children's Feelings About School. *Child Development, 72*(4), 1198-1213.

Weare, K. (2000). *Promoting Mental, Emotional and Social Health: A whole school approach*. New York: NY: Routledge.

Weissberg, R., Caplan, M., and Harwood, R. (1991). Promoting Competent Young People in Competence-Enhancing Environments: A Systems-Based Perspective on Primary Prevention. *Journal of Consulting and Clinical Psychology, 59*(6), 830-841.

Wright, B. D. (1999). Fundamental Measurement for Psychology. In S. E. Embretson and S. L. Hershberger (Eds.), *The New Rules of Measurement: What every psychologist and educator should know* (pp. 65-104). Mahwah, NJ: Lawrence Erlbaum Associates.

APPENDIX A

Teachers' Relationships with Students Questionnaire
(Student Views)

The child is asked to think about each statement in relation to their current classroom teacher, and to rate a response according to the response format below. The child is told that all responses will remain confidential.

Response Format

Almost always   **4**

Most of the time   **3**

Some of the time   2

Not at all   1

Item no.	Item wording	Response	
		This is what does happen	What I "Wish" would happen
Sub-group: Connectedness			
1-2	My teacher likes me.	_____	_____
3-4	My teacher and I get along well together.	_____	_____
5-6	My teacher is interested in what I think and feel, and in what I do.	_____	_____
7-8	My teacher and I care about each other.	_____	_____
Sub-group: Availability			
9-10	I can go up to my teacher any time.	_____	_____
11-12	I can ask my teacher for help.	_____	_____
13-14	If my teacher is busy, I can still go and get help.	_____	_____
Sub-group: Communication Skills			
15-16	My teacher listens to me.	_____	_____
17-18	My teacher listens when I talk about personal/private things.	_____	_____
19-20	My teacher listens to me and helps me to feel better.	_____	_____

Are there any comments you would like to make about you and your teacher?

_____
_____
_____
_____

APPENDIX B

Item Fit to the Measurement Model (Student Measure)

Item No.	Location	SE	Residual	df	Chi-square	Probability
Item 1	-1.68	0.21	0.80	125.35	2.40	0.28
Item 2	0.84	0.16	-0.26	125.35	1.47	0.46
Item 3	-1.79	0.22	-0.27	125.35	0.03	0.98
Item 4	0.99	0.14	-0.77	125.35	1.01	0.59
Item 5	-0.74	0.18	-0.62	125.35	0.82	0.65
Item 6	1.15	0.13	0.67	125.35	0.32	0.85
Item 7	-0.19	0.16	-1.34	125.35	3.82	0.12
Item 8	0.87	0.14	-1.51	125.35	2.52	0.26
Item 9	-0.60	0.18	-0.63	125.35	0.71	0.69
Item 10	1.30	0.14	1.44	125.35	0.82	0.66
Item 11	-1.12	0.21	-0.93	125.35	2.02	0.35
Item 12	0.20	0.16	0.85	125.35	0.88	0.63
Item 13	0.43	0.15	1.90	124.41	14.01	0.00
Item 14	2.57	0.15	0.82	125.35	2.04	0.34
Item 15	-1.47	0.23	-0.32	125.35	1.50	0.46
Item 16	0.37	0.15	-0.83	125.35	2.01	0.35
Item 17	-0.36	0.17	-0.65	125.35	0.58	0.74
Item 18	0.55	0.14	0.28	125.35	1.55	0.45
Item 19	-1.71	0.23	-0.68	125.35	2.68	0.24
Item 20	0.41	0.15	-1.14	125.35	3.81	0.13

1. Location is item difficulty in logits.
2. SE is Standard Error.
3. Residual is the difference between actual value and expected value, calculated according to the measurement model.
4. df is degrees of freedom.
5. 19 out of 20 items fit the measurement model with a probability greater than 0.05.
6. All values are given to two decimal places because the errors are to two decimal places.

APPENDIX C

Item Thresholds for Student Measure

Thresholds Mean	1	2
Item 1	-1.68	-3.40	0.13
Item 2	0.84	-0.62	2.29
Item 3	-1.80	-3.39	-0.20
Item 4	0.99	0.36	1.63
Item 5	-0.74	-2.14	0.65
Item 6	1.15	0.77	1.52
Item 7	-0.19	-0.64	0.27
Item 8	0.87	0.47	1.27
Item 9	-0.60	-1.42	0.21
Item 10	1.30	0.80	1.80
Item 11	-1.12	-1.83	-0.40
Item 12	0.19	-1.13	1.51
Item 13	0.43	-0.12	0.97
Item 14	2.57	2.06	3.08
Item 15	-1.47	-2.32	-0.61
Item 16	0.37	-0.38	1.12
Item 17	-0.36	-0.79	0.06
Item 18	0.55	0.32	0.78
Item 19	-1.71	-3.11	-0.30
Item 20	0.41	-0.30	1.12

1. Thresholds are points between adjacent response categories where the odds are 1:1 of answering the adjacent categories.
2. Mean thresholds are the item difficulties in logits.

3. All values are given to two decimal places because the errors are to two decimal places.
4. The thresholds for each item are ordered in line with the ordering of the response categories.

APPENDIX D

Students with Lowest Teacher-Student Relationship Measures (N=20)

ID	Raw Score	Student Measure	SE	Residual
051	0	-6.01	-	-
050	6	-2.28	0.53	-0.97
079	8	-1.78	0.47	+0.72
063	10	-1.37	0.43	-0.13
049	13	-0.86	0.40	+2.06
069	14	-0.71	0.39	-0.24
059	16	-0.43	0.37	+1.40
093	17	-0.29	0.37	-0.91
061	17	-0.29	0.37	-0.41
137	18	-0.15	0.36	+1.48
023	18	-0.15	0.36	-0.63
102	19	-0.02	0.36	-2.49
070	19	-0.02	0.36	+0.92
080	19	-0.02	0.36	+0.02
091	19	-0.02	0.36	+0.69
067	19	-0.02	0.36	+0.01
120	20	+0.10	0.36	-0.58
100	20	+0.10	0.36	-0.59
095	20	+0.10	0.36	+0.92
021	20	+0.10	0.36	-2.16

1. ID is student identification number.
2. Raw score is the total score on the 20 questionnaire items with three response categories 0, 1, 2 (minimum raw score is 0, maximum is 40).
3. Student measure is in logits (minimum linear measure is -6.01 logits, maximum is +5.49).
4. SE is standard error in logits.
5. Residual is the standardised difference between the actual score and the score estimated according to the measurement model.
6. All values are given to two decimal places because the errors are to two decimal places.

APPENDIX E

Students with Highest Teacher-Student Relationship Measures (N=29)

ID	Raw Score	Student Measure	SE	Residual
044	36	+2.72	0.56	-0.79
004	36	+2.72	0.56	-0.22
036	36	+2.72	0.56	-0.52
003	36	+2.72	0.56	+0.02
092	36	+2.72	0.56	-0.80
038	36	+2.72	0.56	-0.93

138	36	+2.72	0.56	-0.27
018	36	+2.72	0.56	-0.78
134	36	+2.72	0.56	+1.00
013	36	+2.72	0.56	-0.66
017	37	+3.06	0.63	-1.03
111	37	+3.06	0.63	-1.10
014	37	+3.06	0.63	-0.37
086	37	+3.06	0.63	-1.03
040	37	+3.06	0.63	-0.62
129	37	+3.06	0.63	+0.37
074	38	+3.53	0.75	-0.99
034	38	+3.53	0.75	-0.40
039	38	+3.53	0.75	-0.64
057	38	+3.53	0.75	-0.80
127	39	+4.28	1.02	-1.17
047	39	+4.28	1.02	-1.17
011	39	+4.28	1.02	-0.30
001	39	+4.28	1.02	-1.17
089	39	+4.28	1.02	-1.17
064	40	+5.49	-	-
041	40	+5.49	-	-
055	40	+5.49	-	-
077	40	+5.49	-	-

1. ID is student identification number.
2. Raw score is the total score on the 20 items with three response categories 0, 1, 2 (minimum raw score is 0, maximum is 40).
3. Student measure is in logits (minimum linear measure is -6.01 logits, maximum is +5.49).
4. SE is standard error in logits (RUMM does not estimate for maximum scores).
5. Residual is the standardised difference between the actual score and the score estimated according to the measurement model (RUMM does not estimate for maximum scores).

In: Applications of Rasch Measurement in Education   ISBN: 978-1-61668-026-8
Editor: Russell Waugh   © 2010 Nova Science Publishers, Inc.

Chapter 6

A RASCH MEASURE OF CAREER DECISION-MAKING SELF-EFFICACY

Thomas Kin Man Leung[1] and Russell F. Waugh[2]
[1.] Ching Chung Hau Po Woon Secondary School, Hong Kong
[2.] Graduate School of Education, University of Western Australia

ABSTRACT

This paper is part of a larger study of career decision-making with Hong Kong students. Career Decision-Making Self-efficacy Scale (Betz, Klein and Taylor, 1996) was translated into Chinese. The scale involved 25 items answered in five response categories scored from 1 to 5 (not confident at all, very little confidence, moderate confidence, much confidence, and complete confidence). Students came from grade 8 (13 years old) to grade 12 (21 years old) and included 212 females and 179 males. A Rasch analysis was used to create a linear, uni-dimensional scale with 17 items for 185 students. The item-trait chi-square was $\chi^2 = 34.45$, df = 34, $p = 0.45$ showing a very good overall fit to the measurement model. The Student Separation Index was 0.9 and the Cronbach Alpha was 0.89 showing good scale reliability. All 17 items fitted the measurement model with p>0.06. The 17 items were ordered from easy to hard providing good information relating to student career decision-making.

INTRODUCTION

This chapter divides into two sections. The first section introduces the reader to the background related to the research on Career Decision-Making and Attitudes towards Career Counseling presented in Chapters Six and Seven. The second section presents the rasach analysis of the Career Decision-Making Self-efficacy Scale (Betz, Klein and Taylor, 1996). A summary of the main findings from RUMM2020 program analysis is also given at the end of this chapter.

SECTION ONE: RESEARCH BACKGROUND

Youth Unemployment in Hong Kong

A survey conducted by the Hong Kong government in August 2002 revealed that 'Labour-related problems' was the issue that caused the Hong Kong public the most concern, followed by 'economy-related problems' and the 'need for life-long learning' (Hong Kong SAR Government, 2002). The unemployment rate in Hong Kong was 2.2% in 1997 and then rose to 4.7% in 1998, 7.7% in early 2002 and 8.3% in 2003 ("Unemployment Rate Broke the Record", 2003), due to the poor economy and the vast number of leavers and graduates from schools and universities. Among the unemployed, youth unemployment caused the most public concern because it was considered to lead to social instability. A term known as 'Lose-lose teenagers' was invented by the Hong Kong media to describe young people who 'lost' both their chance of further studies and the chance of employment. Young teenagers usually have difficulties in finding a job because they have high expectation on jobs but little commitment ("High Expectation and Low Commitment", 2006).

Youth unemployment for school leavers was much more serious than unemployment for other age groups in Hong Kong, with approximately one out of every four (25%) school leavers found to be unemployed in 2000 ("Thirty Percent Teenagers", 2000). It has been found that young people were more vulnerable and more seriously affected by unemployment than people at other ages (Fryer, 1997; Hammer, 1996). The youth unemployment problems are very important issues because the problems may be repeated if a youth got a job and later got fired (Hammer, 1996). Further, the youth unemployment problems have potentials to cause social instability (Duster, 1987).

To tackle youth unemployment (as most of them are school leavers), the Hong Kong SAR government launched some several new 'education' programmes, includes: (1) Youth Pre-employment Training Programme, (2) Yi Jin Project, Associate Degree Programmes and Community Colleges (HK SAR Government, 2001a).

The Youth Pre-employment Training Programme started in 1999. It was especially designed for school leavers aged between 15 and 19 years and was aimed at preparing them to enter the work of work (Hong Kong SAR Government, 2001b). Besides education and career programmes, the Hong Kong SAR government also launched the 'one company one vacancies' campaign, aimed at increasing job vacancies available for the school leavers.

Criticisms on Personal Qualities of Youths at Workplaces

A survey on 12,000 graduates of the Youth Pre-employment Training Programme revealed that 3800 (31%) of them decided to go on to further study, and the other 6500 (54%) decided on getting a job ("Youth Lack Career Counseling", 2001). Despite the fact that many young people joined the Youth Pre-employment Training Programme, the program was criticized as not able help school leavers to be optimistic about their future ("Youth Lack Career Counseling", 2001). Some graduates of the Training Program still did not know what they wanted to do and many quit their jobs shortly after completion of their training ("Youth Lack Career Counseling", 2001). The Hong Kong Polytechnic University Policy Research

Center conducted 20 in-depth case studies on youth unemployment in 2001 ("Youth Lack Career Counseling", 2001). Findings revealed that young school leavers with less academic achievement and working experience had difficulties maintaining their jobs for months ("Youth Lack Career Counseling", 2001). This kind of segmented working experience was not helpful to the career development of youth. The report stated that those young people in Hong Kong were suffering from a lack of career counseling in schools and a lack of psychological preparation for entering the workforce ("Youth Lack Career Counseling", 2001). The term psychological preparation refers to the attitude aspect of career guidance. It includes attitudes towards career and self-understanding.

Young people in Hong Kong have been criticized by employers for lacking commitment and enthusiasm for work ("Lack of Enthusiasm", 2001). The World Carnival Limited launched the Hong Kong Winter Carnival 2001 and recruited 300 temporary staff in 2001. The company conducted a recruitment interview on December 2, 2001, which attracted many young people. However, only 66 of the 500 applicants were employed, a number that was far below the expectations. The company director criticized young people in Hong Kong, in a news article, for their lack of commitment and enthusiasm for work ("Lack of Enthusiasm", 2001). This news article attracted lots of discussion about the career attitudes of young people in Hong Kong in the public at that time. The public blamed young people for poor career attitude and low career maturity. Furthermore, the public blamed the education systems (schools) in Hong Kong provided too much emphasis on academic achievement and neglected the psychological aspect, such as career maturity, of young people ("Youth Lack Career Counseling", 2001).

The poor career attitude among young people discussed in the above paragraph might be related to insufficient career guidance programmes available in secondary schools. Hok Yau Club, a Non-government Organization in Hong Kong, conducted a survey of 2003 students and found that 43% of students were dissatisfied with the career guidance provided by their schools ("Unemployment Rate is Increasing", 2001). Over 60% of students reported that their schools had not provided them with self-evaluative activities related to careers ("Unemployment Rate is Increasing", 2001). The survey result implied that career guidance in the Hong Kong education system has to be reviewed and stengthened. The following paragraphs introduce the context of this study, the education system in Hong Kong and the development of guidance in Hong Kong respectively.

The Education System in Hong Kong

In the 2006-2007 academic year, there are 669 primary schools (including 46 international schools), 566 secondary schools (including 23 international schools), 61 special schools, one Institute of Vocational Education with nine campuses, two approved post-secondary colleges, nine universities and one Institute of Education in Hong Kong (Education and Manpower Bureau, Hong Kong government, 2007). There were all together about 478,440 secondary school students in Hong Kong in the academic year 2005 to 2006. Overall teacher to student ratio in secondary schools is 1: 38.1 (Education and Manpower Bureau, Hong Kong government, 2007).

The schooling system in Hong Kong followed the traditional British system: 6 years primary school, 7 years secondary school including 2 years matriculation and 3 years university studies. Students in Hong Kong are required by law compulsorily to attend free schooling until the age of 15 years (or Secondary 3). There are two important public examinations in Hong Kong: the Hong Kong Certificate of Education Examination (for Secondary 5 students at aged 16-17 years) and the Hong Kong Advanced Level Examination (for Secondary 7 students at aged 17-18 years). The Hong Kong education system is now undergoing a new senior secondary curriculum reform. Starting from 2009, the existing 6+7+3 schooling system will be changed to 6+6+4 system. The existing two public examinations will be combined to one, the Hong Kong Diploma of Secondary Education (HKDSE) Examination, starting in 2012.

Historical Development of Guidance in Hong Kong

Guidance is a helping process in which clients gain self-understanding and the self-direction necessary to make informed choices and to develop the behaviour necessary to move toward self-selected goals in intelligent or self-correcting ways (Miller, Fruehling, and Lewis, 1978). It has three main focuses: (1) developmental or psychological, (2) vocational, and (3) academic aspect (Hui, 1994).

Guidance in Hong Kong began in the 1950s with a heavy emphasis on career guidance (Hui, 1994). At that time, guidance in Hong Kong schools focused on careers because both occupation information and university places were limited. Most students in the 1960's joined the workforce after study. On the other hand, psychological guidance or educational guidance were not well developed until 1980s.

In 1960's, the economy of Hong Kong was relatively poor. Riots broke out after the Star Ferry announced its intention to increase its fare by one cent in 1967. Riot police were called in to put down the riots. After that, the government became aware of the importance of education and social services for the youths in maintaining social stability. After a series of consultation and survey, the Hong Kong government then published a paper called 'the White Paper: Social Welfare into the 1980's'. The paper mandated that secondary schools should be provided with school social workers to provide student guidance (Hui, 1994). The introduction of the social service was aimed at both foster personal development of youth and preventing youth anti-social behaviours. Starting from 1980, secondary schools were provided with school social workers. School social workers, are rather independent in their roles, were employed by Non-government Organizations.

Furthermore, the Education Commission Report No.3 (Education Commission, 1982) further strengthened the guidance system in secondary schools. The report recommended that the government should provide each secondary school with five more teachers to be responsible for remedial teaching, guidance and counseling, and extra-curricular activities. Guidance teams, each composed of several 'guidance teachers', were then established in secondary schools in the late 1980's to work with the school social workers (Hui, 1994). In early 1980s, there was also no specialized pre-service training for guidance teachers. Guidance teachers, in fact, are subject teachers who teach any one of the knowledge-subjects and are appointed by the school principal to be provided guidance to students as one of their non-teaching duties. Leung, Leung and Chan (2003) conducted a survey on 114 counseling teachers in Hong Kong and found that most guidance teachers were aware of their professional limits, and were willing to seek ways to improve their competency.

Scope of Career Guidance and Guidance in Hong Kong Secondary Schools

The historical development and mission of guidance teachers is different from that of career guidance teachers although they both serve to foster student development. The scope of guidance service, also known as educational guidance, was mainly remedial casework and preventive programmes, mainly on developmental issues, self-concept and social skills. On the other hand, the scope of career guidance service was provision of career information to assist students in application for further studies. Due to their different nature and for historical reasons, career guidance and educational guidance service in most schools are provided by two separate teams. With the increase in university and matriculation school places in the 1980's, the focus of career guidance was shifted from job-hunting to further studies. Career guidance teachers provided students with information about further study, coordinating administration work about applications for examination and universities and being responsible for communicating with universities, whereas, educational guidance teachers and social workers take care of the emotional, psychological development, and adjustment of students.

In 1990, the Education Commission Report No. 4 advocated a 'whole school approach' to guidance (Hui, 1994). Later, in 1992, the Education Department established an Educational Counseling Unit under the Psychological Service Section (Hui, 1994). However, the collaboration between education guidance teachers and career guidance teachers is weak

The Developmental Aspect of Career Guidance

The Chinese words of 'career guidance' do not limit their meaning to 'occupations', as people in other countries understand it. The Chinese term of career guidance, in fact, means two aspects: 'Further studies' and 'vocational' guidance with two explicit aims: 'guidance on further studies' and 'guidance on occupation'.

Career guidance in Hong Kong was perceived as having a remedial, more than a developmental nature (Yau, 1990). Leung (2002) also criticized that students and teachers were focused too heavily on career information instead of career development, interest development and career maturity of students. Career guidance should be developmental and should be offer to students at all grade levels. The practice of career guidance in Hong Kong and its criticisms are further elaborated in the next section.

Implementation of Career Guidance in Hong Kong Schools

Research about career guidance in Hong Kong is limited. One of earliest published research studies using data collected in Hong Kong was done by Yau in 1987. She sent questionnaires to 139 secondary schools and found that only 24% of schools in Hong Kong had career masters. The report showed that the most popular career guidance activities in schools at that time were mass talks on career or further studies, collecting career information, and communicating with organizations and individual career counseling (Yau, 1990). Difficulties perceived by career guidance teachers were: insufficient manpower, heavy teacher workload, and passive students (Yau, 1990).

There is a career guidance master/mistress who is responsible for career guidance in each secondary school in Hong Kong in 2006. It is a senior teaching position for heading the career guidance team in any school (Yau, 1990). The team may consist of two or more members to provide career guidance, or more appropriately, provide career education. However, according to Super's model of career maturity (Super, 1990), career development of students depends not only on career information but also on the self-concept of students. That is, career information can strengthen the career competency of students. On the other hand, self-understanding, self-perception and the attitudes towards careers among students have to be considered in the process of career guidance, and, these seem to be attended to mainly by the guidance teachers in secondary schools in Hong Kong (Yuen, Shea, Leung, Hui, Lau, and Chan, 2003).

Nowadays, career guidance service in most Hong Kong schools is focused mainly on students in Secondary 3, 5 and 7. Secondary Three students need to decide on whether they would join the Arts, Commerce or Science stream in Form four. Career guidance teachers collaborate with teachers of various subjects to offer talks to students for selecting which stream is appropriate for individual students. On the other hand, Secondary Five students have to sit for the Hong Kong Certificate Examination and to compete for Secondary Six places. Those with good examination results can be promoted to Secondary Six, whereas those students with average examination results have to apply for other vocational training programmes hosted by other educational institutes. The chance of advancing to Form Six was less than 30% (Leung, 2002). Career guidance teachers provide Secondary Seven students with information about admission requirements for their own schools or other schools, subject selection information, information about occupations and the course offered by the Institutes of Vocational Education. Secondary Seven students have to select university majors and sit for the Hong Kong Advanced Level Examination. Students have to complete the joint universities application form. Career guidance teachers will provide information about entrance requirements for various programmes in various universities. In addition, career guidance teachers are responsible for checking the style and grammar of self-descriptive essays submitted by students to universities. Career guidance teachers may also provide information about careers and study overseas.

Limitations of Career Guidance in Hong Kong Schools

Career guidance teachers are actually full-time subject teachers in Hong Kong schools. They may have little teaching workload reduction by their principals for their career guidance duties. The pre-service training of career guidance teachers is limited. Career guidance, like other non-teaching duties, is allocated by the principal to each teacher. Some career guidance teachers have not received formal career guidance training. Career guidance teachers usually take part-time evening in-service training programmes at the universities sponsored by the government.

There is little integration between the work of career guidance teachers and that of guidance teachers (Hui, 1994). Guidance teachers are responsible for individual counseling or group activities, and work closely with the school social worker, whereas career guidance teachers do not. It is perceived that guidance teachers are responsible for the growth of students whereas career guidance teachers provide a one-shot service, for example, offering the latest information about further study.

Academic achievement, instead of career maturity, are emphasized by teachers in Hong Kong because it is believed that having good academic results will allow students to enter a good school or get a good job eventually. Career attitude and maturity do not count significantly for university admission when compared to academic achievement. On the other hand, there is no adverse problem if the career development of students is weak. Teachers enjoy seeing students prefer to study than to work. There is an old Chinese saying that, "Everything is inferior unless studying is superior." As a result, principals and teachers do not put career development of students at high priority as long as students gain good examination results and can further their studies.

In addition, career development of students in Hong Kong has not been properly evaluated because: (1) career maturity has been neglected in the past; and (2) there was no standardized, valid local instrument for assessing the career maturity of students in the Hong Kong context. However, with the Education Reform (Education Commission, 2000) proposed by the Hong Kong government, schools are urged to provide opportunities for the all-round development of their students. Parents have also begun to express concern about their children's 'careers' in addition to their 'further studies'. Some schools have begun to be aware of the importance of 'employment potential' or 'career planning' of their students. Some of the difficulties that schools face include a lack of literature for understanding career development of students in the Hong Kong context and the lack of a local instrument for assessing the career maturity of Hong Kong students.

Purpose of the the Study

The papers in Chapters Six and Seven were designed to investigate the measurement of Career Decision-Making Self-Efficacy (Betz, Klein and Taylor, 1996) and Attitude Towards Career Counseling (Rochleon, Mohr and Hargrove, 1999) to investigate career maturity among Hong Kong secondary school students. The study has two aims:

1. To translate into Chinese and test the Career Decision-Making Self-Efficacy (Betz, Klein and Taylor, 1996) and Attitude Towards Career Counseling (Rochleon, Mohr and Hargrove, 1999) for students in the Hong Kong context.
2. To assess the psychometric properties of the above two career-related scales using a Rasch measurement model.

Note: Professor Aaron Rochlen (PhD) at the University of Texas at Austin (Department of Educational Psychology) has kindly given permission to use the Attitude Towards Career Counseling Questionnaire in this research study and to publish the items in this book. Professor Nancy E. Betz (PhD) at Ohio State University (Department of Psychology) has kindly given permission to use the Career Decision Making Self-Efficacy Questionnaire in this research study and to publish the items in this book. Further use by others requires permission from the copyright holders.

Research Questions

Research Question 1: What are the psychometric properties of the two career related variables Career Decision-Making Self-Efficacy and Attitude towards Career Counseling when analysed with the RUMM2020 computer program (Andrich, Sheridan, and Luo. 2005).

Research Question 2: What are the easiest items and the hardest items in each of the measures of the above two variables?

Research Question 3: How do the measures of each of the above two career related variables differ by grade level or gender?

Significance of the Study

Career guidance in the Hong Kong education system needs to be reviewed for it to be kept in line with improvements in the western countries. With the lack of evaluation instruments, career guidance teachers could not evaluate how well career education is implemented in schools. Career Decision-Making Self-efficacy Scale (Betz, Klein and Taylor, 1996) and Attitude towards Career Counseling Scale (Rochleon, Mohr and Hargrove, 1999) are useful instruments for screening students and evaluating the effectiveness of career guidance programmes. There is no known literature (as far as the researcher could determine), reporting the item difficulties of Career Decision-Making Self-efficacy Scale (Betz, Klein and Taylor, 1996) and Attitude towards Career Counseling Scale (Rochleon, Mohr and Hargrove, 1999) each on the same linear scale as the person measures. Based on the results of this study, reliable linear instruments with linear measurement could be developed. The instruments could provide insight to improve career guidance practice in schools and may further contribute to effective evaluation of the career guidance system in Hong Kong.

SECTION TWO: RASCH ANALYSIS OF CAREER DECISION MAKING SELF-EFFICACY SCALE

This section presents the results of the data analysed using the computer program Rasch Unidimensional Measurement Models (RUMM2020) (Andrich, Sheridan, and Luo, 2005) and is divided into three parts. Part One introduces the preliminary Rasch analysis results for the data from the initial 25 items of the Career Decision Making Self-Efficacy questionnaire (Betz, Klein and Taylor, 1996). The global test of fit, item-trait interaction, Person Separation Index, threshold levels of items and the individual item fits are reported. Part Two explains how a linear measurement of Career Decision Making Self-Efficacy was constructed after the deletion of eight non-fitting items. Part Three summarizes the Rasch analysis of the final 17 good-fitting items of Career Decision Making Self-Efficacy in creating a unidimensional, linear scale. Tables relating to global item and person fit, individual item fit, individual item thresholds, and graphs for category responses, item characteristics, and targeting are presented. A summary of the main findings from RUMM2020 program analysis is then given at the end.

Part One: Preliminary Rasch Analysis

In order to fit a Rasch measurement model, items must be ordered by difficulty from easy to hard, and persons (with low to high measures along the scale) have to agree with these item difficulties. That is, persons with low measures should only answer the easy items positively (but not the medium and hard items); persons with medium measures should answer the easy and medium items positively (but not the hard items); and persons with high measures should answer the easy, medium and hard items positively. When there is a good agreement about the difficulties of the items for different students along the scale, a unidimensional measure is created. This agreement is indicated by the item-trait interaction statistic generated by the RUMM2020 computer program. When the chi-square probability of the item-trait interaction statistics is greater than 0.05, there is no significant interaction between the responses to the items and the location values (measures) of the persons along the scale (Andrich and van Schoubroeck, 1989, p.480).

Table 1. Global Test of Fit for the Career Decision Making Self-Efficacy (I=25, N=185)

Item-Person Interactions				
Items			Persons	
Location	Fit Residual		Location	Fit Residual
Mean 0.00	0.13		-0.21	-0.41
SD 0.46	1.09		1.04	1.85

(1) The item means are constrained to zero by the measurement model.
(2) When the standardized fit residuals have a mean near zero and SD near one, the data are likely to fit the Rasch measurement model. The person fit residuals indicate that the fit to the measurement model is not so good.
(3) The standard errors are in two decimal places, so numbers are given to two decimal places.

Global Tests of Fit

At the beginning of the analysis, all 25 items of the Career Decision Making Self-Efficacy were included. The summary of the test of fit statistics is presented in the Table 1. The global item fit statistics are satisfactory (with a mean near zero and a standard deviation near one), but the global person fit statistics are not so satisfactory.

The item-trait interaction chi-square is 82.36, df=50, and p=0.003 (see Table 2), which indicates the person measures interact significantly with the item difficulties, resulting in a poor fit to the Rasch measurement model. This means that a uni-dimensional measure where a single parameter measures each person for all items and a single parameter measures each item difficulty for all persons cannot be created. Therefore, items need to be deleted to improve fit to the model for the Career Decision-Making Self-Efficacy.

Table 2. Dimensionality and Fit to the Rasch Measurement Model of the Career Decision Making Self-Efficacy Measure (I=25, N=185)

Item-Trait Interaction		Reliability Indices
Total Item Chi Square	81.08	Separation Index = 0.92
Total Degree of Freedom	50.00	Cronbach Alpha = 0.92
Total Chi Square Probability	0.00	
Power of test-of-fit: EXCELLENT (based on Separation Index)		

(1) The item-trait interaction chi-square indicates that there is significant person-item interaction along the scale.

(2) The person separation index = 0.92 means that the proportion of observed variance considered true is 92%. It shows that there is a good separation of measures along the scale, compared with the errors of measurement, which are comparatively smaller. This also implies that the power of the tests-of-fit to the model is excellent.

Table 3. Uncentralized Item Thresholds for the Career Decision Making Self-Efficacy (I=25)

Item	Threshold Mean	Thresholds 1	2	3	4
1.	+0.06	-3.10	-0.55	2.25	1.62 *
2.	+0.07	-2.85	-0.54	0.98	2.69
3.	+0.69	-2.30	0.31	1.65	3.12
4.	+0.74	-2.66	-0.60	1.27	4.95
5.	-0.11	-3.61	-0.55	1.09	2.63
6.	-0.06	-3.28	-0.92	0.76	3.23
7.	-0.06	-4.18	-0.39	1.79	2.56
8.	-0.27	-3.45	-0.79	0.68	2.49
9.	-0.31	-3.18	-0.55	0.96	1.51
10.	+1.05	-1.52	0.85	1.55	3.32
11.	-0.09	-4.09	-0.40	1.29	2.82
12.	+0.51	-3.75	-0.44	1.26	4.96
13.	+0.47	-2.42	0.06	1.85	2.40
14.	-0.76	-5.02	-1.79	1.07	2.70
15.	+0.09	-2.74	-0.79	1.26	2.64
16.	+0.05	-4.55	-0.35	1.41	3.70
17.	+0.19	-2.87	-0.62	1.05	3.20
18.	-0.68	-4.01	-1.08	0.60	1.77
19.	-0.52	-2.96	-1.36	0.70	1.53
20.	-0.11	-2.73	-0.97	0.63	2.62
21.	+0.20	-3.24	-0.48	1.69	2.82
22.	-0.69	-3.33	-2.00	0.44	2.11
23.	-0.57	-3.60	-1.35	0.60	2.09
24.	+0.07	-3.02	-0.40	1.16	2.54
25.	+0.04	-3.05	-1.17	1.70	2.70

(1) All items have five response categories (4 thresholds).

(2) Thresholds are points between adjacent categories where the odds are 1:1 of answering either category.

(3) Mean threshold is the item difficulty in logits.

(4) * = disordered threshold.

Item Thresholds.

Table 4. Item difficulties for Career Decision Making Self-Efficacy (I=25)

Item	Location	SE	Residual	Chi-Square	Probability
Item 15	+0.09	0.10	+0.36	0.10	0.95
Item 12	+0.52	0.11	+0.77	0.16	0.92
Item 9	-0.34	0.10	-0.52	0.48	0.78
Item 24	+0.07	0.10	-0.53	0.92	0.63
Item 2	+0.04	0.10	+0.91	1.00	0.61
Item 3	+0.70	0.10	-1.33	1.15	0.56
Item 19	-0.54	0.10	+0.83	1.20	0.55
Item 21	+0.20	0.11	-0.92	1.89	0.39
Item 22	-0.71	0.11	+0.85	1.98	0.37
Item 4	+0.74	0.11	+2.58	2.02	0.36
Item 23	-0.55	0.10	+0.48	2.49	0.29
Item 18	-0.65	0.10	+1.20	2.65	0.27
Item 5	-0.10	0.10	-0.39	2.65	0.27
Item 6	-0.09	0.10	-0.78	2.74	0.25
Item 25	+0.05	0.11	-0.56	2.88	0.24
Item 8	-0.26	0.10	-0.57	3.52	0.17
Item 14	-0.79	0.12	-0.72	4.08	0.13
Item 11	-0.08	0.11	-1.23	4.16	0.12
Item 10	+1.04	0.10	+1.04	4.24	0.12
Item 17	+0.19	0.10	+1.83	4.42	0.11
Item 7	+0.02	0.11	-0.39	5.09	0.08
Item 20	-0.11	0.10	-1.49	6.00	0.05
Item 16	+0.08	0.11	-1.28	7.02	0.03*
Item 1	+0.03	0.11	+1.11	8.05	0.02*
Item 13	+0.45	0.10	+1.81	11.49	0.00*

(1) Location is item difficulty in logits and SE is standard error.
(2) Residual is the difference between the actual and predicted values.

Table 5. Item-Trait Interaction and Reliability Indices for Career Decision Making Self-Efficacy (I=17, N=185)

Item-Trait Interaction		Reliability Indices
Total Item Chi Square	36.08	Separation Index =0.90
Total Degree of Freedom	34.00	Cronbach Alpha =0.90
Total Chi Square Probability	0.37	
Power of test-of-fit: EXCELLENT (based on Separation Index)		

The preliminary item threshold table for the 25-items of Career Decision-Making Self-Efficacy is presented in Table 3. The thresholds of Item 1 were disordered indicating that the response categories were not answered consistently and logically by the students. This item needs to be deleted.

Item Difficulties

From Table 4, it can be seen that three items have a poor fit to the measurement model (items 13, 1 and 16) and need to be deleted for the next analysis.

Part Two: Further Analyses after Deletion of Items

After the initial analysis where three poor fitting items were deleted (items 13, 1 and 16), it was found that the next analysis still did not produce a good fit to the measurement model. Items 17, 6 and 20 now did not fit the measurement model and so they were deleted and the analysis repeated. While it may seem odd that these three items did fit the measurement model with 25 items but not with 22 items, this is not unusual. In Rasch measurement, all the items have to 'hang together' to fit the measurement model and form a unidimensional scale. A further analysis showed that item 14 did not now fit the measurement model and this item was deleted. The final analysis was performed with 17 items after eight items were deleted (items 1, 4, 6, 13, 14, 16, 17, 20) from the original Career Decision-Making Self-Efficacy data. Part Three now explains the results of this final analysis.

PartThree: Final Rasch Analysis with the 17 Items

Testing for Dimensionality

The Item-trait interaction is 39.01, df=36 and p=0.34 (see Table 5). This indicates that there is no significant interaction between the person measures and the item difficulties along the scale. That is, the data for the 17 items now have a very good fit to the Rasch measurement model and a unidimensional trait, which is called Career Decision-Making Self-Efficacy, has been measured.

The Person Separation Index = 0.90 (and Cronbach Alpha = 0.90) indicating that the person measures are well separated along the scale in comparison to the errors. Based on this Person Separation Index, the power of the tests-of-fit is good. This means that it is possible to tell whether persons with higher locations than others with lower locations tend to obtain higher scores on items or not (RUMM Laboratory, 2004).

Table 6. Global Test of Fit for the Career Decision Making Self-Efficacy Measure (I=17, N=185)

Item-Person Interactions				
Items			Persons	
Location	Fit Residual		Location	Fit Residual
Mean	0.00	0.17	-0.18	-0.42
SD	0.49	0.92	1.10	1.64

(1) The item means are constrained to zero by the measurement model.

(2) As the item and person fit statistics have means near zero, and standard deviations near one, there is an acceptable global fit to the model.

(3) The standard errors are two decimal places, so numbers are given to two decimal places.

(4) The Person Separation Index = 0.90 meaning that the proportion of observed variance considered true is 90%. It shows that there is a good separation of measures along the scale, compared with the errors of measurement, which are comparatively smaller. This also implies that the power of the tests-of-fit to the model is excellent.

Table 7.Individual Item Fit for Career Decision Making Self-Efficacy (Items =17)

Item	Location	SE	Residual	Chi-Square	Probability
2	+0.11	0.10	+1.57	0.27	0.87
3	+0.74	0.11	-1.26	2.31	0.32
5	-0.08	0.11	+0.15	2.03	0.36
7	-0.04	0.12	-0.09	2.35	0.31
8	-0.25	0.11	-0.34	1.37	0.50
9	-0.29	0.10	-0.48	0.11	0.95
10	+1.12	0.10	+1.09	4.46	0.11
11	-0.06	0.11	-1.11	4.77	0.09
12	+0.58	0.12	+0.98	0.12	0.94
15	+0.12	0.10	+0.63	0.63	0.73
18	-0.66	0.10	+1.90	6.82	0.03
19	-0.49	0.10	+0.94	0.53	0.77
21	+0.23	0.11	-0.81	3.93	0.14
22	-0.67	0.11	+0.31	1.51	0.47
23	-0.55	0.10	+0.38	1.30	0.52
24	+0.12	0.10	-0.56	1.49	0.48
25	+0.08	0.11	-0.45	2.08	0.35

(1) No residual exceeds specific limits of greater or less than 2.00 logits.
(2) Location means item difficulties and SE means standard error.
(3) Residual means responses predicted from the Rasch measurement parameters and responses provided by the lecturers.
(4) Probability means the calculated chance of such occurrence, based on the chi-square value.

Table 8. Uncentralized Item Thresholds for Career Decision Making Self-Efficacy (I=17)

Item	Threshold Mean	Thresholds 1	2	3	4
2	+0.06	-2.85	-0.55	0.97	2.66
3	+0.69	-2.34	0.30	1.64	3.18
4	+0.78	-2.69	-0.62	1.28	5.17
5	-0.12	-3.65	-0.56	1.08	2.63
7	-0.08	-4.23	-0.40	1.78	2.54
8	-0.29	-3.54	-0.78	0.66	2.48
9	-0.34	-3.25	-0.53	0.94	1.48
10	+1.05	-1.55	0.85	1.54	3.34
11	-0.11	-4.13	-0.40	1.26	2.84
12	+0.54	-3.83	-0.45	1.26	5.19
15	+0.07	-2.77	-0.80	1.25	2.60
18	-0.70	-4.03	-1.07	0.59	1.71
19	-0.53	-2.94	-1.38	0.70	1.48
21	+0.18	-3.29	-0.48	1.67	2.82
22	-0.70	-3.34	-2.02	0.43	2.12
23	-0.59	-3.68	-1.39	0.59	2.12
24	+0.06	-3.07	-0.41	1.14	2.58
25	+0.03	-3.09	-1.18	1.67	2.69

(1) All items have four ordered thresholds (and five response categories).
(2) Thresholds are points between adjacent categories where the odds are 1:1 of answering either category.
(3)Mean threshold is the item difficulty in logits.

Global Item-Person Fit Statistics

The RUMM 2020 program calculates fit residuals for items and persons. These are the differences between the actual responses and the expected responses as estimated from the parameters of the measurement model. When the mean fit residuals for both items and persons are near to zero, and the standard deviations are near to one, the data fit a Rasch measurement (Waugh, 2006). The summary statistics shown in the following table indicate that there is good consistency of item-person fit and a satisfactory person-item fit.

Fit of Individual Item Residuals

Residuals are the difference between the observed values and the expected values estimated from the parameters of the Rasch measurement model (Waugh, 2006). In other words, the value of the residuals indicates that the difference between the response predicted from the Rasch measurement parameters and response provided by the respondents. It is preferable to have a small value of residuals, within + or - 2.5 logits, and this indicates acceptable agreement between the model predictions and the actual responses. The following table 7 shows the individual item fit for all 17 items.

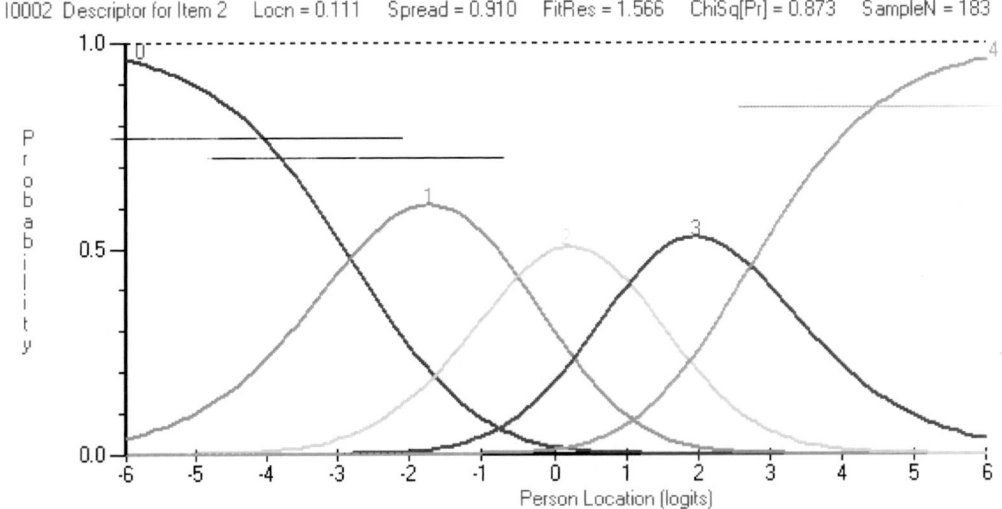

I0002 Descriptor for Item 2   Locn = 0.111   Spread = 0.910   FitRes = 1.566   ChiSq[Pr] = 0.873   SampleN = 183

(1) RUMM changes Response Categories 1,2, 3, 4,5 to 0, 1, 2, 3,4,5 respectively.
(2) Item 2 is located at 0.11 logits unit of item difficulty, with a fit residual of 1.57 and a chi-square value of 0.87.

Figure 1. Response Category Curve of item 2 for Career Decision Making Self-Efficacy.

Table 7 shows that the residuals of the items are between -1.3 and 1.9 logits, which are generally acceptable. This reflects that the data are answered consistently and logically, and they fit the measurement model to an acceptable level. All items have an acceptable fit to the measurement model with a probability greater than p=0.03 and 16 out of 17 items fit the model better than p=0.09.

Ordering of Response Categories

The RUMM2020 computer program provides two checks on the answering of the response categories to examine whether the responses are given consistently and logically. The first is a table of thresholds (presented in Table 8) and the second check is the response category curves (presented in Figure 1).

Item Thresholds

The thresholds are points between adjacent response categories where the odds are 1:1 of answering in either category. There are five response categories in the Career Decision Making Self-Efficacy measure and hence there are four thresholds. If the thresholds are ordered, that means the response categories are answered consistently and logically. The Item thresholds of the 17-item Career Decision Making Self-efficacy measure are listed in the Table 8. The thresholds are well ordered and this indicates that the responses were answered consistently and logically.

Figure 1 shows that persons (students) have answered the response categories consistently and logically for this item. When the person measure increases from -6.0 to -3.0 logits, the probability of answering category 0 (totally not confident) drops from 0.95 to 0.5 while the probability of answering category 1 (with little confidence) rises from 0.05 to 0.50. A similar trend occurs for the other category responses as the person measures increase along the scale. This indicates that as the person measures increase, the persons are answering all the categories consistently and logically. All Item Category Curves of the 17 items of the Career Decision Making Self-Efficacy measure were examined and they showed that the response categories were answered consistently and logically for each of the 17 items.

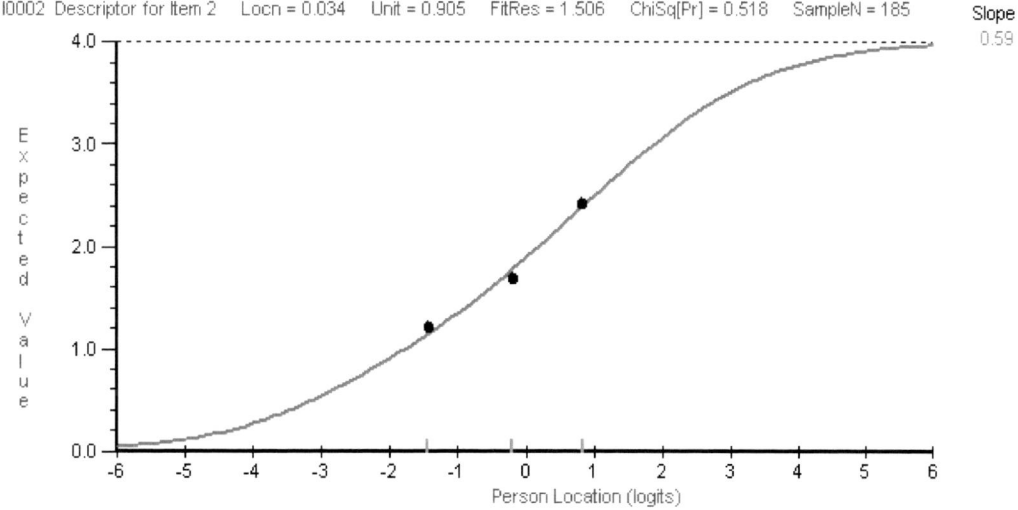

Figure 2. Item 2 Characteristic Curve for Career Decision Making Self-Efficacy.

Item Characteristic Curve

The RUMM2020 generates Item Characteristic Curves for each item so that researcher can examine how well the item differentiates between persons with measures above or below the item location (Waugh, 2006). In other words, the curve shows how the expected values vary for person measures above and below the item difficulty. The Item Characteristic Curve of item 2 of the Career Decision Making Self-Efficacy is shown in Figure 2. It shows how the expected response value of item 2, 'You can choose your university major', varies with different person measures of Career Decision Making Self-Efficacy and shows that the item is acting as it should.

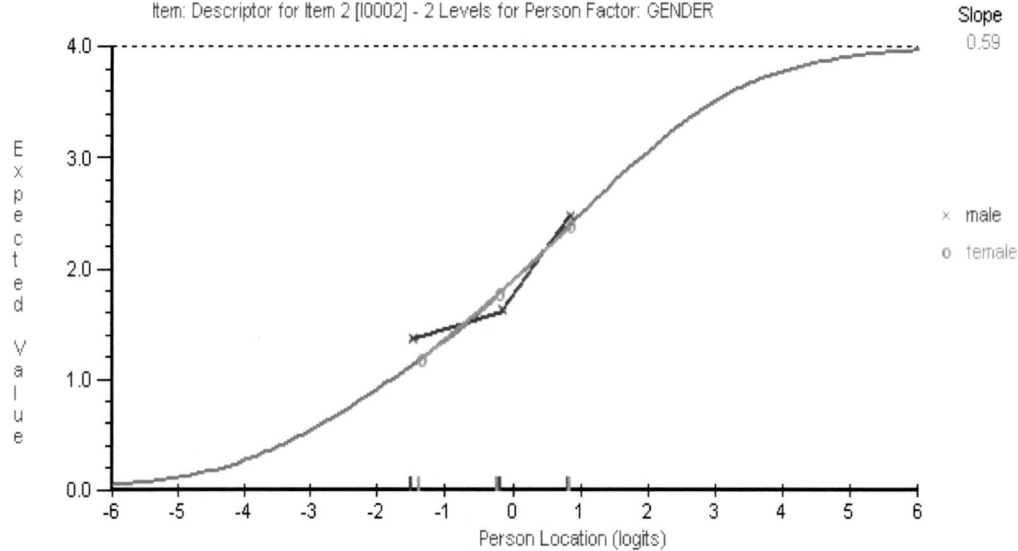

The differences by gender are not significant: $F_{(2,1)}=0.03, p=0.86$.

Figure 3. Item 2 Characteristic Curve for Career Decision Making Self-Efficacy Differentiated by Gender.

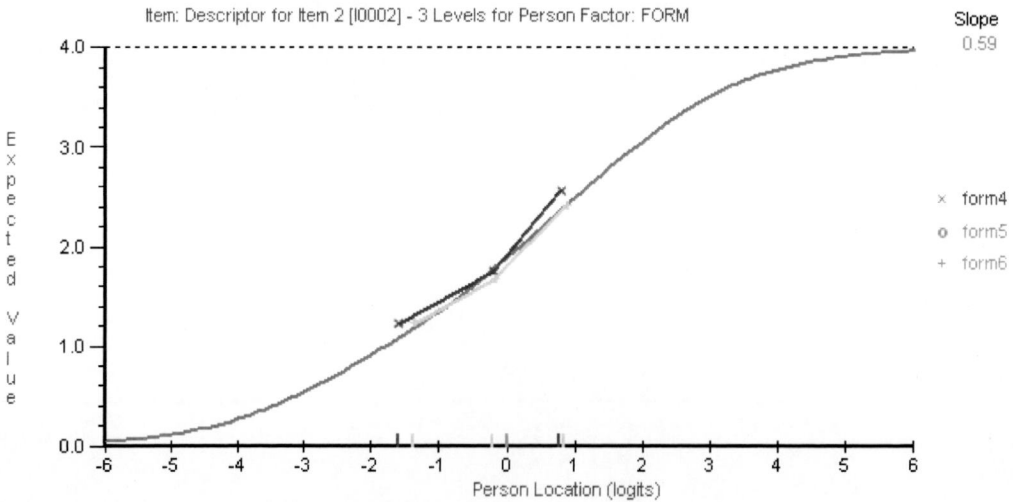

The differences by Form are not significant: $F_{(2,1)}=0.77, p=0.38$.

Figure 4. Item 2 Characteristic Curve for Career Decision Making Self-Efficacy Differentiated by Form.

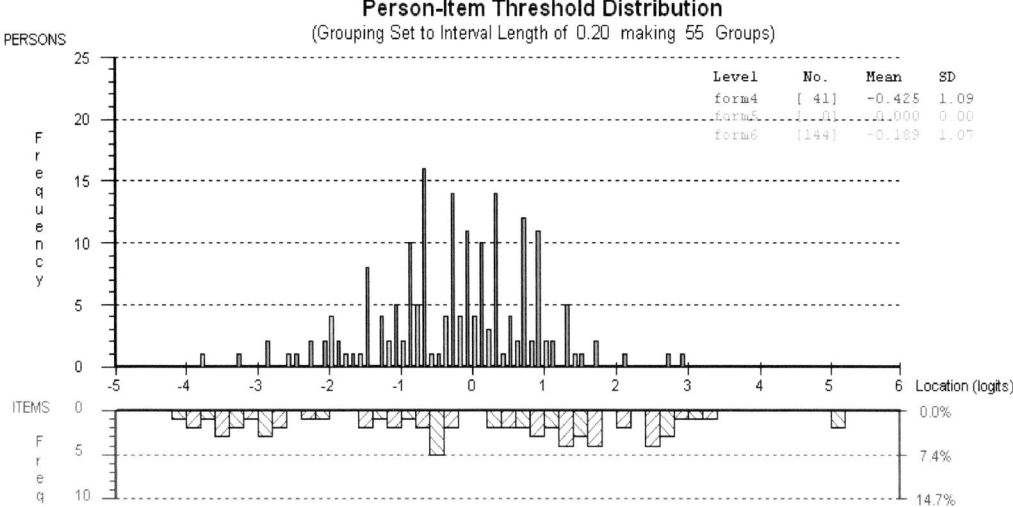

(1) Person measures are on the top of the scale in logits and item thresholds are on the bottom of the scale in logits.

(2) The person measures range from -3.57 logits to 2.99 logits and the item thresholds cover the same range. This indicates that the targeting is good.

(3) The graph has an error in colour due to the computer program. Green should be blue (N=41) and purple should be green (N=144).

Figure 5. Person Measure Item Threshold Distribution Graph of the 17 items Career Decision Making Self-Efficacy Measure by Form.

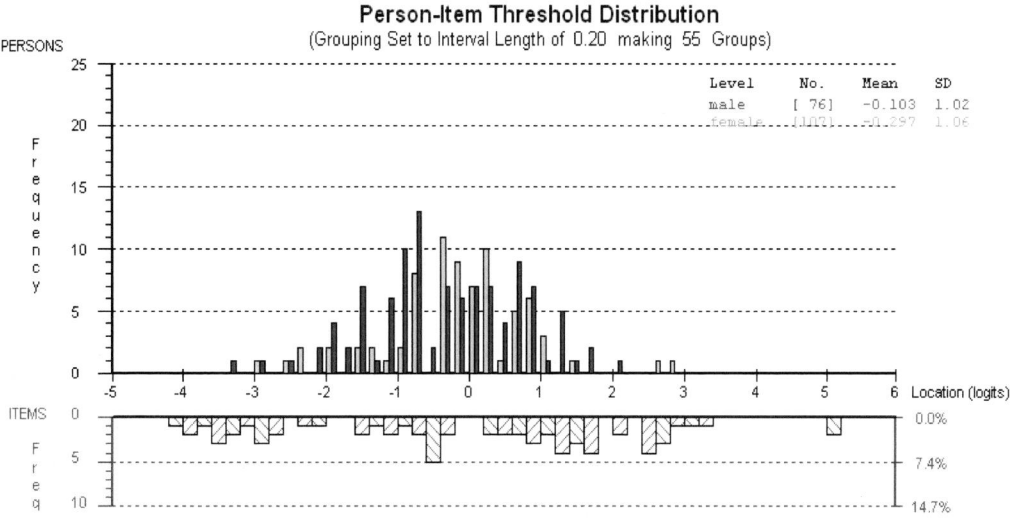

(1) Person measures are on the top of the scale in logits and item thresholds are on the bottom of the scale.

(2) There is a colour error in the graph due to the computer program. Green is males (N=76) and purple is females (N=107).

Figure 6. Person Measure Item Threshold Distribution Graph of the 17 items Career Decision Making Self-Efficacy Measure by Gender.

Item Differential Functioning

The RUMM2020 computer program produces Item Characteristic Curves for all 17 items, differentiated by gender and, separately, by form. These curves and their associated statistics were inspected for differential functioning. There was no significant difference between how males and females answered the items (although item 19 had a p=0.01, based on ANOVA). An example of the Item Characteristic Curve, differentiated by gender, is given in Figure 3. There was no significant difference between how form 6 and form 4 students answered the items (although both items 4 and 5 had a p=0.01, based on ANOVA). An example of the Item Characteristic Curve, differentiated by form, is given in Figure 4.

Table 9. Mean Measures of Career Decision Making Self-Efficacy by Gender (N=183,I=17)

Gender	Number	Mean	Standard Deviation
Male	76	-0.10	1.02
Female	107	-0.30	1.06

Means and standard deviations are in logits.

Table 10. Mean Measures of Career Decision Making Self-Efficacy by Form (N=181,I=17)

Form	Number	Mean	Standard Deviation
Form 4	41	-0.42	1.09
Form 6	144	-0.19	1.07

Means and standard deviations are in logits.

Targeting

Targeting refers to how well the item difficulties (or thresholds) cover the same part of the scale as the person measures. A scale with good targeting should have some easier, medium and harder items that are suitable to respondents with different person measures. The RUMM 2020 program generates two types of person measure/ item difficulty maps. They are 'Person-item Location Distribution Graph' and 'Person Measure and Item Thresholds'. The Person-Item Threshold Graph of the 17 items Career Decision Making Self-Efficacy measure is presented in Figure 5. The graph shows that the targeting of the item thresholds against the measures is good.

Inferences from the Mean Measures

Since the measure of Career Decision Making Self-Efficacy is reliable and shows a good fit to the measurement model, valid inferences can now be made from the measures. Table 9 shows the mean measures by gender. While males have a higher mean measure than females, this is not significant (t=1.22, df=181, p=0.11).

Table 10 shows the mean measures by form. While form 6 has a higher mean measure than form 4, this is not significant (t=1.23, df=181, p=0.11).

Inferences about Easiest and Hardest Items

Table 11 shows the item difficulties for Career Decision Making Self-Efficacy. The lower the item difficulty in logits, the lower the measure of Career Decision Making Self-Efficacy needed to have confidence in a self-efficacy decision and, conversely, the higher the item difficulty, the higher the measure needed to have confidence in a self-efficacy decision.

The four easiest items are, in order from easy to hard: 1(22) Have confidence in defining the lifestyle wanted to live (easiest); 2 (18) Have confidence in figuring out what you are and ready to sacrifice to achieve one's goals; 3 (23) Have confidence in finding information about graduate and professional schools; and 4 (19) Have confidence in talking with a person already employed in a field in which I am interested in.

The four hardest items are, in order from hardest to easier: 17 (10) Have confidence in finding out the employment trends for an occupation over the next ten years (hardest); 16 (4) Have confidence in determining the steps to take if you are having academic trouble with an aspect of your chosen major; 15 (3) Have confidence in making a plan of my goals for the next five years; and 14 (12) Have confidence that I can prepare a good resume. The high difficulty of these items probably reflect the low attention given to, and respect for, career decision making by many students in Hong Kong.

Table 11. Ordered Item Difficulties for Career Decision Making Self-Efficacy (I=17 Items) How much confidence do you have in performing the statement (item)?

No confidence at all	Very little confidence	Moderate confidence	Much confidence	Complete confidence

Item Number and Statement	Item Difficulty
1 (18) Figure out what you are and are not ready to sacrifice to achieve your career goals (Easiest)	-0.70
2 (22) Define the type of lifestyle that you would like to live	-0.70
3 (23) Find information about graduate and professional schools	-0.59
4 (19) Talk with a person already employed in a field in which you are interested in	-0.53
5 (9) Determine what your ideal job would be	-0.34
6 (8) Persistently work at your major or career goal even when you get frustrated	-0.29
7 (5) Accurately assess your abilities	-0.12
8 (11) Choose a career that will fit your preferred lifestyle	-0.11
9 (7) Determine the steps you need to take to successfully complete your chosen major	-0.08
10 (25) Identify some reasonable major or career alternatives, if you are unable to get your first choice	+0.03
11 (24) Successfully manage the job interview process	+0.06
12 (15) Find out about the average yearly earnings of people in an occupation	+0.07
13 (21) Identify employers, firms, and institutions relevant to your career possibilities	+0.18
14 (12) Prepare a good resume	+0.54
15 (3) Make a plan of your goals for the next five years	+0.69
16 (4) Determine the steps to take if you are having academic trouble with an aspect of your chosen major	+0.78
17 (10) Find out the employment trends for an occupation over the next ten years (Hardest)	+1.05

Item difficulties are in logits. Numbers in brackets are original item numbers.

Professor Nancy E. Betz (PhD) at Ohio State University (Department of Psychology) has kindly given permission to use the Career Decision Making Self-Efficacy Questionnaire in this research study and to publish the items in this book.

Further use of the Questionnaire and items by others requires permission from the copyright holder.

Inferences about Students with Low Self-Efficacy

Although it is not reported here for reasons of confidentiality, those students with the lowest measures of Career Decision Making Self-Efficacy can be identified and, because the measure has very good psychometric properties, this can be done with reliability and validity. This means that the career guidance teacher could, on a confidential basis, approach these students and provide them with advice and help. This measure could now be used for secondary schools in Hong Kong.

Those students with very low self-efficacy measures are listed by number in Table 12. These are the students who have said that they have no confidence at all, or very little confidence, in answering the 17 items of the Career Decision Making Self-Efficacy Questionnaire.

Person of ID 2 with the lowest Rasch linear measure (-3.68 logits) has a raw score of 7 which means that he or she answered no confidence at all to 10 items (each scored zero) and very little confidence to 7 items (each scored 1). In practice, the Guidance Counsellor could identify this student and interview him or her to see if the student can be helped in regard to career decision making. As another example, person of ID 19 had a low Rasch linear measure of -1.97 logits and a corresponding raw score of 17. This means that this person probably answered very little confidence to all 17 items of the scale and potentially can also be identified for counseling about career decision making.

Table 12. Persons with the Lowest Measures of Career Decision Making Self-Efficacy

ID	Raw Score	Location	SE	Residual
2	7	-3.68	0.47	+2.28
16	9	-3.28	0.44	-0.75
1	11	-2.93	0.42	+0.76
15	11	-2.93	0.42	-1.23
4	13	-2.59	0.41	-1.77
9	14	-2.43	0.40	+1.89
17	15	-2.27	0.40	+0.93
14	15	-2.27	0.40	+0.96
3	16	-2.12	0.39	-0.24
72	16	-2.12	0.39	+0.45
77	17	-1.97	0.39	-0.53
19	17	-1.97	0.39	-1.09

1. ID is the student identification number.
2. Raw score is total score on the 17 items (scored 0,1,2,3,4) of the scale.
3. Location is the Rasch linear scale measure in logits.
4. SE is the standard error.
5. Residual is the difference between the actual person score and that estimated from the Rasch model parameters.

SUMMARY OF THE RESULTS

Using the RUMM 2020 computer program, a reliable, unidimensional linear scale of Career Decision Making Self-Efficacy was created. Based on a Rasch Measurement Model (Partial Credit Model), the measure had:

(1) Good global item fit statistics;
(2) Acceptable global person fit statistics;
(3) Good individual item fit statistics (all 17 items fitted the model with p>0.05);
(4) A good item-trait interaction, showing that a unidimensional trait was measured;
(5) A good Person Separation Index showing that the person measures were well separated compared to the errors of the measurement;
(6) Ordered item thresholds;
(7) Response categories that were answered consistently and logically
(8) Item difficulties that target the person measures satisfactorily; and
(9) The items showed no significant differential functioning by gender or form.

These results mean that valid inferences could be made from the Career Decision-Making Self-Efficacy Scale (Betz, Klein and Taylor, 1996) such as that the mean measures are not significantly different by gender or form, and the easiest and hardest items can be identified.

REFERENCES

Andrich, D., Sheridan, B., and Luo, G. (2005). Rasch unidimensional measurement models: A windows-based item analysis employing Rasch models (RUMM2020). Perth: RUMM Laboratory.

Andrich, D., and van Schoubroeck, L. (1989). The general health questionnaire: a psychometric analysis using latent trait theory. *Psychological Medicine,* 1989 (19), 469-485.

Betz, N. E., Klein, K. A., and Taylor, K. M. (1996). Evaluation of a short form of the career decision making self-efficacy scale. *Journal of Career Assessment,* 4, 47-57.

Crites, J. O. (1995). *Career maturity inventory [revised form].* New York: Bridges.com.

Duster, T. (1987). Crime, youth unemployment and the Black urban underclass. *Crime and Delinquency, 33* (2), 300-316.

Education and Manpower Bureau, Hong Kong (2007). Retrieved on February 1, 2007, from *http://www.emb.gov.hk/*

Education Commission (1982). Education Commission Report No.3. Hong Kong: Hong Kong Government Printer.

Education Commission (1990). *Education Commission Report No. 4.* Hong Kong: Hong Kong Government Printer.

Education Commission (2000). *Learning for Life, Learning through Life: Reform Proposal for the Education System in Hong Kong.* Hong Kong: Hong Kong SAR Government.

Fryer, D. (1997). International perspectives on youth unemployment and mental health: Some central issues. *Journal of Adolescence,* 20, 333-42.

Hammer, T. (1996). Consequences of unemployment in the transition from youth to adulthood in a life course perspective. *Youth and Society*, 27 (4), 450-468.

High expectation and low commitment (2006, September 24). Singtao Daily. Retrieved September 24, 2006, from http://www.singtao.com

Hong Kong SAR government. (2001a). Introduction to project springboard. Retrieved November 4, 2001, from Education and Manpower Bureau Web site, http://www.info.gov.hk/emb/new/springboard/intro/intro.html

Hong Kong SAR government. (2001b). History of youth pre-employment training program (in Chinese). Retrieved November 4, 2001, from Labor Department Web site, *http://www.yptp.com.hk/index.php*

Hong Kong SAR government. (2002). Increased public concern about labour-related problems. Released on August 5, 2002 by Information Service Department. Hong Kong SAR Government. Retrieved September.14, 2002, from Wisenews Information Limited. *http://www.wisenews.net/hku/*

Hui, E. K. P. (1994). Teaching in Hong Kong: Guidance and counseling. Hong Kong: Longman.

High expectation and low commitment (2006, September 24). Singtao Daily. Retrieved September 24, 2006, from http://www.singtao.com

Lack of enthusiasm and responsibility, teenagers in HK are unemployable. (2001, December 12). The Mingpao News. Retrieved December 28, 2001, from Lam, M. P. (1986). Counseling and psychotherapy (in Chinese). Hong Kong: Commercial Press.

Leung, S. A. (1999). The development of counseling in Hong Kong: Searching for professional identity. *Asian Journal of Counseling*, 6 (2), 77-95.

Leung, S. A. (2002). Career counseling in Hong Kong: Meeting the social challenges. *The Career Development Quarterly,* 50(3), 237-245.

Leung, S. A., Leung, T. K. M., and Chan, E. P. O. (2003). Ethical counseling practice: A Survey of counseling teachers in Hong Kong secondary schools. *Asian Journal of Counseling,* 10 (1), 71-94.

Miller, F. W., Fruehling, J. A. and Lewis, G. J. (1978). Guidance principles and service. Charles E. Merill.

Rochleon, A. B., Mohr, J.J., and Hargrove B. K. (1999). Development of the attitudes towards career counseling scale. *Journal of Counseling Psychology*, 46 (2), 196-206.

RUMM Laboratory (2004). Interpreting RUMM2002. Retrieved June 6, 2007 at: *http://www.rummlab.com.au/*

Super, D. E. (1990). A life-span, life-space approach to career development. In D. Brown, L. Brooks, and associates (Eds.), Career choice and development: Applying contemporary theories to practice (pp. 197- 261). San Francisco: Jossey–Bass.

Thirty percent teenagers were unemployed (in Chinese). (2000, June 26). The Singtao Daily News. Retrieved December 28, 2001, from http://www.singtao.com

Tsang visited labor department and encourage youth (2007, August 10). Singtao Daily. Retrieved August 10, 2007, from http://www.singtao.com

Unemployed rate broke the record (2003, June 18). Apple Daily . Retrieved June 18, 2003, from http://appledaily.atnext.com

Waugh, R. F. (2006). Rasch measurement. In N. J. Salkind (Ed.), The encyclopedia of measurement and statistics (vol.3) (pp.820-825). Thousand Oaks, CA: Sage.

Yau, L. L. (1990). Student guidance (in Chinese). Hong Kong: Chinese University Press.

Yuen, M., Shea, P. M. K., Leung, T. K.M., Hui, E., Lau, P. S. Y., and Chan, R. M.C. (2003). Enhancing students' life skills development. In M. Yuen (Ed.), Life skills development and comprehensive guidance program: Theories and practices. Hong Kong: Faculty of Education, The University of Hong Kong.

Youth lack career counseling (2001, September 30). (in Chinese). Hong Kong Commercial Daily. Retrieved January 6, 2002, from WiseNews at: *http://www.wisenews.net/wisenews-cgi/enterprise/x?200109300010011*

In: Applications of Rasch Measurement in Education
Editor: Russell Waugh

ISBN: 978-1-61668-026-8
© 2010 Nova Science Publishers, Inc.

Chapter 7

A RASCH MEASURE OF ATTITUDE TOWARDS CAREER COUNSELING

Thomas Kin Man Leung[1] and Russell F. Waugh[2]
[1]Ching Chung Hau Po Woon Secondary School, Hong Kong
[2]Graduate School of Education, University of Western Australia

ABSTRACT

This paper follows through from the research in Chapter Six. Attitude Towards Career Counseling Scale (Rochleon, Mohr and Hargrove, 1999) was translated into Chinese. The scale involved 16 items answered in four Likert response categories scored from 1 to 4 (strongly disagree, disagree, agree, and strongly agree). Students came from Secondary 4 (13 years old) to Secondary 6 (15 years old) and included 103 females and 79 males. A Rasch analysis was used to create a linear, uni-dimensional scale with 15 items for 184 students . The item-trait chi-square was $\chi^2 = 33.89$, df = 30, $p = 0.28$ showing a very good overall fit to the measurement model. The Student Separation Index was 0.79 and the Cronbach Alpha was 0.79 showing good scale reliability. All 15 items fitted the measurement model with p>0.04. The 15 items were ordered from easy to hard providing good information relating to student Attitude towards Career Counseling.

BACKGROUND

The background to this paper is given in Chapter Six.
This chapter presents the results of the Rasch analysis for Attitude towards Career Counseling (Rochleon, Mohr and Hargrove, 1999) analysed using the computer program Rasch Unidimensional Measurement Models (RUMM2020) (Andrich, Sheridan, and Luo, 2005). This chapter is divided into two sections. Section One introduces the preliminary Rasch analysis results for the whole 16-item Attitude towards Career Counseling Scale. The table of threshold values is reported showing that one of the items, item 13, has disordered thresholds. The item 13 was then deleted and the Rasch analysis was repeated with the other 15 items of the Attitude towards Career Counseling Scale (Rochleon, Mohr and Hargrove, 1999). Section

Two summarizes the Rasch analysis results of the new 15-item Attitude towards Career Counseling Scale to support the claim that it is a unidimensional linear measurement. Global item and person fit table, item fit table, threshold table, category response curve, item characteristic curve of some good fitting items and target graph are presented. A summary of the main findings from RUMM2020 program analysis is also given at the end of this chapter.

Table 1. Item Thresholds for Attitudes towards Career Counseling (N=184, I=16)

Item	Threshold MEAN	Thresholds 1	2	3
1	0.54	-1.66	-0.27	1.93
2	-0.27	-1.53	0.15	1.39
3	0.38	-1.33	0.20	1.13
4	-0.51	-1.37	0.11	1.26
5	0.19	-1.68	-0.21	1.89
6	-0.10	-0.84	-0.30	1.14
7	0.11	-1.44	-0.67	2.11
8	-0.21	-1.17	-0.26	1.42
9	0.39	-2.03	-0.28	2.31
10	0.19	-2.07	0.17	1.90
11	0.21	-0.93	-0.54	1.47
12	0.13	-1.00	-0.06	1.06
13	-0.11	-0.63	-1.23*	1.86
14	-0.14	-1.54	-0.69	2.23
15	-0.31	-1.34	0.02	1.32
16	-0.48	-1.01	-0.96	1.96

(1) All items have four response categories (3 thresholds).
(2) Thresholds are points between adjacent categories where the odds are 1:1 of answering either category. (3) Mean threshold is the item difficulty in logits. *= disordered threshold.

Preliminary Rasch Analysis of the Attitude towards Career Counseling Scale

There were 16 items in the Attitude towards Career Counseling Scale (Rochleon, Mohr and Hargrove, 1999) and, after excluding several questionnaires with extreme scores, 184 responses were analysed with the RUMM2020 program. The item thresholds are listed in Table 1. Respondents chose one out of four Likert response categories (strongly disagree score 1, disagree score 2, agree score 3 and strongly agree score 4). The RUMM 2020 computer program calculates thresholds that are points between adjacent categories where there are odds of answering 1:1 in either category. When the response categories are answered consistently, the thresholds are ordered in line with the ordering of the response categories. The analysis showed that one item (item 13) had disordered thresholds indicating that the students did not answer this item consistently and logically.

Rasch Analysis Results of the 15-item Attitudes towards Career Counseling Measure

After deletion of item 13 which has disordered thresholds, the Rasch analysis was repeated. This section presents the re-analysis results with this scale created in order to support the claim that the measure is now unidimensional and linear. The analyses include: global fit of items and persons, individual item fit, item thresholds, response category curve and item characteristic curve for selected item.

Global Items-Person Fit Statistics

The summary of statistics of the 15-item Attitudes towards Career Counseling is presented in Table 2. The item-trait interaction chi-square = 33.89, df = 30, p=0.28. This indicates that there is no significant interaction between the person measures along the trait and the item difficulties. This means that there each person's attitude can be represented by a single parameter in his or her interaction with each item and that a unidimensional trait has been measured. The global item and person fit statistics are given in Table 3. When the data fit the Rasch measurement model, the fit statistics have a mean near zero and standard deviation near one. In this case, the items have a slightly better fit than the persons, but both are acceptable.

Table 2. Item-trait Interaction for Attitude towards Career Counseling (N=184, I=15)

Item-Trait Interaction		Reliability Indices
Total Item Chi Square	33.89	Separation Index = 0.79
Total Degree of Freedom	30.00	Cronbach Alpha = 0.79
Total Chi Square Probability 0.28		
Power of test-of-fit: GOOD (based on Separation Index)		

Table 3. Global Test-of-Fit Statistics for the Attitude towards Career Counseling Measure (N=184, I=15)

Item-Person Interactions				
Items			Persons	
	Location	Fit Residual	Location	Fit Residual
Mean	0.00	0.22	0.56	-0.51
SD	0.32	0.78	0.79	1.77

(1) The item means are constrained to zero by the measurement model.
(2) The means of the item and person fit statistics are 0.22 and -0.51 respectively. The standard deviations of the item and person fit statistics are 0.77 and 1.77 respectively. As the item and person fit statistics have a mean near zero, and standard deviations near one, they indicate that the data fit the Rasch Measurement Model.
(3) The standard errors are two decimal places, so numbers are given to two decimal places.

The Person Separation Index is 0.79 which indicates an acceptable person separation in comparison to the errors. This implies that the person locations are well spread out across the continuum (scale) compared to the errors and hence it is possible to tell whether persons with higher locations than others with lower locations tend to obtain higher scores on items or not (RUMM Laboratory, 2004). The item mean =0.00 (SD =0.32) and person mean = 0.56 (SD =

0.79) indicates that the targeting is acceptable and this is shown later when the targeting graphs are produced.

Table 4. Individual Item Fits to the Model for Attitude towards Career Counseling (I=15)

Item	Location	SE	Residual	df	Chi-Square	Probability
1	+0.52	0.10	+1.30	167.87	6.22	0.04
2	-0.28	0.10	+0.47	167.87	0.90	0.64
3	+0.37	0.09	+1.05	167.87	0.67	0.71
4	-0.52	0.10	-1.15	167.87	5.41	0.07
5	+0.18	0.11	+1.32	167.87	0.06	0.97
6	-0.10	0.09	-0.45	167.87	0.85	0.66
7	+0.10	0.11	-0.33	167.87	4.07	0.13
8	-0.22	0.10	-0.48	167.87	1.77	0.41
9	+0.38	0.11	+0.98	167.87	1.20	0.55
10	+0.18	0.11	+1.01	167.87	2.25	0.33
11	+0.21	0.10	+0.06	167.87	4.03	0.13
12	+0.13	0.09	+0.48	167.87	0.76	0.69
14	-0.15	0.12	-0.23	167.87	2.05	0.36
15	-0.32	0.10	-0.40	167.87	1.87	0.39
16	-0.48	0.12	-0.27	167.87	1.06	0.59

(1) No residual exceeds specific limits of greater or less than 2.00
(2) Location means item difficulties and SE means standard error.
(3) Residual means the difference between responses predicted from the Rasch measurement parameters and responses provided by the persons.
(4) Probability means the calculated chance of fit to the measurement model, based on the chi-square value and the degrees of freedom (DF).

Table 5. Item Thresholds for Attitude towards Career Counseling (N=183, I=15)

Item	Threshold Mean	Thresholds 1	2	3
1	+0.52	-1.13	+0.25	+2.45
2	-0.28	-1.81	-0.14	+1.12
3	+0.37	-0.96	+0.58	+1.50
4	-0.52	-1.90	-0.41	+0.74
5	+0.18	-1.51	-0.02	+2.06
6	-0.10	-0.94	-0.40	+1.04
7	+0.10	-1.33	-0.55	+2.19
8	-0.22	-1.38	-0.48	+1.20
9	+0.38	-1.62	+0.10	+2.67
10	+0.18	-1.89	+0.35	+2.07
11	+0.21	-0.73	-0.33	+1.68
12	+0.13	-0.88	+0.07	+1.20
14	-0.15	-1.68	-0.83	+2.05
15	-0.32	-1.67	-0.30	+1.01
16	-0.48	-1.46	-1.44	+1.46

(1) All items have three thresholds appropriately ordered in line with the four response categories.
(2) Thresholds are points between adjacent categories where the odds are 1:1 of answering either category.
(3) Mean threshold is the item difficulty in logits.

Item Residuals

Residuals are the difference between the observed values and the expected values estimated from the parameters of the Rasch measurement model. Table 4 shows the individual item fit for all 15 items.

The value of the residuals indicates that the difference between the responses predicted from the Rasch measurement parameters and responses provided by the respondents are within +/-2, and this indicates good agreement between the model predictions and the actual responses. The actual residuals of the items (from Table 4) are between -1.15 and 1.29. This reflects that the data are answered consistently and logically, and they fit the measurement model. All items have an acceptable fit to the measurement model with a probability greater than p>0.04.

Ordering of Response Categories

The RUMM 2020 computer program provides two checks on the answering of the response categories to examine whether the responses are given consistently and logically. The first is a table of thresholds (presented in Table 5) and the second check is the response category curves (presented in Figure 1).

Item Thresholds

The next step is to examine the item thresholds. The table of item thresholds of the 15-item Attitude towards Career Counseling measure is presented in the Table 7.5. The thresholds are points between adjacent response categories where the odds are 1:1 of answering in either category.

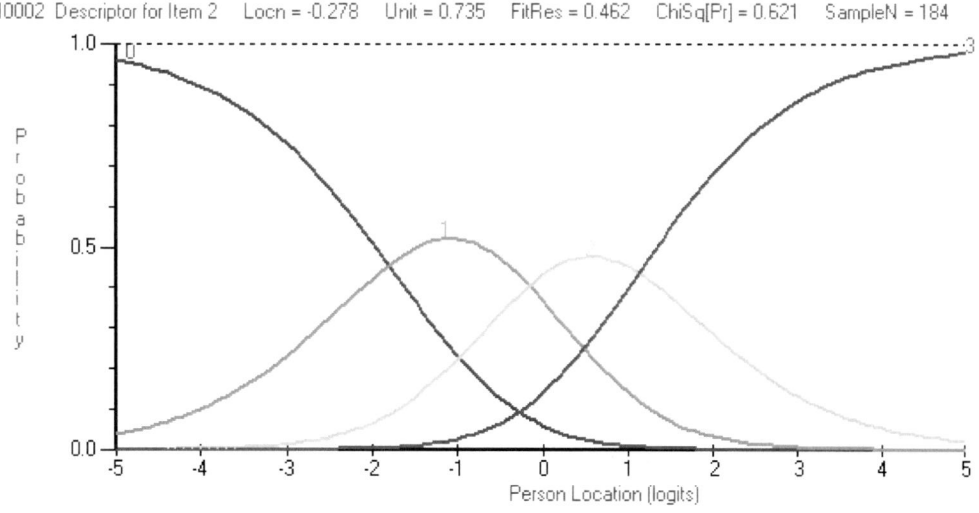

(1) The RUMM2020 computer program changes Response Categories 1,2, 3 and 4 to 0, 1, 2 and 3 respectively.
(2) Item 2 is located at 0.28 logits (item difficulty) with a fit residual of +0.46 and a probability of fit p= 0.62.

Figure 1. Characteristic Curve of Item 2 of Attitude towards Career Counseling.

There are four response categories in Attitude towards Career Counseling measure and hence there are three thresholds. If the thresholds are ordered, that means the response categories are answered consistently and logically. The thresholds are well ordered and this indicates that the responses were answered consistently and logically.

Response Category Curves

The Response Category Curves are also used for checking consistency of responses. The Response Category Curve of item 2 (item 2, difficulty = 0.28, probability of fit = 0.64) of the measure is displayed in Figure 1. All the other Response Category Curves were satisfactory.

The Response Category Curve in Figure 1 shows that, as the person measures increase along the scale, the probability of answering in the higher response categories increases, as required of good measurement. Each of the Category Curves of the 15 items of Attitude towards Career Counseling measure were examined and they were all satisfactory although, in some items, the persons did not use some categories as often as others. This was most probably due to the relatively low number of persons (N=184), rather than a more ideal number for Rasch analysis that would be closer to N=400.

Item Characteristic Curves

The Item Characteristic Curves show how well the item differentiates between persons with measures above or below the item location. In other words, the curve shows how the expected values vary for person measures above and below the item difficulty. The Item Characteristic Curve of Item 2 of the Attitude towards Career Counseling measure is shown on Figure 2.

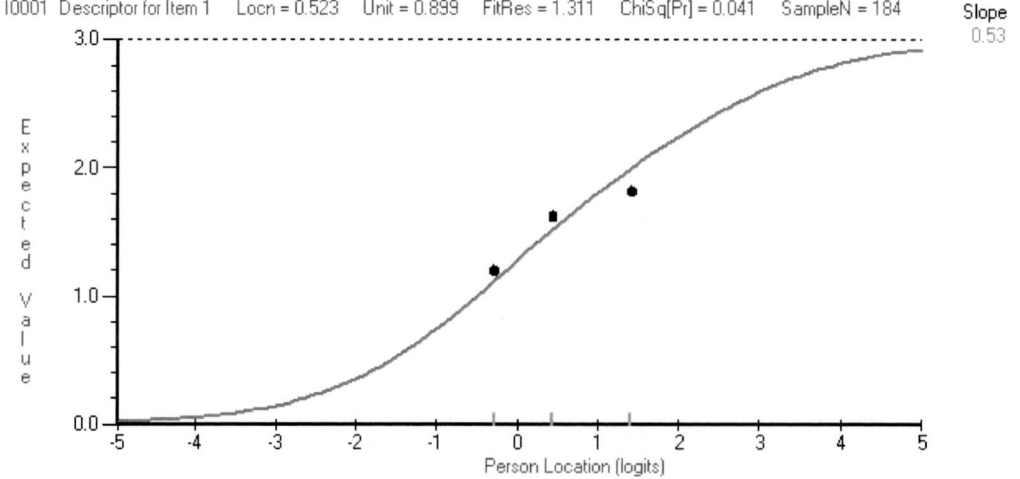

Figure 2. The Item Characteristic Curve for Item 2 of Attitude towards Career Counseling.

Item Differential Functioning

The RUMM2020 computer program produces Item Characteristic Curves for all 15 items, differentiated by gender and, separately, by Form (grade level). These curves and their associated statistics were inspected for differential functioning. There was no significant difference between how males and females answered the items or between how Form 6 and Form 4 students answered the items. An example of the Item Characteristic Curve, differentiated by gender is given in Figure 3 and by form in Figure 4.

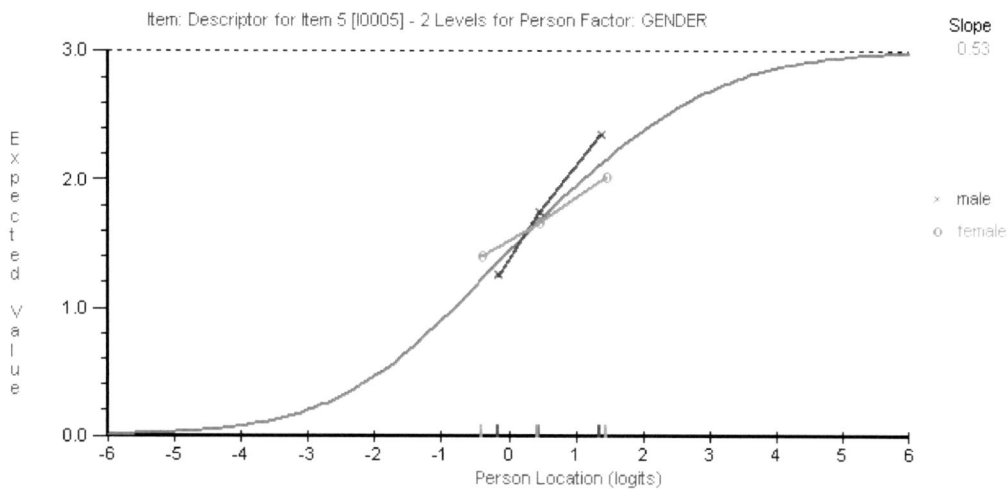

The differences by gender are not statistically significant: $F_{(2,1)}=0.64$, $p=0.42$.

Figure 3. Item 5 Characteristic Curve for Attitude towards Career Counseling Differentiated by Gender.

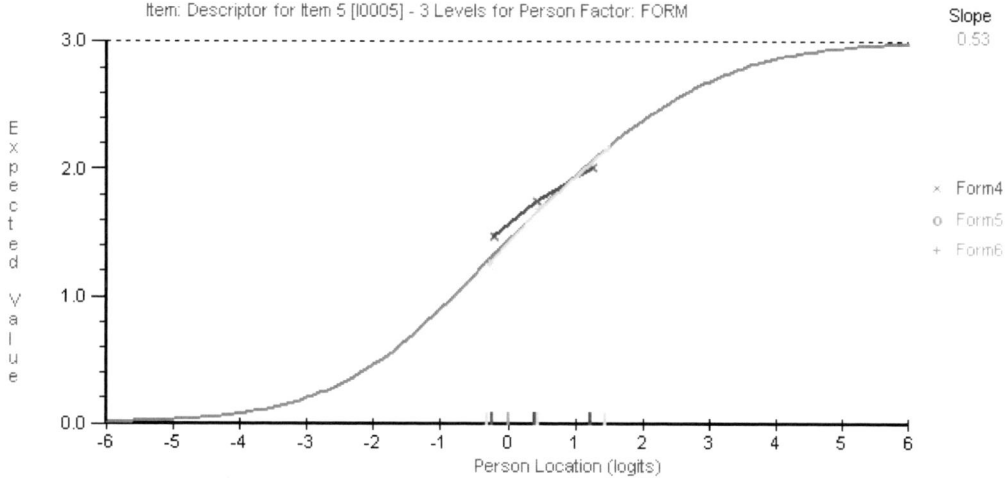

The Differences by Form are not statistically significant: $F_{(2,1)}=0.03$, $p=0.87$.

Figure 4. Item 5 Characteristic Curve for Attitude towards Career Counseling Differentiated by Form.

Targeting

Targeting refers to how well the item difficulties are distributed along the scale in respect to the person measures. A scale with good targeting should have some easier, medium and harder items that are suitable to respondents with different person measures. The RUMM2020 program generates a Person Measure/Item Thresholds graph showing how the person measures are distributed along the variable and how the item thresholds are distributed along the same variable (measured in logits). Figure 5 shows that the targeting of the item thresholds against the person measures is good.

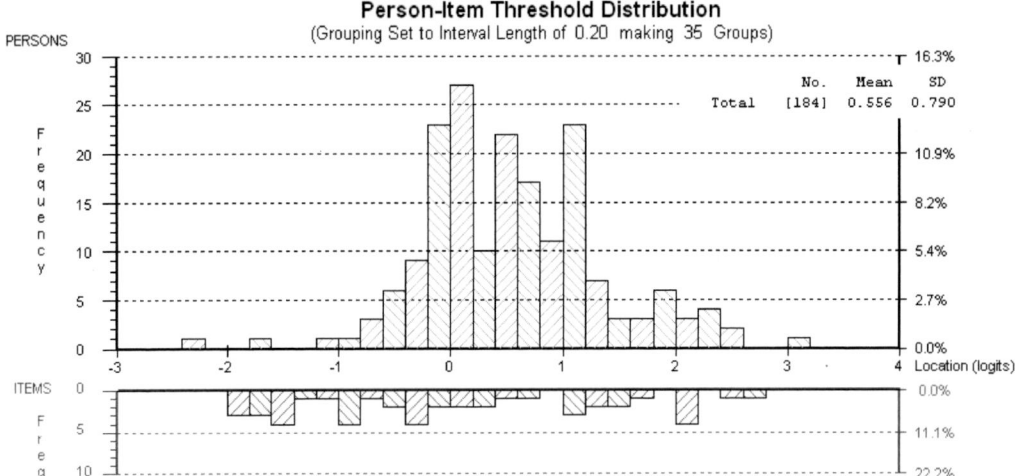

(1) Person measures are on the top of the scale in logits and item thresholds are on the bottom of the scale.

(2) The person measures range from -2.3 logits to +3.1 logits and the item thresholds range from -2.00 logits to +2.9 logits showing that the targeting is good.

Figure 5. Person Measure-Item Threshold Graph for the Attitude towards Career Counseling.

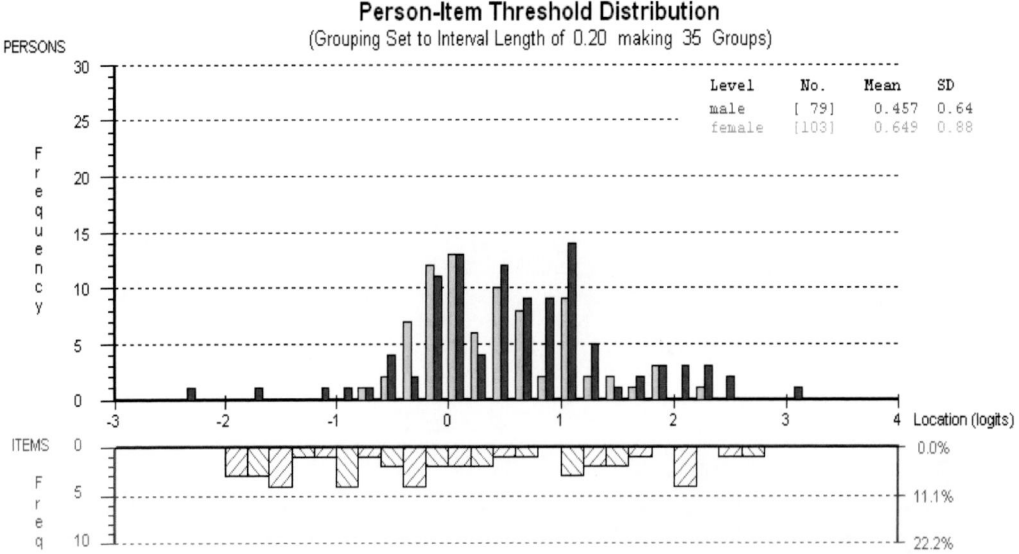

There is a colour error in the graph due to the RUMM program. Green is males (79) and purple is females (103).

Figure 6. Person Measure-Item Threshold Graph for the Attitude towards Career Counseling By Gender.

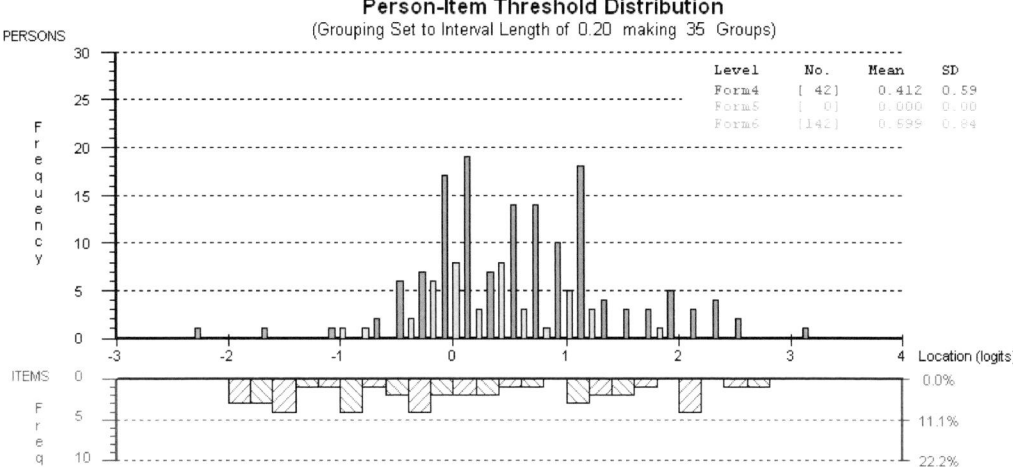

There is a colour error in the graph due to the RUMM program. Green is Form 4 (42) and Purple is Form 6 (142).

Figure 7. Person Measure-Item Threshold Graph for the Attitude towards Career Counseling By Form.

Table 6. Ordered Item Difficulties for Attitude towards Career Counseling (I=15 Items) Do you: Strongly Disagree, Disagree, Agree or Strongly Agree with the Items

Item Number and Statement	Item Difficulty
1 (4) Talking to a career therapist is not a sign of weakness. *	-0.52 (easiest)
2 (16) Career counseling is a valuable resource in making a career choice	-0.48
3 (15) I would not be too embarrassed to ever schedule an appointment with a career counsellor. *	-0.32
4 (2) Having to see a counsellor to talk about career-related concerns is not a sign of indecisiveness. *	-0.28
5 (8) In all likelihood, a career counseling experience for me would not be very depressing. *	-0.22
6 (14) Career counseling can be an effective way to learn what is best suited to my interests	-0.15
7 (6) I don't fear the negative stigma associated with seeing a career counsellor. *	-0.10
8 (7) If a career-related dilemma aroused me, I would be pleased to know that career counseling services are available.	+0.10
9 (12) Having to see a counsellor to talk about career issues is a very private matter that should not be discussed with anyone.	+0.13
10 (5) If I was in a career transition, I would value the opportunity to see a career counsellor	+0.18
11 (10) My feelings about counseling in general would not make me hesitant to see a career counsellor.*	+0.18
12 (11) If I were seeing a career counsellor, I would not be against anyone knowing about it.*	+0.21
13 (3) If I were having trouble choosing a major, I would not hesitate to schedule an appointment with a career counsellor	+0.37
14 (9) With so many different ways to get help on career-related decisions, I see career counseling as relatively important .	+0.38
15 (1) I could easily imagine how career counseling could be beneficial to me.	+0.52 (hardest)

Item difficulties are in logits. Numbers in brackets are original item numbers. * Some items have been reversed for their correct scale meaning.

Professor Aaron Rochlen (PhD) at the University of Texas at Austin (Department of Educational Psychology) has kindly given permission to use the Attitude Towards Career Counseling Questionnaire in this research study and to publish the items in this book. Further use of the Questionnaire and items by others requires permission from the copyright holder.

Measures by Gender and Form

The data analysis has shown that there is a good fit to the measurement model and that the data form a reliable, unidimensional scale and so valid inferences can be made from this scale. Figure 6 shows the Person Measures/Item Thresholds by gender. The females have a higher Attitude to Career Counseling measure than the males but this is not statistically significant (t = 1.63, df = 180, p=0.06).

Figure 7 shows the Person Measures/Item Thresholds by form. Form 6 students have a higher Attitude to Career Counseling measure than Form 4 students but this is not statistically significant (t = 1.33, df = 180, p= 0.09).

Inferences About the Easiest and Hardest Items

Table 6 shows the item difficulties for Attitude towards Career Counseling. The lower the item difficulty, the lower the measure of Attitude to Career Counseling needed to answer positively and, conversely, the higher the item difficulty, the higher the measure of Attitude towards Career Counseling needed to answer positively.

The four easiest items for Attitude to Career Counseling are, in order from easy to hard: 1(4) Agreeing that talking to a therapist regarding career issues is not a sign of weakness (easiest); 2 (16) Agreeing that career counseling is a valuable resource in making a career choice; 3 (15) Agreeing that I would not be too embarrassed to schedule an appointment with a career counsellor; and 4 (2) Agreeing that having to see a counsellor to talk about career-related concerns is not a sign of indecisiveness.

The four hardest items are, in order from hardest to easier: 15 (1) I could easily imagine how career counseling could be beneficial for me (hardest); 14 (9) With so many different ways to get help on career-related decisions, I see career counseling as relatively important; 13 (3) If I were having trouble choosing a major, I would not hesitate to schedule an appointment with a career counsellor; and 12 (11) If I was seeing a career counsellor, I would not be against anyone knowing about it. These items are probably difficult because some students in Hong Kong have a negative stigma against career counseling.

Inferences about Students with Low Attitude towards Career Counseling

Those students with the very lowest Attitude are listed by number in Table 7. These are the students who have said that they strongly disagree, or disagree, in answer to the 15 items of the Attitude towards Career Counseling Questionnaire. Person of ID 7 with the lowest Rasch linear measure (-2.33 logits) has a raw score of 5 which means that he or she answered strongly disagree to all 10 items (each scored zero) and disagree to 5 items (each scored 1). In practice, the Guidance Counsellor could identify this student and interview him or her to see if the student's Attitude to Career Counseling can be improved (or least find out why it is so poor). As another example, person of ID 9 had a low Rasch linear measure of -0.36 logits and a corresponding raw score of 20. This means that this person answered disagree to 10 items of the scale (scored 1) and agree to only five items (scored 2), and potentially can also be identified for counseling about improving his or her attitude. In another words, the Attitude towards Career Counseling Scale could be used as a screening instrument for career counseling in schools. Career counsellor could, on a confidential basis, approach these students and provide them with advice and help. This measure could now be used for all secondary schools in Hong Kong.

Table 7. Persons with Lowest Measures of Attitude towards Career Counseling

ID	Raw Score	Location	SE	Residual
7	5	-2.33	0.47	+0.57
6	9	-1.65	0.38	+2.63
8	13	-1.13	0.35	+0.02
10	15	-0.90	0.34	-1.27
27	16	-0.79	0.34	+1.71
107	17	-0.68	0.33	+3.01
12	17	-0.68	0.33	-1.72
26	18	-0.57	0.33	+0.83
36	18	-0.57	0.33	-0.39
24	18	-0.57	0.33	+1.40
1	19	-0.47	0.33	+1.56
11	19	-0.47	0.33	-0.65
35	19	-0.47	0.33	-1.57
5	20	-0.36	0.33	+2.79
53	20	-0.36	0.33	-2.09
57	20	-0.36	0.33	-1.74
9	20	-0.36	0.33	-0.64

(1) ID is the student identification number.
(2) Raw score is total score on the 15 items (scored 0,1,2,3) of the scale.
(3) Location is the Rasch linear scale measure in logits.
(4) SE is the standard error.
(5) Residual is the difference between the actual person score and that estimated from the Rasch model parameters.
(6) Numbers are given to two decimal places because the errors are to two decimal places.

SUMMARY OF THE RESULTS

Using the RUMM2020 computer program, a reliable linear scale of Attitude towards Career Counseling Measure was created. Based on a Rasch Measurement Model (Partial Credit Model), the measure had:

(1) Acceptable global item fit statistics and acceptable global person fit statistics;
(2) Good individual item fit statistics (all 15 items fitted the model with p.>0.04);
(3) A good item-trait interaction, showing that a unidimensional trait was measured (chi-square =33.89, df=30, p=0.28);
(4) A good Person Separation Index showing that the person measures were well separated compared to the errors of the measurement (PSI= 0.80) and good reliability (Cronbach Alpha =0.80) ;
(5) Ordered item thresholds showing that the response categories were answered consistently and logically;
(6) Item thresholds that target the person measures well.

The results presented in this chapter mean that valid inferences could be made from the scale. Thus it was concluded that the mean measures for males and females were not statistically significantly different and the mean measures for Secodary 6 and Seconary 4 were not statistically significantly different.

REFERENCES

Andrich, D., Sheridan, B., and Luo, G. (2005). *Rasch unidimensional measurement models: A windows-based item analysis employing Rasch models* (RUMM2020). Perth: RUMM Laboratory.

Rochleon, A. B., Mohr, J.J., and Hargrove B. K. (1999). Development of the attitudes towards career counseling scale. *Journal of Counseling Psychology,* 46 (2), 196-206.

In: Applications of Rasch Measurement in Education
Editor: Russell Waugh
ISBN: 978-1-61668-026-8
© 2010 Nova Science Publishers, Inc.

Chapter 8

BACKGROUND TO THE CHINESE LANGUAGE TESTING AT CAMBRIDGE "A" LEVEL STANDARD (FOR CHAPTERS 9 AND 10)

Ong Chun Ghee[1] and Russell Waugh[2]
[1]. Dunman High School
[2]. Graduate School of Education,
University of Western Australia

MOCK 'A' LEVEL CHINESE LANGUAGE TEST

The Mock 'A' Level Chinese Language Test was modelled after the present Singapore-Cambridge GCE 'A' Level examinations, of which the teaching and examination syllabus are offered by the Singapore Ministry of Education (2006c) and Singapore Examinations and Assessment Board (2008b). Following the GCE 'A' Level Chinese Language and Literature H2 examination syllabus, the Mock 'A' Level Test contains 32 test items in two papers (see Appendix B and C), with each paper taking three hours to complete. In 2008 Singapore GCE 'A' Level examinations, the Chinese Language and Literature H2 Paper 1 was a three-hour paper on 30th October and the Paper 2 was also a three-hour paper on 31st October (Singapore Examinations and Assessment Board, 2008c). Simulating the actual examination arrangements, the Mock 'A' Level Test was conducted over two days to ensure that the research participants experienced less fatigue taking the two papers.

After six hours of examinations, the Mock 'A' Level Test was assessed according to the marking scheme as described below in Table 1. Note that the marking scheme was devised solely by Ong Chun Ghee because the Chinese Language and Literature H2 subject syllabus provided by the Ministry of Education (2006c) does not provide any specific scoring rubrics or marking scheme.

Table 1. Marking Scheme of Mock GCE 'A' Level Chinese Language Test

Paper / Item no.	Task (Marks)	Scoring Rubrics			
		Content (17 marks)		Expression (18 marks)	
P 1 / Item 1-2	Write an essay of more than 600 words. The test user chooses one of the four topics or titles provided (35) *Due to the marking scheme, the essay writing task is broken up into two components, namely content (Item 1) and expression (Item 2)*	15-17	Able to provide thoughtful insights about the topic	15-18	Excellent readability, good writing flair and vocabulary knowledge
		12-14	Able to develop more substantial content from the question topic	12-14	Few or no spelling mistakes, essay is easy to read
		9-11	Answers to the question, presented sufficient points	9-11	Few spelling mistakes, the paragraphs do not link up well
		6-8	Partly relevant to the question topic, some related points included	6-8	Little grammar and spelling mistakes, some sentences do not link up
		3-5	Totally irrelevant to the question topic, out of point	3-5	Some grammar and spelling mistakes, few paragraphs incomprehensible
		0-2	Little or nothing written, out of point	0-2	Poor sentence structure, whole essay does not make any sense
P 1 / Item 3-5	Translate ancient Chinese vocabulary terms (6)	No scoring rubrics available, as these are dichotomous items with standard answers provided			
P 1 / Item 6-7	Translate ancient Chinese sentences (8)	0-3	More than half of the sentence wrongly translated	4-8	Few or no mistake in translation
P 1 / Item 8	Briefly answer one question relevant to the same passage (6)	0-1	Almost all or all of the key points are answered wrongly	4-5	At least three key points are answered correctly
		2-3	At least two key points are answered correctly	6	All key points are answered correctly
P 1 / Item 9	Briefly answer one short question about from an ancient Chinese passage (5)	0-1	Almost all or all of the key points are answered wrongly	4-5	At least two key points are answered correctly
		2-3	At least one key points are answered correctly	6	All key points are answered correctly
P 1 / Item 10	Fill in the blanks in a modern Chinese cloze passage (5)	No scoring rubrics available, as the five questions are dichotomous items with standard answers provided			
P 1 / Item 11	Answer one comprehension question of a short passage (4)	0-2	Almost all or all of the points are answered wrongly	3-4	At least two key points are answered correctly
P 1 / Item 12	Answer one comprehension question from the same passage (5)	Scoring rubrics is the same as Item 5			
P 1 / Item 13	Answer one comprehension question from the same passage (6)	Scoring rubrics is the same as Item 4			

Paper / Item no.	Task (Marks)	Scoring Rubrics			
P 1 / Item 14	Answer one multiple-choice question about a new passage (2)	No scoring rubrics available, as this is a dichotomous item with standard answers provided			
P 1 / Item 15	Briefly answer one comprehension question of the same passage (2)	0-1		Almost all or all of the points are answered wrongly	
P 1 / Item 16	Tick two statements that best describe the same passage (4)	No scoring rubrics available, as this is a dichotomous item with standard answers provided. Each correct tick earns 2 marks			
P 1 / Item 17-18	Summarize the same passage into an abstract of 120 words (12) *Similar to the essay writing task in Item 1 and 2, the summary writing consist of two components, namely content (8) and expression (4)	Content		Expression	
		6-8	Five or all of the six key points are included.	4	Fluent expression with at most one grammar mistake
		3-5	Two to four key points are included.	2-3	Few grammar mistakes
		0-2	One or no key point included	0-1	Many disjointed sentences and grammatical errors
P 2 / Item 19-20; 21-22; 23-24; 25-26	Write four short critiques of about selected Tang, Song dynasty and modern poetry (40) *Each critique (10 marks) consists of two components – outlining the analysis key points (Item 19, 21, 23, 25 for the four critiques) and elaborating arguments (Item 20, 22, 24, 26 for the four critiques)	4-5 per item	All key points are clearly defined	4-5 per item	Relevant and in-depth review with all vital quotes listed
		2-3 per item	Partly relevant to the question, at least two points are included	2-3 per item	Elaboration is not focused enough with some irrelevant quotes
		0-1 per item	Little or nothing written, totally out of point	0-1 per item	No elaboration with little or no quotes
P 2 / Item 27-28; 29-30; 31-32	Write three analyses of one short novel, a three-scene drama play and a Chinese sword-fighting novel (60) *Each analysis (20 marks) consists of two components – outlining the analysis key points (Item 27, 29, 31 for the three analyses) and elaborating arguments (Item 28, 30, 32 for the three analyses)	9-10 per item	All key points are clearly defined	9-10 per item	Relevant and in-depth review with all vital quotes listed
		6-8 per item	Most key points are defined	6-8 per item	Focused elaboration with most quotes provided.
		3-5 per item	Only two to three key points are defined	3-5 per item	Elaboration is not focused enough with some irrelevant quotes
		0-2 per item	Little or nothing written, totally out of point	0-2 per item	No elaboration with little or no quotes

Source: Designed by Ong Chun Ghee for this study (2009)

The Mock 'A' Level Test covers a wide range of language assessment modes, ranging from cloze passage to literature analysis. In the various assessment sections, test item difficulties vary significantly from elementary syntax and semantic knowledge to advanced analytic and interpretive skills in literature review writing. The wide range of item-difficulties and the numerous test items set in a single test may affect the test reliability, as the thresholds of the test items are more complex to be ordered from easy to hard. This implies that the Mock 'A' Level Test may be susceptible to inconsistent scoring. The long hours of assessment may likely aggravate the problem, as the Chinese Language and Literature H2 papers take a total of six hours of writing assessment during the GCE 'A' Level examinations (Singapore Examinations and Assessment Board, 2008c).

In addition, the test sample size may likely be constricted due to the fact that there is only an estimate of 400 language students studying GCE 'A' Level Chinese language in the Chinese Language Elective Programme and Bicultural Studies Programme[1] each year, and not many of them are willing to prepare for and go through the six-hour mock language test research. The sample size of possibly less than 150 participants may cause inconsistency in scoring, as RUMM 2020 usually needs about 300 to 500 persons to yield reliable measurement scales.

In order to overcome these constraints of assessment format and sampling size, the 32 test items in the Mock 'A' Level Test were categorized into three separate parts, namely the *basic*, *intermediate* and *advanced* language skill categories and analyzed separately. The classification of items into the three categories will be described in the next section where the theoretical Form-Semantic-Pragmatic Language Learning Model (Goh and Silver, 2004, 2006) is reviewed to explain the ordering of the item-difficulty categories.

CATEGORISATION OF ITEM-DIFFICULTIES IN MOCK 'A' LEVEL CHINESE LANGUAGE TEST

According to the Form-Semantic-Pragmatic Language Learning Model (Goh and Silver, 2004, 2006), advanced literacy and pragmatics are observed in the later stages of language learning, while basic knowledge in form and semantics are developed earlier. Applying this language learning model to the Mock 'A' Level Test, the basic, intermediate and advanced language skill categories can be established according the types of language competency involved.

Firstly, the basic language skill category includes test items that involve route learning with only elementary grammar and vocabulary knowledge required. These basic language skills can be represented by the language Form and Semantic components in Goh and Silver's Form-Semantic-Pragmatic Language Learning Model (2004, 2006). In these two components, knowledge of grammar and vocabulary are considered foundational language skills that can be assessed in conventional test formats such as cloze passages and vocabulary quizzes. Hence, the Mock 'A' Level Test items such as the cloze passage and the ancient Chinese vocabulary translation in Paper 1 (see Appendix B) can be classified under this category where foundational language skills are needed for most test users to answer these items correctly.

---

1 While it is an obligatory requirement for Chinese Language Elective Programme students to study GCE 'A' Level Chinese Language and Literature H2, it is optional for Bicultural Studies Programme students to study Chinese at 'A' Level.

Secondly, the intermediate language skill category contains items that require higher levels of literacy in reading and writing. According Goh and Silver (2004, 2006) and Christie (2002), literacy competency undergoes significant developments for adolescent learning languages, and is usually evident after the language form and basic semantic knowledge are acquired. An example is the Mock 'A' Level Paper 1 essay writing task (see Table 1) in which test users need to exhibit writing literacy in their works, and hence usually find more challenging than cloze passages.

Lastly, the advanced language skill category involves advanced literacy and analytical expression skills. These higher levels of language competency can be represented by the advanced pragmatic component in the same Form-Semantic-Pragmatic Language Learning Model (Goh and Silver, 2004). According to the learning model, mature adolescents who have acquired the pragmatic skills are "able to analyse and present points of view regarding abstract concepts", and to "develop and present arguments in a logical manner" (Goh and Silver, 2006, p. 238). For these advanced language learners, writing topical essays may not necessarily provide the platform to exhibit higher levels of language skills, as writing such essays usually involve little creativity[2] with students mostly focused on topic relevance and error-free expression. On the other hand, the Paper 2 literature analyses (see Items 19 to 32 in Table 1), which require students to review and evaluate literature works, are more likely to elicit language performances at higher competency levels. In these literature analyses, students are expected to outline key points and further elaborate with supporting quotes from the literature texts. While defining the key points can be relatively easier to prepare from study notes, selecting the appropriate quotes and elaborating arguments to answer the question are more challenging. The students may even have to express their own views and provide alternative perspectives to add depth to their reviews. All these assessment needs certainly require advanced levels of analytical and expression skills to be employed, and hence the Paper 2 literature analyses (elaborating arguments) are classified under the advanced language skill category.

After defining the three language skill categories, all the Mock 'A' Level Test items were rated and classified into the respective categories.

Although the Form-Semantic-Pragmatic Language Learning Model (Goh and Silver, 2004, 2006) helps to determine the characteristics of each category, a pilot test still needs to be conducted with the students to confirm the categorization of every test item. In the pilot test conducted with three junior college students, the participants were briefed about the items they needed to categorise and were allowed to rate "basic", "intermediate" or "advanced" for each test item or component. At the end of the pilot test, it was interesting to note that while all three pilot test participants agreed unanimously on the items rated as "basic", some participants revealed that there were components in the a single test item which ought to be classified separately in intermediate and advanced categories. For example, the Paper 2 literature analysis required that the test participants to outline the key points and elaborate the arguments with literature quotes. The test participants acknowledged that the former should be categorized as "intermediate", while the latter categorised as "advanced", because the two components demand distinct levels of skills. This categorization is applied to all literature analysis test items (P2/19 to P2/32) in the Mock 'A' Level Test, as shown in Table 2.

---

[2] An example is the 2005 GCE 'A' Level examinations' essay topic -- "Discuss about money and life" (" 论金钱与人生"), which produced mostly essays of similar content about physical and spiritual wealth.

Table 2. Categorisation of test items in the pilot testing of Mock 'A' Level Test

Paper/ Item no.	Assessment Task		Language Skill Category
P1/1	Write an essay of at least 600 words. The marking scheme consists of "content" and "expression" components	Content	Intermediate
P1/2		Expression	Intermediate
P1/ 3-5	Ancient Chinese vocabulary translation question 1 to 3		Basic
P1/6-7	Ancient Chinese sentence translation question 1 to 2		Intermediate
P1/8-9	Ancient Chinese comprehension question 1 to 2		Basic
P1/10	Modern Chinese cloze passage		Basic
P1/11-13	3 comprehension questions based on the cloze passage		Basic
P1/14	1 multiple-choice comprehension question on a modern Chinese passage		Basic
P1/15	1 free-response question on the same passage in P1/14		Basic
P1/16	Tick 2 statements that represent the passage in P1/14		Basic
P1/17-18	Summarize the P1/14 passage into an 120-word abstract		Basic
P2/19, P2/21, P2/23, P2/25	4 short critiques on ancient and contemporary poems. Each critique is assessed in two parts, namely "outlining key points" and "elaborating arguments" components	Outlining answer key points	Intermediate
P2/20, P2/22, P2/24, P2/26		Elaborating arguments	Advanced
P2/27, P2/29, P2/31	3 long critiques each analyses 1 short novel, 1 drama play and 1 novel. Each critique is assessed in two parts, namely "outlining key points" and "elaborating arguments" components	Outlining answer key points	Intermediate
P2/28, P2/30, P2/32		Elaborating arguments	Advanced

Sources: Ministry of Education (2006c, pp.1-2), Ong (2009).

As shown in Table 2, the pilot testing had helped to create successfully three item-difficulty categories with 14 items in the basic category, 14 items in the intermediate category, and 13 items in the advanced category. The even distribution of the test items ensures that the each categorical part of the Mock 'A' Level Test can be analysed in the RUMM 2020 (Andrich, Sheridan and Luo, 2005) to yield individual tests of fit. However, the test items classified within its individual category will still need to be ranked in item-difficulty in preparation for data collection and analysis. Hence, the second part of the pilot testing has to be conducted to determine the internal ordering of test items within each of the three categories, all of which will be explained in the next three sections.

ORDERING OF DIFFICULTIES IN THE BASIC MOCK 'A' LEVEL TEST

According to the item-difficulty ratings in Table 2, the basic category consists of 14 test items (P1/3 to P1/5 and P1/8 to P1/18). The first three test items in Paper 1 (P1/3 to P1/5) are vocabulary translations of selected ancient Chinese passages, of which the vocabulary translation items P1/3, P1/4 and P1/5 are unanimously rated as the easiest of all during the pilot test. This is because the three items can be answered by regurgitating the modern Chinese translation answers from prepared study notes, such as the published notes by Nanyang Junior College (2006, pp. 7-68). Similarly, P1/8 and P1/9 are ancient Chinese comprehension questions that can be answered using the same prepared study notes, but with more content to memorize and therefore ranked as the next easiest in the basic category. In answering all of these five test items, all of the pilot test participants concurred that they only needed to prepare and regurgitate the study notes of the seven selected ancient Chinese proses stated in the GCE 'A' Level syllabus (Singapore Examinations and Assessment Board, 2008b).

Table 3. Similarities between the Mock GCE 'A' Level Chinese Language Test Paper 1 and the GCE 'O' Level Higher Chinese Language examinations

Paper / Item no.	Mock GCE 'A' Level Language Test Paper 1 (Marks)	GCE 'O' Level Higher Chinese Language Examinations
P1/10	Cloze passage (5)	Cloze passage
P1/11	1 free-response comprehension question on the cloze passage (4)	5 multiple-choice questions, 3 free-response questions and 4 vocabulary questions on 2 comprehension passages
P1/12	1 free-response comprehension question on the same cloze passage (5)	
P1/13	1 free-response comprehension question on the same cloze passage (6)	
P1/14	1 multiple-choice question on another comprehension passage (2)	
P1/15	1 free-response question requiring a one-sentence answer (2)	
P1/16	Tick 2 statements that best summarize the same passage in P1/14 (4)	12 free-response questions on another 2 comprehension passages and summarize 1 of the 2 passages into an 80-word abstract
P1/17-18	Summarise the passage in P1/14 into a 120-word abstract (12)	

Sources: Ministry of Education (2005c, 2006c).

The next eight basic category items in Paper 1 (P1/10 to P1/18) include various comprehension questions and cloze passages, of which the assessment formats pilot test participants found to be very close to that assessed during their secondary school examinations (Singapore Examinations and Assessment Board, 2008a). In investigation of their feedback, the GCE 'A' Level Chinese Language and Literature Paper 1 and GCE 'O' Level Higher Chinese Language examinations are compared in Table 3 and at least three similarities in assessment format are found.

Among all the similar test items in Table 3, cloze passage in P1/10 was rated the easiest after the ancient Chinese translation questions. The cloze passage in the Mock 'A' Level Test provides five blanks with ten choice words to select from the box (see Appendix B). In one participant's opinion, the chances of getting the cloze passage answers correct are "almost 50/50, better than the 1-in-4 multiple choice questions", which led the participants to rank the cloze passage as easier than the multiple choice questions in the Mock 'A' Level Test. After the cloze passage, three short comprehension questions P1/11, P1/12 and P1/13 were ranked next.

These three questions were designed in the "describe-define-exemplify[3]" format, which is similar to the secondary GCE 'O' Level comprehension in the Higher Chinese Language papers.

The two multiple-choice questions P1/14 and P1/16 reminded the pilot test participants of their secondary school comprehension papers. However, these two questions were slightly more challenging as the passages were generally longer than the cloze passage in the previous set of comprehension questions (P1/11, P1/12 and P1/13).

Table 4. Ordering of item-difficulties in the Basic Mock 'A' Level Test

Paper / Item	Task (Marks)	Ordering
P1/3	Translate ancient Chinese vocabulary terms (2) (easiest)	1
P1/4	Translate ancient Chinese vocabulary terms (2)	1
P1/5	Translate ancient Chinese vocabulary terms (2)	1
P1/8	One comprehension question on an ancient Chinese passage (6)	2
P1/9	One comprehension question on an ancient Chinese passage (5)	3
P1/10	Cloze passage (5)	4
P1/11	1 free-response comprehension question on the cloze passage (4)	5
P1/12	1 free-response comprehension question on the cloze passage (5)	6
P1/13	1 free-response comprehension question on the cloze passage (6)	7
P1/14	1 multiple-choice question on another passage (2)	8
P1/16	Tick 2 statements that best summarize the passage in P1/14 (4)	9
P1/15	1 free-response comprehension question (2)	10
P1/17	Summarize the passage in P1/14 – Content (8)	11
P1/18	Summarize the passage in P1/14 – Expression (4) (hardest)	12

Source: Ong Chun Ghee (2009).

Therefore, P1/14 and P1/16 were ranked eighth and ninth respectively after the cloze passage, with P1/16 rated as slightly more difficult because it required the participants to choose two out of four statements that best represent the passage theme. After the two multiple-choice questions, one short free-response comprehension test item P1/15 was ordered to be more difficult. It was because this two-mark question required students to conclude the meaning of the entire passage in a few concise sentences. The pilot test participants found this question hardest among all comprehension free-response questions and hence ranked P1/15 at the tenth place.

The last two items in P1/17 and P1/18 left are the "content" and "expression" components in summary writing. Although the total score of the summary writing is 12 marks, test participants had been briefed that the summarized abstract would be assessed in two parts, which are the "content" key points (8 marks) and "expression" sentence fluency (4 marks). Between the two components, the participants ranked P1/18 (expression) harder than P1/17 (content) because they felt that many content key points could be easily lifted from the passage, while handling grammar expression to summarize all sentences into a 120-word abstract was much more challenging.

---

[3] In GCE 'O' Level Higher Chinese Language papers, the comprehension section contains three to four questions, which are designed in such an order that the first question requires the student to describe or paraphrase content; the second question needs the student to define meanings; and the last question requires the student to exemplify the passage theme and provide his or her own views.

After analyzing the pilot test feedback and explaining the ordering of all the 14 items in the basic language skill category, the ranking from easy (1) to hard (12) can be summarized in Table 4.

ORDERING OF DIFFICULTIES IN THE INTERMEDIATE MOCK 'A' LEVEL TEST

As shown in Table 2, the intermediate language skill category includes essay writing (P1/1 for "content" component and P1/2 for "expression" component) and the ancient Chinese comprehension (P1/8 and P1/9) in Paper 1, as well as the "outlining answer key points" component literature analyses in Paper 2 (P2/19, P2/21, P2/23, P2/25, P2/27, P2/29 and P2/31). The ordering of difficulty for all these 11 intermediate category test items is again based on the pilot test feedback.

In this category, the ancient Chinese sentence translation questions P1/6 and P1/7 were rated in the pilot test as the two easiest test items. In these two translation questions, participants needed to recall from their study notes the meanings of ancient Chinese vocabulary terms in the questions, and combined these vocabulary translations to form sentences translated in modern Chinese. To the pilot test participants, translating the ancient Chinese sentences required mainly memory work and good syntactical knowledge to use auxiliaries and prepositions in translation. Hence, the two items were collectively ranked as the least challenging questions.

The next two test items in difficulty order are the "content" and "expression" components in essay writing question of Paper 1. Essay writing at the GCE 'A' Level standards (Ministry of Education, 2006c) demands at least 600 words with more content, while grammar and style are not specified to be any different from GCE 'O' Level standards. The pilot test participants therefore agreed that it is easier to have error-free in expression than working out sufficient content to meet the minimum word length.

The remaining test items in the intermediate language skill category all require analytical thinking to outline the relevant key points to answer to the questions. However, for the four short literature analysis questions on the ancient and modern Chinese poetry, pilot test participants found it easier to outline the key answers for the selected poems. The main reason cited by the participants was that the analyses of poetry could have been well prepared beforehand as the syllabus-selected readings are all short and famous poems (Singapore Examinations and Assessment Board, 2008b). Hence, the test items of P1/19, P1/21, P1/23 and P1/25 were ranked respectively right after the essay task in the intermediate category of the Mock 'A' Level Test.

The last three test items of P1/27, P1/29 and P1/31 are analyses of longer literature texts, which generally have a wider range of possible answers. Because there is a greater amount of content to analyse in the lengthy texts, the "outlining key point" component of every test item is split into two. For example, P1/27 will register as two items, namely P1/27a and P1/27b, of which the latter is expected to be more difficult, as the pilot test showed the next two or three key points were usually harder to generate.The pilot test also revealed that the difficulty ordering of the three test items was proportionate to the length of the literature text assessed. In other words, the three pilot test students rated their difficulties from easy to hard in the order of P1/27, P1/29 and followed by P1/31, which are analyses of a short novel, a drama play and a novel respectively. According to their feedback, a full-length novel was the most difficult to prepare for as the characters, content themes and stylistics involved were a lot more complex than the drama play and the short novel.

After explaining the differences of the 14 items in the intermediate category, the overall difficulty ordering of the second part of the Mock 'A' Level Chinese language test can be summarized in Table 5.

Table 5. Ordering of item-difficulties in the Intermediate Mock 'A' Level Test

Paper / Item	Task (Marks)	Ordering
P1/6	Translate ancient Chinese sentences (4) (easiest)	1
P1/7	Translate ancient Chinese sentences (4)	1
P1/2	Write an essay of more than 600 words. Out of a total of 35 marks, 17 marks are awarded to the "content" component, while 18 marks are awarded to the "expression" component. P1/2 refers to the "expression" component (18)	2
P1/1	Same essay test item. P1/1 refers to the "content" component (17)	3
P2/19	First question on ancient and modern Chinese poetry analysis – "outlining key points" component (5)	4
P2/21	Second question on ancient and modern Chinese poetry analysis – "outlining key points" component (5)	5
P2/23	Third question on ancient and modern Chinese poetry analysis – "outlining key points" component (5)	6
P2/25	Fourth question on ancient and modern Chinese poetry analysis – "outlining key points" component (5)	7
P2/27a	Short novel analysis – "outlining key points" component for first two points (4)	8
P1/27b	Short novel analysis – "outlining key points" component for next two or three points (4)	9
P2/29a	Drama play analysis – "outlining key points" component for first two points (4)	10
P2/29b	Drama play analysis – "outlining key points" component for first two points (4)	11
P2/31a	Novel analysis – "outlining key points" component for first two points (4)	12
P2/31b	Novel analysis – "outlining key points" component for first two points (4) (hardest)	13

Source: Ong (2009).

ORDERING OF DIFFICULTIES IN THE ADVANCED MOCK 'A' LEVEL TEST

The advanced category of the Mock 'A' Level Test consist only of seven Paper 2 literature analysis test items (P2/20, 2/22, P2/24, 2/26, P2/28, P2/30 and P2/32), as rated by the pilot test participants earlier in Table 2. According to the pilot test analysis explained in the previous sections, every test item in the advanced category represents the assessment component of elaborating the arguments and essay organisation in the literature critique, which is contrary to the other assessment component of outlining the key points in the intermediate category.

All pilot test participants agreed that the elaborating and analysing further in the literature analyses demanded more rigour in writing, especially when they were expected to substantiate their arguments by citing quotes from the literature text. As the test requirements for the literature analyses became more challenging, the pilot test participants then revealed the need to know more about the scoring rubrics in elaborating key points when writing their literature analyses. However, till December 2008, there had not been any formal assessment framework published for literature analyses in the GCE 'A' Level Chinese Language and Literature H2 papers (Ministry of Education, 2006c). This problem was particularly evident in the P2/28, P2/30 and P2/32 test items, which each carried 20 marks and generally 12 to 14 marks were given for "elaborating argument" in the analyses. To overcome this constraint, the present study devised a three-part scale for the P2/28, P2/30 and P2/32 test items, which implied that each test item would be further split into three smaller assessment components, such as P2/28a, P2/28b and P2/28c. The subdivided components assessed the elaboration on different key points as well as the overall structure and flow of arguments in the analysis. As a result, the number of test items in the advanced category increased to 13 items for the pilot testing assessment, as shown in Table 6.

Table 6. Ordering of item-difficulties in the Advanced Mock 'A' Level Test

Paper / Item	Task (Marks)	Ordering
P2/20	Elaborating arguments in the critique on an ancient poem (5)	1
P2/22	Elaborating arguments in the critique on another ancient poem (5)	2
P2/24	Elaborating arguments in the critique on a contemporary poem (5)	3
P2/26	Elaborating arguments in the critique on another ancient or contemporary poem (5)	4
P2/28a	Elaborating arguments on the first two key points in the critique on a short novel (4)	5
P2/28b	Elaborating arguments on the next two key points in the critique on the short novel (4)	6
P2/28c	Overall content structure of the critique on the short novel (4)	7
P2/30a	Elaborating arguments on the first two key points in the critique on the selected drama play (4)	8
P2/30b	Elaborating arguments on the next two key points in the critique on the selected drama play (4)	9
P2/30c	Overall content structure of the critique on the drama play (4)	10
P2/32a	Elaborating arguments on the first two key points in the critique on the selected novel (4)	11
P2/32b	Elaborating arguments on the next two key points in the critique on the novel (4)	12
P2/32c	Overall content structure of the critique on the novel (4)	13

Source: Ong (2009).

When the 13 test items were pilot tested according to their levels of difficulty, the four poetry analysis components were rated as the easier test items, while the next nine short novel, drama play and novel analysis items were ranked in the same respective order proportional to the length of literature texts. The only difference in the advance category ordering is that the subdivided components in P2/28, P2/30 and P2/32 test items needed to be further ranked. Among the subdivided components, the "overall organisation and structure" component was rated by pilot test participants to be more difficult than the elaboration of the key points, because the participants all found it easier to apply their study notes and literature text in answering the key points, as compared to structuring the entire analysis appropriately in answering the question. With the final nine items ordered, the overall ranking of item-difficulties can be finalised as shown in Table 6.

In summary, the marking scheme and pilot testing of the Mock 'A' Level Chinese Language Test were planned to collect appropriate data for the Rasch RUMM2020 analysis. In order to ensure accuracy in the data analysis, the Mock 'A' Level Test was divided into three parts in which each part has 13 to 14 test items ordered in respective levels of difficulty. This measurement strategy can help to overcome possible constraints in sampling and hence will be applied to the Authentic Chinese Language Test. The next section shall introduce the Authentic Chinese Language Test and explain the similar processes in pilot testing and item-difficulty ordering of the test items.

AUTHENTIC CHINESE LANGUAGE TEST

The design of an Authentic Chinese Language Test (see Appendix A) begins with simulated real-world tasks targeting specific language use in ability domains where adolescent language talents are expected to perform. Advanced language competencies such as creativity and pragmatics are the main important criteria in designing the authentic test items. Despite instilling creativity and authentic contexts in the test design, the study syllabus content for the authentic test should not depart from the present GCE 'A' Level Chinese Language and Literature H2 curriculum (Ministry of Education, 2006c), otherwise the test participants would need to study two different syllabi for both the authentic test and the Mock 'A' Level Test. Similarly, the marking scheme of the authentic test should also be aligned as much as possible with the Mock 'A' Level Test, so that the students taking the tests will not adapting to two entirely different assessment systems.

In following the Mock 'A' Level Test assessment format (see Tables 4, 5 and 6), the Authentic Chinese language test assigns not more than five marks for every test item. For each test item in the authentic test, a five-point marking scale, which was earlier introduced in Table 5, is devised from the six-trait writing model (Spandel, 2009). The five-point scale can assess a test item as a writing trait component, such as sentence fluency and voice (Spandel, 2009). In other words, an authentic writing task carrying 20 marks can be made up of four writing-trait components, each of which uses the five-point scale as scoring rubrics (see Appendix A). The entire test could therefore consist of over 20 test items with only four to five writing tasks designed, provided that each writing task is capable of assessing the six writing traits in Spandel's model (2009).

There are two types of writing tasks in the authentic test, namely the essay writing and analytic writing task, both of which assess different aspects of the writing-trait components. Therefore, there will be two sets of scoring rubrics created to cater for these writing tasks, as illustrated in Chapter Three (see Table 4 and 5). The Authentic Test scoring rubrics, unlike the Mock 'A Level Test rubrics, do not award marks for regurgitation of text and norm-referenced test items. Instead, these scoring rubrics assess pragmatic and creative language competency in designed authentic writing tasks such as script writing, lyrics composition and copywriting. As a testing instrument focused on authentic testing and advanced literacy, the Authentic Language Test thus does not need the same assessment load as the Mock 'A' Level

Test does. The Authentic Test took one and a half hour less than the Mock 'A' Level Test to complete, as it consists of only five major writing tasks.

Table 7. Marking Scheme of Authentic Chinese Language Test

Task (Marks)	Test Item No.	Scoring Rubrics (Marks)	
Write a newspaper report, short prose, short critique or a movie script synopsis of at least 600 words according to the requirements stated in the writing task (30)	1	Content and ideas (5)	Refer to Table 3.4 for scoring rubrics of each writing-trait test item
	2	Organisation (5)	
	3	Voice (5)	
	4	Word Choice (5)	
	5	Sentence fluency (5)	
	6	Conventions (5)	
Write a brief analysis comparing two ancient Chinese literature works. The format has to be a symposium report that can be presented in a school symposium (20)	7	Content and ideas (5)	Refer to Table 3.4 for scoring rubrics of each writing-trait test item
	8	Organisation (5)	
	9	Sentence fluency (5)	
	10	Conventions (5)	
According to the task requirements, convert one of the ancient or contemporary Chinese poems into a creative writing product such as modern song lyrics, a prose or a to-be-published critique (20)	11	Ideas and creativity (5)	Refer to Table 3.5 for scoring rubrics of each writing-trait test item
	12	Organisation (5)	
	13	Sentence fluency (5)	
	14	Conventions (5)	
According to the task requirements, rewrite one of the novels and drama play into a play script synopsis, a teaching plan or a copywriting draft. Test user need to complete two out of the three writing tasks provided (15 x 2 = 30)	15	Ideas and creativity (5)	Refer to Table 3.5 for scoring rubrics of each writing-trait test item
	16	Voice (5)	
	17	Conventions (5)	
	18	Ideas and creativity (5)	
	19	Voice (5)	
	20	Conventions (5)	

Source: Ong (2009), Spandel (2009, pp.401-403).

The first task involves creative writing set in four different authentic contexts, where the test user can choose one task that matches his or her strategic competency (Bachman, 1990, p.104-106). A total of 30 marks is assigned to this task, with each five-point scale attributed to six writing-trait categories, such as 'voice' and 'word choice' (Spandel, 2009). The second writing task involves comparative analysis of two ancient Chinese proses and drafting a simple symposium report to address 'a student audience' (Appendix A). Because the second task is more focused on the analytical aspects of writing literacy, only four categories of 'ideas and content', 'convention', 'organisation' and 'sentence fluency' are assessed, totalling to 20 marks assigned to this question. The third writing task combines creative writing and literature analysis based on the selected ancient and contemporary poems in the present GCE

'A' Level syllabus (Singapore Examinations and Assessment Board, 2008b). In the third writing task, the test users express their literature knowledge in creative forms of authentic writing products, such as modern song lyrics and museum introductory write-ups. Similar to the previous writing task, the assessment involves the same four categories, only with the 'ideas and content' category modified to 'ideas and creativity' to place more emphasis on the creativity criteria. The last two writing tasks are role-playing assessment tasks, in which the test user plays an authentic role of a playwright, an art critic or a teacher, and creates two writing products based on the novels and drama plays selected in the GCE 'A' Level syllabus. Each of these two tasks is assigned 15 marks, with three writing-trait categories – 'ideas and creativity', 'conventions' and 'voice', selected to assess the targeted language competences. 'Voice' is the most important test item in the last two tasks where the test user needs to adopt the language tone and strategic mechanisms (Bachman, 1990; Spandel, 2009) to fit the writer's role specified in the question.

After explaining the design of the scoring rubrics and writing tasks in the Authentic Chinese Language Test, the overall marking scheme can be summarized in Table 7.

Table 7 indicates that the Authentic Chinese Language Test has twenty test items that need to be ordered in difficulty levels and analysed in the Rasch measurement model (Andrich, 1988; Master, 1982, 1988; Rasch, 1960/1980). Similar to the Mock 'A' Level Test, the Authentic Test also needs to analysed separately in different parts, so as to overcome possible sampling constraints. However, unlike the Mock 'A' Level Test, the Authentic Test has less test items and hence will be split into only two parts, which are the *intermediate* and *advanced* language competency categories. The categorisation in the authentic test is still based on the principles from Goh and Silver's language learning model (2004, 2006).

All the test items in the Authentic Test are classified as at least intermediate language competency, due to the standards of writing literacy assessed in the writing tasks. In all the authentic writing tasks, simulated real-world contexts are designed in the test requirements to ensure that advanced literacy and pragmatic competences are evaluated in every writing product (Bachman, 1990; Christie, 2005; Mueller, 2006). Therefore, the design of the Authentic Chinese Language Test attributes a minimum of intermediate language competency to all the test items, and leaves the advanced category to be defined.

The advanced competency category differs from the intermediate category by merit of the three writing traits – creativity, convention and voice (Spandel, 2009). All test items of 'convention' and 'voice' writing traits are categorised as advanced competency as they are more directly linked with authentic assessment, which is an assessment mode uncommon in Singapore Chinese language lessons. In fact, the present formats of the GCE 'O' Level and GCE 'A' Level Chinese language examinations (Ministry of Education, 2005c, 2006c) and the Chinese language teaching climate in Singapore do not allow much curriculum space to assess the students using the authentic approach (Liu et al., 2004; Shen, 2003). Hence, it is generally more challenging for Singapore students to produce Chinese writings that can meet the requirements of authentic assessment and to even at a standard that is "ready to be published" (Spandel, 2009). Meeting the standards of 'convention' and 'voice' writing traits in the authentic test is therefore a level higher than the standards of other writing traits such as 'sentence fluency' and 'word choice'. Another group of advanced category items are the 'content and creativity' writing traits in Item 11 and 15 (Table 7), which involves re-creating literature works to produce literary adaptations. Combining literary knowledge and creative expression proves to be more difficult for Singapore students, as they are accustomed to solely doing literature analysis, as shown in the Mock 'A' Level Test. Due to these reasons, 'convention', 'voice' and 'content and creativity' writing-trait test items are classified as advanced language competency, while the rest of the test items are by default in the intermediate category.

After classifying individual test items into the two parts of the authentic test, the next section proceeds to explain the ordering of difficulties of the test items within each part of the test. Pilot testing is also conducted to assist in the ordering process. Similar preparations are made to ensure both the Authentic and Mock 'A' Level Chinese Language Tests are able to provide reliable data for analysis.

ORDERING OF DIFFICULTIES IN INTERMEDIATE AUTHENTIC TEST

To determine the ordering of the test item difficulties in the intermediate category, a pilot test similar to that of the Mock 'A' Level Test needs to be conducted. The pilot testing of the authentic language test involves the same participants who took part in the Mock 'A' Level Test, so as to maintain a consistency of the standards between the two types of Chinese language tests.

The pilot test participants were first briefed about the standards of rubrics as they needed to be aware that they would be rating the writing traits as individual test-items. Several examples illustrated in Spandel's six-trait writing guide (2009) were shared with the pilot test participants to ensure they acquired full understanding of the concepts of different writing traits. During the pilot test, these participants were reminded to be conscious of the different aspects of writing performances they were expected to exhibit in their essays. At the end of the pilot test, the participants were interviewed as a group to know more about the categorisation of the test items and the ordering of different test items in each respective category. The final rating results are shown in Table 8.

As the entire pilot test is conducted to rate both intermediate and advanced category test items together, the participants could possibly make changes to the categorisation as planned in the last section. According to Table 8, the pilot test participants rated two advanced category test items (see underlined Item 3 and 6) under intermediate category and the two items were ranked among the first six easier items. Upon investigation, the participants reflected that though the "voice" and "convention" standards seemed to be of higher standard in many writing tasks, these two test items in the first essay writing task were much assisted by the instructions provided in the questions, as shown in the following example from the authentic language test (see Appendix A).

Imagine you are a drama critic. After watching Lao She's play "Cha Guan", you need to write a report to be published on the front page of the "Fukan" section in "Lianhe Zaobao" (Singapore Chinese newspaper)
a. You need to design headlines for the front-page report
b. You need to write a report about this play according to your headlines. Your content should attract your readers as a front-page report.

As shown in the example above, one question in the first writing task consists of two parts, in which scaffolding instructions are provided to help test users devise the writing components needed to achieve good 'convention' and 'voice' standards. Therefore, the students taking part in the pilot test agreed that the Item 3 and 6 (see Table 8) should be instead ranked within the intermediate category.

In the overall ranking of difficulty levels among the ten intermediate test items, the first six easier items are all from the first writing task. The pilot test participants revealed that the first writing task provided scaffolding instructions that helped to place all the test items in the first task as the easiest group of test items. The participants proceeded to rank 'content and ideas' harder than 'word choice', 'organisation' and 'voice'.

Table 8. Ordering of item-difficulties in the Intermediate Authentic Test

Test Item	Writing Task	Writing-Trait Test Item (Marks)	Ordering
4	Essay (Creative/Informational)	Word Choice (5) (easy)	1
2	Essay (Creative/Informational)	Organisation (5)	2
3	*Essay (Creative/Informational)*	*Voice (5)*	3
1	Essay (Creative/Informational)	Content and ideas (5)	4
5	Essay (Creative/Informational)	Sentence fluency (5)	5
6	*Essay (Creative/Informational)*	*Conventions (5)*	6
7	Ancient Chinese "Symposium Report"	Content and ideas (5)	7
8	Ancient Chinese "Symposium Report"	Organisation (5)	8
9	Ancient Chinese "Symposium Report"	Sentence fluency (5)	9
13	Creative Poetry Analysis	Sentence fluency (5)	10

Source: Ong (2009).

They felt that the 'contents and ideas' item was more challenging as they had to 'devise imaginary content' to make their written products as authentic as possible. After that, they put 'sentence fluency' harder than content for the reason that stringing all the sentences in the whole essay of at least 600 words was most challenging, especially when the sentence styles must cater to the context specified in the writing task. Similarly, the participants also found 'convention' standard difficult as the presentation style also needed to cater to the writing context, though there was some assistance provided by the task instructions.

The next group of test items ordered through the pilot testing was the ancient Chinese 'symposium report'. The 'sentence fluency' test item in the ancient Chinese task was also ordered as more difficult than the 'content' and 'organisation', similar to the 'sentence fluency' test item in the first writing task. Again 'sentence fluency' of the creative poetry analysis was also ordered among the more difficult items. The main difference between the last two items was that creative writing expression seemed to be more challenging as the participants did not practise much creative writing while they were studying at junior colleges.

All the test items were ordered from easy to difficult in the intermediate category of the authentic language test, with reasons provided by the pilot test participants. The same pilot testing was also conducted to order the advance category test items by difficulty.

Table 9. Ordering of item-difficulties in the advanced category of authentic language test

Test Item	Writing Task	Writing-Trait Test Item (Marks)	Ordering
10	Ancient Chinese "Symposium Report"	Convention (5) (easy)	1
11	Creative Poetry Analysis	Ideas and creativity (5)	2
12	Creative Poetry Analysis	Organisation (5)	3
14	Creative Poetry Analysis	Convention (5)	4
15	Write a curator's prologue for a novel	Ideas and creativity (5)	5
16	Write a curator's prologue for a novel	Voice (5)	6
17	Write a curator's prologue for a novel	Conventions (5)	7
18	Recreate literature into a script synopsis	Ideas and creativity (5)	8
19	Recreate literature into a script synopsis	Voice (5)	9
20	Recreate literature into a script synopsis	Conventions (5) *(hard)*	10

Source: Ong (2009).

ORDERING OF DIFFICULTIES IN ADVANCED AUTHENTIC TEST

As explained earlier in the introduction of the Authentic Chinese Language Test, all of the 'convention', 'voice' and 'idea and creativity' writing traits are categorised as advanced category test items. However, the 'convention' and 'voice' writing traits in the first writing task were categorised under the intermediate category during the pilot test. That left ten test items for the participants to rank, using the same interview process to collect feedback, and finalize the item-difficulty ordering for the advanced category part of the authentic test. The result of the difficulty ordering is shown in Table 9.

Of all the test items, the ancient Chinese 'convention' writing trait was deemed the easiest in the pilot test. As discussed during the pilot test interviews, the format of the 'symposium report' was rated to be comparatively easier than the more creative expressions required from the other questions, in which tasks like writing modern song lyrics and a script synopsis seemed to be more 'unconventionally out-of-the-classroom' according to these junior college participants. That also explained why Item 10, 14, 17 and 20 were ranked respectively from easy to difficult for all the 'convention' writing-trait test items. The most difficult 'convention' test item was converting a selected drama play, which is set during the 1898-1947 period, into a contemporary play. In order to recreate the play, the pilot test participants not only needed to apply their content knowledge of the literature, but they also had to consider various elements of drama such as props and costumes, shown in the question as follows (see Appendix A):

> "If there is a local theatre group attempting to re-write Lao She's 'Cha Guan' as a modern drama play, what do you think how the three scenes in 'Cha Guan', which represent three different eras in China's history, should be replaced with?
> Write a concept draft for a modern 'Cha Guan' play (12 marks). Your script draft should include the following:
> a. Characters   b. Stage setup   c. Story outline"

Similar to the ordering of the 'convention' among the creative poetry task and the literature re-creation writing tasks, the 'ideas and creativity' test items were also ranked in the same order from easy to hard, with the writing of curator's prologue being more challenging than the creative poetry analysis (see Item 11, 15 and 18 in Table 9). Lastly, for the 'organisation' and the two 'voice' test items in Item 12, 16 and 19 ranked respectively, the poetry 'organisation' test item was ordered to be less difficult than the two 'voice' test items during the pilot test. Two pilot test participants commented that with the poetry task assigned 20 marks and the reconstructing literature task assigned 30 marks, they wrote less content for the former task and thus spent less effort trying to organise the content. On the contrary, the 'voice' writing trait to be portrayed in the literary reconstruction tasks was more complex as they were required to engage with the readers within the stipulated task contexts. Therefore, the pilot test end results showed the 'voice' test items were ordered to be more challenging than the poetry 'organisation' test item.

After explaining the ordering of test items in the advanced category of the Authentic Chinese Language Test, the entire test instrument is prepared, with ten test items each in the intermediate and advanced category for data analysis. Along the way, a pilot test and post-test interviews were conducted to align the different perspectives of the test maker and the test taker. The ordering results were then finalized and explained in the previous few sections.

All the ordering and classification of item-difficulties in both Mock 'A' Level and Authentic Chinese Language Test are established, with the language tests piloted and ready for implementation in the research.

REFERENCES

Andrich, D. (1988b). *Rasch models for measurement.* Sage university paper on quantitative applications in the social sciences, series number 07/068. Newbury Park, CA: Sage Publications.

Andrich, D. (2004). Controversy and the Rasch model: A characteristic of incompatible paradigms? *Medical Care, 42*(1), 7-16.

Andrich, D., Sheridan, B. S., and Luo, G. (2005). *RUMM2020: Rasch unidimensional models for measurement.* Perth, Western Australia: RUMM Laboratory.

Andrich, D., and van Schoubroeck, L. (1989). The general health questionnaire: a psychometric analysis using latent trait theory. *Psychological Medicine, 19*, 469-485.

Avery, L. D., Li Z., Little, C. A., and VanTassel-Baska, J. (2004). A curriculum study of gifted-student learning in the language arts. In C. A. Tomlinson (Ed.), *Differentiation for gifted and talented students* (pp. 165-186). California, CA: Corwin Press.

Bachman, L. F., and Palmer, A. S. (1996). *Language testing in practice.* Oxford, UK: Oxford University Press.

Beijing Language and Culture University (2006). *HSK test center.* Retrieved Aug 4, 2007, from http://www.blcu.edu.cn/blcuweb/english/research.asp.

Betts, G. T. (1991). The autonomous learner model for the gifted and talented. In N. Colangelo and G. A. Davis (Eds.), *Handbook of gifted education* (pp. 142-153). Boston, MA: Allyn and Bacon.

Brown, J. D., and Hudson, T. (1998). The alternatives in language assessment. *TESOL Quarterly*, *32*(10), 653-675.

Chan, W. Y. (2008). Exploring patchwork assessment for A-level statistics. In K. Tan, and K. H. Koh (Eds.), *Authentic assessment in schools* (pp. 85-98). Singapore: Prentice Hall.

Chew, C. H. (2001, December). *Shehui bianqian yu yuwen jiaoyu de gaige [Changes in Society and its relevance to revamp in language education]*. Paper presented at a symposium conducted at the Fourth International Conference for China Language Education Curriculum and Pedagogy, Hong Kong, China.

Clark, M. (2004). By the numbers: The rationale for Rasch analysis in placement testing. *Second Language Studies, 22*(2), 61-90.

Cohn, S. J. (1981). What is giftedness? A multidimensional approach. In A. H. Kramer (Ed.), *Gifted children: Challenging their potential* (pp. 33-45). New York, NY: Trillium Press.

Christie, F. H. (2002). The development of abstraction in adolescence in subject English. In M. J. Schleppegrell, and M. C. Colombi. (Eds.), *Developing advanced literacy in first and second languages: meaning with power* (pp. 45-66). New Jersey, NJ: Lawrence Erlbaum Associates.

Christie, F. H. (2005). *Advanced literacy development for the years of adolescence*. Paper presented at the conference conducted at the Charles Darwin Symposium Series 2005, Darwin, Australia.

ERIC Clearinghouse on Disabilities and Gifted Education. (2000). *Gifted students and alternative assessment*. Retrieved Jun 3, 2006, from *http://www.hoagiesgifted.org/eric/faq/gt-altas.html*.

Feldhusen, J. F., and Kolloff, M. B. (1986). The Purdue three-stage model for gifted education at the elementary level. In J. S. Renzulli (Ed.), *Systems and models for developing programs for the gifted and talented* (pp. 126-153). Mansfield Center, CT: Creative Learning Press.

Gagné, F. (2004). Giftedness and talent: Reexaming a reexamination of the definitions. In R. J. Sternberg (Ed.), *Definitions and Conceptions of Giftedness* (pp. 79-94). California, CA: Corwin Press.

Gardner, H. (1983). *Frames of mind: The theory of Multiple Intelligences*. New York, NY: BasicBooks.

Gardner, H. (1987). Developing the spectrum of human intelligences. *Harvard Educational Review, 57*(2), 187-193.

Gardner, H. (1993). *Multiple Intelligences: The theory in practice*. New York, NY: BasicBooks.

Gardner, H., Károlyi, C.V., and Ramos-Ford, V. (2003). Multiple Intelligences: A perspective on giftedness. In N. Colangelo, and G.A. Davis (Eds.), *Handbook of Gifted Education* (pp. 100-111). Boston, MA: Allyn and Bacon.

Goh, C. M., and Silver, R. E. (2004). *Language acquisition and development*. Singapore: Prentice Hall.

Goh, C. M., and Silver, R. E. (2006). *Language learning: Home, school and society* . Singapore: Pearson Education South Asia Pte Ltd.

Goh, N. H. (2005). *Chunfeng chuifu, qiaomu chouya – Huayuwen zai xinjiapo de xianzhuang yu qianzhan [Present and future state of Chinese language in Singapore]*. Retrieved Aug 9, 2007, from http://huayuqiao.org/articles/wuyuanhua/.

Gulikers, J. T. M., Bastiaens, T. J., and Kirschner, P. A. (2007). Defining authentic assessment: Five dimensions of authenticity. In A. Haves, and L. McDowell (Eds.), *Balancing dilemmas in assessment and learning in contemporary education* (pp. 73-86). New York, NY: Routledge.

Herman, J. L., Aschbacher, P. R., and Winters L. (1992). *A practical guide to alternative assessment*. Alexandria, VA: Association for Supervision and Curriculum Development.

Hoe, W. M., and Tong, I. (2006, May). *Authentic assessment through innovative project work in Jurong Secondary School.* Paper presented at a conference conducted at the International Association for Educational Assessment, Singapore.

Jarmer, D., Kozol, M., Nelson, S., and Salsberry, T. (2000). Six-trait writing improves scores at Jennie Wilson Elementary. *Journal of School Improvement 1*(2), 29-32.

Johnson, D. T. (1996). Assessment in the language arts classroom. In D.T. Johnson, B.L. Neal, and J. VanTassel-Baska (Eds.), *Developing verbal talent: ideas and strategies for teachers of elementary and middle school students* (pp. 241-257). Boston, MA: Allyn and Bacon.

Koh, K. H. (2008). Authentic assessment and its technical quality. In K. Tan, and K. H. Koh (Eds.), *Authentic assessment in schools* (pp. 34-54). Singapore: Prentice Hall.

Koh, K., and Gong W.G. (2008). Assessment and the teaching of Mandarin Chinese in Singapore schools. *New Horizons in Education Journal, 56* (2), 43-51.

Koh, K., and Luke, A. (in press). Authentic and conventional assessment in Singapore schools: An empirical study of teacher assignments and student work. *Assessment in Education Journal*

Lan, C. P. (2001). Chinese teaching testing method and its effects to the quality of the Chinese language teaching. *Language and Translation, 2*, 56-59.

Lim, C. C. (2008). Authentic assessment and Understanding by Design. In K. Tan, and K. H. Koh (Eds.), *Authentic assessment in schools* (pp. 157-171). Singapore: Prentice Hall.

Liu, Y., Kotov, R., Abdul Rahim, R., and Goh, H. H. (2004). *Chinese language pedagogic practice: A preliminary snapshot description of Singaporean Chinese language classrooms.* Retrieved Aug 8, 2007, from http://www.crpp.nie.edu.sg/publications/rrs

Luke, A., Freebody, P., Lau, S., and Gopinathan, S. (2005). Towards research-based innovation and reform: Singapore schooling in transition. *Asia Pacific Journal of Education, 25*(1), 1-23.

Lynch, B. K. (1996). *Language program evaluation.* Cambridge, UK: Cambridge University Press.

Marland, S. P. (1972). *Education of the gifted and talented: Report to the Congress of the United States by the U.S. commissioner of education.* Washington, D.C.: U.S. Government Printing Office.

McLean, D. L. (1990). Time to replace the classroom test with authentic measurement. *The Alberta Journal of Educational Research, 36*(1), 78-84.

Meyer, C. A. (1992). What's the difference "authentic" and "performance" assessment? *Educational Leadership, 49*(8), 39-40.

Ministry of Education. (1992a). *Gifted Education Programme Handbook.* Singapore.

Ministry of Education. (1992b). *Report of Chinese Language Review Committee.* Singapore.

Ministry of Education. (2002). *Report of the Junior College/Upper Secondary Education Review Committee.* Retrieved Jan 3, 2006, from *http://www.moe.gov.sg/jcreview/ index.htm.*

Ministry of Education. (2004a). *From secondary to post-secondary education.* Retrieved April 4, 2007, from http://www.moe.gov.sg/corporate/eduoverview/Sec_sectopost.htm.

Ministry of Education. (2004b). *Gifted education programme.* Retrieved May 30, 2005, from http://www.moe.gov.sg/gifted/index.htm.

Ministry of Education. (2004c). *GCE 'A' Level curriculum.* Retrieved Dec 4, 2006, from http://www.moe.gov.sg/corporate/eduoverview/PreU_ALevelCurri.htm.

Ministry of Education. (2004d). *Nurturing a core of students with advanced knowledge of Chinese language and culture.* Retrieved Dec 4, 2006, from *http://www.moe.gov.sg/ press/2004/pr20040903.htm.*

Ministry of Education. (2004e). *Language elective programmes.* Retrieved Dec 4, 2006, from http://www.moe.gov.sg/elective/LEP%20Content%20Page.htm.

Ministry of Education. (2004f). *Gifted education programme enrichment model.* Retrieved Jun 4, 2007, from http://www.moe.gov.sg/gifted/Enrichment_Model.htm.

Ministry of Education. (2005a). *4th language elective programme (Chinese) centre to be set up in 2006.* Retrieved Aug 4, 2005, from *http://www.moe.gov.sg/press/2005/* pr20050409.htm.

Ministry of Education. (2005b). *Chinese language elective programme.* Retrieved Sept 15, 2005, from *http://www.moe.gov.sg/elective/CLLEP.pdf.*

Ministry of Education. (2005c). *2006 PSLE and 'O' Level mother tongue language and higher mother tongue language interim examination formats.* Retrieved Mar 22, 2008, from *http://www.moe.gov.sg/press/2005/pr20050422.htm.*

Ministry of Education. (2005d). *Parliamentary replies - 28 Feb 2005.* Retrieved Jan 22, 2008, from http://www.moe.gov.sg/media/parliamentary-replies/2005/ pq28022005.htm.

Ministry of Education. (2006a). *Flexibility and choice.* Retrieved Dec 15, 2006, from http://www.moe.gov.sg/corporate/yearbook/2006/pdf/flexibility-and-choice.pdf.

Ministry of Education. (2006b). *Bicultural studies programme (Chinese).* Retrieved Jun 12, 2007, from http://www.moe.gov.sg/spotlight/2004/splt_bspc.htm.

Ministry of Education. (2006c). *Singapore-Cambridge General Certificate of Education (advanced) level examination syllabuses: H1 Chinese Language / H2 Chinese Language and Literature / H3 Chinese Language and Literature.* Singapore.

Ministry of Education. (2006d). *Speech by Mr Gan Kim Yong, Minister of State, Ministry of Education and Ministry of Manpower, at the 2006 national inter-secondary school translation competition cum prize-presentation ceremony on Saturday, 8 April 2006, at 12 noon at lt4, Nanyang Junior College.* Retrieved Jun 12, 2007, from http://www.moe.gov.sg/speeches/2006/sp20060408b.htm

Ministry of Education. (2007). *Gifted education programme-special programmes.* Retrieved Jan 12, 2007, from *http://www.moe.gov.sg/gifted/SP.htm.*

Ministry of Education. (2008). *Gifted education programme: development and growth.* Retrieved Aug 17, 2008, from *http://www.moe.gov.sg/education/programmes/*gifted-education-programme/development-and-growth/.

Ministry of Education. (2009). *Special and express streams to merge from 2008.* Retrieved May 5, 2009, from http://www.schoolbag.sg/archives/2007/08/ special_and_express _streams_to.php.

Mueller, J. (2006). *Authentic Assessment Toolbox.* Retrieved April 25, 2006, from http://jonathan.mueller.faculty.noctrl.edu/toolbox/whatisit.htm.

Nanyang Junior College. (2006). Wen yan wen, tang shi, song ci shang xi : da xue xian xiu
    ban H2 hua wen yu wen xue [Ancient Chinese, Tang dynasty poetry and Song dynasty
    poetry: Pre-university H2 Chinese language and literature]. Singapore: Lingzi Media Pte
    Ltd.

Newmann, F. M., and Associates. (1995). *Authentic achievement: Restructuring schools for
    intellectual quality*. San Francisco, CA: Jossey-Bass.

North, B., and Schneider, G. (1998). Scaling descriptors for language proficiency scales.
    Language Testing, 15(2), 217-263.

Passow, A. H. (1996). Talent identification and development in the language arts. In D.T.
    Johnson, B.L. Neal, and J. VanTassel-Baska, (Eds.), *Developing verbal talent: ideas and
    strategies for teachers of elementary and middle school students*. (pp. 23-32). Boston,
    MA: Allyn and Bacon.

Passow, A. H. (2004). The nature of giftedness and talent. In R. J. Sternberg (Ed.),
    Definitions and conceptions of giftedness (pp. 1-10). California, CA: Corwin Press.

Renzulli, J. S. (1984, April). The three ring conception of giftedness: A developmental model
    for creative productivity. 68th Annual Meeting of the American Educational Research
    Association, LA, USA.

Resnick, L. B., and Resnick, D. P. (1992). Assessing the thinking curriculum: New tools for
    educational reform. In B. R. Gifford and M. C. O'Connor (Eds.), *Changing assessments:
    Alternative views of aptitude, achievement, and instruction* (pp. 37-75). Boston: Kluwer
    Academic Publishers.

Seah-Tay, H. Y. (2005). *Investigating the intellectual quality of alternative assessments at
    Nanyang Girls' High School*. Retrieved Jul 8, 2007, from *http://www.nygh.moe.edu.sg/
    RnD/research_2005_06.htm*.

Shen, S. H. (2003). Xinjiapo zhongxue zuowen jiaoxue [Teaching Chinese composition in
    Singapore secondary schools]. *Huawen Laoshi, 16*(2), 6-13.

Singapore Department of Statistics. (2000a). *Singapore census of population, 2000: Advance
    data release no. 3, literacy and language*. Retrieved 25 Oct, 2008, from
    http://www.singstat.gov.sg/pubn/papers/people/c2000adr-literacy.pdf.

Singapore Department of Statistics. (2000b). *Census of population 2000: Education,
    language and religion*. Retrieved 25 Oct, 2008, from *www.singstat.gov*.sg/pubn/
    popn/c2000sr2/cop2000sr2.pdf.

Singapore Examinations and Assessment Board. (2008a). *GCE O level examination: Exam
    syllabuses for school candidates*. Retrieved Aug 15, 2008, from *http://www.seab.gov.sg/
    SEAB/oLevel/syllabusSchool.html*.

Singapore Examinations and Assessment Board. (2008b). *GCE A Level examination: Exam
    syllabuses for school candidates*. Retrieved Aug 15, 2008, from *http://www.seab.gov.sg/
    SEAB/aLevel/syllabusSchool_Info.html*.

Singapore Examinations and Assessment Board. (2008c). *GCE A Level examination: 2008
    examination timetable*. Retrieved Oct 15, 2008, from http://www.seab.gov.sg.

Spandel, V. (2009). *Creating writers through 6-trait writing assessment and instruction* (5th
    ed.). Boston: Pearson Education.

Stern, H. H. (1992). *Issues and options in language teaching*. Oxford: Oxford University
    Press.

Sternberg, R. J. (2004). Introduction to definitions and conceptions of giftedness. In R.J. Sternberg (Ed.), *Definitions and Conceptions of Giftedness* (pp. xxiii-xxv). California, CA: Corwin Press.

Tan, K. and Koh, K.H. (2008) (Eds.), *Authentic assessment in schools.* Singapore: Prentice Hall.

Tan, K., and Lim, C. (2008). Authentic assessment: What does it actually mean? In K. Tan, and K. H. Koh (Eds.), *Authentic assessment in schools* (pp. 3-18). Singapore: Prentice Hall.

Tannenbaum, A. J. (2003). Nature and nurture of giftedness. In N. Colangelo, and G. A. Davis (Eds.), *Handbook of Gifted Education* (pp.45-56). Boston, MA: Allyn and Bacon.

Van Merriënboer, J. J. G. (1997). *Training complex cognitive skills: A four-component instructional design model for technical training.* Englewood Cliffs, NJ: Educational Technology Publications.

Van Tassel-Baska, J. (1996). The process of talent development. In D.T. Johnson, B.L. Neal, and J. VanTassel-Baska (Eds.), *Developing verbal talent: ideas and strategies for teachers of elementary and middle school students* (pp. 3-20). Boston, MA: Allyn and Bacon.

Waugh, R.F., Bowering, M. and Chayarathee, S. (2005). Creating scales to measure reading comprehension, and attitude and behaviour, for Prathom 6 (grade 6) students taught ESL through a cooperative learning method in Thailand. In R.F. Waugh (Ed.), *Frontiers in Educational Psychology* (pp.183-220). New York: Nova Science Publishers.

Waugh, R. F., and Cavanagh, R. F. (2002, December). *Linking classroom environment with educational outcomes using a Rasch measurement model.* Paper presented at the conference of the Australian Association for Research in Education, Brisbane, Australia.

Waugh, R. F., and Chapman, E. S. (2005). An analysis of dimensionality using factor analysis (true-score theory) and Rasch measurement: What is the difference? Which method is better? *Journal of Applied Measurement, 6*(1), 80-99.

Wiggins, G. P. (1990). The Case for Authentic Assessment. *ERIC Clearinghouse on Tests Measurement and Evaluation (ERIC Identifier ED328611).*

Wiggins, G. P. (1993). *Assessing student performance.* San Francisco: Jossey-Bass Publishers.

Wiggins, G. P., and McTighe, J. (1998 and revised 2005). *Understanding by design.* Alexandria, VA: Association for Supervision and Curriculum Development.

Wright, T., and Bolitho, R. (1993). Language awareness: a missing link in language teacher education? *ELT Journal, 47*(4), 292-304.

Zhang, C. Z. (2000). Tan Dangqian Yuwen Jiaoxue Cunzai de Wenti he Gaige Yijian [Discuss about the current problems and revamps in language teaching]. *Curriculum, Teaching Material and Method, 1*, 20-23.

Zhu, Y., and Tan-Foo, K. F. (2005). *An analysis of Singapore secondary students' performance on one authentic open-ended mathematics task.* Retrieved Jun 15, 2007, from *http://www.crpp.nie.edu.sg/file.php/393/RRS05-008_final_version_.pdf*

APPENDIX A: AUTHENTIC CHINESE LANGUAGE TEST

[Date of Test]
0830hr - 1300hr

语文能力真实性评量测试
Authentic Language Assessment

Duration: 4 hours and 30 minutes

考生须知:

1 本试卷共有六页。考生必须在所提供的答卷稿纸上作答。

2 本试卷共分四个部分：写作测试、古文阅读分析、文学分析一、文学分析二

3 第一部分（写作测试）共四题，任选一题作答，占30分

4 第二部分（古文阅读分析）仅有一题必答，占20分

5 第三部分（文学分析一）共两题，任选一题作答，占20分

6 第四部分（文学分析二）共三题，任选两题作答，占30分

7 考生可带规定文本进入考场，却不准把词典或笔记带入考场。

8 作答时不必抄题，但须写明题目号数。

9 细读每一组的指示后才作答。

一、写作测试（30分）

四题任选一题，字数不得少过600字。

1. 假设你现在于一间报馆工作，编辑突然派你到坊间调查国人对于新加坡大量引

   入外来人才的看法。结果，你收集了许多公众人士对这问题的想法。

   a. 试列表归类你所记录的不同看法（5分）

   b. 按照你的列表，写一篇新闻报导，其中内容必须清楚阐述公众对于此问

   题的不同意见，并在最后一段提出自己的看法（25分）

2. 身为散文作家的你，对于王维"诗中有画，画中有诗"的境界情有独钟。请尝试以王

   维诗歌《山居秋暝》为题，创作一篇同名散文来表现你对这位唐朝伟大诗人的敬仰

   （30分）

3. 假设你是位艺术评论记者，昨天在观看了老舍的《茶馆》戏剧，要为这部作品写一份

   戏剧评论，刊登在《联合早报》副刊首页。

   a. 你需要设计首页头版标题（5分）

   b. 你必须按照自己所设的标题，写一份戏剧评论报告，内容力求吸引读者

   的兴趣（25分）

4. 你是一位剧作家，需要写一份电影故事构思，明天交给电影公司。公司要求一部能吸

引青年观众的爱情喜剧片。

   a. 你需要为电影故事取一个名字，并写明主要的人物以及场景（5分）

   b. 你必须交上一份1小时电影短片的故事构思，构思文本力求简练明晰（25分）

二、古文阅读分析（20分）

　　宋代学者赵与时在《宾退录》中说："读诸葛孔明（诸葛亮）《出师表》而不堕泪者，其人必不忠。读李令伯（李密）《陈情表》而不堕泪者，其人必不孝。……"

　　试比较以下两个取自于诸葛亮《出师表》与李密《陈情表》的语段，找出两者令人不禁"堕泪"之处，并从中整理出一篇可以在发表会宣读的简短文学报告，字数不能少于300字（占15分）。文学报告应该具备一个标题及副标题（占5分），而报告的开头应为："各位老师、各位同学，你们好！今天我要发表的文学报告题目是……"

李密《陈情表》语段一：

　　伏惟圣朝以孝治天下，凡在故老，犹蒙矜育，况臣孤苦，特为尤甚。且臣少事伪朝，历职郎署，本图宦达，不矜名节。今臣亡国贱俘，至微至陋，过蒙拔擢，宠命优渥，岂敢盘桓，有所希冀？但以刘日薄西山，气息奄奄，人命危浅，朝不虑夕。臣无祖母，无以至今日；祖母无臣，无以终余年。母孙二人，更相为命，是以区区不能废远。臣密今年四十有四，祖母刘今年九十有六，是臣尽节于陛下之日长，报养刘之日短也。乌鸟私情，愿乞终养。

语段一语译：

　　我想圣朝是以孝道来治理天下的，凡是故旧老人，尚且还受到怜惜养育，何况我的孤苦程度更为严重呢？而且我年轻的时候曾经做过蜀汉的官，历任郎中和尚书郎，本来图的就是仕途通达，无意以名誉节操来炫耀。现在我是一个低贱的亡国俘虏，实在卑微到不值一提，承蒙得到提拔，而且恩命十分优厚，怎敢犹豫不决另有所图呢？但是只因为祖母刘氏已是西山落日的样子，气息微弱，生命垂危，朝不保夕。臣下我如果没有祖母，是活不到今天的，祖母如果没有我的照料，也无法度过她的余生。我们祖孙二人，互相依靠，相濡以沫，正是因为这些我的内心实在是不忍离开祖母而远行。臣下我今年四十四岁了，祖母今年九十六岁了，臣下我在陛下面前尽忠尽节的日子还长着呢，而在祖母刘氏面前尽孝尽心的日子已经不多了。我怀着乌鸦反哺的私情，企求能够准许我完成对祖母养老送终的心愿。

诸葛亮《出师表》语段二:

臣本布衣,躬耕南阳,苟全性命于乱世,不求闻达于诸侯。先帝不以臣卑鄙,猥自枉屈,三顾臣于草庐之中,谘臣以当世之事,由是感激,遂许先帝以驱驰。后值倾覆,受任于败军之际,奉命于危难之间:尔来二十有一年矣。先帝知臣谨慎,故临崩寄臣以大事也。受命以来,夙夜忧虑,恐付托不效,以伤先帝之明;故五月渡泸,深入不毛。今南方已定,甲兵已足,当奖帅三军,北定中原,庶竭驽钝,攘除奸凶,兴复汉室,还于旧都:此臣所以报先帝而忠陛下之职分也。至于斟酌损益,进尽忠言,则攸之、依、允等之任也。愿陛下托臣以讨贼兴复之效,不效则治臣之罪,以告先帝之灵;若无兴复之言,则责攸之、依、允等之咎,以彰其慢。陛下亦宜自谋,以谘诹善道,察纳雅言,深追先帝遗诏。臣不胜受恩感激!今当远离,临表涕泣,不知所云。

语段二语译:

我本来是一介平民,在南阳亲自种田,只求能在乱世中暂且保全性命,不奢求在诸侯面前有什么名气。先帝不因我身世卑微、见识短浅,反而降低自己的身份,三次到草庐里来访问我,向我征询对当今天下大事的意见,我因此十分感激,于是答应先帝愿为他奔走效劳。后来遇到失败,我在战败的时候接到委任,在危难的时候奉命出使东吴,从那时到现在已经二十一年了。先帝(刘备)知道我谨慎,因此在临终前把国家大事托付给我(诸葛亮)。自从接受任命以来,我日夜忧虑叹息,担心不能将先帝的托付的事情办好,有损先帝的圣明。所以我在五月渡过泸水,深入到荒凉的地方。现在南方已经平定,兵器已经准备充足,应当鼓舞并率领三军,向北方平定中原。希望全部贡献出自己平庸的才能,铲除奸邪凶恶的曹魏,复兴汉室,回到原来的都城洛阳。这是我用来报答先帝并忠于陛下的职责的本分。至于对政事的斟酌兴废,进献忠诚的建议,那是郭攸之、费祎、董允等人的责任。

希望陛下把讨伐奸贼、复兴汉室的任务交给我,如果没有完成,就请治我重罪,来告慰先帝在天之灵。如果没有劝勉陛下宣扬圣德的忠言,就责备郭攸之、费祎、董允等人的怠慢,来揭露他们的过失;陛下自己也应该认真考虑国家大事,征询治理国国的好办法,听取正确的意见,深切追念先帝的遗训。如果能够这样,我就受恩感激不尽了。现在我就要辞别陛下远行了,面对奏表热泪纵横,不知说了些什么。

三、文学分析（一）

两题任选一题作答，占20分。

1. **唐诗宋词**：你在一次画展看到这幅画：

Picture of a Chinese landscape painting.

Not included here for copyright reasons

在你阅读过的几首诗词中，你认为杜甫的《登高》、王维的《山居秋暝》、苏轼的《念奴娇》或是李清照的《武陵春》最能体现出这幅画的境界？为什么？（20分）

或

2. **新诗**：试以郑愁予的《错误》或徐志摩的《再别康桥》诗歌给你的启示，编写一首流行歌曲的歌词，其歌词的格式必须具备以下成分：（20分）

     a.   主歌歌词四段，每段至少八行

     b.   副歌两段，每段至少六行。

四、文学分析（二）

三题中任选两题，共 30 分。

1. 现代短篇小说

鲁迅的小说《药》这部小说着重揭示百姓思想的"毒疮"，借用人血馒头的象征赤裸裸地表现出了民族"吃人"的弱点。假设新加坡将设立鲁迅文学博物馆，试为鲁迅的《药》写一篇不超过 1000 字的作品简介，呈现这篇小说的思想精髓。（15 分）

2. 现代戏剧《茶馆》

如果有一间剧场把老舍的《茶馆》改为现代版本，你认为《茶馆》里面三幕各自代表的三个时代背景该如何被取代？（3 分）

试为剧场提供一个现代版《茶馆》的故事构思（12 分），构思中必须具备以下成分：

    a. 人物身份

    b. 场景布局

    c. 情节流程

3. 现代武侠小说《雪山飞狐》

倪匡曾评金庸的《雪山飞狐》这篇小说的结尾是"一个解不开的死结"，也是"金庸所卖弄的狡狯"。如果你要把这篇小说的结尾情节教授给一批高中二年级语文能力水平中上的学生，你会采取怎样的教学策略？你的教学计划必须具备以下成分（15 分）：

    a. 教学策略的步骤流程

    b. 教学所会用到的工具或习题

TRANSLATION FOR AUTHENTIC CHINESE LANGUAGE TEST

(Page 1)
Instructions to the Candidates

1. This paper consists of six pages. Candidates are to write their answers in answer booklets provided separately.
2. This paper consists of four sections: Writing test, ancient Chinese comprehension and analysis, literature analysis part 1, and literature analysis part 2.
3. Section 1 (writing test) has four questions, from which the candidate needs to choose only one question to attempt (30%).
4. Section 2 (ancient Chinese comprehension and analysis) has only one question, which the candidate must attempt (20%).
5. Section 3 (literature analysis part 1) has two questions, from which the candidate needs to choose only one question to attempt (20%).
6. Section 4 (literature analysis part 2) has three questions, from which the candidate needs to choose *two* questions to attempt (30%).
7. Candidates are allowed to bring in only syllabus textbooks specially printed for this examination. Dictionaries and notes are *strictly disallowed*
8. Candidates need only to copy the question number when answering the questions, there is no need to copy any question in the answer booklet
9. Candidates must carefully read the instructions in every section before attempting the questions

(Page 2)
Section 1: Writing Test (30 %)

Attempt One Question only. Your Essay should be less than 600 Words

1. Suppose you are now working in a press, and your editor needs you to do a quick survey on how local Singaporeans feel about the massive influx of foreign talents. At the end of the day, you have collected many feedbacks from the public.

    a. Draw a table to list down and categorise the feedbacks (5 marks)
    b. Write a newspaper report on your survey, with every paragraph stating different viewpoints about the issue. Make sure that you state your stand and personal view on this issue in your last paragraph. (25 marks)

2. As a writer, you have been researching on Tang dynasty famous poet Wang Wei and his sublime art of drawing sceneries with words. Using the same title as Wang Wei's famous poem "Shan Ju Qiu Ming", try to write a short prose to describe how you feel about this ingenious poet. (30 marks)

3. Imagine you are a drama critic. After watching Lao She's play "Cha Guan", you need to write a report to be published on the front page of the "Fukan" section in "Lianhe Zaobao" (Singapore Chinese newspaper).

    a. You need to design headlines for the front-page report (5 marks)
    b. You need to write a report about this play according to your headlines. Your
    c. content should attract your readers as a front-page report (25 marks).

4. Suppose you are a scriptwriter, and you need to write a script concept draft for an upcoming movie project. Your company requires you to write a script for a love comedy that can attract teenage audience.

    a. You need to give a name to your story. You also need to state the main characters and stage sets needed (5 marks).
    b. You need to write a script story for a one-hour short movie. Your story outline should be clear and concise (30 marks).

(Page 3)
Section 2: Ancient Chinese Comprehension and Analysis (20%)

Song dynasty scholar Zhao Yu Shi commented in his book "Bin Tui Lu" : "If you read Zhu Ge Liang's 'Chu Shi Biao' and not weep, then you know nothing about patriotism; if you read Li Mi's 'Chen Qing Biao' and not weep, then you know nothing about filial piety".

Referring the passages provided below, find out from the two works by Zhu Ge Liang and Li Mi, the key parts that can move readers to tears. Write a short literary comparison report (15 marks) for these two works and the report should be made ready for a mini-symposium in your school. The report should be not less than 300 words and should have a title and a sub-heading (5 marks). It should also starts with an introduction like this: "Good morning, teachers and fellow classmates, today I. am going to read my symposium report titled ... ..."

[An excerpt from Li Mi's "Chen Qing Biao" in ancient Chinese]
[Translation for the above passage in modern Chinese]

(Page 4)

[An excerpt from Zhu Ge Liang's "Chu Shi Biao"]
[Translation for the above passage]

(Page 5)
Section 3: Literature Analysis Part 1 (20%)

Attempt One Question only

1. Ancient Chinese Poetry:
Suppose you see this painting below in an art gallery:

[Picture of a Chinese painting]

From the many poems that you had read, which poems among Du Fu's "Deng Gao", Wang Wei's "Shan Ju Qiu Ming", Su Shi's "Nian Nu Jiao" and Li Qing Zhao's "Wu Ling Chun" do you think best fit the painting? Why do you think so? (20 marks)

or

2 . Contemporary Poetry :
Compose a modern mandarin pop song lyric from the content of either Zheng Chou Yu's poem "Cuo Wu" or Xu Zhi Mo's poem "Zai Bie Kang Qiao". Your lyric must consist of the below:

    a.   Four verses. Each verse must have a minimum of eight lines
    b.   Two choruses. Each chorus must have a minimum of six lines

(Page 6)
Section 4: Literature Analysis Part 2 (30%)

Attempt Two Questions out of the Three Questions in this Section

1 . Modern Short Novels
Lu Xun, in his novel "Yao", emphasized on revealing the cultural shortcomings of the Chinese people, and he used the symbol of a "bloody bun" to signify the so-called "Chinese cannibalism". If Singapore were to set up a Lu Xun literary museum, try to write a short introduction of not more than 1000 words about this novel by Lu Xun. Your writing should be able to portray the essence of the novel (15 marks).

2 . Modern Drama Play
If there is a local theatre group attempting to re-write Lao She's "Cha Guan" as a modern drama play, what do you think how the three scenes in "Cha Guan", which represent three different eras in China's history, should be replaced with? (3 marks)
Write a concept draft for a modern "Cha Guan" play (12 marks). Your script draft should include the following:

    a. Characters   b. Stage setup   c. Story outline

3 . Sword-fighting Novel

Ni Kuang once commented that Jin Yong's novel "Xue Shan Fei Hu" had an ending that proved to be "too difficult to resolve" and it is just a "cunning trick by the author". Imagine you are teaching this part of the novel to a class of junior college year 2 students with good language skills. What type of teaching strategy would you adopt? Write a teaching plan draft with the following elements:

a. A systematic flowchart of teaching strategy b. Teaching tools or worksheets

APPENDIX B: OCK GCE 'A' LEVEL CHINESE LANGUAGE TEST PAPER 1

GCE 'A' Level H2 Chinese Language and Literature
MOCK EXAMINATIONS

8121/1	2006 Mock
9121/1	[Date of Test]
	0830 — 1130

H2 华文与文学
试卷一

Chinese Language and Literature H2

Paper 1

考生须知:

1 本试卷共有七页, 分为两个部分分印。

2 第一部分和第二部分的答案应全写在同一套答卷上。

3 应用华文词典

   a. 第一部分: 考生可以翻查词典。

   (规定应用词典时间: 1 小时 15 分钟)

   b. 第二部分: 考生作答时<u>不可以</u>翻查词典。

   c. 考生必须在第一部分作答卷右上角写上词典及其出版社的名称。

4 细读每一组的指示后才作答。

第一部分

一、作文（**35分**）

任选一题，字数不得少过**600**字。

1. 试以《夏日炎炎》为题，写一篇描写文或记叙文

2. 试根据一下漫画的内容，写一篇记叙文

Picture of a man in a factory making spectacles.

Not included here for copyright reasons

3. 请以"我与日记"为题写一篇文章。文体没有限制，但不能写成诗歌

4. 试根据下列一段文字给你的启示，写一篇议论文，并自拟题目

在追求人生目标的过程中，我们有时也会被途中的细枝末节和一些毫无意义的琐事，分散了精力，扰乱了视线，以至中途停顿下来，或是走上岔路，而放弃了自己原先追求的目标。

第二部分

二、阅读理解（一）（共 25 分）

　　逮奉圣朝，沐浴清化。前太守臣逵，察臣孝廉；后刺史臣荣，举臣秀才。臣以供养无主，辞不赴命。诏书特下，拜臣郎中；寻蒙国恩，除臣洗马。猥以微贱，当侍东宫，非臣陨首所能上报。臣具以表闻，辞不就职，诏书切峻，责臣逋慢；郡县逼迫，催臣上道；州司临门，急于星火。臣欲奉诏奔驰，则以刘病日笃；欲苟顺私情，则告诉不许。臣之进退，实为狼狈。

1. 试解释下列画线的词语：（6 分）

1.1　寻蒙国恩，除臣洗马：＿＿＿＿＿＿＿＿＿＿＿＿＿＿＿＿＿＿

1.2　猥以微贱，当侍东宫，非臣陨首所能上报：＿＿＿＿＿＿＿＿＿＿

1.3　诏书切峻，责臣逋慢：＿＿＿＿＿＿＿＿＿＿＿＿＿＿＿＿＿＿

2.　试把下列句子改写成白话文（8 分）

2.1 逮奉圣朝，沐浴清化。前太守臣逵，察臣孝廉；后刺史臣荣，举臣秀才。

＿＿＿＿＿＿＿＿＿＿＿＿＿＿＿＿＿＿＿＿＿＿＿＿＿＿＿＿＿＿＿＿

＿＿＿＿＿＿＿＿＿＿＿＿＿＿＿＿＿＿＿＿＿＿＿＿＿＿＿＿＿＿＿＿

2.2 臣欲奉诏奔驰，则以刘病日笃；欲苟顺私情，则告诉不许。

＿＿＿＿＿＿＿＿＿＿＿＿＿＿＿＿＿＿＿＿＿＿＿＿＿＿＿＿＿＿＿＿

＿＿＿＿＿＿＿＿＿＿＿＿＿＿＿＿＿＿＿＿＿＿＿＿＿＿＿＿＿＿＿＿

3. 你认为李密通过什么途径辞诏"辞不赴命"？（6 分）

＿＿＿＿＿＿＿＿＿＿＿＿＿＿＿＿＿＿＿＿＿＿＿＿＿＿＿＿＿＿＿＿

＿＿＿＿＿＿＿＿＿＿＿＿＿＿＿＿＿＿＿＿＿＿＿＿＿＿＿＿＿＿＿＿

嗟夫！予尝求古仁人之心，或异二者之为，何哉？不以物喜，不以己悲；居庙堂之高则忧其民；处江湖之远则忧其君。是进亦忧，退亦忧。然则何时而乐耶？其必曰"先天下之忧而忧，后天下之乐而乐"乎。

范仲淹　《岳阳楼记》

4. 作者所追求的所谓"仁人之心"蕴含着什么意义？作者范仲淹是如何定义忧国忧民之精神？试从以上语段找出两点加以说明（5分）

_____

_____

三、阅读理解（二）（共20分）

有句老话叫"知易行难"，懂得道理很容易，付诸行动却很难。聪明人喜欢"眉头一皱计上心来"的潇洒，但是，他们往往只限于"脑力激荡"，而不善于与人打交道，5.1 _____，结果聪明反被聪明误。历史上的周瑜何等聪明，但结局却是悲剧。现代企业管理中，无数次商场上的起起落落，似乎都证明了这个5.2 _____的真理。

有人这么界定"聪明"的含义———一个人的智商高出普通人的正常值，这样的人就是我们生活中常说的聪明人。顺着这个5.3 _____，我们会发现很多成功的企业家并不绝顶聪明；相反的，他们可能还曾是差生。有个统计数字显示，他们中最多只有不超过10%的人智商超群，其余90%的智商绝对只是普通人水平。但是，他们成功了。我们或许还能够回想起企业界一些5.4 _____般的人物，他们嗅觉灵敏，脑筋活络；他们能够迅速洞察消费者的心理，精心包装各种产品并迅速形成市场规模，然后又迅速消失……时至今日，这些聪明人又在哪里？聪明本不是坏东西，但它可能坏事，它只是初步的，我们必须通过5.5

_____ 去把聪明转变成智慧，因为智慧而进步，在智慧的基础上行动，

够事半功倍。

5. 从下列表中选择适当的词语写在横线上（5分）

流星	练习	刚愎自用	自强不息	实践
复杂	朴素	快马	逻辑	道理

5.1 _____

5.2 _____

5.3 _____

5.4 _____

5.5 _____

6. 文中为什么说"知易行难"是聪明人常遇到困难的原因？（4分）

_____

_____

7. 读了这篇文章，你认为作者怎么定义聪明人与成功的联系？（5分）

_____

_____

8. 作者对聪明人抱着哪些主观的看法？试举例加以阐述作者的论点（6分）

_____

_____

四、阅读理解（三）（共 20 分）

　　有心人倡议让孩童读经，如空谷跫音。此建议很有远见，用心良苦。在科技发达，资讯汹涌如潮的今时今日，提倡读经，似乎有点不切实际。但经书是前人智慧的结晶，如能背而诵之，融成身心不可分割的部分，前人的智慧变成自身的智慧，受用无穷。

　　我觉得让孩童读经还不够，应该也让他们学写大、小楷，并希望能从课业发展成为生活的一种嗜好。习字，是一种艺术熏陶。这种文字和艺术相结合的独特艺术，唯中华文化才有，应该珍惜。

　　写字，简单的纸、笔、墨、砚，不必花什么钱，可以成就一门艺术，也可以怡情养性。

　　过去的中学课业里，每周都规定要交几篇大小楷。写得端正的字老师都用红墨水圈上鸡蛋，以资鼓励。每周几篇的大小楷当然培养不出书法家，但这是秧苗，是指引你到艺术殿堂的开端；而且写字也大可不必以成书法家为目的，写字本身就充满情趣；此情趣惟有拿起笔来，浸淫其中，自有体会。

　　古时候形容嗜好书法之勤者，"凡家之衣帛，必书而后练之，临池学书，池水尽黑。"我小时候也嗜好书法，但勤快程度，与古人相距十万八千里。虽然经常一写就是好几个小时，但做不到天天如是，不然几年下来，果真身边有池，写完字洗笔洗砚，池水不黑也会变色。

　　所谓"字无百日功"，虽然说的是练字必须假以时日的刻苦磨练，无捷径可走，但如果掌握方法，百日的苦练，是可以看出功效的。

　　念中学时曾经参加一个钢笔书法函授班，指导老师将中文分解为横、竖、点、撇、捺等基本笔法，先要求学员从基本笔法练起，在大方格的习字簿上，一横一横的画，一竖一竖的写。稳定笔势后，再像搭建房子一样，将这些基本笔画建构成字。这种练法的特色是不需临帖，而在你现有字体的基础上，规范凝聚成你原有风貌的字体。这种方法非常有效，三个星期即可改变你字体的面貌。

　　写字，还可以养生。

　　古代之论书者，每每提到写字之先，要"默坐静思，随意所适"，"贵乎沉静，意在笔先"，要"收视反听，心正气和"。练字的准备工夫和练习气功的原则并无二致。人们常说练字可以长寿，看来所言不虚。

9. 这篇文章的中心论点是：（2 分）

（1）天天练字，乃长寿之秘方
（2）写字养性，胜于读经背诵
（3）练字之妙，在于修身养性
（4）练字之法，独有勤奋二字

10. 文章的最后一段哪八个字最能表达书法养性之道？为什么？（2 分）

_____

_____

11. 下列对文章的分析，哪两项是正确的? 请在适当的格子里打 "√"（4分）

1	书法不只是一个情趣，也是德育美育之道	
2	读经是不够的，应该也孩子学写书法，并发展成为一种嗜好	
3	书法乃中华文化瑰宝，蕴含了许多修身养性之道理	
4	练书法能延年益寿，与练习气功的原则并无二致	

12. 试将第二至五段所写成约 120 字的短文（12分）

TRANSLATION OF THE CHINESE LANGUAGE AND LITERATURE H2
PAPER 1

(Page 1)
Instructions to the Candidates

1. This paper consists of seven pages. It is formatted separately into two main sections (as the second section paper will not be given out until the dictionary allowance time of 1 hour and 15 minutes is over)
2. The answers of both section 1 and 2 are to be written in the same answer booklet

3. Use of Chinese dictionaries

    a. Section 1: candidates are allowed to refer to their dictionaries Duration allowed for use of dictionaries: First 1 hour 15 minutes)
    b. Section 2: candidates are NOT allowed to refer to their dictionaries

4. Candidate must write the name of the dictionary publisher on the top right corner of the first page of answer booklet
5. Please read the instructions carefully before attempting the questions

(Page 2)
Section 1

I. Essay Writing 35%

Choose One Question and Write an Essay not less than 600 Words

1. Write a narrative or descriptive essay with the title "A hot summer"
2. Write a narrative essay according to the content of the picture below:
[Drawing]
3. Write an essay with the title "The diary and I". There is no restriction on the style of writing, except that poetry will not be accepted
4. Write an argumentative essay according to the content of the passage below. You are to give your essay a title.

In the pursuit for life goals, we tend to be boggled down by miscellaneous and meaningless issues, losing our focus with half-hearted efforts, and even straying away until we eventually give up our goals set initially.

(Pages 3 - 5)
Section 2

II. Comprehension Part 1 Total 25%
[An excerpt from ancient Chinese literature "Chen Qing Biao" by Li Mi]

1. Translate the vocabulary terms below into modern Chinese – 6 marks
    [Three underlined vocabulary terms from the ancient Chinese excerpt are set as questions]
2. Translate the sentences below into modern Chinese – 8 marks
    [Two sentences from the ancient Chinese excerpt are set as questions]
3. How do you think did Li Mi manage to reject the imperial edict's call to assume the responsibility of an officer? – 6 marks
4. [An excerpt from ancient Chinese literature "Shi Shuo" by Han Yu]

How do you interpret the meaning of "Ren Ren Zhi Xin" (the "heart" of a holy man) How did the author Fan Zhong Yan define patriotism? Please draw two arguments from the passage to work your answers – 5 marks

III. Comprehension Part 2 [Cloze Passage] Total 20%

[A modern Chinese passage that discusses about the "over-use" of intelligence that often works against clever people. On contrary, many so-called "not-so-intelligent" people often end up as high flyers, as they are more willing to put in hard work and stay focus on their simple goals]

5. Choose the correct words from the box for the answers of the cloze passage question – 5 marks

meteoric	practice	arrogant	self-renewal	put to practice
complicated	simple	quick as a running horse	logic	meaning

6. Why did the author feel that the logic of "things are easier said than done" often proves to be too much for clever people? - 4 marks
7. How did the author link the definition of a true clever man to the meaning of success? - 5 marks
8. How did the author personally feel about clever people? Try to give your own examples to argue for the author's viewpoints. - 6 marks

(Pages 6 - 7)

IV. Comprehension Part 3 Total 20%

[A modern Chinese passage that encourages the use of Chinese calligraphy as a form of moral education]

9. The main theme of the passage is: -- 2 marks

(1) practice calligraphy daily, will promote longevity
(2) practice calligraphy will be better than just memorizing words of wisdom
(3) the essence of practice calligraphy lies on its effect on one's moral well-being
(4) practice calligraphy needs a lot of hard work
10. Which one of the "eight-character–words of wisdom" sums up the essence of Chinese calligraphy? Why do you choose these words? – 2 marks
11. Which two of the statements represent the themes of the passage? Tick the boxes beside the correct statements – 4 marks

1	Chinese calligraphy is not only a hobby, it is a way to improve one's moral and character
2	Studying words of wisdom is not enough, children should be taught Chinese calligraphy
3	Chinese calligraphy is a gem in Chinese culture, it encompasses many truths about life's well-being
4	Chinese calligraphy can promote longevity, having the same effect as practicing Qigong

12. Rewrite paragraph 2 to 5 into a short summary of 120 words – 12 marks

APPENDIX C: MOCK GCE 'A' LEVEL CHINESE LANGUAGE TEST PAPER 2

GCE 'A' Level H2 Chinese Language and Literature

MOCK EXAMINATIONS

8121/2 9121/2	2006 Mock [Date of Test] 1430hr - 1730hr

H2 华文与文学

试卷二

Chinese Language and Literature H2

Paper 2

考生须知：

1   本试卷共有三页，分为四个部分，共有十二题。

2   考生可带规定文本进入考场，却<u>不准把词典或笔记带入考场</u>。

3   第一部分共有三组六题，考生须选答四题：考生从中每一组必选答一题，第四题

       再从三组中任选一题作答。

4   考生须在第二、三、四部分每一部分中任选一题作答，每题二十分。

5   作答时不必抄题，但须写明题目号数。

6   细读每一组的指示后才作答。

第一部分：简答题（四题，共占40分）

第一部分共三组六题，从各组中选答一题，第四题从三组中任选一题作答。

第一组：唐诗

1. 杜甫在《登高》其中哪两个诗句最能体现出诗人孤单悲秋的心情？为什么？（1
   分）

2. 王维在《山居秋暝》中如何通过诗句结构的安排达到"诗中有画，画中有诗"的艺术
   境界（10分）

第二组：宋词

3. 苏轼在《念奴娇》中通过缅怀三国英雄周瑜表现出什么感慨情绪？（10分）

4. 李清照在《武陵春》一词中如何体现出忧愁哀伤的风格？（10分）

第三组：新诗

5. 郑愁予在诗歌《错误》中如何体现出浪漫的艺术风格？（10分）

6. 《再别康桥》一诗怎么表现出作者理想幻灭的失落情绪？（10分）

第二部分：现代短篇小说（任选一题，占20分）

7. 鲁迅在《药》小说中如何通过人物的塑造传达出揭示百姓思想愚昧迷信的主题？

   （20分）

8. 试分析王蒙《最宝贵的》中严一行与蛋蛋两父子的矛盾（20分）

第三部分：现代戏剧（任选一题，占20分）

9. 老舍在《茶馆》所安排的三幕时代背景有何共同点？（10分）如此时代背景的安排

   又与王利发的悲剧下场有何联系？（10分）

10. 《茶馆》第二幕中的"莫谈国事"字条"保存了下来，而且字写得更大"，这一场

景安排暗示了第二幕时代里的哪些社会问题？（**10**分），又怎么刻画了王掌柜的思

想变化？（**10**分）

第四部分：武侠小说（任选一题，占 **20** 分）

11. 作者如何在《雪山飞狐》中借助胡斐与苗若兰的爱情带出胡斐与苗人凤结尾

决斗的心理矛盾？（**14**分）你对于小说的结尾情节有什么看法？（**6**分）

12. 《雪山飞狐》在故事叙述方面具备什么特色？（**10**分）作者如何采用不同的叙述观

点有效地勾画出主角人物的轮廓？（**10**分）

TRANSLATION OF THE CHINESE LANGUAGE AND LITERATURE H2 PAPER 2

(Page 1)
Instructions to the Candidates

1. This paper consists of three pages. It has four sections with twelve questions
2. Candidates are allowed to bring in only syllabus textbooks specially printed for this examination. Dictionaries and notes are *strictly disallowed*
3. Section 1 consists of three subsections with six questions, from which candidates must answer four questions. Candidates must answer one question from every subsection, and choose the fourth question from any one of the three subsections
4. For Section 2, 3 and 4, candidates must choose to answer one of the questions from each section. Each question is 20 marks
5. Candidates need only to copy the question number when answering the questions, there is no need to copy any question in the answer booklet
6. Candidates must carefully read the instructions in every section before attempting the questions

(Page 2)
Section 1: Short-answer Questions (Answer Four Questions, Total 40%)

There are three subsections with six questions, from which candidates must answer one question from every subsection, and choose the fourth question from any of the three subsections

Subsection 1: Tang Dynasty Poetry

1. Which of the two lines from Du Fu's "Deng Gao" express his lonely sad feelings about his past? Why do you think they are the most appropriate lines? (10 marks)
2. How did Wang Wei manage to display the "sublime art of visual poetry" in his work "Shan Ju Qiu Ming"? (10 marks)

Subsection 2: Song Dynasty Ci Poetry

3. Through reminiscence of hero Zhou Yu in his work "Lian Nu Jiao", what emotion did poet Su Shu want to express? (10 marks)
4. How did Li Qing Zhao exhibit her plaintive yet elegant style of writing in her work "Wu Ling Chun" (10 marks)

Subsection 3: Contemporary Poetry

5. Analyse Zheng Chou Yu's romanticistic style of writing in his work "Cuo Wu" (10 marks)
6. How did the poem "Zai Bie Kang Qiao" express the poet's sense of loss and disillusion? (10 marks)

Section 2: Contemporary Short Novels (Choose and Answer One Question only, 20%)

7. How did Lu Xun express the theme of superstition and fatuity among the Chinese commoners through the characters in his work "Yao" ? (20 marks)
8. Analyse the conflict between Yan and his son in the short novel "Zui Bao Gui De". By Wang Meng. (20 marks)

(Page 3)
Section 3: Contemporary Drama Play (Choose and Answer One Question only, 20%)

9. What is the common theme behind the three different historic sets in Lao She's play "Cha Guan"? (10 marks) How does these historic sets relate to the demise of the main character Wang Li Fa? (10 marks)

10. The second scene in the drama play "Cha Guan" started with the same notices "No politics please" pasted all over, except that the notices are written in larger characters. What political problems does this special arrangement implicate? (10 marks) and how does this difference in the pasted notices bring forth the change in Wang Li Fa's (boss of tea house) character? (10 marks)

Section 4: Sword-fighting Novel (Choose and Answer One Question only, 20%)

11. How did the author of "Xue Shan Fei Hu", through the love story between Hu Fei and Miao, manage to describe the psychological turmoil in the "last duel" ending where Hu Fei was forced to fight Miao's father to death? (14 marks) What do you think of the ending of the novel story? (6 marks)

12. What are the special narrative techniques used in the novel "Xue Shan Fei Hu" (10 marks) How did the author used different points of view to introduce the main character – Hu Fei? (10 marks)

In: Applications of Rasch Measurement in Education
Editor: Russell Waugh
ISBN: 978-1-61668-026-8
© 2010 Nova Science Publishers, Inc.

Chapter 9

RASCH MEASURES OF A MOCK CHINESE LANGUAGE TEST AT CAMBRIDGE "A" LEVEL STANDARD

Ong Chun Ghee[1] and Russell Waugh[2]
[1]. Dunman High School
[2]. Graduate School of Education, University of Western Australia

ABSTRACT

This paper is part of a larger study into the measuring of achievement of Chinese language talents at Cambridge 'A' Level in Singapore. A Mock 'A' Level paper was prepared and administered to N=101 students who aimed to attend university the following year from a population of 405. Students completed the test in a formal setting over six hours on a voluntary basis. They came from three different Junior Colleges and included 75 females and 26 males. The test was divided into three parts that were separately Rasch analysed to create three uni-dimensional, linear scales. For the 'Basic Test' of 10 items, the item-trait chi-square was $\chi^2 = 20.28$, df = 20, $p = 0.44$; for the 'Intermediate Test' of 14 items it was $\chi^2 = 33.19$, df = 28, $p = 0.14$; and for the 'Advanced Test' of 11 items it was $\chi^2 = 29.38$, df = 22, $p = 0.13$, showing a reasonable overall fit to the measurement model. The Student Separation Index was 0.61, 0.82 and 0.91 respectively and the Cronbach Alpha was 0.65, 0.82 and 0.89 respectively, showing acceptable scale reliability. Differential Item Functioning was tested and the items were found to be performing satisfactorily. The items in each test were ordered from easy to hard providing good information relating to the difficulty of the items and performance of the students.

MOCK 'A' LEVEL CHINESE LANGUAGE TEST

This chapter presents the Rasch analysis (Rasch, 1960/1980) of the Mock 'A' Level Chinese Language Test in three separate parts, namely the basic, intermediate and advanced categories. Each analysis uses output data produced by the Rasch Unidimensional Measurement Model (RUMM 2020) program (Andrich, Sheridan and Luo, 2005), and determines if all three parts of the language test are reliable and have a good fit to the Rasch measurement model.

In producing tests-of-fit during data analysis, there were two pertinent problems present that required some adjustments to be made. Firstly, the scoring responses for some of the test items were not logical and consistent. As a result, some of the thresholds were not ordered in line with the scoring marks, and the test scores then would not fit the Rasch measurement model. Notably, there was an intermediate category essay test item being assessed in a wide score range from 0 to 18 marks (see previous chapter) as the mock paper needed to simulate the GCE 'A' Level scoring system (Ministry of Education, 2006c). Test items like this often resulted in poor discrimination between the scores, causing the differences between, for example 12, 13 and 14 marks, to be inconsistent due to low numbers of students in these categories. Although this problem could be resolved by breaking up the total scores into smaller components requiring the markers to mark these components in scores of lesser marks, it would be less authentic for the Mock 'A' Level Test in simulating the GCE 'A' Level assessment system. A more viable solution was to group adjacent scoring responses together to form a more consistent scoring system. For example the scores of 12, 13 and 14 will be grouped together as one score for the Rasch analysis to ensure ordered item thresholds.

The second problem with the Rasch analysis was that some test items did not fit the Rasch measurement model. These were the items on which students could not agree about their levels of difficulty and which subsequently led to the entire test not fitting the measurement model. An example of such items was the translation of ancient Chinese vocabulary terms in the basic category. Regurgitation of memorized content is adequate to score in this test item. Regurgitating model answers might appear easy for all students who had memorized their notes, yet this "easy" item did not yield full marks for many students who simply could not recall the exact translated answers during the test. Hence, some of these items might be removed during the test analysis in order to create a better fit for the measurement model.

In light of the adjustments made to overcome analysis constraints, the data analyses manage to derive reasonably accurate measurement scales for the three parts of the Mock 'A' Level Test. The following sections report on the Rasch measurement fit statistics for each part of the test and explain how the unidimensional scales of language ability measurement were created with the RUMM 2020 program.

The program provides output statistics such as student-item interactions (chi-square), Student Separation Index, item and student fit to the measurement model, global item and student fit residuals and the consistency of use of scoring categories. The program also provides targeting graphs, Item Characteristic Curves to check on item discrimination and item differential functioning across selected aspects.

Table 1. Scoring adjustment in the Basic Mock 'A' Level Language Test

Item	Score Adjustment	Item	Score Adjustment
P1/4	0=0, 1=1, 2=1	P1/12	0=0, 1=0, 2=1, 3=1, 4=1, 5=2
P1/5	0=0, 1=1, 2=1	P1/13	0=0,1=0, 2=1,3=1,4=1, 5=2, 6=2
P1/8	0=0, 1=0, 2=0, 3=1, 4=1, 5=2, 6=2	P1/14	0=0,1=1, 2=1
P1/9	0=0, 1=0, 2=0, 3=1, 4=1, 5=2	P1/16	0=0,1=1, 2=1, 3=1, 4=2
P1/10	0=0, 1=1, 2=2, 3=2, 4=2, 5=3	P1/17	0=0,1=0, 2=1,3=1,4=1,5=1, 6=1, 7=1, 8=2

Source: Designed by Ong (2009) for this study from the RUMM analysis.

OVERALL FIT TO THE MEASUREMENT MODEL

The program computes a statistic to determine the overall fit of the data to the measurement model. For each student on each item, the expected value (according to the measurement model) is compared with the observed mean of scores that students with the same total score obtained on each item. If the observed and expected values are not significantly different, then there is no significant interaction between the responses to the items and the location values (measures) of the students along the trait. This item-trait interaction is represented by a chi-square statistic and, when there is no significant interaction, this is what it means to have a unidimensional trait. The following sections report this statistic for the three parts of the Mock 'A' Level Test respectively.

Basic Mock 'A' Level Test

There were initially 14 test items ordered in the Basic Mock 'A' Level Test. During the initial analysis, four test items, namely P1/3, P1/11, P1/15 and P1/18, were found to be poorly fitting and hence were removed for the final analysis. Also, the initial scoring system was adjusted to ensure consistency of the item scoring. The adjustments are shown in Table 1.

The remaining ten ordered test items (I = 10, N = 101) were used to create a linear scale showing good overall fit to the measurement model. The item-trait interaction chi-square of χ^2 = 20.28, df = 20.00, p = 0.44 shows that there is no statistically significant interaction between the student measures and the item difficulties along the scale. All the items fit with a probability of $p > 0.09$ and the Student Separation Index is 0.61 (and Cronbach Alpha is 0.65). While the reliability is acceptable, it needs to be improved. Considering these statistics, the basic Mock 'A' Level Test would seem to be a test that needs some improvements.

Intermediate Mock 'A' Level Test

The Intermediate Mock 'A' Level Test initially had 14 items ordered in difficulty from easy to hard. There were problems obtaining sufficient students for some test items, such as P1/2, where scoring ranges from 0 to 17 marks, to attain good discrimination. As the present study could only obtain N = 101, there were insufficient responses to score all of the marks over the wide scoring range. Hence, the program was unable to calculate some thresholds for these test items. Therefore, adopting the same solution as with the Basic Mock Test, the scoring system for the Intermediate Mock Test also needed to be adjusted as shown in Table 2.

After the scoring adjustment, the program analysis output showed that all 14 intermediate test items (I = 14, N = 101) yielded a total item-trait interaction chi-square of χ^2 = 36.19, df = 28.00, p = 0.14. This shows that there is no statistically significant interaction between the student measures and the item difficulties along the scale and that there is a good fit to the measurement model. The Student Separation Index was 0.82 (and the Cronbach Alpha equals 0.82). It is evident that the Intermediate Mock 'A' Level Test is a reliable scale with a good fit to the measurement model.

Table 2. Scoring adjustment in the Intermediate Mock 'A' Level Test

Item	Score Adjustment	Item	Score Adjustment
P1/6	0=0, 1-3=1, 4=2	P2/25	0=0, 1-3=1, 4=2, 5=3
P1/7	0=0, 1-3=1, 4=2	P2/27a	0=0, 1-3=1, 4=2
P1/2	0=0, 1-4=1, 5-9=2, 10-18=3	P2/27b	0=0, 1-3=1, 4=2
P1/1	0=0, 1-4=1, 5-9=2, 10-18=3	P2/29a	0=0, 1-3=1, 4=2
P2/19	0=0, 1-4=1, 5=2	P2/29b	0=0, 1-3=1, 4=2
P2/21	0=0, 1-4=1, 5=2	P2/31a	0=0, 1-3=1, 4=2
P2/23	0=0, 1-4=1, 5=2	P2/31b	0=0, 1-3=1, 4=2

Source: Designed by Ong (2009) for this study from the RUMM output.

Table 3. Scoring adjustments in the Advanced Mock 'A' Level Test

Item	Score Adjustment	Item	Score Adjustment
P2/22	0=0, 1=1, 2=1, 3=1, 4=2, 5=3	P2/30b	0=0, 1=1, 2=1, 3=1, 4=2
P2/24	0=0, 1=1, 2=1, 3=1, 4=2, 5=3	P2/30c	0=0, 1=1, 2=1, 3=2, 4=3
P2/26	0=0, 1=1, 2=1, 3=1, 4=2, 5=3	P2/32a	0=0, 1=1, 2=1, 3=1, 4=2
P2/28b	0=0, 1=1, 2=1, 3=2, 4=3	P2/32b	0=0, 1=1, 2=1, 3=2, 4=3
P2/28c	0=0, 1=1, 2=1, 3=2, 4=3	P2/32c	0=0, 1=1, 2=1, 3=2, 4=3
P2/30a	0=0, 1=1, 2=1, 3=2, 4=3		

Source: Designed by Ong (2009) for this study from the RUMM output.

Advanced Mock 'A' Level Test

The Advanced Mock 'A' Level Test initially had 13 test items ordered by difficulty and despite scoring adjustments being made as shown in Table 3, two test items P2/20 and P2/28a needed to be removed in order to construct a linear scale (I = 11, N = 101) with good agreement about all item difficulties along the scale.

The final constructed measure yielded an item-trait interaction chi-square value of χ^2 = 29.38, df = 22.00, p = 0.13. All 11 items fitted with a probability of $p > 0.09$. The Student Separation Index was 0.91 (and Cronbach Alpha was 0.89). It is evident that the Advanced Mock 'A' Level Test is a reliable scale with a good fit to the measurement model.

OTHER RUMM OUTPUT STATISTICS

Student Separation Index

The Student Separation Index is an important criterion used to determine the quality of test construct. A good language test will have the measures of language ability well separated in comparison to the errors, which are expected to be relatively small. The standard errors of measurement for the Basic, Intermediate and Advanced categories of the Mock 'A' Level Tests are about 0.20 logits, compared to the corresponding Student Separation Indices of 0.61, 0.82 and 0.91. While the Intermediate and Advanced Mock 'A' Level Tests both show good separation of measures compared to their mean error values, the Basic Mock 'A' Level

Test shows not so good separation of measures compared to errors. The implication drawn is that this measure is not as reliable as those from the other two measures. The reliability might be improved by adding some extra harder items in any future use of the test.

Item Fit to the Measurement Model

In the output analysis, individual item fits to the measurement model are presented in tabular form. The fit statistics for all test items in the three categories of the Mock 'A' Level Tests are collated in Table 4, Table 5 and Table 6.

Table 4. Fit of items to Rasch Measurement Model (Basic Mock 'A' Level Test)

Item No.	Location	SE	Residual	df	ChiSq	Prob
Item 1	NF					
Item 2	-0.53	0.31	-0.75	89.20	1.05	0.59
Item 3	-1.54	0.42	-0.34	89.20	0.60	0.74
Item 4	-0.07	0.20	-0.98	89.20	2.49	0.29
Item 5	+0.38	0.19	-1.24	89.20	4.82	0.09
Item 6	-1.79	0.24	0.89	89.20	2.49	0.29
Item 8	+0.80	0.23	-1.19	89.20	2.24	0.33
Item 9	+0.40	0.20	-1.26	89.20	0.60	0.74
Item 10	-0.25	0.29	0.29	89.20	1.57	0.46
Item 11	NF					
Item 12	+0.94	0.18	1.56	89.20	4.34	0.11
Item 13	+1.65	0.30	-0.74	89.20	0.07	0.97
Item 14	NF					

Source: Designed by Ong (2009) for this study from the RUMM analysis.

Table 5. Fit of items to Rasch Measurement Model (Intermediate Mock 'A' Level Test)

Item No.	Location	SE	Residual	df	ChiSq	Prob
Item 1	+4.16	0.52	-0.64	91.64	0.70	0.71
Item 2	+2.76	0.21	3.07	91.64	12.02	0.00
Item 3	+0.68	0.71	0.25	91.64	1.43	0.49
Item 4	-3.25	0.71	0.29	91.64	3.41	0.18
Item 5	-1.33	0.43	-1.00	91.64	0.41	0.82
Item 6	-1.97	0.30	-1.65	91.64	2.71	0.26
Item 7	-0.42	0.25	-0.66	91.64	0.55	0.76
Item 8	+0.29	0.20	1.42	91.64	1.95	0.38
Item 9	+2.05	0.23	-1.75	91.64	3.53	0.17
Item 10	-0.75	0.25	-0.71	91.64	0.30	0.86
Item 11	-1.33	0.22	-2.44	91.64	4.52	0.10
Item 12	-0.35	0.22	-1.39	91.64	1.02	0.60
Item 13	-0.46	0.20	-1.95	91.64	1.87	0.40
Item 14	-0.086	0.20	-1.26	91.64	1.78	0.41

Source: Designed by Ong (2009) for this study from the RUMM analysis.

As shown in the Table 4, 11 items of the Easy Mock 'A' Level Test fitted the measurement model with probabilities greater than, or equal to, p = 0.09. For the Intermediate Mock 'A' Level Test, Table 5 shows that all its 14 items fitted the measurement model with probabilities greater than, or equal to, p = 0.10 (except for item 2). For the Advanced Mock 'A' Level Test, 11 items fitted the measurement model with probabilities greater than, or equal to, p = 0.01. All the item-fits in the three parts of 'A' Level mock tests support other fits to the measurement, implying that three reasonably consistent scales have been created in the present study.

Table 6. Fit of items to Rasch Measurement Model for (Advanced Mock 'A' Level Test)

Item No.	Location	SE	Residual	df	ChiSq	Prob
Item 1	NF					
Item 2	-1.58	0.20	0.63	88.27	4.15	0.13
Item 3	+0.17	0.17	2.26	88.27	2.50	0.29
Item 4	NF					
Item 5	-0.97	0.17	-0.79	88.27	1.50	0.47
Item 6	+0.44	0.19	-1.01	88.27	3.29	0.19
Item 7	+0.83	0.16	0.52	88.27	1.89	0.39
Item 8	-0.59	0.16	-0.02	88.27	0.32	0.85
Item 9	+0.14	0.24	-0.82	88.27	4.78	0.09
Item 10	+0.53	0.15	0.31	88.27	0.45	0.80
Item 11	-0.20	0.22	-0.03	88.27	9.64	0.01
Item 12	+0.43	0.22	-0.44	88.27	0.75	0.69
Item 13	+0.80	0.15	-0.51	88.27	0.11	0.94

Source: Designed by Ong (2009) for this study from the RUMM analysis.

Notes for Tables 4, 5 and 6.

1. Location refers to the difficulty of the item on the linear scale.
2. SE refers to standard error, that is, the degree of the uncertainty in a value. In this case, the standard error for each item is reasonable, ranging from 0.18 to 0.42 logits (for Table 6.4), 0.20 to 0.71 logits (for Table 6.5) and 0.15 to 0.24 logits (for Table 6.6) for the basic, intermediate and advanced part of Mock 'A' Level Test respectively.
3. Residual represents the difference between the expected value on an item, calculated according to the Rasch measurement model, and its actual value.
4. df (degrees of freedom) refers to the number of scores in a distribution that are free to change without changing the mean of the distribution.
5. ChiSq means chi-square.
6. Prob means probability, and refers to the levels of certainty to which an item fits the measurement model, based on its chi-square.
7. N/F means no fit (hence, the test item was removed from the final linear scale)
8. All values are given to two decimal places because the errors are to two decimal places.

Item-Student Fit Residuals

Fit residuals refer to the differences between the actual test score values and the expected test score values. If the test score data fits the measurement model, these fit residuals, when standardized, would have an approximately normal distribution with mean value = 0 and standard deviation value = 1. For each of the three categories in the Mock 'A' Level Tests, the standardized fit residuals have a mean near zero and a standard deviation near one, for both the item difficulties and the student measures (see Table 7).

Table 7. Global item and student fit residuals for the three Mock 'A' Level Tests

'A' Level Mock Tests	Statistic	Item locations	Item residuals	Student locations	Student residuals
Basic	Mean	0.00	-0.38	+1.66	-0.39
	SD	1.08	0.98	+1.20	0.99
Intermediate	Mean	0.00	-0.60	+0.30	-0.42
	SD	1.93	1.47	+1.63	0.67
Advanced	Mean	0.00	0.01	+0.57	-0.39
	SD	0.77	0.93	+1.80	1.26

Source: Designed by Ong (2009) for this study from the RUMM analysis.
1. Item location is item difficulty in logits
2. Person location is the student measure in logits
3. SD is standard deviation
4. The mean item difficulty is constrained to zero by the RUMM 2020 program
5. Fit residuals are the difference between the actual values and the expected values calculated according to the measurement model (standardised) (a good fit for these data). They have a mean near zero and an SD near 1.
6. All values are given to two decimal places because the errors are to two decimal places.

The standardized fit residual data for the basic test have mean values of -0.38 (items), -0.39 (students) and standard deviation values of 0.98 (item), 0.99 (students), which indicate good consistency of student responses to the test items. The standardized fit residual data for the intermediate test have a mean value of -0.60 (items), -0.42 (students) and standard deviation value of 1.47 (items), 0.67 (students), which still provide a reasonable consistency of student-item responses. The standardized fit residuals for the advanced test have a mean value of 0.01 (items), -0.39 (students) and a standard deviation value of 0.93 (items), 1.26 (students), which show a good consistency of student-item responses.

While it is important to measure the minimal differences between the ideal fit values and exact values in test scoring, the thresholds between category responses also need to be measured to ensure that the scoring responses are well aligned to the level of item difficulties along the same linear scale of measurement. The next part of the Rasch analysis looks into these threshold values and determines the consistency of the scoring categories for the three tests.

Consistency of Use of Scoring Categories

A reliable language test will have its scoring categories consistently applied by the test markers. Even if there is only one test marker, the consistency of scoring still needs to be tested. The RUMM program produces item thresholds for each item. Thresholds are points between scoring categories where the odds are 1:1 of scoring in adjacent categories. Since the scoring categories are conceptually ordered from low to high in order that students with higher scores should have corresponding higher measures, the thresholds should be ordered too, in line with the ordering of the scoring categories. For the Mock 'A' Level Test, Tables 8, 9 and 10 show the thresholds for all test items in the basic, intermediate and advanced categories, respectively. The thresholds are ordered in line with the scoring categories, as required for good measurement.

Table 8. Item thresholds (Basic Mock 'A' Level Test)

Item No.	Mean location	Threshold 1	Threshold 2	Threshold 3
Item 2	-0.53	-0.53		
Item 3	+1.54	-1.54		
Item 4	-0.07	-0.62	+0.49	
Item 5	+0.38	-0.98	+1.75	
Item 6	+1.79	-5.55	-2.88	+3.08
Item 8	+0.80	-1.69	+3.29	
Item 9	+0.40	-1.52	+2.32	
Item 10	-0.25	-0.25		
Item 12	+0.94	-0.30	+2.18	
Item 13	+1.65	-1.53	+4.84	

Source: Designed by Ong (2009) for this study from the RUMM analysis.

Table 9. Item thresholds (Intermediate Mock 'A' Level Test)

Item No.	Mean location	Threshold 1	Threshold 2	Threshold 3
Item 1	4.16	-3.53	11.79	4.21*
Item 2	2.75	-2.05	2.03	8.28
Item 3	0.68	-5.09	6.45	
Item 4	3.25	-11.62	5.13	
Item 5	1.33	-6.59	3.94	
Item 6	1.97	-6.57	2.64	
Item 7	-0.42	-3.23	2.39	
Item 8	0.29	-1.41	1.99	
Item 9	2.05	-4.67	0.88	9.94
Item 10	-0.75	-3.62	2.13	
Item 11	1.33	-3.54	0.88	
Item 12	-0.35	-2.62	1.92	
Item 13	-0.46	-2.25	1.32	
Item 14	-0.09	-1.88	1.71	

Source: Designed by Ong (2009) for this study from the RUMM analysis.

Notes on Table 8, 9 and 10.

1. Thresholds are points between adjacent response categories where the odds are 1:1 of answering the adjacent categories.
2. Mean thresholds are the item difficulties in logits.
3. The thresholds for each item are ordered in line with the ordering of the response categories.
4. All values are given to two decimal places because the errors are to two decimal places.
5. Items 1, 7, 11 and 14 are unfit for the measurement model and are hence deleted from the basic category of the mock test. For the advanced category of the mock test, items 1 and 4 are also deleted for similar reason.
6. Item 1 in the intermediate category of the mock test shows disordered thresholds.
7. Item 1 has a disordered threshold because there are no scores in the highest category.

Table 10. Item thresholds (Advanced Mock 'A' Level Test)

Item No.	Mean location	Threshold 1	Threshold 2	Threshold 3
Item 2	1.58	-8.43	0.19	3.51
Item 3	0.17	-2.46	0.10	2.87
Item 5	-0.97	-3.84	-0.78	1.71
Item 6	0.44	-3.02	0.29	4.05
Item 7	0.83	-1.28	0.79	2.97
Item 8	-0.59	-2.30	-0.74	1.28
Item 9	0.14	-2.53	2.81	
Item 10	0.53	-1.18	0.39	2.39
Item 11	-0.20	-2.56	2.15	
Item 12	0.43	-1.80	2.66	
Item 13	0.80	-1.10	0.79	2.71

Source: Designed by Ong (2009) for this study from the RUMM analysis.

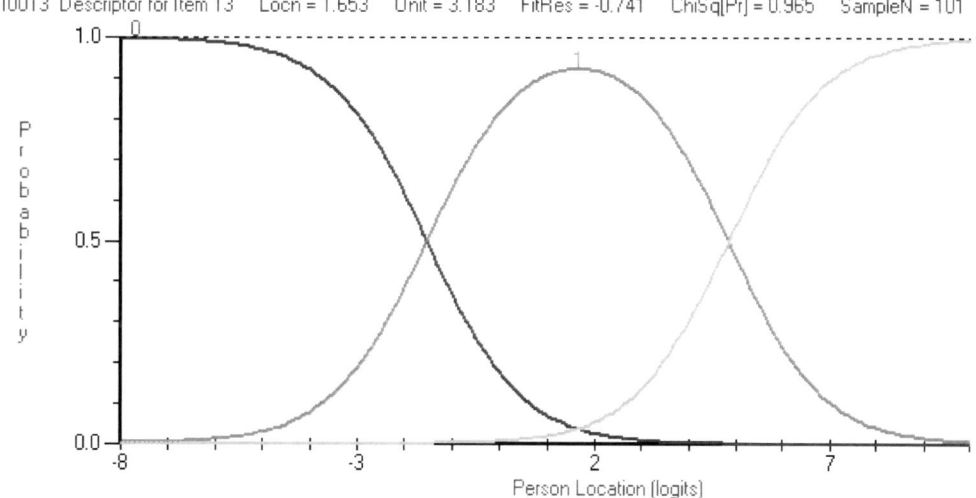

Figure 1. Scoring Category Curve for Item 13 (Basic Mock 'A' Level Test).

The thresholds for Basic and Advanced Mock 'A' Level Tests have all of their thresholds ordered in alignment with the scoring categories. For example, Item 6 in the basic category (see Table 6.8) has the highest mean location in item difficulty at 1.79 logits and produces an ordered set of thresholds from low to high (-5.55, -2.88, 3.08), with also a high upper threshold value of 3.08 logits. Likewise, Item 2 in the advanced category (see Table 10) being a hard item with mean location of 1.58 logits, also has an ordered set of thresholds (-8.43, 0.19, 3.51) with high upper threshold value of 3.51 logits.

The intermediate category has Item 1 being the only test item that shows disordered thresholds (-3.53, 11.79, 4.21) but this is because there are no students in the highest scoring category. Otherwise, the rest of the 13 thresholds are well ordered, such as Item 2 and 9, which are hard items with well-ordered thresholds and good upper threshold values of 8.28 and 9.94 logits respectively.

Besides threshold values, the program also produces category scoring curves for each test item. Each set of category scoring curves display the probabilities of students scoring in different scoring categories corresponding to their ability measures (person location) as shown in Figure 1.

Figure 1 shows an example of a scoring category curve for a relatively difficult test item in the Basic Mock 'A' Level Test – Item 13 which has its thresholds ordered from low to high. The category curves for scores of 0, 1 and 2 show that Item 13 is scored in a logical and consistent way. At the lowest person locations, there is a high probability of scoring zero. As the person location increases, the scoring probability for the category zero decreases and the scoring probability of the category 1 increases. At about 2 logits, the scoring probability for category 0 is low (not quite zero) and the scoring probability for category 2 is about zero. At this point the scoring category 1 has its highest probability (about 0.9). As the person location increases further, the probability of scoring 1 decreases and the probability of scoring 2 increases. Hence, the scoring category curves produced by RUMM 2020 program are important data to prove that the scoring categories were used consistently and logically. The rest of the test items in the 'A' Level Mock Tests were checked for consistency and logical scoring through their scoring category curves, but are not reported here to avoid unnecessary repetition.

ITEM DIFFERENTIAL FUNCTIONING

All the items for all three Mock 'A' Level Tests were checked for item differential functioning. Ideally, the items should not favour (or disfavour) any particular groups of students. That is, for example, the items should not favour boys, such that girls are disadvantaged in answering any of the items in the three tests. The RUMM program does this through Item Characteristic Curves, differentiated by the designated independent variable and statistically checked through an F-test. In the present study, the designated independent variables used were pre-entry junior college grades (JC1, JC2, JC3), gender (Male, Female), age (16, 17, 18 years), prior GCE 'O' Level grades (A1, A2, B3, B4), home language (Mandarin, English, Dialects, Other), social language (Mandarin, English, Dialects, Other) and family income (<$1499 per month, $1500-$3000, $3001-$6000, >$6000). It is important that the items should not advantage (or disadvantage) students from any of these groups and so a check was made on all items, for all three tests, across all seven independent variables.

Differential Item Functioning in the Basic Mock 'A' Level Test

All the 10 test items in the Basic Mock 'A' Level Test show no statistically significant item differential functioning by age, home language and social language. However, there are significant interactions by gender, junior college grade, prior GCE 'O' Level grades and family income for three test items in the Basic Mock 'A' Level Test.

Firstly, the gender factor influences the ability measure (person location) in Item 10 as shown in the Item Characteristic Curve in Figure 4; while the remaining nine test items such as Item 12 show no significant item differential functioning by gender, as shown in Figure 2.

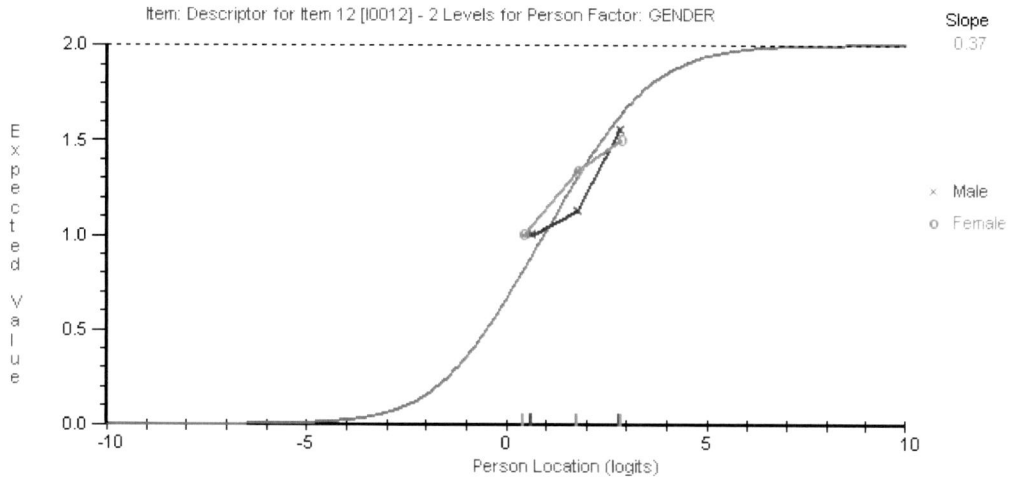

Figure 2. Item 12 Characteristic Curve by Gender (Basic Mock 'A' Level Test).

As compared to Item 12 (Figure 2), Item 10 (Figure 3) clearly shows a statistically significant interaction effect caused by gender differences. Males have a lower expected value for Item 10 than females at the low group measure, while having a higher expected value than females at the high group value. The overall F-test statistics for Item 10 are F $(2, 1) = 5.21$, $p = 0.007$ for three groups of ability measures and two groups of gender (degrees of freedom are hence F $(2, 1)$) in the Item Characteristic Curve in Figure 3. The probability $p = 0.007$ refers to the statistical probability that the significant F value of 5.21 is due to a chance fluctuation, or due to a real effect caused by real differences between males and females taking the language tests. As the probability limit (critical value) is usually taken as $p = 0.01$, the statistical probability $p = 0.007$ of Item 10 means that the differences between the genders are highly likely to be real differences due to real effects between the groups.

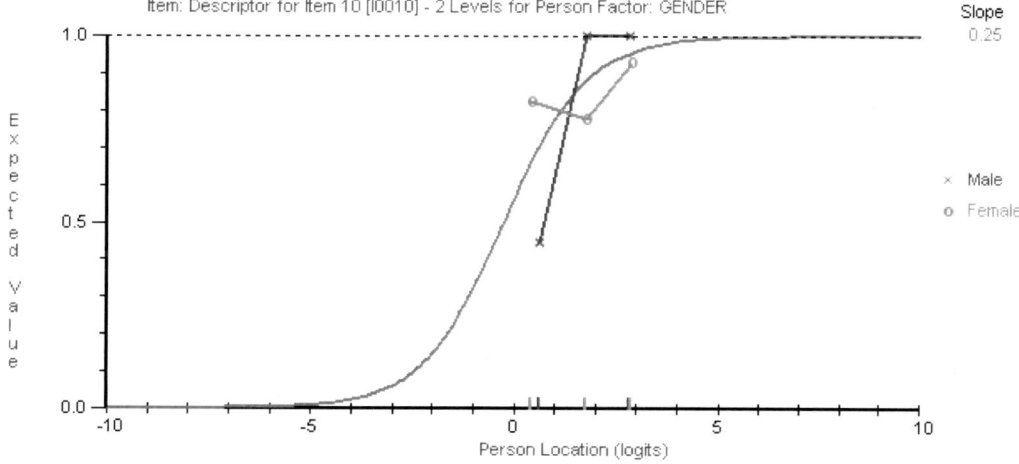

Figure 3. Item 10 Characteristic Curve by Gender (Basic Mock 'A' Level Test).

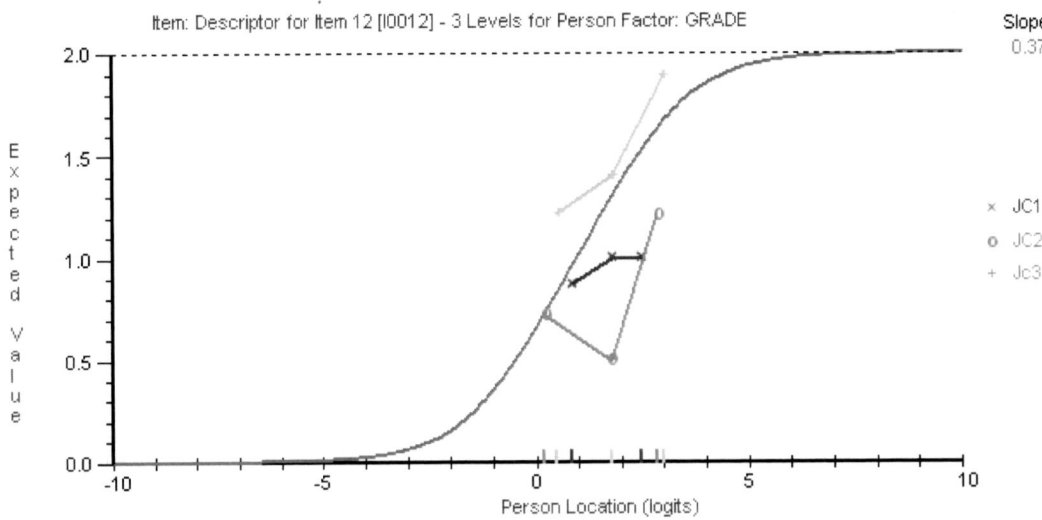

Figure 4. Item 12 Characteristic Curve by Junior College (Basic Mock 'A' Level Test).

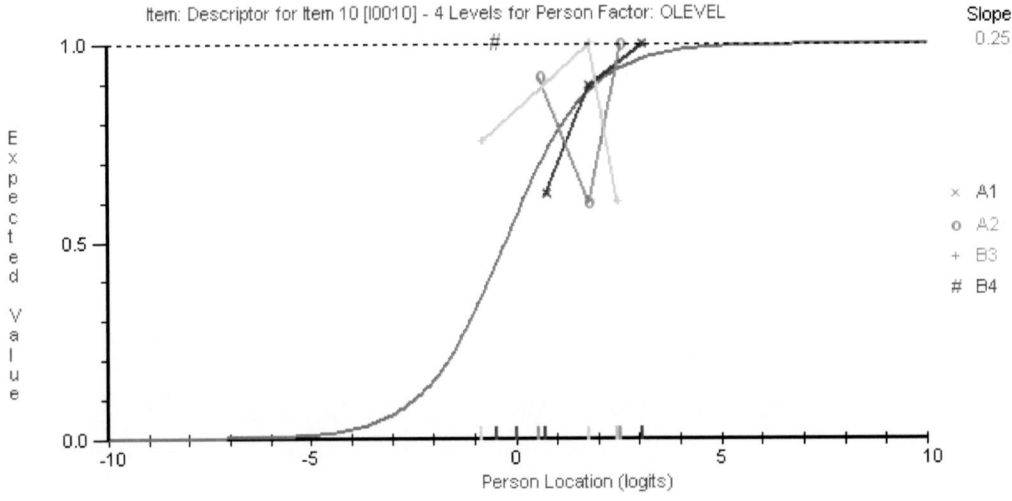

Figure 5. Item 10 Characteristic Curve by Prior Grades (Basic Mock 'A' Level Test).

Secondly, there is also a statistically significant interaction effect caused by junior college grades (JC1, JC2, JC3) in Item 12. According to the Item Characteristic Curve in Figure 6.4, Item 12 reports a significant main effect among these three groups of students.

The Item Characteristic Curve in Figure 4 reflects the F-test values of F $(2,2) = 11.57$, $p = 0.00$ as a significant main effect, for which all JC1 and JC2 students have lower expected values than JC3 students at all group measures. This result is not unexpected as students with high prior achievement are expected to do better than those with lower prior achievement in later years, on average. Most Junior College 1 students had just covered their 'A' Level syllabus when they participated in the research and hence their performance levels were not expected to be on a par with their Junior College 3 seniors.

Thirdly, prior GCE 'O' Level Higher Chinese Language grades, which have four categories of students (A1, A2, B3 and B4), also produce similar item differential functioning across three groups of ability measure, as shown in Figure 5.

Out of all items, only Item 10 shows statistically significant item differential functioning at $F (3, 2) = 5.56$, $p = 0.0004$, as an interaction effect. At low measures, students with B3 'O' Level grades produce higher Chinese ability measures. At high measures, students with A1 and A2 'O' Level grades produce higher Chinese ability measures, which are expected as these high-ability students are likely to continue with consistent academic performance when they progress from secondary to junior college levels.

Lastly, family income is the fourth factor which shows significant item differential functioning for Item 13 in the basic category test. Item 13 reports a main effect with $F (3, 2) = 6.25$, $p = 0.0007$. As shown in Figure 6, students with family monthly income of $1500 produce highest expected values over students with other family incomes, especially at the higher group measures.

In summary, out of the possible 10 test items, only three test items (Item 10, 12, 13) exhibit item differential functioning by four person traits and background factors. Therefore, the Basic Mock 'A' Level Test as a whole, does not exhibit a strong advantage or disadvantage to different groups of students too much; there is only a very minor advantage or disadvantage on three items across four independent variables.

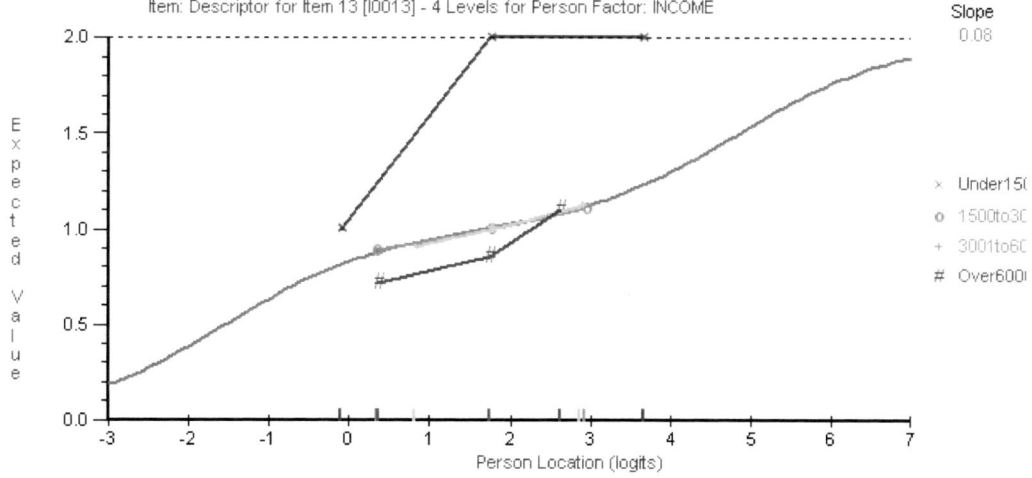

Figure 6. Item 13 Characteristic Curve by Family Income (Basic Mock 'A' Level Test).

Differential Item Functioning in the Intermediate Mock 'A' Level Test

The Item Characteristic Curves produced for the Intermediate Mock 'A' Level Test were checked for item differential functioning by school grade, gender, age, prior GCE 'O' Level grade, home language, social language and family income. In order to avoid unnecessary repetition, the Item Characteristic Curves of the Intermediate Mock 'A' Level Test are not shown here as they are similar to those given for the Basic Mock 'A' Level Test (see Figure 3 to Figure 6). However, one of the test items with item differential functioning by grade and home language will be discussed in this section.

For gender, age, prior GCE 'O' Level grade, social language and family income, all 14 test items in the Intermediate Mock 'A' Level Test show no statistically significant item differential functioning at p (critical)=0.01. For prior junior college grade and home language, only Item 5 has item differential functioning with interaction effects. Firstly, Item 5 shows item differential functioning by prior school grades (JC1, JC2, JC3) with F (2, 2) = 7.72 , p = 0.000 as an interaction effect. JC1 students at the medium measures produce the highest language ability measures but not at the lower and higher levels where JC1, JC2 and JC3 students produce around the same results.

Secondly, Item 5 also shows item differential functioning by home language, which has four categories of students speaking Mandarin, English, Chinese dialects[1] and other languages at home respectively. For Item 5, F-test statistics show F (3, 2) = 15.15, p = 0.000 as an interaction effect. Students speaking English language at home tend to produce the highest Chinese measures at the medium measures, but not at the lower and higher levels where English-speaking, Mandarin-speaking and dialect-speaking students are about the same.

Compared with the Basic Mock 'A' Level Test, the Intermediate Mock 'A' Level Test has less items with item differential functioning by person traits. This latter test is able to discriminate ability measures fairly, regardless of prior grades, gender, age, prior GCE 'O' Level grades, home language, social language and family income.

Differential Item Functioning in the Advanced Mock 'A' Level Test

All 11 items in the Advanced Mock 'A' Level Test show no statistically significant item differential functioning by gender, age, prior GCE 'O' Level grades, home language, social language and family income. Only Item 13 shows item differential functioning by prior school grade among three groups of students (JC1, JC2, JC3), yielding F-test values of F (2, 2) = 6.36 , p = 0.003 as a main effect. Junior College 1 (JC1) students produce the highest Chinese language ability measures at all points along the scale, performing better than JC2 and JC3 students. This could probably be expected as it was earlier mentioned in Basic 'A' Level Test that the JC1 and the JC2 students would be unlikely to outperform their JC3 seniors. Despite showing item differential functioning in one of its test items, the Advanced Mock 'A' Level Test in overall does not exhibit a strong advantage or disadvantage to different groups of students.

In summary, the three Mock 'A' Level Tests all have test items that show item differential functioning by various situation variables. In particular, there are some items that significantly discriminate between some groups of students, such as the males and females. Some interaction or main effects in the Item Characteristic Curves have been explained for variables such as school grades and 'O' Level achievements. However, other factors such as gender and family income require more research to investigate the differences.

While Item Characteristic Curves for individual test items provide evidence for item differential functioning, it is also important to analyse the entire set of test items by checking

---

[1] The Chinese dialects in this present study refer mostly to southern Chinese dialects, such as Southern Min dialect (otherwise known as Hokkien), Cantonese and Teochew.

the person-item threshold distribution against the item difficulties: that is, a check of targeting. Hence, the next section proceeds to analyse the targeting for the three Mock 'A' Level Tests.

TARGETING

The program produces Person-Item Threshold Distribution graphs that show item thresholds mapped against all student measures. In addition, Person-Item Threshold Distribution can also be computed for analyses through different background variables, such as gender and prior school grade. Ideally, a reliable test should show good targeting of language ability measures against the item difficulties (or item threshold distribution), and a fair distribution of student measures covering the item thresholds, despite gender, age and other traits. The following sub-sections will show the Person-Item Threshold Distribution graphs for the three Mock 'A' Level Tests separately.

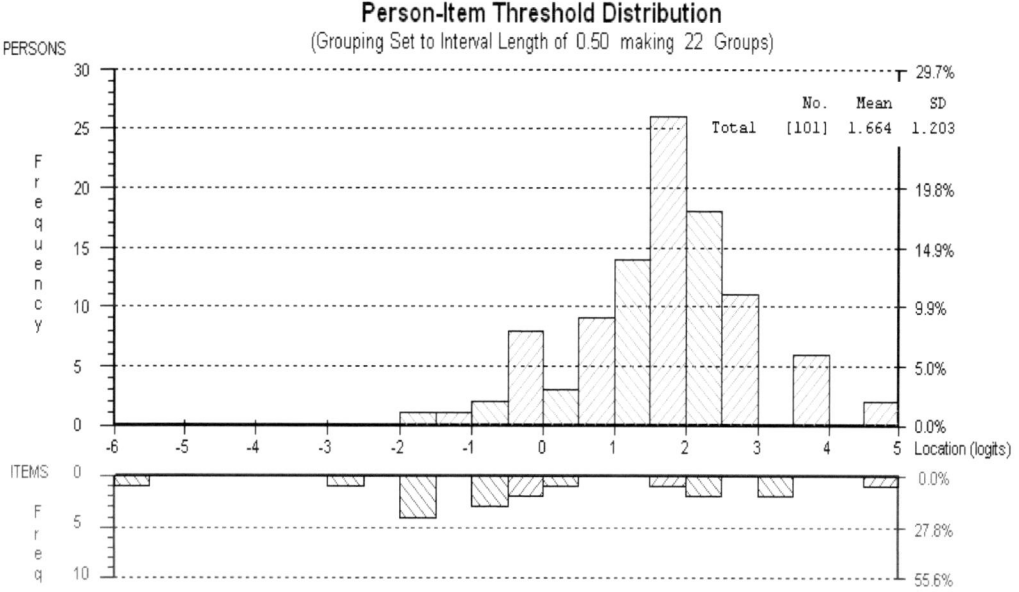

Notes on Figures 6.7, 8, 9, 10, 11, 12 and 13.
1. The scale is in logits, that is, the log odds of answering the response categories.
2. Person ability measures (low to high) are given on the upper side in logits.
3. Item thresholds (easy to hard) are given on the lower side in logits.

Figure 7. Targeting Graph for the Basic Mock 'A' Level Test.

Targeting in the Basic Mock 'A' Level Test

As shown in Figure 7, the Person-Item Threshold Distribution graph shows the item thresholds for the Basic Mock 'A' Level Test ranging from very easy (-5.5 logits) to very hard (+5.0 logits); and the students' language ability measures calibrated on the same scale range from reasonably low (-1.8 logits) to very high (about + 4.5 logits). With the range of item difficulties matching the majority of the range of ability measures, there is evidently good targeting of language ability measures against item difficulties in the Basic Mock 'A' Level Test. This is generally a requirement for good measurement.

Figure 8 shows person measures and item locations differentiated by Junior College grades (JC1, JC2, JC3). The JC3 students have the highest mean measures as compared to JC1 and JC2 students (+1.71, +1.67 and +1.52 logits for JC3, JC2 and JC1 students respectively), which is expected, but this is not statistically significant (F[2,98] = 0.16, p = 0.85). The JC3 students also have the widest range of ability measure from considerably low (about − 1.6 logits) to very high (about + 4.8 logits), compared to JC1 (about -0.5 to + 2.6 logits) and JC2 (about -1.3 to + 3.6 logits) students. There are some test items that still fail to target the lowest person measures (from -5.5 to -2.5 logits). If some more easy items could be added, the overall measure would be improved.

Besides the targeting graph differentiated by prior school grades, other similar graphs differentiated by gender, prior GCE 'O' Level grades, home language, social language and family income are shown in Figure 9, Figure 10, Figure 11, Figure 12 respectively.

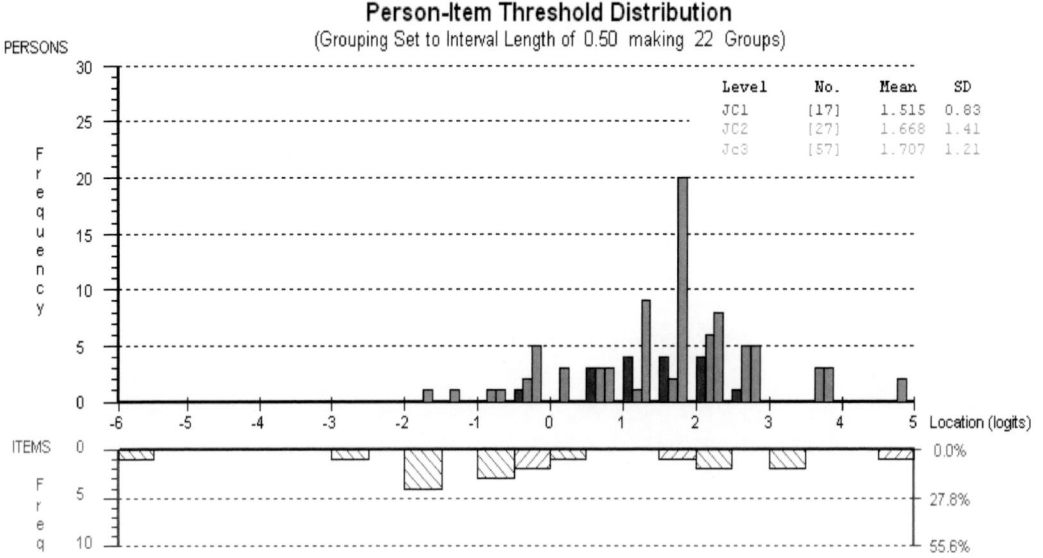

Figure 8. Targeting Graph for the Basic Mock 'A' Level Test with Ability Measures Differentiated by Junior College Grades.

As shown in Figure 9, male students have slightly higher mean measures than female students, +1.72 and +1.64 logits for the males and females respectively, but this is not statistically significant (F [1,99] = 0.08, p = 0.77). While there are more females (13.33%) than males (7.69%) in the lower ability measure range of -0.3 to -1.8 logits, there are also more high-achieving females (9.33%) than males (3.85%) at the upper limit ability measure range of +3.5 to +4.8 logits.

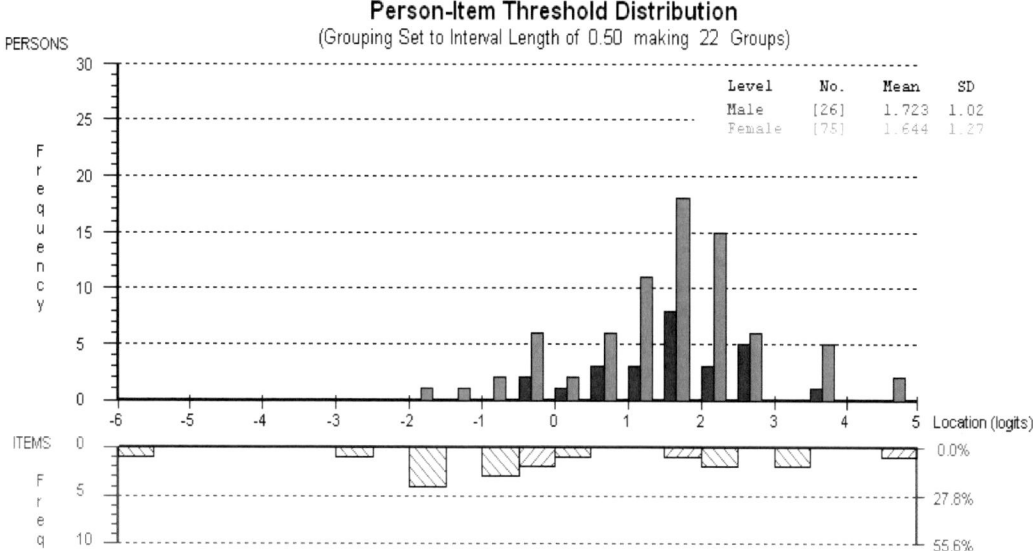

Figure 9. Targeting Graph for the Basic Mock 'A' Level Test with Ability Measures Differentiated by Gender.

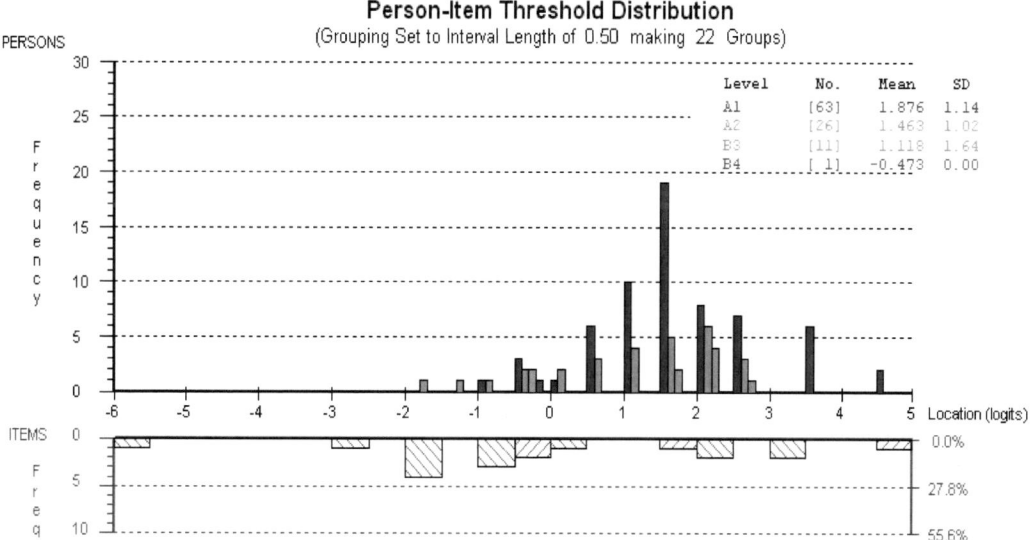

Figure 10. Targeting Graph for the Basic Mock 'A' Level Test with Ability Measures Differentiated by Prior 'O' Level Grades.

Compared to the targeting graph differentiated by gender, Figure 6.10 displays a more complex person-item threshold distribution with four categories of 'O' Level achievement. As expected, the A1 students have the highest mean of +1.88 logits, while the B4 students have the lowest mean of -0.47 logits, and this is statistically significant at the $p = 0.05$ level (F [3,97] = 2.85, $p = 0.04$). It is evident, as expected, that the GCE 'O' Level high-achievers continue to excel at junior colleges, as 23.81% of the A1 students are in the upper ability measure range of +2.5 to +4.5 logits.

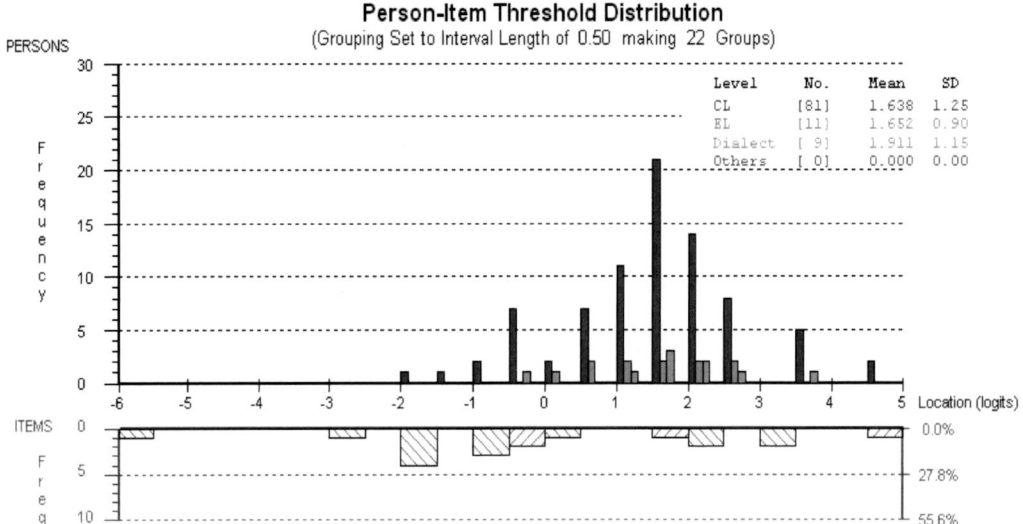

Figure 11. Targeting Graph for the Basic Mock 'A' Level Test with Ability Measures Differentiated by Home Language.

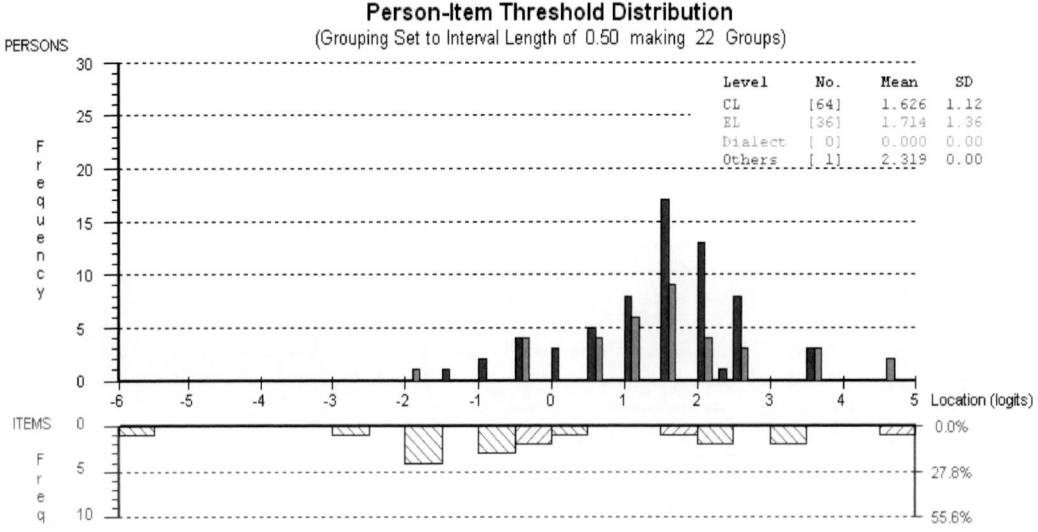

Figure 12. Targeting Graph for the Basic Mock 'A' Level Test with Ability Measures Differentiated by Social Language.

Among the three groups of students who speak different language at home, Figure 11 shows that dialect-speaking students have the highest mean measures at +1.91 logits, as compared to the Mandarin-speaking (CL) and the English-speaking (EL) students who have similar low mean measures of +1.64 and +1.65 logits respectively. For these dialect-speaking students, they are all proficient in speaking Mandarin and English in school, as they have undergone at least 11 years of bilingual education. This means that these students are effectively tri-lingual and likely to have a heightened sense of language awareness. With better language awareness, students are more motivated in language learning, which may in turn explain their high-achieving performances. Interestingly, the next two Mock 'A' Level Tests also report similar trends for the dialect-speaking students.

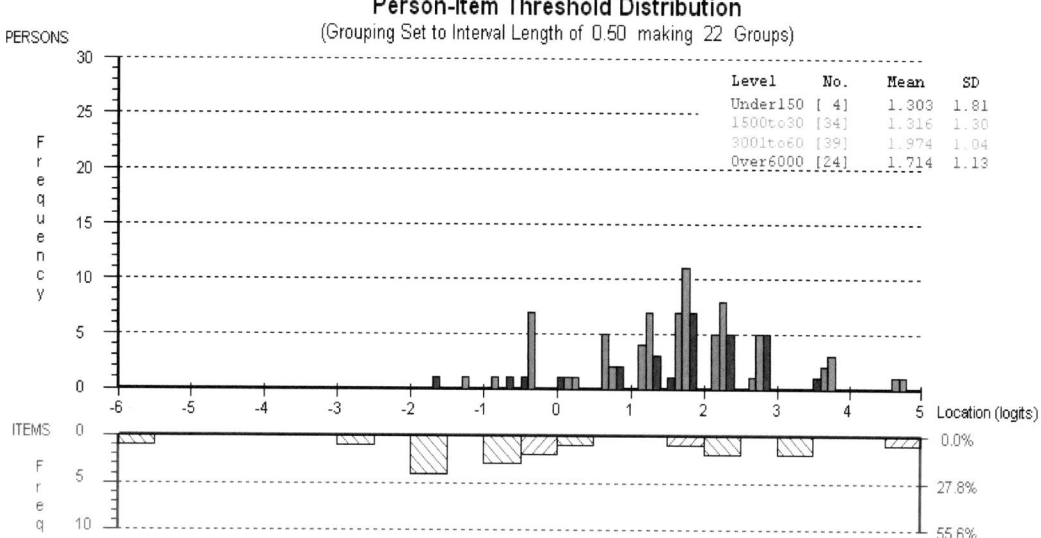

Person-Item Threshold Distribution
(Grouping Set to Interval Length of 0.50 making 22 Groups)

Level	No.	Mean	SD
Under150	[4]	1.303	1.81
1500to30	[34]	1.316	1.30
3001to60	[39]	1.974	1.04
Over6000	[24]	1.714	1.13

Figure 13. Targeting Graph for the Basic Mock 'A' Level Test with Ability Measures Differentiated by Family Income.

Compared with the previous graph, the targeting graph in Figure 12 has no dialect-speaking students. This is expected as Chinese dialects are generally spoken at home, rather than in social settings in school[2]. With only two main groups of Mandarin-speaking (CL) and English-speaking (EL) students, the EL students have slightly higher mean measures (+1.71 logits) than the CL students (+1.63 logits). The differences between students speaking different social languages are not significant (F [3, 97] =0.14, p = 0.94).

As shown in Figure 13 above, the upper income groups of $3001 and above have higher mean measures (+1.97 and +1.71 logits) than those of the lower income groups (+1.30 and +1.32 logits) but this is not statistically significant (F [3,97] = 2.0, p = 0.12). Students from under-privileged families generally fare worse in the language test. However, that does not infer that the students will perform better if their families are more privileged, as the middle income group ($3001-$6000) students have higher mean measures than the top income group ($6001 and above).

Targeting in the Intermediate Mock 'A' Level Test

Compared to the Basic Mock 'A' Level Test, the Intermediate Mock 'A' Level Test has a wider range of item thresholds from − 11.5 logits to +11.5 logits. Student ability measures cover a smaller − the lowest measure is -6.0 logits and the highest measure is +4.0 logits.

---

[2] Singapore government launched the Speak Mandarin Campaign in 1979 to discourage the use of non-Mandarin Chinese dialects among Chinese Singaporeans. Ever since the use of Chinese dialects is generally confined in homes and young Singaporeans speak Mandarin rather than dialects in schools.

Nevertheless, considering the majority of the test items cover a range of -6.5 to +5.0 logits, there is satisfactory targeting of measures against item difficulties in the Intermediate Mock 'A' Level Test.

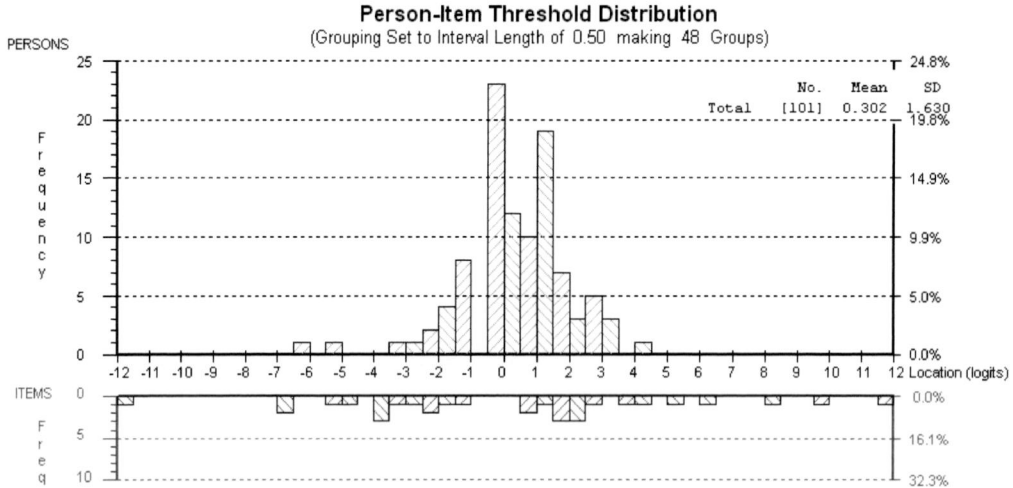

Figure 14. Targeting Graph for the Intermediate Mock 'A' Level Test.

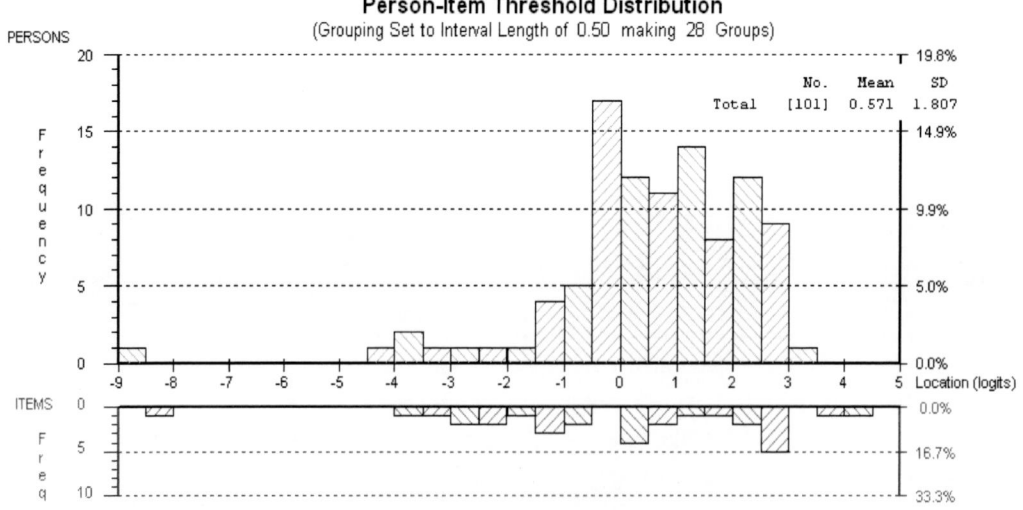

Figure 15. Targeting Graph for the Advanced Mock 'A' Level Test.

In order to avoid unnecessary repetition, the targeting graphs differentiated by other variables are not shown here. One distribution graph differentiated by gender shows that there are more females (21.33% among all females) than males (19.2% among all males) in the lower measure range of -6.5 to -1.2 logits. Meanwhile, the ability measure range of the males (-3.5 to +4.2 logits) is higher than that of the females (-6.3 to +3.2 logits). Both observations suggest that male students generally do better in the Intermediate Mock 'A' Level Test, but this is not statistically significant (F [1,99] =0.14, $p = 0.71$).

Overall, the Person-Item Threshold Distribution graphs differentiated by other factors all show a fair calibration of students' measures without significant discrimination against any person trait. However, all distribution graphs suggest the Intermediate Mock 'A' Level Test can be further improved if there are less difficult items from +5.0 logits onwards (see Figure 6.14), so that a better targeting of students' measures can be achieved.

Targeting in the Advanced Mock 'A' Level Test

The Advanced Mock 'A' Level Test was designed to be the most difficult of all Mock 'A' Level Tests, but it appears that the Intermediate Mock 'A' Level Tests has the more difficult items. The hard items for the Advanced Mock 'A' Level Test only cover the range from about 0 to +4.5 logits, but targeting appears to be satisfactory.

In Figure 15, the graph shows that the students' measure range starts from very low at -8.8 logits to considerably high at +3.3 logits, while the item thresholds range from -8.0 to +4.5 logits. This implies that there is good targeting of measures against item difficulties in the Advanced Mock 'A' Level Test.

Similar to the previous test, the Person-Item Threshold Distribution graphs differentiated by person traits are also not displayed here to avoid repetition. All the graphs have been checked, and there is no significant discrimination or unbalanced distribution by any gender, age, school grades and other factors. Compared with the other two tests, the Advanced Mock 'A' Level Test shows better targeting of ability measures with no need for adjustment.

In: Applications of Rasch Measurement in Education
Editor: Russell Waugh

ISBN 978-1-61668-026-8
© 2010 Nova Science Publishers, Inc.

Chapter 10

RASCH MEASURES OF AN AUTHENTIC CHINESE LANGUAGE TEST AT CAMBRIDGE "A" LEVEL STANDARD

Ong Chun Ghee[1] and Russell Waugh[2]

[1]. Dunman High School
[2]. Graduate School of Education, University of Western Australia

ABSTRACT

This paper is part of a larger study into the measuring of achievement of Chinese language talents at Cambridge 'A' Level in Singapore. An authentic 'A' Level paper was prepared and administered to N=101 students who aimed to attend university the following year from a population of about 400. Students completed the test in a formal setting over six hours on a voluntary basis. They came from three different Junior Colleges and included 75 females and 26 males. The test was divided into two parts that were separately Rasch analysed to create two uni-dimensional, linear scales. For the 'Intermediate Test' of 10 items, the item-trait chi-square was $\chi^2 = 18.55$, df = 20, $p = 0.55$; and for the 'Advanced Test' of 10 items it was $\chi^2 = 36.52$, df = 20, $p = 0.01$, showing a reasonable overall fit to the measurement model. The Student Separation Index was 0.83 and 0.86 respectively and the Cronbach Alpha was 0.82 and 0.83 respectively, showing acceptable scale reliability. Differential Item Functioning was tested and the items were found to be performing satisfactorily. The items in each test were ordered from easy to hard providing good information relating to the difficulty of the items and performance of the students.

INTRODUCTION

Background to this chapter is provided in Chapter Eight. In the present chapter, the Authentic Chinese Language Test was analyzed in two separate parts, namely the intermediate and advanced categories of the authentic test. The RUMM 2020 program (Andrich, Sheridan and Luo, 2005) was used to determine if both parts of the authentic language test are constructed with reliability and validity, and if they have a good fit to the Rasch measurement model.

Due to the research scope in the present study, it was not possible to engage large numbers of Chinese language talents to ensure consistent and logical scoring in all the test items. Therefore, to produce tests-of-fit during data analysis, some scoring adjustments need to be made for the Authentic Chinese Language Tests.

OVERALL FIT TO THE MEASUREMENT MODEL

The RUMM 2020 (Andrich, Sheridan and Luo, 2005) program was run through a series of analyses with the Authentic Chinese Language Tests to investigate the overall fit of the data to the measurement model. Item-trait interaction and its relevant chi-square statistics are instrumental in determining whether uni-dimensional traits exist in the measuring scales from the Authentic Chinese Language Tests. These statistics are provided in the following two sections, where both parts of the Authentic Chinese Language Test are analyzed for significant interactions and scale linearity. If the two tests have good overall fits to the measurement model, they should show minimal statistically significant interaction between the student measures and the item difficulties along the scale, and have all the tests items fit with a probability of $p > 0.09$ with Student Separation Index near 0.90.

Intermediate Authentic Chinese Language Test

All ten test items ordered in the Intermediate Authentic Chinese Language Test were found to be of good fit to the measurement model. However, due to sampling size constraints faced in the research, the initial scoring system had to be adjusted, as shown in Table 1, to improve the consistency of item scoring.

After scoring was adjusted, the ten ordered test items (I = 10, N = 101) were used to construct a linear scale, showing good overall fit to the measurement model. The item-trait interaction chi-square ($\chi^2 = 18.59$, df = 20.00, $p = 0.55$) shows that there is no statistically significant interaction between the student measures and the item difficulties along the scale. All test items fit with a probability of $p > 0.09$ with the Student Separation Index value of 0.83 and Cronbach Alpha value of 0.82. These statistics show that the student ability measures are well separated in comparison to the errors in the Intermediate Authentic Chinese Language Test, and that the test is internally reliable.

Table 1. Scoring adjustment in the Intermediate Authentic Test

Test Item No.	Score Adjustment	Test Item No.	Score Adjustment
4	0=0, 1=0, 2=1, 3=1, 4=2, 5=3	6	0=0, 1=0, 2=1, 3=1, 4=2, 5=2
2	0=0, 1=0, 2=1, 3=1, 4=2, 5=3	7	0=0, 1=0, 2=1, 3=1, 4=2, 5=3
3	0=0, 1=0, 2=1, 3=1, 4=2, 5=3	8	0=0, 1=0, 2=1, 3=1, 4=2, 5=2
1	0=0, 1=0, 2=1, 3=1, 4=2, 5=3	9	0=0, 1=0, 2=1, 3=1, 4=2, 5=3
5	0=0, 1=0, 2=1, 3=1, 4=2, 5=3	13	0=0, 1=0, 2=1, 3=1, 4=2, 5=3

Source: Designed by Ong (2009) for this study from the RUMM analysis.

Table 2. Scoring adjustment in the Advanced Authentic Test

Test Item No.	Score Adjustment	Test Item No.	Score Adjustment
10	0=0, 1=0, 2=1, 3=1, 4=1, 5=2	16	0=0, 1=0, 2=1, 3=1, 4=2, 5=3
11	0=0, 1=0, 2=1, 3=1, 4=2, 5=3	17	0=0, 1=0, 2=1, 3=1, 4=2, 5=3
12	0=0, 1=0, 2=1, 3=1, 4=2, 5=3	18	0=0, 1=0, 2=1, 3=1, 4=1, 5=2
14	0=0, 1=0, 2=1, 3=1, 4=1, 5=2	19	0=0, 1=0, 2=1, 3=1, 4=1, 5=2
15	0=0, 1=0, 2=1, 3=1, 4=1, 5=2	20	0=0, 1=0, 2=1, 3=1, 4=1, 5=2

Source: Designed by Ong (2009) for this study from the RUMM output.

Table 3. Comparison between the Authentic Tests and Mock 'A' Level Tests

Chinese Language Tests	χ^2	df	p	SSI	Cronbach Alpha (α)
Intermediate Authentic	18.59	20.00	0.55	0.83	0.82
Advanced Authentic	36.52	20.00	0.01	0.86	0.83
Mock 'A' Level Basic	20.28	20.00	0.44	0.61	0.65
Mock 'A' Level Intermediate	36.19	28.00	0.14	0.82	0.83
Mock 'A' Level Advanced	29.38	22.00	0.13	0.91	0.89

Source: Designed by Ong (2009) for this study from the RUMM analysis.

1. χ^2 refers to the total item chi-square value; df refers to the degrees of freedom.

2. p refers to the total chi-square probability that the deviation of the observed frequencies from the expected frequencies is due to chance alone.

3. SSI refers to Student-Separation Index.

Advanced Authentic Chinese Language Test

The Advanced Authentic Chinese Language Test also had 10 items conceptually ordered in difficulty from easy to hard. However, in order to obtain a uni-dimensional measurement scale, the scoring system for the test needed to be adjusted as shown in Table 2.

The output showed that all 10 items of the Advanced Authentic Test (I = 10, N = 101) had an item-trait interaction chi-square of χ^2 = 36.52, df = 20.00, p = 0.01, indicating that there was a significant interaction between the measures and the item difficulties. This appeared to be primarily due to one item (item 19) whose removal did not improve the overall fit to the measurement model. Two other items (13 and 20) did not fit the measurement model as well as would be liked, but the best overall fit was still with the original 10 items. It appeared that approximately half the students with average ability measures rated Item 19 as difficult, while the other half rated it as easy. Despite the removal of Item 19 from the measurement scale, there was still a significant interaction with low statistical probability, and the best possible test-of-fit was with all the ten items including Item 19.

Nevertheless, the Advanced Authentic Chinese Language Test produced good Student Separation Index (SSI = 0.86) and Cronbach Alpha values (α = 0.83). These statistics imply that in most of the test items, ability measures are well separated in comparison to the errors, suggesting that the test is still internally reliable and has a strong power to detect any non-fit to the measurement model.

In review, the Authentic Chinese Language Test could have been better constructed if certain items, such as Item 19, can be modified to give a better fit to the measurement model.

Other possible solutions, such as increasing the sample size to N = 400, would also help to improve the quality of test construct.

Comparison between Authentic Chinese Language Tests and Mock 'A' Level Tests

Compared to the other three Mock 'A' Level tests, the item-trait interaction statistics of the Intermediate Authentic Chinese Language Test suggest that it has the best overall fit to the Rasch measurement model. As shown in Table 3, the item-trait chi-square for the Intermediate Authentic Chinese Language Test (χ^2 = 18.59, df = 20, p = 0.55) is not statistically significant. It has a high Cronbach Alpha value (0.82) and a high Student-Separation Index value (0.83) indicating good internal reliability and good power for the tests-of-fit.

Table 4. Fit of items to Rasch Measurement Model (Intermediate Authentic Test)

Item No.	Location	SE	Residual	df	ChiSq	Prob
Item 1	0.74	0.18	-0.06	87.30	2.92	0.23
Item 2	-0.31	0.18	0.71	87.30	2.11	0.35
Item 3	-0.19	0.18	-1.27	87.30	2.98	0.23
Item 4	-0.86	0.18	0.14	87.30	1.20	0.55
Item 5	-0.36	0.20	-0.99	87.30	2.65	0.27
Item 6	-0.53	0.24	-0.50	87.30	0.09	0.96
Item 7	0.12	0.16	-0.43	87.30	0.14	0.93
Item 8	0.73	0.27	-0.32	87.30	0.46	0.80
Item 9	0.31	0.20	0.23	87.30	1.40	0.50
Item 10	0.33	0.18	2.73	87.30	4.63	0.10

Source: Designed by Ong (2009) for this study from the RUMM analysis.
Notes for Tables 4 and 5.
1. Location refers to the difficulty of the item on the linear scale.
2. SE refers to standard error, that is, the degree of the uncertainty in a value. In this case, the standard error for each item is reasonable, ranging from 0.18 to 0.27 logits (for Table 7.4), 0.16 to 0.26 logits (for Table 7.5) for the Intermediate and Advanced Authentic Chinese Language Tests respectively.
3. Residual represents the difference between the expected value on an item, calculated according to the Rasch measurement model, and its actual value.
4. df (degrees of freedom) refers to the number of scores in a distribution that are free to change without changing the mean of the distribution.
5. ChiSq means chi-square.
6. Prob means probability, and refers to the levels of certainty to which an item fits the measurement model, based on its chi-square.
7. All values are given to two decimal places because the errors are to two decimal places.

OTHER RUMM OUTPUT STATISTICS

Item Fit to the Measurement Model

Table 4 shows that the Intermediate Authentic Test has all ten items fitting the measurement model, with probabilities larger than $p = 0.09$, creating a reliable scale with good individual item fits to the Rasch measurement model.

On the other hand, the Advanced Authentic Test only has nine of its items fitting the measurement model, with probabilities greater than, or equal to, $p = 0.07$. As shown in Table 5, Item 9 is the only exception in the Advanced Authentic Test, having problems fitting the model with probability of $p = 0.00$. The Advanced Authentic Test can be improved if Item 9 (originally 19) were re-designed so that most students could agree about its difficulty.

Besides checking individual item fit for both authentic language tests, it is also important to analyze the item-student fit residuals to ensure good consistency of student responses to the test items. The next section hence proceeds to report the item-student fit statistics for the authentic language tests.

Table 5. Fit of items to Rasch Measurement Model (Advanced Authentic Test)

Item No.	Location	SE	Residual	df	ChiSq	Prob
Item 1	0.71	0.26	1.04	85.00	3.21	0.20
Item 2	-0.41	0.18	0.79	85.00	1.90	0.39
Item 3	0.47	0.18	1.14	85.00	5.31	0.07
Item 4	-0.15	0.26	-0.54	85.00	0.26	0.88
Item 5	-1.28	0.26	0.20	85.00	0.80	0.67
Item 6	0.54	0.20	-1.51	85.00	1.06	0.59
Item 7	0.32	0.16	-0.16	85.00	3.09	0.21
Item 8	-0.33	0.18	-1.45	85.00	2.70	0.26
Item 9	0.51	0.20	-1.90	85.00	13.36	0.00
Item 10	-0.38	0.17	-1.87	85.00	4.81	0.09

Source: Designed by Ong (2009) for this study from the RUMM analysis.

Item-Student Fit Residuals

In an ideal measurement scale, the standardized fit residuals should yield an approximately normal distribution with mean value = 0 and standard deviation value = 1, with minimal differences between the actual and expected test score values. The standardized fit residuals of both Intermediate and Advanced Authentic Tests have a mean near zero and a standard deviation near one (as shown in Table 6). The Intermediate Authentic Test has mean values of -0.02 (items), -0.31 (students) and standard deviation values of 1.11 (item), 1.11 (students), showing reasonable consistency of student responses to the test items. Similarly, the Advanced Authentic Test has mean values of -0.43 (items), -0.60 (students) and standard deviation values of 1.20 (item), 1.44 (students), showing that it is a reasonably consistent test measure.

Comparing statistics between the Intermediate Authentic Test and the Advanced Mock 'A' Level Test, both tests are similarly close to the ideal mean values for their standardized item fit residuals (+0.02 and +0.01 logits respectively) and item standard deviation values (+0.11 and -0.07 logits respectively), as shown in Table 7. The student standardized fit residuals for the Intermediate Authentic Test and the Advanced Mock 'A' Level Test (means = -0.31 and -0.39 logits respectively) and (SDs = +0.11 and +0.26 logits respectively) show a slightly less consistent pattern, although they are still acceptable.

While the consistency of scoring responses is analysed with the item-student fit residual statistics, the scoring categories in the authentic tests also need to be checked for consistency. Hence, the next section continues by examining the consistency of use of scoring categories and verifying that the test item thresholds are ordered in alignment with the scoring categories.

Table 6. Global item and student fit residuals for the Authentic Tests

Authentic Chinese Language Test	Statistics	Item locations	Item residuals	Student locations	Student residuals
Intermediate	Mean	0.00	0.02	-0.35	-0.31
	SD	0.54	1.11	1.49	1.11
Advanced	Mean	0.00	-0.43	-0.60	-0.60
	SD	0.62	1.20	1.60	1.44

Source: Designed by Ong (2009) for this study from the RUMM analysis.

Table 7. Comparison of global item and student fit residuals between the Authentic Test and the Mock 'A' Level Test

Language Tests	Statistics	Item residuals	Student residuals
Intermediate Authentic Chinese Language Test	Mean	0.02	-0.31
	SD	1.11	1.11
Difference between actual and ideal Mean = 0:		+0.02	-0.31
Difference between actual and ideal SD = 1:		+0.11	+0.11
Advanced Mock 'A' Level Chinese Language Test	Mean	0.01	-0.39
	SD	0.93	1.26
Difference between actual and ideal Mean = 0:		+0.01	-0.39
Difference between actual and ideal SD = 1:		-0.07	+0.26

Source: Designed by Ong (2009) for this study from the RUMM analysis.

Notes on Tables 6 and 7.

1. Item location is item difficulty in logits.
2. Person location is the student measure in logits.
3. SD is standard deviation.
4. The mean item difficulty is constrained to zero by the RUMM 2020 program.
5. Fit residuals are the difference between the actual values and the expected values calculated according to the measurement model.
6. All values are given to two decimal places because the errors are to two decimal places.

Consistency of Use of Scoring Categories

Thresholds for each item in the Authentic Chinese Language Tests are expected to be ordered in line with the ordering of the scoring categories if the tests are reliable measures of language abilities. Tables 8 and 9 display the thresholds for the Intermediate and Advanced Authentic Tests and threshold values are shown to be well ordered and aligned with the scoring categories.

Table 8. Item thresholds (Intermediate Authentic Test)

Item No.	Mean location	Threshold 1	Threshold 2	Threshold 3
Item 1	0.74	-2.46	0.90	3.78
Item 2	-0.31	-3.76	0.01	2.81
Item 3	-0.18	-3.63	0.51	2.58
Item 4	-0.86	-4.05	-0.70	2.17
Item 5	-0.35	-4.09	-0.55	3.57
Item 6	-0.53	-3.13	2.07	
Item 7	0.12	-2.51	1.03	1.85
Item 8	0.73	-2.34	3.80	
Item 9	0.31	-3.52	1.14	3.30
Item 10	0.33	-2.85	0.30	3.54

Source: Designed by Ong (2009) for this study from the RUMM analysis.

Table 9. Item thresholds (Advanced Authentic Test)

Item No.	Mean location	Threshold 1	Threshold 2	Threshold 3
Item 1	0.71	-2.19	3.60	
Item 2	-0.41	-3.79	-0.11	2.67
Item 3	0.47	-2.74	0.60	3.55
Item 4	-0.15	-2.86	2.56	
Item 5	1.28	-4.16	1.60	
Item 6	0.54	-3.20	0.99	3.84
Item 7	0.32	-1.94	0.59	2.30
Item 8	-0.33	-1.71	1.05	
Item 9	0.51	-1.21	2.23	
Item 10	-0.38	-1.18	0.43	

Source: Designed by Ong (2009) for this study from the RUMM analysis.
Notes on Table 8 and 9.
1. Thresholds are points between adjacent response categories where the odds are 1:1 of answering the adjacent categories.
2. Mean thresholds are the item difficulties in logits.
3. The thresholds for each item are ordered in line with the ordering of the response categories.
4. All values are given to two decimal places because the errors are to two decimal places.

According to Table 8, the Intermediate Authentic Test has all of its thresholds ordered in alignment with the scoring categories. All ten items have their threshold values ordered from low to high. In addition, Item 1 and 8, being the more difficult items with mean locations of 0.74 and 0.73 logits, expectedly yield the highest upper threshold values of 3.78 and 3.80

logits respectively. Similarly, Table 9 shows that the Advanced Authentic Test also has all its thresholds ordered. For example, Item 6 has produced an ordered set of thresholds from low to high (-3.20, 0.99, 3.84). At the same time, with a comparatively high mean location in item difficulty at 0.54 logits, Item 6 also managed a high upper threshold value of 3.84 logits.

Unlike the Mock 'A' Level Tests of which the intermediate category test has problems with producing ordered thresholds for all its test items, both Intermediate and Advanced Authentic Tests have yielded ordered thresholds for all their test items. This shows that the scoring was reliable and consistent with its conceptual structure.

Another way to examine scoring reliability is to analyse the Scoring Category Curves produced by the RUMM 2020 program. Figure 1 shows an example of a Scoring Category Curve for the Intermediate Authentic Test's Item 1, which has its thresholds ordered from low to high, as shown in Table 8.

At the lowest student measures, there is a high probability of scoring category 0 and a low probability of scoring category 1. As the student measures increase, the probability of scoring category 0 decreases and the probability of scoring category 1 increases. As the student measures increase the probability of scoring in the lower category decreases and the probability of scoring in the higher category increases. At the highest student measures, the probability of scoring in the highest category tends to 1 and the probability of scoring in a lower category tends to zero. This is consistent with the intended scoring rubric and is consistent with good measurement. Similar consistent scoring curves for the other items were computed by RUMM 2020, but they are not displayed in this section to avoid unnecessary repetition.

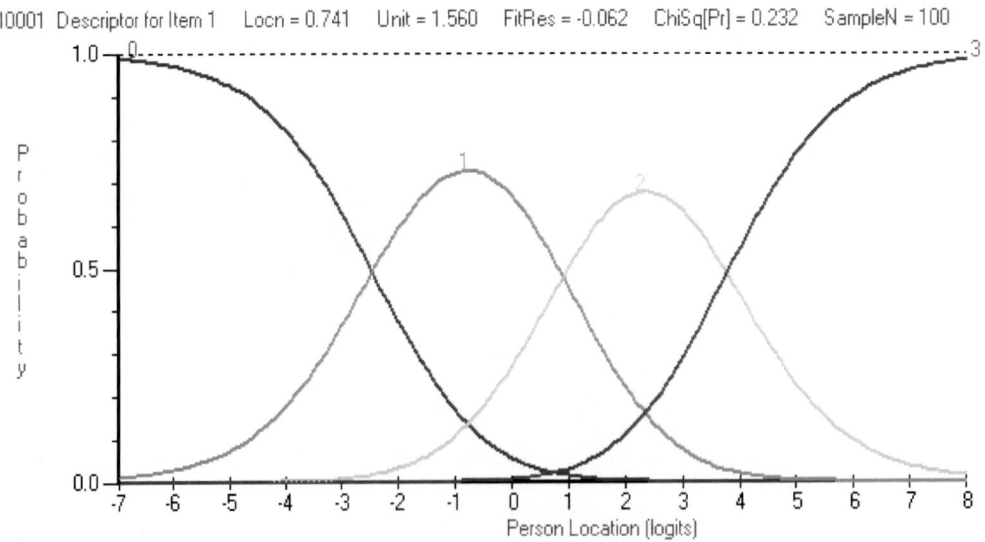

Figure 1. Scoring Category Curve for Item 1 (Intermediate Authentic Test).

In summary, the ordered thresholds and the scoring category curves reported prove that the scoring categories in the Authentic Chinese Language Tests were used consistently and logically. However, in order to further affirm the reliability of the test construct, there is a need to check the item differential functioning to ensure that no particular group of students is discriminated against or favoured while using the tests. The following section therefore continues by analysing the item differential functioning statistics for the authentic tests.

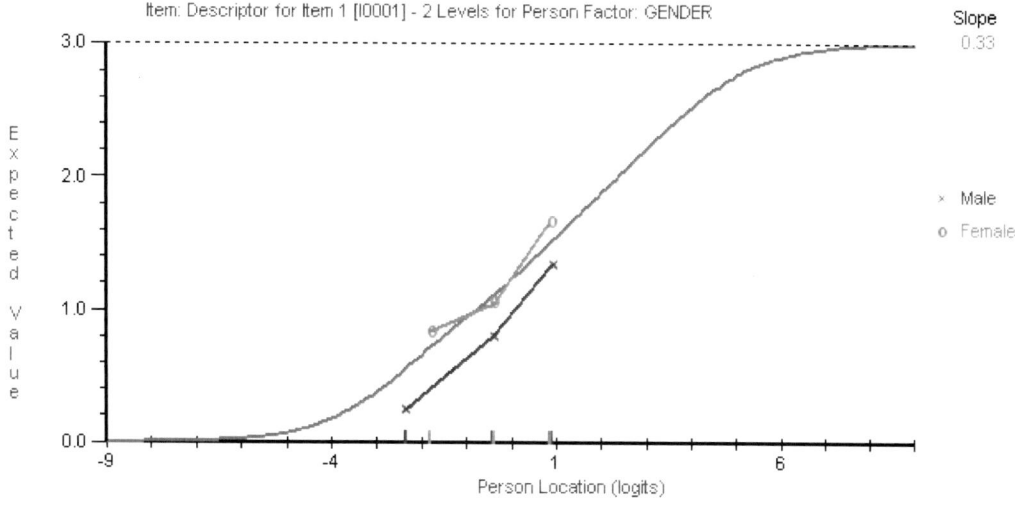

Figure 2. Item 1 Characteristic Curve by Gender (Intermediate Authentic Test).

ITEM DIFFERENTIAL FUNCTIONING

While checking for item differential functioning, the RUMM program generates the relevant Item Characteristic Curves and F-test statistics similar to those generated for the Mock 'A' Level Tests. The seven designated independent variables involved are the same ones studied in the Mock 'A' Level Tests . These variables are to be checked against every test item to ensure that all groups of students are neither disadvantaged nor privileged by means of their person traits or background factors.

Differential Item Functioning in the Intermediate Authentic Chinese Language Test

All ten test items in the Intermediate Authentic Test show no statistically significant item differential functioning with age, prior school grade, prior GCE 'O' Level grades, home language and family income. However, a few items have significant interactions by gender and social language.

Item 1 shows a statistically significant effect caused by gender differences, as shown in the Item Characteristic Curves in Figure 2. In Figure 2, Item 1 shows a statistically significant main effect, favouring females [$F(2, 1) = 10.2$, $p = 0.002$]. The significant main effect refers to the trend that all females have higher expected values than the males at all group measures. These gaps are likely to be real differences due to real effects between the groups, as the related statistical probability is $p = 0.002$, which is lower than critical probability value of $p = 0.01$.

Besides gender differences, languages spoken in social settings (social language) also caused item differential functioning in Item 2 of the authentic test items. As shown in Figure 3, Item 2 exhibits a statistically significant main effect with social language, favouring English [$F(2, 1) = 5.57$, $p = 0.005$]. All English-speaking students (EL) have higher expected values than the Mandarin-speaking students (CL) at all group measures.

The trend that English-speaking students (36 out of 101 students) in social settings generally fare better in a Chinese language test can be explained by the fact that many of these students are actually effectively bilingual speakers who are likely to speak Mandarin at home. From the questionnaire data, there are only 11 students speaking English at home, and 81 students speaking Mandarin at home, hence there can be only be at most 11 students speaking only English at home and in social settings. This implies that a majority of the EL group students in Figure 3 are effectively bilingual and therefore likely to attain higher levels of language awareness, performing better than their peers in the language tests. This trend is further validated by the targeting graphs in the next section, where many students speaking Mandarin at home are found to perform well in the test, despite being likely to speak English in schools and in other social settings.

To summarize, all test items, except Item 1 and Item 2, have no statistically, significant item differential functioning with the designated independent variables, such as age and prior school grades. These item differential functioning statistics show that the Intermediate Authentic Test is a reliable test in which most of its test items (but not all) are not biased against any group of students.

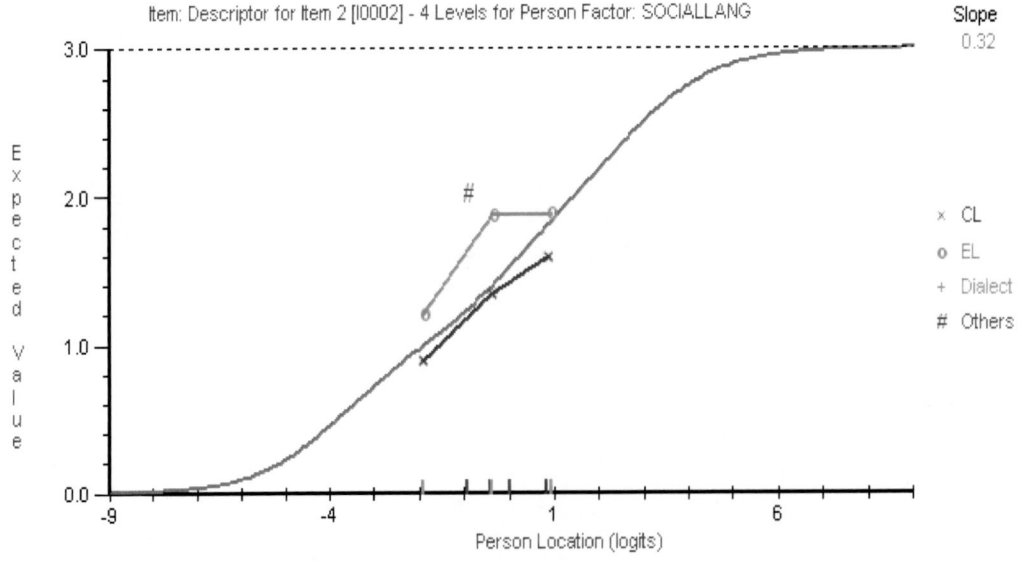

Figure 3. Item 2 Characteristic Curve for Social Language (Intermediate Authentic Test).

Differential Item Functioning in the Advanced Authentic Chinese Language Test

Similar to the intermediate part of the Authentic Chinese Language Test, the Advanced Authentic Test was analyzed through a series of checks for item differential functioning. For gender, age, prior GCE 'O' Level grades, home language, social language and family income, all ten test items in the Advanced Authentic Test show no statistically significant item differential functioning at p(critical) $= 0.01$. The only variable that causes significant interaction with one of the test items are the junior college grades (JC1, JC2, JC3), as shown in Figure 4.

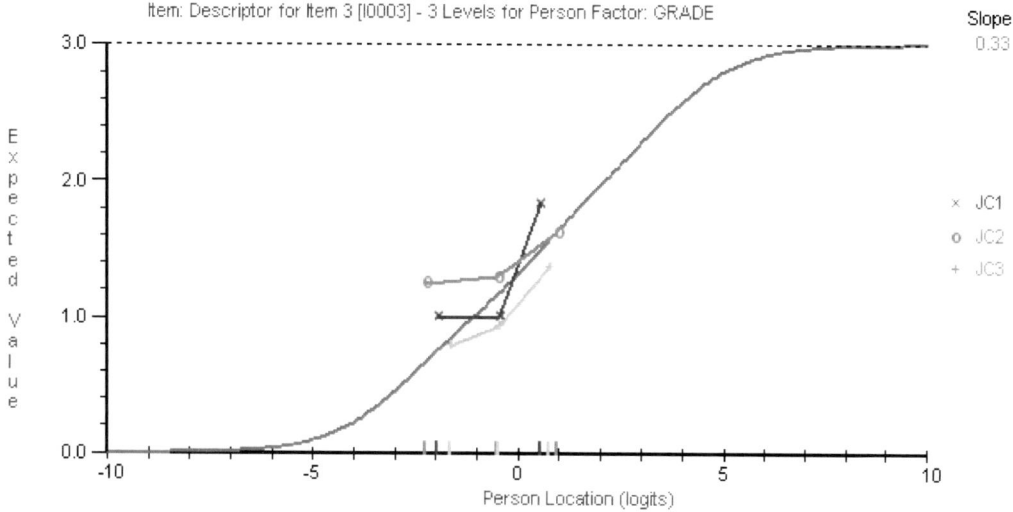

Figure 4. Item Characteristic Curve for Item 3 (Advanced Authentic Test).

Figure 4 shows that Item 3 has item differential functioning by Junior College grades, dis-favoring JC3 [$F (2, 2) = 5.61$, $p = 0.005$] as a main effect. The JC3 students have produced the worst expected values of language ability at all measures along the scale. This phenomenon contradicts earlier observations for the Mock 'A' Level Tests in which the JC3 students generally outperformed their juniors (JC1 and JC2). In this case, Item 3 of the Advanced Authentic Test may need to be modified to ensure fair distribution of scoring responses across all three levels of students. One possible modification is to reword the question and provide scaffolding to emphasize the need for organization of the content.

Compared to the Mock 'A' Level Tests, the Authentic Chinese Language Tests have only three test items with item differential functioning by person traits and other variables. In terms of possible bias in test construct, the Authentic Chinese Language Tests provide more reliability and less discrimination across all groups of students, which can be further validated by means of targeting graphs. Hence, the following section proceeds to discuss the Person-Item Threshold Distribution graphs for all item thresholds among all students.

TARGETING

The purpose of checking the targeting of ability measures against item difficulties is to ensure there is a fair distribution of students scoring correctly in all items from easy to difficult. In addition, ideal targeting should not discriminate against any background variables or person traits. Therefore, good distribution patterns in Person-Item Threshold Distribution graphs will display consistent frequency trends for all groups of students, without certain groups of students doing better or worse compared to other groups.

Targeting in the Intermediate Authentic Chinese Language Test

As shown in Figure 5, the Person-Item Threshold Distribution graph displays a range of item thresholds from -4.2 logits (easy) to +4.0 logits (difficult). This scale of varying item difficulties is well matched by the scale of corresponding student ability measures in which 98.02% of the students fall within the range of -4.2 logits to +3.7 logits. This shows good targeting of language ability measures against item difficulties for the Intermediate Authentic Test. Compared to the Intermediate and Advanced Mock 'A' Level Tests respectively, the Intermediate Authentic Test has demonstrated better targeting in its test design, as it has the least number of items unable to target any ability measure.

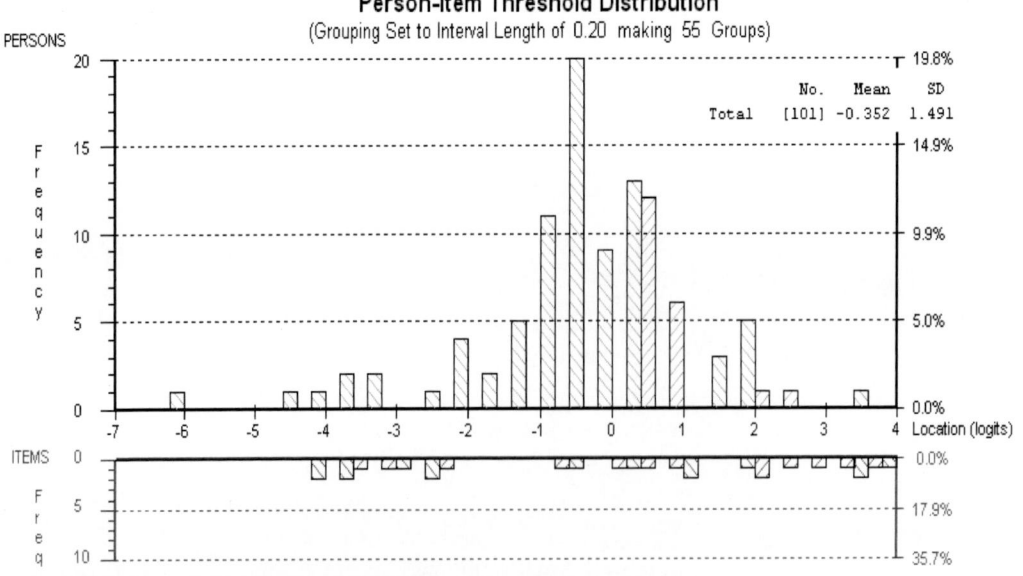

Notes on Figures 5, 6, 7, 8, 9, 10, 11 and 12.
1. The scale is in logits, that is, the log odds of answering the response categories.
2. Person ability measures (low to high) are given on the upper side in logits.
3. Item thresholds (easy to hard) are given on the lower side in logits.

Figure 5. Targeting Graph for the Intermediate Authentic Test.

In Figure 6, student ability measures and item locations are differentiated by Junior College and the respective person-item thresholds are mapped out for different groups of students. The JC2 students occupy the upper range in the ability measure scale (from +2.2 to +3.2 logits). Meanwhile, more JC3 students occupy the lower range with 10.52% of these students having very low mean measures from -3.2 to -6.2 logits, whereas only 4.70% of JC2 students have very low mean measures within the same range. The differences here are not statistically significant [F (2, 98) = 0.29, p = 0.75]. It can also be noted that there are too few students with high ability measures being targeted within the upper range from +2.5 to +4.0 logits.

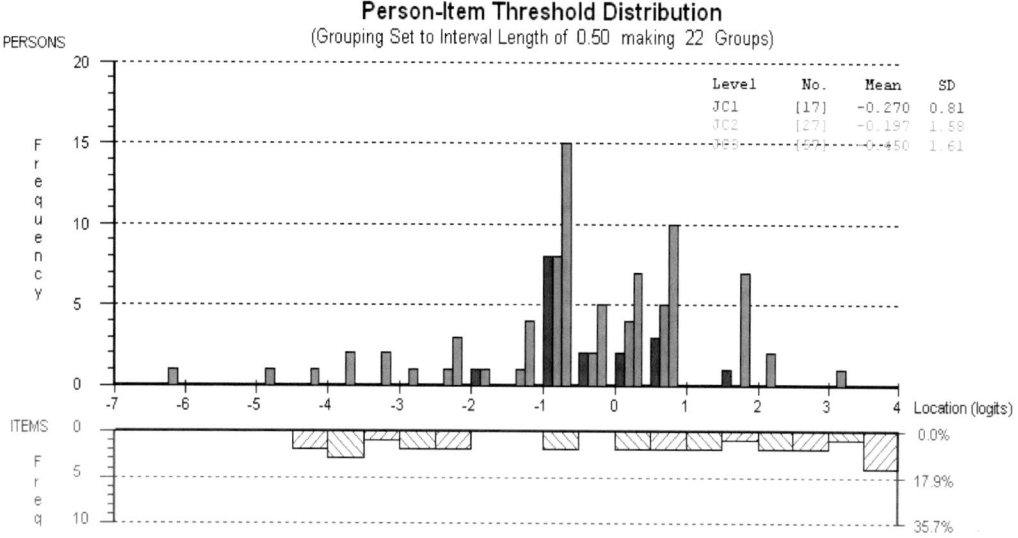

Figure 6. Targeting Graph for the Intermediate Authentic Test with Ability Measures Differentiated by Junior College.

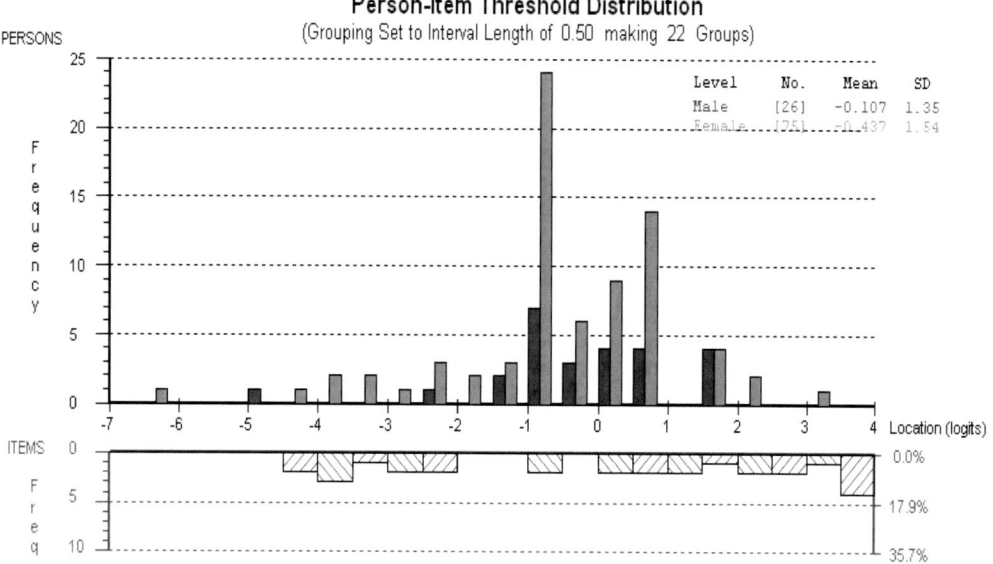

Figure 7. Targeting Graph for the Intermediate Authentic Test with Ability Measures Differentiated by Gender.

Similar targeting graphs differentiated by other variables were computed and these are shown in Figure 7 (gender), Figure 8 (prior GCE 'O' Level grades), Figure 9 (home language), Figure 10 (social language) and Figure 11 (family income).

Figure 7 shows that both males and female students have different mean measures of -0.11 and -0.44 logits respectively. The overall performance of the male students is slightly better than their counterparts, which is consistent with the previous analyses, but this is not statistically significant [F $(1, 99) = 0.95$, $p = 0.33$].

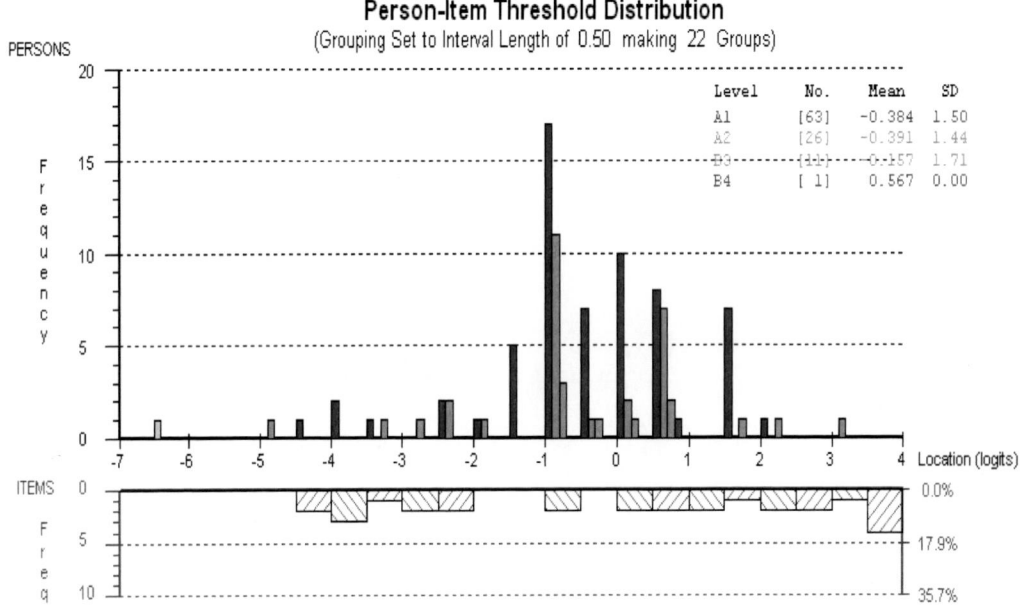

Figure 8. Targeting Graph for the Intermediate Authentic Test with Ability Measures Differentiated by Prior 'O' Level Grades.

The targeting graph differentiated by prior GCE 'O' Level grades, as shown in Figure 8, shows an unexpected distribution between the A grade students and the B grade students. Both A1 and A2 students have lower mean measures at -0.38 and -0.39 logits respectively, while the B3 students have a higher mean measure value of -0.16 logits, but these are not statistically significant [F $(3,92) = 0.20$, $p = 0.89$]. It seems that the better 'O' Level performers did not continue to excel in the Authentic Tests in the present research, while the B3 and B4 students did unexpectedly well. One possible explanation is that the authentic assessment approach has reduced the amount of assessment associated with rote learning, such as vocabulary translation of ancient Chinese. Hence, the B grade students may be less impeded by the constraints in the 'O' Level and 'A' Level test formats and found the present authentic test approach a fairer platform to assess their language abilities.

Figure 9 shows the targeting graph differentiated by languages spoken at home. The dialect-speaking students have the highest mean measure at +0.73 logits, but this is not statistically significant [F $(3,97) = 0.28$, $p = 0.84$].

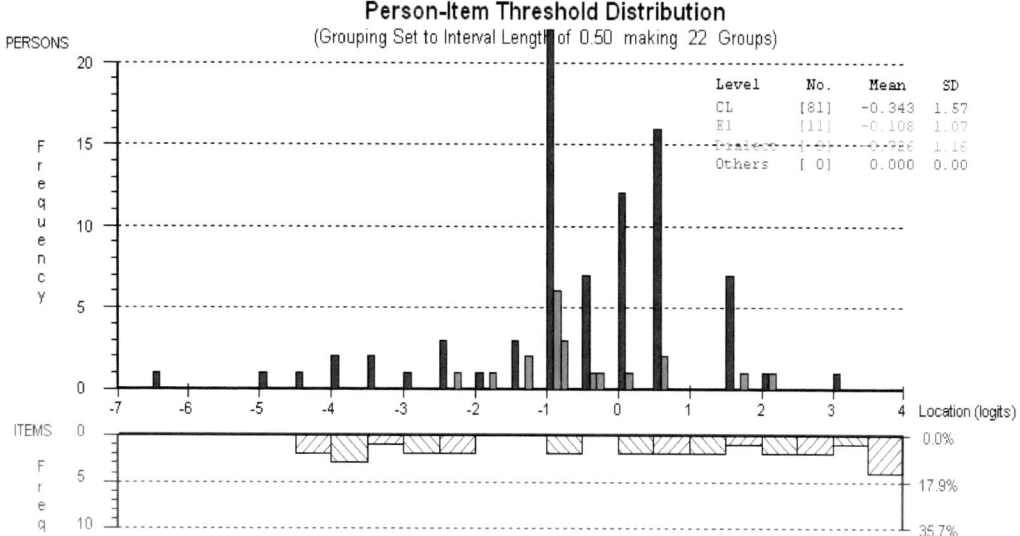

Figure 9. Targeting Graph for the Intermediate Authentic Test with Ability Measures Differentiated by Home Language.

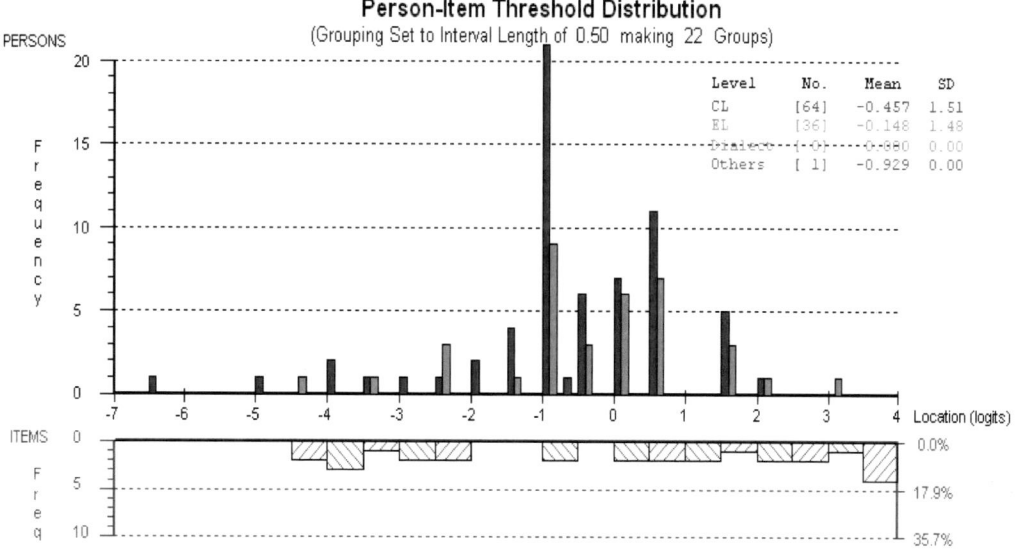

Figure 10. Targeting Graph for the Intermediate Authentic Test with Ability Measures Differentiated by Social Language.

One possible reason why the English-speaking students are performing better is that these students in Singapore are likely to be exposed to more English books, media and other learning resources, which generally have more content on creative and authentic learning compared to Chinese language resources. Therefore, when these English-speaking students took the Authentic Test, they are likely to be able to adapt to the styles of authentic and creative assessment designed in the test. However, these differences are not statistically significant [F $(3, 97) = 0.37, p = 0.77$].

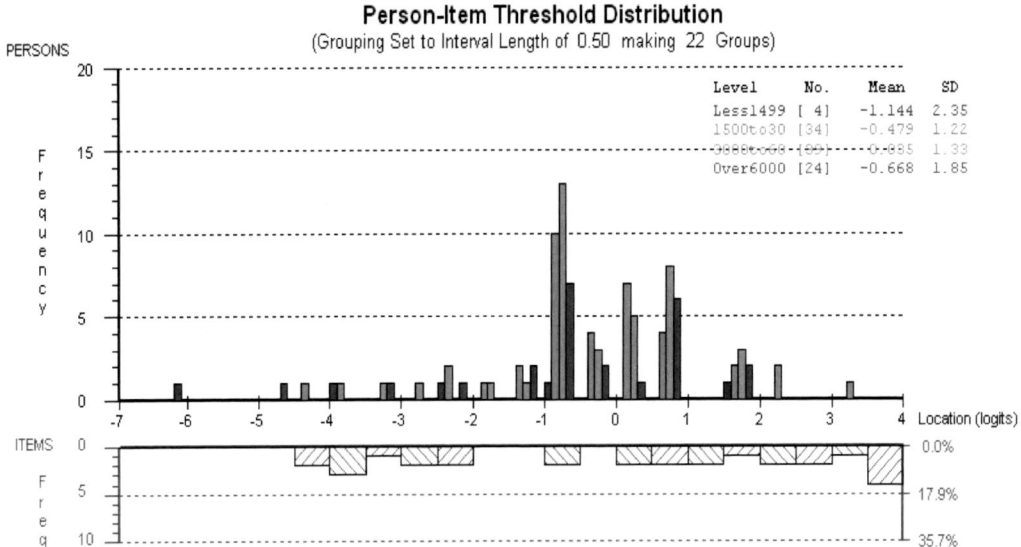

Person-Item Threshold Distribution
(Grouping Set to Interval Length of 0.50 making 22 Groups)

Figure 11. Targeting Graph for the Intermediate Authentic Test with Ability Measures Differentiated by Family Income.

Similar to the targeting graphs differentiated by languages most often spoken, the targeting graph for different groups of family income, as shown in Figure 11, also shows trends consistent with the targeting graphs in the Mock 'A' Level Tests. The students in the mid-income groups with monthly income brackets of $1500 to $3000 and $3001 to $6000, have higher mean measures of -0.48 and +0.04 logits respectively, whereas the lower income group students have very low mean measures of -1.14 logits. Nevertheless, there is no correlation between family income and ability measures, as students from the highest income group (over $6000), who have low mean measure of only -0.67 logits, do not fare better than the mid-income groups. The differences are not statistically significant either [F (3, 97) = 1.73, p = 0.17]. This performance trend is very similar to that in the Mock 'A' Level Test and these analysis data may serve as preliminary references to educators to identify and help the weaker students in junior colleges.

The next section proceeds to provide similar targeting analysis for the Advanced Authentic Test. However, in order to avoid unnecessary repetitions, targeting graphs differentiated by variables will not be displayed in the following section.

Targeting in Advanced Authentic Chinese Language Test

As seen in Figure 12, the targeting graph shows that there is better targeting of ability measures against item difficulties in the upper scale range from -0.8 to +2.8 logits. On the other hand, 4.95% students with very low measures of -4.7 logits and below do not have their ability measures well targeted.

Figure 12 shows that the targeting for the Advanced Authentic Test is very satisfactory but the test could have been better designed if some easier items had been added (with difficulties from -4 to -6 logits).

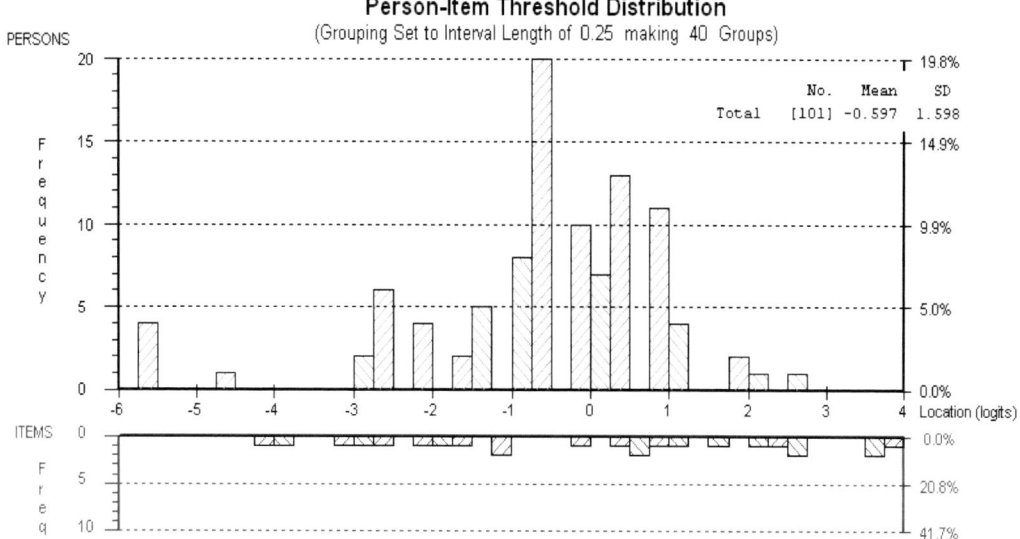

Figure 12. Targeting Graph for the Advanced Authentic Test.

Table 10. Comparison of mean measures between the Authentic Test and the Mock 'A' Level Test

Language Tests	Mean	Standard Deviation
Basic Mock 'A' Level Chinese Language Test	+1.66	1.20
Intermediate Mock 'A' Level Chinese Language Test	+0.30	1.63
Advanced Mock 'A' Level Chinese Language Test	+0.57	1.81
Intermediate Authentic Chinese Language Test	-0.35	1.49
Advanced Authentic Chinese Language Test	-0.60	1.60

Source: Designed by Ong (2009) for this study from the RUMM analysis.

The mean student measures for all the Mock 'A' Level Tests and Authentic Tests are given in Table 10, but these cannot be validly compared because they are not on the same linear scale. The scales are equated in the next chapter and valid comparisons are made there.

Besides the overall Person-Item Threshold Distribution graph, other targeting graphs differentiated by variables report trends mostly similar to that in the Intermediate Authentic Test. For example, in the distribution graph differentiated by home language, the dialect-speaking students have higher mean measures than the other groups of the students. Similarly, the English-speaking students fare better than the Mandarin-speaking students, due to reasons previously explained in the Intermediate Authentic Test section.

Despite the similarities, there are still minor differences among the targeting graphs between the Intermediate and Advanced Authentic Tests. In the Advanced Authentic Test targeting graph differentiated by the prior school grades shown in Figure 13, the JC2 students have lower mean measure of -0.77 logits, compared to their JC1 juniors who have relatively higher mean measures at -0.63 logits. Although the difference between the JC1 and JC2 students are not statistically significant [F (2,98) = 0.25, p = 0.78], it is understandable that the JC2 students might be more geared towards their 'A' Levels preparation and hence are less motivated in completing the more creative components in the Advanced Authentic Test.

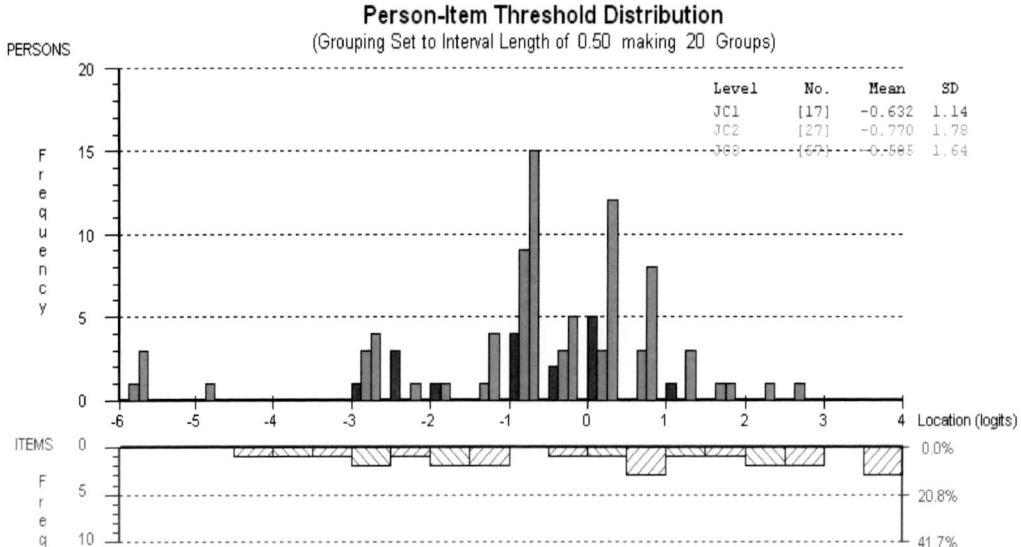

Figure 13. Targeting Graph for the Advanced Authentic Test with Ability Measures Differentiated by Junior College.

In summary, both the Intermediate and Advanced Chinese Language Tests have a reasonable fit to the measurement model and reliable scales have been created in which students are not much advantaged or disadvantaged across seven main independent variables. While some minor re-wording of some items could be made to improve some individual item fits, it is clear that the test questions are a good basis for measuring Chinese Language ability and valid inferences can be made from these scales.

ITEM DIFFICULTIES ACROSS THE FIVE TESTS COMPARED

Using the appropriate Translation Constant with the Basic Mock 'A' Level Test as the anchor variable, the item difficulties across the five tests were calculated and are set out in Table 11. The Table shows that the items of the Intermediate Mock 'A' Level Test are split into two sections, one easy and one hard. The two Authentic Tests contain no easy items and have items generally more difficult than the Mock 'A' Level Tests, although the Intermediate Mock 'A' Level Test has the three hardest items. The Basic Mock 'A' Level Test is clearly the easiest, although the Intermediate Mock 'A' Level Test has the easiest item, and the Intermediate Mock 'A' Level Test is clearly harder than the Advanced Mock 'A' Level Test. These results support the earlier analysis that the Basic Mock 'A' Level Test is probably less valid than the other four tests and is not providing any information which other tests may lack. In conclusion, the Intermediate Mock 'A' Level Test and the two Authentic Tests would appear to be the best measures of Chinese language ability for the Chinese language talents participating in the present study.

Table 11. Item Difficulties across the Five Tests Compared on the Same Scale

Basic Mock 'A' Level Test	Intermediate Mock 'A' Level Test	Advanced Mock 'A' Level Test	Intermediate Authentic Test	Advanced Authentic Test
	-1.89 (4)			
-1.79 (6)				
-1.54 (3)				
-0.53 (2)	-0.61 (6)	-0.49 (2)		
-0.25 (10)				
-0.07 (4)	+0.03 (5,11)			
+0.38 (5)		+0.39 (5)		
+0.40 (9)				
		+0.50 (8)		
	+0.61 (10)			
+0.80 (8)				
+0.94 (12)	+0.90 (13)	+0.89 (8)		
	+0.94 (7)			+0.98 (5)
	+1.01 (12)			
	+1.27 (14)	+1.23 (9)	+1.15 (4)	
		+1.26 (3)		
		+1.52 (6,12)	+1.48 (6)	
+1.65 (13)	+1.65 (8)	+1.62 (10)	+1.65 (2,5)	
		+1.90 (7,13)	+1.82 (3)	+1.88 (2,8,10)
	+2.04 (3)		+2.13 (7)	+2.11 (4)
			+2.33 (9,10)	
				+2.58 (7)
			+2.75 (1,8)	+2.73 (3)
				+2.79 (6,9)
				+2.97 (1)
	+3.41 (9)			
	+4.12 (2)			
	+5.52 (1)			

Source: Designed by *Ong (2009)* for this study from the equating analysis.

1. A few item difficulties (where there are duplicates) have been changed by 0.01 or 0.02 logits (still within the error of measurement) to fit them neatly in the Table.
2. The item difficulties have been equated onto the same scale using the original Rasch-created difficulties and an appropriate Translation Constant.
3. The number in brackets refers to the test item number.

In Table 11, all the test items are equated onto the same scale and each test has its easiest and hardest items to help define the limits of overall language competency assessed in the present study. For Basic Mock 'A' Level Test, the easiest test items are Item 6 and 3, which refer to the cloze passage (P1/10) and ancient Chinese vocabulary translation (P1/5) questions respectively; while the hardest item is Item 13, which is scoring for content in summarising a modern Chinese passage (P1/17). In the Intermediate Mock 'A' Level Test, the easiest part would be scoring for content in essay writing (P1/1), while its most difficult part would be translating an Ancient Chinese sentence (P1/6). For Advanced Mock 'A' Level Test, the easiest item is elaborating arguments in an ancient poem analysis (P2/22) and the hardest items are scoring for the organisation of the content structure in one short novel and a full length novel (P2/28c and P2/32c).

The Authentic Tests also have their easiest and hardest items. For the Intermediate Authentic Test, the easiest item (Test Item 1) is scoring for the contents and ideas in the first essay writing task, in which scaffolding and contextual information are provided in the questions; while one of the hardest items (Test Item 8) is scoring for the organisation in writing the symposium report on two ancient Chinese passages. For the Advanced Authentic Test, it is easiest to score for ideas and creativity in writing a curator's prologue for a novel in Test Item 15; while it is most difficult to score in finding the right convention to write the symposium report in Test Item 10. For both Authentic Tests, it is interesting to note that test items linked to language pragmatic competence and organisational competence (Bachman, 1990), which are introduced earlier in Chapter Three, generally seem more difficult to the students.

In summary, this analysis equated all the Mock 'A' Level and Authentic Chinese Language Tests, and concluded that, using the Basic Mock 'A' Level Test as the anchor variable, all the other scales can be linked onto the same linear scale. This shows that:

1. The Basic Mock 'A' Level Test has a small range of moderately easy items;
2. The Intermediate Mock 'A' Level Test has a very wide range of item difficulties from the easiest to the very hardest;
3. The Advanced Mock 'A' Level Test has a medium range of moderately difficult items;
4. The Intermediate Authentic Test has a small range of moderately hard items; and
5. The Advanced Authentic Test has a small range of moderately hard items with some harder than the Intermediate Authentic Test.

INDEX